D0085181

GLOBAL GEOPOLITICAL FLASHPOINTS

GLOBAL GEOPOLITICAL FLASHPOINTS

An Atlas of Conflict

Ewan W. Anderson

FITZROY DEARBORN PUBLISHERS

CHICAGO • LONDON

© The Stationery Office 2000

A Cataloging-in-Publication record for this book is available from the Library of Congress.

First published in the UK and USA 2000

Published in the United Kingdom by
The Stationery Office Limited, 51 Nine Elms Lane, London SW8 5DR

Published in the United States of America by
Fitzroy Dearborn Publishers, 919 North Michigan Avenue,
Chicago, Illinois 60611

ISBN 1-57958-137-4   Fitzroy Dearborn

Printed in the United Kingdom by Hobbs the Printers Ltd, Totton, Hampshire

Dedication ■   To my sons, Greg, Liam and Lew for all their support during numerous personal flashpoints.

CONTENTS

CONTENTS

PREFACE

Since late 1989 there has been a fundamental global geopolitical change. The certainties of the bipolar world have been shattered, to be replaced by increasing volatility. One key result has been the acceptance of intervention by bodies such as the United Nations (UN) and the North Atlantic Treaty Organisation (NATO) into the internal affairs of states. Thus, by the turn of the century, there have been conflicts in Iraq, Kosovo and East Timor, initiated with humanitarian aims. Changes during the 1990s have necessitated a reassessment of potential flashpoints, which have increased as the decade has progressed.

In this atlas, current and potential flashpoints are discussed. For each, the importance of its location is examined and the development of the particular geopolitical issue is traced. The current status of the flashpoint is then assessed and a short bibliography on the subject is listed. Core references are noted below:

Banks, A. and Muller, T. (1998) *Political Handbook of the World 1998*, Basingstoke: Macmillan

Krieger, J. (1993) *The Oxford Companion of the World*, Oxford: Oxford University Press

Szajkowski, B. (1993) *Encyclopaedia of Conflicts, Disputes and Flashpoints in Eastern Europe, Russia and the Successor States*, Harlow: Longman

Each entry is illustrated with a map, compiled and drawn for the atlas under the direction of Don Shewan at 'City Cartographic', London Guildhall University. Assistance with the production of the maps was given by Drew Ellis (London Guildhall University); Edward Oliver (Queen Mary & Westfield College, London University) and Owen Tucker (Cambridge University).

In any such volume, it is impossible to cover all areas of instability. Furthermore, the rapidity of geopolitical change, particularly on a local scale, militates against the possibility of producing a volume which is up to the minute. However, the great majority of current flashpoints have been covered and every effort has been made to include all locations with the potential for conflict. This has entailed a very extensive data search and for this I am particularly grateful to Louise Waite. A former distinguished student of Durham University's Geography Department, Louise has been a meticulous and thoughtful research colleague. As with so many of my publications, I am also greatly indebted to Bid Austin for her careful typing and editing and Barry Austin for his thorough checking of the manuscript. For any errors, I take responsibility.

Ewan Anderson
Durham
October 1999

ABBREVIATIONS AND ACRONYMS

ADEMA	Alliance pour la Démocratie au Mali
AG	Action Group
ALN	Armée de Liberation Nationale
ANC	African National Congress
APC	All People's Congress
APRA	Alianza Popular Revolucionaire Americana
ASEAN	Association of South-East Asian Nations
BCP	Basotho Congress Party
BEAC	Barents Euro-Arctic Council
BIOT	British Indian Ocean Territory
BJP	Bharatiya Janata Party
BNP	Basutoland National Party
BSEC	Black Sea Economic Co-operation
BSPP	Burma Socialist Program Party
CAEU	Central Asian Economic Union
CTBT	Comprehensive Test Ban Treaty
CENTO	Central Treaty Organisation
CIA	Central Intelligence Agency
CIS	Commonwealth of Independent States
CNR	Conseil de Reconciliation Nationale
CNTR	National Council for Timorese Resistance
CPT	Communist Party of Tajikistan
CSRC	Conflict Studies Research Centre
CTBT	Comprehensive Test Ban Treaty
DFOR	Dissuasion Force
DPP	Democratic Progressive Party
DPRK	Democratic People's Republic of Korea
DPT	Democratic Party of Turkmenistan
dwt	dead-weight tonnage
EAC	East African Community
EBRD	European Bank for Reconstruction and Development
EC	European Community
EEC	European Economic Community

ECOMOG	ECOWAS Monitoring Group
ECOWAS	Economic Community of West African States
EEZ	Exclusive Economic Zone
ELN	National Liberation Army
ENI	Ente Nationale Idrocarburi
EOKA	National Organisation of Cypriot Fighters
EPLF	Eritrean People's Liberation Front
EPRDF	Ethiopian People's Revolutionary Democratic Front
ETA	Euzkadi ta Askatasuna
EU	European Union
FAR	Rebel Armed Forces
FARC	Revolutionary Armed Forces of Colombia
FIS	Front Islamique de Salut
FLEC	Front for the Liberation of Cabinda
FLN	Front de Liberation Nationale
FNLA	National Front for the Liberation of Angola
FORD	Forum for the Restoration of Democracy
FPR	Rwandan Patriotic Front
FPRY	Federal People's Republic of Yugoslavia
FRETELIN	Revolutionary Front for Independence
FSU	Former Soviet Union
GAP	South-east Anatolian Project
GCC	Gulf Co-operation Council
GDP	gross domestic product
GIA	Group Islamique Armé
GNP	gross national product
GPC	General People's Congress
ha	hectares
HDP	People's Democratic Party
HDZ	Croatian Democratic Union
IAEA	International Atomic Energy Agency
IBRD	International Bank for Reconstruction and Development
IBRU	International Boundaries Research Unit
ICJ	International Court of Justice
ICT	International Criminal Tribunal
IFOR	Implementation Force
IISS	International Institute for Strategic Studies
IMF	International Monetary Fund

INPFL	Independent National Patriotic Front of Liberia
IRA	Irish Republican Army
IRP	Islamic Renaissance Party
KANU	Kenya African National Union
KDP	Kurdish Democratic Party
KLA	Kosovo Liberation Army
km	kilometres
KMT	Kuomintang
KWP	Korean Workers' Party
LCD	Lesotho Congress for Democracy
LPDR	Lao People's Democratic Republic
LPRP	Lao People's Revolutionary Party
m	metres
M-13	13th November Movement
MERCOSUR	Common Market of the Southern Cone
MIA	Mouvement Islamique Armé
MINURSO	UN Mission for the Referendum in Western Sahara
mm	millimetre
MMD	Movement for Multiparty Democracy
MNC	Multinational Corporation
MNR	Nationalist Revolutionary Movement
MNRD	Mouvement National Rwandais pour le Developpement
MOSOP	Movement for the Survival of the Ogoni People
MPLA	Popular Movement for the Liberation of Angola
MPM	Mouvement Populaire Mahorais
MRTA	Tupac Amaru Revolutionary Movement
MSP	Movement for a Peaceful Society
NATO	North Atlantic Treaty Organisation
NCNC	National Council of Nigeria and the Cameroons
NDPL	National Democratic Party of Liberia
NLF	National Liberation Front
nml	nautical miles (1 nml = 1.852 km)
NPC	Northern People's Congress
NPFL	National Patriotic Front of Liberia
NPP	National Patriotic Party
NPRC	National Provisional Ruling Council
NPT	Non-Proliferation Treaty
NRC	National Reconciliation Commission

NSC	National Salvation Council
NSP	National Salvation Party
NUP	Nationalist United Party
OAS	Organisation of American States
OAU	Organisation of African Unity
OIC	Organisation of the Islamic Conference
OLF	Oromo Liberation Front
OSCE	Organisation for Security and Co-operation in Europe
PA	Palestinian Authority
PDPA	People's Democratic Party of Afghanistan
PDRY	People's Democratic Republic of Yemen
PfP	Partnership for Peace
PKI	Indonesian Communist Party
PKK	Kurdish Workers' Party
PLO	Palestine Liberation Organisation
PNC	People's National Congress
PNG	Papua New Guinea
PNV	Partido Nacionalista Vasco
PPP	People's Progressive Party
PRC	People's Republic of China
PUK	Patriotic Union of Kurdistan
RCC	Revolutionary Command Council
RDA	Rassemblement Démocratique Africain
RDK	Republican Movement of Crimea
RF	Rhodesian Front
RIIA	Royal Institute of International Affairs
RND	National Democratic Rally
ROC	Republic of China
RPP	Republican People's Party
RSFSR	Russian Soviet Federal Socialist Republic
RUF	Revolutionary United Front
SADC	Southern African Development Community
SADCC	Southern African Development Co-ordination Council
SADF	South African Defence Forces
SADR	Sahrawi Arab Democratic Republic
SAS	Special Air Services
SEATO	South-East Asia Treaty Organisation
SFOR	Stabilisation Force

SHP	Social Democratic Populist Party
SL	Sendero Luminoso (Shining Path)
SLA	South Lebanon Army
SLORC	State Law and Order Restoration Council
SLPP	Sierra Leone People's Party
SNA	Somali National Alliance
SNM	Somali National Movement
SPDC	State Peace and Development Council
SPLA	Sudan People's Liberation Army
SRC	Supreme Revolutionary Council
SSR	Soviet Socialist Republic
START	Strategic Nuclear Arms Reduction Treaty
SUMED	Suez–Mediterranean
TCP	Turkmen Communist Party
TDP	Tajik Democratic Party
TMT	Turkish Resistance Organisation
TPLF	Tigre People's Liberation Front
TSP	Tajik Socialist Party
TWP	True Whig Party
UAE	United Arab Emirates
UCP	Uzbek Communist Party
UDI	Unilateral Declaration of Independence
UDPM	Union Démocratique du Peuple Malien
UK	United Kingdom
UN	United Nations
UNAMIR	UN Assistance Mission for Rwanda
UNCLOS	UN Convention on the Law of the Sea
UNEF	UN Emergency Force
UNFP	Union Nationale des Forces Populaires
UNHCR	UN High Commissioner for Refugees
UNIP	United National Independence Party
UNITA	National Union for the Total Independence of Angola
UNITAF	United Task Force
UNOSOM	UN Operation in Somalia
UNPROFOR	UN Protection Force
URNG	Guatemalan National Revolutionary Unity
US	United States
USA	United States of America

UTO	United Tajik Opposition
VLCCs	Very Large Cargo Carriers
VMRO-DPMNE	Internal Macedonian Revolutionary Organisation–Democratic Party for Macedonian National Unity
WMO	World Meteorological Organisation
YAR	Yemen Arab Republic
YSP	Yemeni Socialist Party
ZANU	Zimbabwe African National Union
ZAPU	Zimbabwe African People's Union

INTRODUCTION

Flashpoints are identified as current, dormant or potential areas of geopolitical instability. In most cases, flashpoints are likely to exert an influence well beyond their point of origin, but in some cases, such as that of Sierra Leone, while the overall effect within the region may not be widespread, the instability is so devastating that they can be designated local flashpoints. Afghanistan, Eritrea, Kashmir, Kosovo and South Lebanon are examples of current flashpoints. Dormant flashpoints include the Chagos Archipelago, Cabinda, Moldova, Liancourt Rocks and the Kola Peninsula. Potential flashpoints are more difficult to predict, but Taiwan, the Black Sea, Gibraltar and Kaliningrad are among several examples which could become active in the future.

Instability may result from strategic/military, political, economic, social or even environmental factors. In many cases, several of these factors are combined and a large number either concern boundaries directly or impinge upon them. The Spratly Islands are identified in strategic and economic terms, whereas Kashmir is strategic and social and Suriname is social and economic. However, some flashpoints have a clear primary consideration. The Wakhan Panhandle, the McMahon Line, Bosnia and the Tunbs Islands are all military-strategic. The Aegean, Kurdistan, Angola and Cyprus are political. Bab el Mandeb, the Hawar Islands, the Benguela Railway, the Black Sea and the Caspian Sea are essentially economic. The Basque Country, Bessarabia, East Timor, Northern Ireland and Transylvania are primarily flashpoints resulting from social issues. In the Russian Federation and most of the states of the Former Soviet Union (FSU), there are major environmental problems.

It is clear that flashpoints are not necessarily restricted in area and, in many examples, it would imply a spurious accuracy to attempt to identify a point. For example, Afghanistan as a state is a flashpoint. At different periods of the civil war it would be possible to identify individual passes or cities as flashpoints, but it appears more realistic to designate the whole country. Flashpoints can therefore be relatively small areas or points, occasionally linear features or lines, but are most commonly areas. Islands such as Abu Musa and the Liancourt Rocks are good examples of specific points, as are, on a rather larger scale, the Golan Heights and Chechnya. The Strait of Malacca, the Benguela Railway and the Sino-Indian boundary (the McMahon Line) are all examples of linear features. Most of the flashpoints in this volume are, however, either states or sections of states. Good examples of the latter are Kurdistan, the Hatay and Transylvania.

All of the case studies are defined as geopolitical flashpoints in that they represent the interplay of geography and politics. As is clear from the factors giving rise to flashpoints, the geographical component may derive from any aspect of the subject: physical, political, economic, social or military. A key variable is location. Straits and isolated islands with a potential for large Exclusive Economic Zone (EEZ) claims are good examples. Many flashpoints, such as Rwanda, Burundi, Guyana, Transylvania and Northern Ireland, result from ethnic, religious or other societal cleavages. Some, such as Mururoa Atoll, Tacna and the Hatay, include a component of historical geography. Economic concerns can influence in some way most territorial claims, but in particular, the relationship between isolated island groups and the potential for petroleum exploration is significant.

Thus, in identifying geopolitical flashpoints, a wide range of issues is addressed. These illustrate the breadth of geography and the large number of possible interrelationships with politics.

Legend

———	Major Road	—·—·—	International boundary
··············	Railway	— — —	Previous International boundary
⤳	River	- - - -	Disputed boundary
▪▪▪▪▪▪▪	Canal	········	Administrative boundary
- - - - - -	Navigation route	··········	Ceasefire Line
●	Major City/town	**IRAN**	Country name
■	Overseas possession	*Maldive*	Island name
·	Additional City/town	HATAY	State/province name
▲	Mountain	*ANDES*	Physical feature
⥇	Locks		Area of disputed ownership
⬭	Mountain pass		
	Location of main map	}	Areas annexed by another country
	Topography		

 Marsh

 Swamp

 Major salt pan

Minor salt pan

Software used for producing maps in the atlas include:

Mountains High Maps ® Copyright © 1998 Digital Wisdom, Inc.
Map Art Geopolitical Series ® Copyright © 1996 Cartesia
Map Art Terrain Series ® Copyright © 1996 Cartesia
Geoatlas World Vector ® Copyright © 1997 Graphi-Ogre

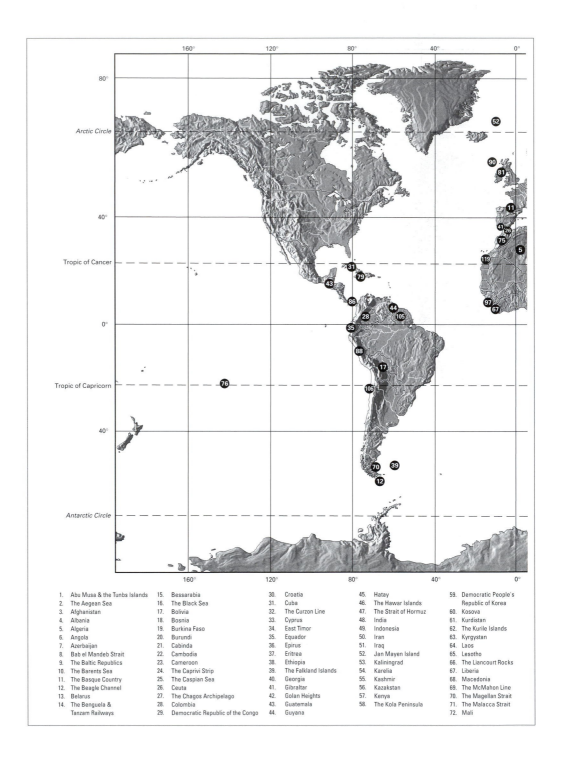

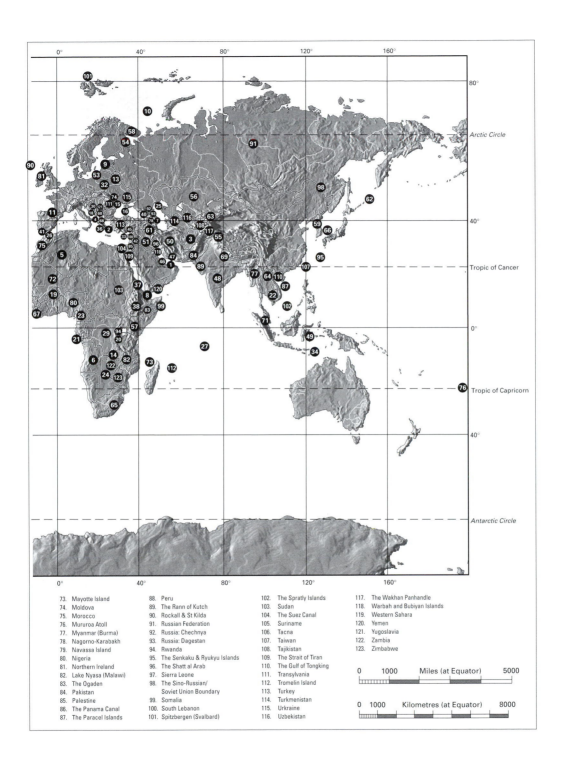

73. Mayotte Island	88. Peru	102. The Spratly Islands	117. The Wakhan Panhandle
74. Moldova	89. The Rann of Kutch	103. Sudan	118. Warbah and Bubiyan Islands
75. Morocco	90. Rockall & St Kilda	104. The Suez Canal	119. Western Sahara
76. Mururoa Atoll	91. Russian Federation	105. Suriname	120. Yemen
77. Myanmar (Burma)	92. Russia: Chechnya	106. Tacna	121. Yugoslavia
78. Nagorno-Karabakh	93. Russia: Dagestan	107. Taiwan	122. Zambia
79. Navassa Island	94. Rwanda	108. Tajikistan	123. Zimbabwe
80. Nigeria	95. The Senkaku & Ryukyu Islands	109. The Strait of Tiran	
81. Northern Ireland	96. The Shatt al Arab	110. The Gulf of Tongking	
82. Lake Nyasa (Malawi)	97. Sierra Leone	111. Transylvania	
83. The Ogaden	98. The Sino-Russian/	112. Tromelin Island	
84. Pakistan	Soviet Union Boundary	113. Turkey	
85. Palestine	99. Somalia	114. Turkmenistan	
86. The Panama Canal	100. South Lebanon	115. Ukraine	
87. The Paracel Islands	101. Spitzbergen (Svalbard)	116. Uzbekistan	

0   1000   Miles (at Equator)   5000

0   1000   Kilometres (at Equator)   8000

1

ABU MUSA AND THE TUNBS ISLANDS

Abu Musa is a small island, approximately 5 kilometres (km) across, located at the southern end of the Persian/Arabian Gulf, 100 nautical miles (nml) from the Strait of Hormuz. It is approximately 37 nml from Iran and 30 nml from Sharjah (United Arab Emirates [UAE]). It is on the easterly side of a loosely knit group of islands and, other than the Tunbs, is the nearest to Hormuz. The population is approximately 800. Apart from the strategic relevance of the island, it is potentially important for petroleum exploitation.

■ *Situation*

The Greater and Lesser Tunbs Islands, significantly smaller than Abu Musa, lie some 8 nml apart. The nearest Iranian island, Qeshm, is only 15 nml away and both Tunbs Islands are on the Iranian side of the median line. The EEZ for Abu Musa and the Tunbs Islands, together, would cover some 1,500 nml^2.

Sovereignty over Abu Musa and the Tunbs has long been disputed between Persia (Iran) and the Emirates of Sharjah and Ras al Khaymah (UAE). In the middle of the 19th century, possession of all three islands was taken by the Qawasim family of the then Trucial Coast (now UAE) and this ownership was recognised by Britain. Persia, with a stronger geographical claim on the Tunbs, installed customs officials on the islands in 1904, but these were withdrawn after British protests. A little later, Britain forcibly ejected iron miners of a German company from Abu Musa. In international maritime law, such evidence of government ownership of a sovereignty can be very important in arbitration. A further example occurred when Britain erected a lighthouse on Greater Tunb in 1913.

■ *Issue*

In 1921, the Qawasim family split and the two emirates separated. Abu Musa was considered to belong to Sharjah and the Tunbs Islands to Ras al Khaymah. There were again problems in 1928 when an Arab *dhow* was seized by Persian customs officials at Greater Tunb. Persia restated its claims despite the fact that there had been, in 1928, a verbal agreement between London and Tehran to accept the *status quo*. The *status quo* in this case was that Persia had sovereignty over the island of Sirri, 25 nml due west of Abu Musa, but that sovereignty over Abu Musa and the Tunbs rested with the emirates. A median line between Iran and the UAE shows clearly that the Tunbs Islands, and indeed Sirri, are on the Iranian side and Abu Musa is on the UAE side.

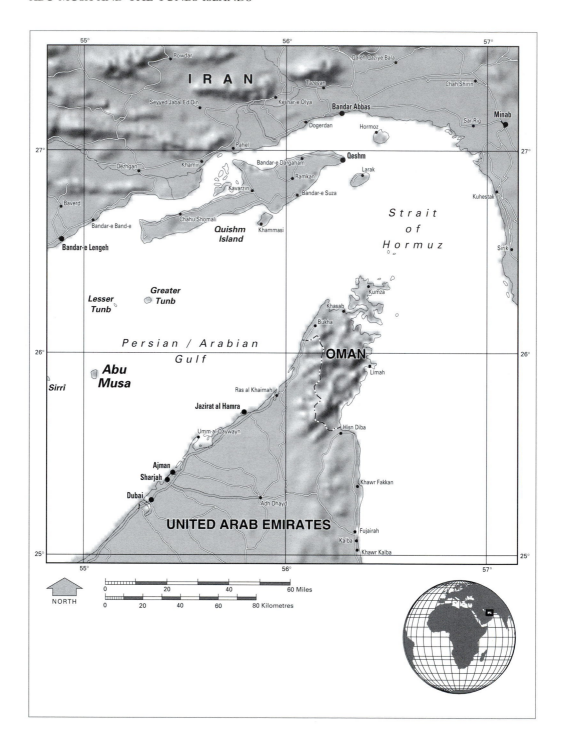

Following the announcement of Britain's withdrawal from the Gulf in 1968 and the burgeoning flow of oil through the Strait of Hormuz (see p. 141), the issue of the islands' sovereignty was revived. Iran feared a power vacuum in the region in the post-British period which might result in the disruption of oil flow through Hormuz. Immediately before British withdrawal in November 1971, agreement was reached between Iran and Sharjah which allowed the former to take control over the strategic areas of Abu Musa. These consisted of the northern half of the island, overlooking the main sea-line of communication. In return, Iran would pay Sharjah annually £0.5 million for nine years or until Sharjah's oil revenues reached £3 million per annum.

On 30 November 1971, just two days before the official British withdrawal and also the announcement of the independence of the UAE, Iranian troops occupied Abu Musa. They also backed their claim to the Tunbs Islands which were captured after a skirmish with a small British–Ras-al-Khaymah detachment. This action caused a storm of criticism throughout the Arab world.

During the Iran–Iraq War, the issue of the islands arose again and, in 1982, Iran threatened to block the Strait of Hormuz. In April 1992, Iran deployed troops to Abu Musa and reiterated its territorial claim. There was a meeting between the UAE and Iran over the issue in November 1995, and in 1998 there were further bilateral discussions. In December 1998, the UN requested that the UAE and Iran hold talks to resolve the dispute.

■ *Status*

As a result of their strategic location, the islands remain highly significant. Most of Iran's oil exports transit the Gulf, although thought has been given to overcoming the potential problem by the construction of a pipeline at least as far as Bandar Abbas. Arab oil exports are not quite so vulnerable in that there are pipelines to both the Red Sea and the Mediterranean. Furthermore, the UAE and Saudi Arabia have considered the possibility of pipelines to the Indian Ocean coast. For the Arabs, the islands remain strategic, but there is the additional fear associated with any move by Iran. The recent *rapprochement* between Saudi Arabia and Iran may have lessened the threat in Arab eyes. The 1971 agreement between Sharjah and Iran left the status of Abu Musa ambiguous, since both countries claimed full sovereignty. A 4 km-long boundary delimiting the Iranian from the UAE sector does appear on certain maps, but it has not been demarcated. In general, the UAE and Iran have enjoyed good relations, but the islands provide a constant irritant.

Strategically, the Tunbs are of even greater significance than Abu Musa. The Tunbs remain under Iranian control and their position places them firmly within Iranian jurisdiction. As a result of their strategic location, all three islands are likely to retain a high profile.

Reading ■   Amirahmadi, H. (1996) *Small Islands, Big Politics: The Tunbs and Abu Musa in the Gulf*, Basingstoke: Macmillan

Mojtahed-Zadeh, P. (1990) Iran's role in the Strait of Hormuz, 1970–1990, in N. Beschorner, St J.B. Gould and K. McLachlan (eds), *Sovereignty, Territoriality and International Boundaries in South Asia, South West Asia and the Mediterranean Basin*. Proceedings of a seminar held at the School of Oriental and African Studies, University of London, pp. 96–108

Peterson, J.E. (1985) The Islands of Arabia: their recent history and strategic importance, *Arabian Studies*, VII, pp. 23–35

Swearington, W.D. (1981) Sources of conflict over oil in the Persian/Arabian Gulf, *The Middle East Journal*, 35(3), pp. 314–30

2

THE AEGEAN SEA

Strategically, the Aegean is of great importance because it lies in the approaches to the Turkish Straits. Following the demise of the Soviet Union, the Black Sea has been transformed from a Soviet cul-de-sac into a potential major development area. Furthermore, beyond it the Caspian Sea Basin has important, if possibly exaggerated, petroleum resources. The natural outlet for the Black Sea and much of the trade from the Caspian is the Turkish Straits and this has increased the geopolitical relevance of the Aegean. The sea lies between Greece and Turkey and is dominated by islands, almost all of which are under Greek sovereignty. This raises problems of equitable maritime boundary delimitation between the two countries. Furthermore, Greece and Turkey's problem over the Aegean is only one of a number of key issues, predominant among which is Cyprus (see p. 97). Both Greece and Turkey are members of NATO and their relationship could critically influence the future security of the eastern Mediterranean.

■ *Situation*

Benefiting from the demise of the Ottoman Empire and the defeat of Italy in World War II, Greece has progressively established sovereignty over the islands of the Aegean. One large island, Gokceada (Imbros), and one medium-sized island, Bozcaada (Tenedos), are both under Turkish sovereignty. These islands are the nearest to the Dardanelles, the outlet of the Turkish Straits.

■ *Issue*

The sovereignty of the islands is not disputed: what is at issue is the method by which the maritime boundary should be delimited. If the median line between the Greek-owned island and the Turkish coast is taken as the boundary, then effectively the whole of the Aegean would belong to Greece. The Turkish case is that the median line should be calculated from the two mainlands, but this is rejected by Greece. A further issue is that both sides presently claim territorial waters of 6 nml, but Greece has indicated its desire to increase these to 12 nml. If this were to occur, the Greek share of the Aegean would rise from 35 to 66 per cent, but Turkey's would only increase from 9 to 10 per cent. On 16 November 1994, Turkey threatened to declare war if Greece made such an increase.

Strict application of the 1958 UN Convention on the Continental Shelf allows islands to have full effect, but there are many instances where some other proportion, normally half effect, has been agreed. Turkey can cite the judgement over the United Kingdom (UK) Channel Islands and the case between Australia and Papua New Guinea (PNG) in which islands in the Torres Strait lie close to the PNG coastline. More recently, the agreement between the UK and Argentina over the Falklands has been based on the set-aside of sovereignty (see p. 116).

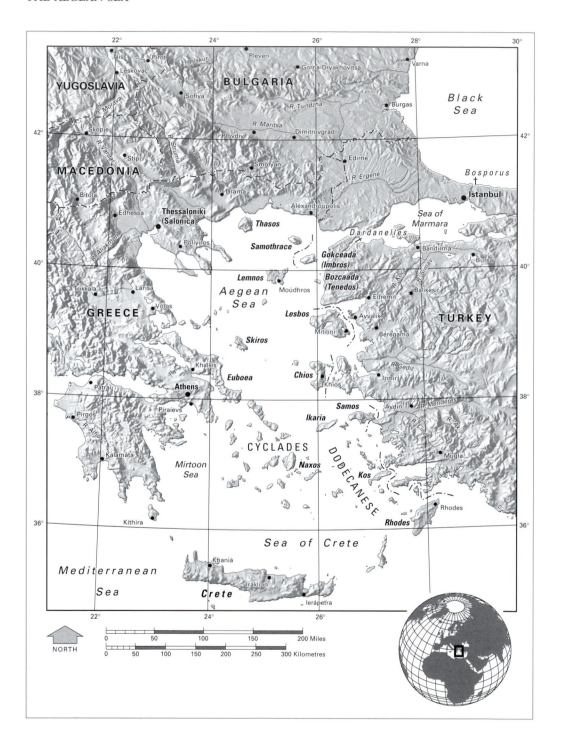

The main issues on which the dispute is focused are: ■ *Status*
a) the territorial sea;
b) the continental shelf;
c) air space, sovereignty and control; and
d) the re-militarisation of the Greek islands.

Tension rose considerably in January 1996 when Greece and Turkey came to the brink of war over an uninhabited islet in the eastern Aegean, known as Imia to the Greeks and Kardak to the Turks. The incident originated on 26 December 1995 when a Turkish coaster ran aground on the islet and refused help from Greek tugs. This illustrates how a seemingly minor event can have major geopolitical repercussions. Given future developments forecast on the Black Sea littoral and in the Caspian Sea Basin, and the parlous state of Greek–Turkish relations, the Aegean is destined to remain a major potential flashpoint.

■ *Reading*

Arvanitopoulos, C. (1998) *The International Legal Status of the Aegean*, Athens, Greece: Ministry of Mass Media (pamphlet)

Beeley, B.W. (1989) The Turkish–Greek boundary: change and continuity, in *International Boundaries and Boundary Conflict Resolution*, Conference Proceedings, Durham: International Boundaries Research Institute (IBRU), University of Durham, pp. 29–40

Munir, M. (1976) The Aegean conflict: is reconciliation possible? *The Middle East*, No. 24, October, pp. 8–12

Rozakis, C.L. (1975) *The Greek–Turkish Dispute over the Aegean Continental Shelf*, Kingston, Rhode Island: Law of the Sea Institute, University of Rhode Island

3

AFGHANISTAN

Situation ■ With an area of 652,000 km^2 and a population of just over 20 million, Afghanistan is a sparsely populated, largely mountainous landlocked state. It shares boundaries with Iran, Turkmenistan, Uzbekistan, Tajikistan and Pakistan, all of which have, over the recent past, exhibited degrees of instability. As there are ethno-linguistic links with all five countries, Afghanistan can be seen as a regional flashpoint. In Afghanistan, what was a Cold War conflict involving the Soviet Union and the United States of America (USA) has metamorphosed into a post-Cold War ethno-nationalist contest for power.

Issue ■ Following a treaty with Britain, Afghanistan became a recognised state in 1879, but was subsequently fashioned as a buffer between British and Russian spheres of influence. This is seen most obviously with the Wakhan Panhandle, designed to keep Russia from the Indian subcontinent (see p. 360). Under Amanullah Khan, Afghanistan won independence in the third Anglo–Afghan war of 1919. The monarchy was overthrown in 1973 when a republic was proclaimed and, following a further coup in 1978, the Marxist-Leninist People's Democratic Party of Afghanistan (PDPA) took power. The new party lacked popular support and the rule by decree and mass terror which it initiated resulted in revolt. Within two years, by 1957, it had split into two factions – Khalq and Parcham. The association of Afghanistan with freedom fighters (*mujahidin*) and refugees began at this time.

With continuing instability in a Marxist state in its boundary area, the Soviet Union sent troops into the country in September 1979 and installed a Parchami-dominated PDPA leadership. Other interpretations of the Soviet action include the expansion of the Soviet Union to provide more leverage in the Middle East and the start of an attempt to gain a port along the Makran coast. The effect was worldwide condemnation and large-scale support for the resistance from the USA, Saudi Arabia, Pakistan and China. By 1987 it was estimated that 1.25 million people had been killed and that the fighting had generated more than 5 million refugees who had moved to Pakistan and Iran. One side effect of this was that Pakistan received massive aid and was considered a close ally of the USA.

In the long struggle over the most taxing of environmental conditions, the Soviet troops could not establish lasting ascendency and, under Mikhail Gorbachev, the decision was taken to withdraw. The Soviet Union, the USA, Pakistan and Afghanistan signed four agreements in Geneva to this effect, but no agreement was reached on the composition of

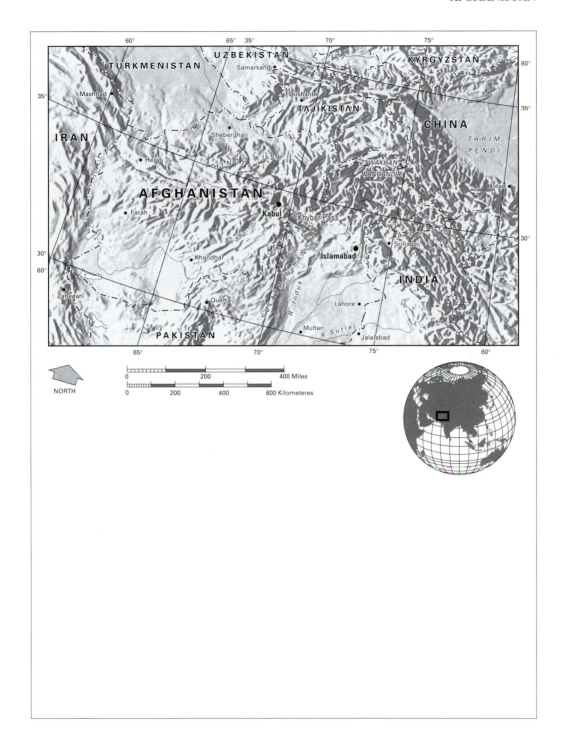

NORTH

0   200   400 Miles

0   200   400   600 Kilometeres

the possible future government. Following withdrawal, both the USA and the Soviet Union continued to aid their clients and the government lost control of most of the periphery. With the demise of the Soviet Union in 1991, Mohammed Najibullah, who had held power insecurely, was removed and a loose coalition of *mujahidin* leaders established the Islamic state of Afghanistan on 6 May 1992.

However, there was little overall agreement among the *mujahidin* leadership and the next key event was the entry of the *taliban* (Islamic students) who captured the city of Khandahar. Despite some setbacks, the *taliban* continued to take over areas of the country, including the city of Jalalabad and, in September 1996, Kabul. After 17 years of civil war, stability seemed a possibility, but anti-*taliban* forces remained, backed among others by India, Russia and Uzbekistan.

Status ■ Although it controls Kabul and approximately 60 per cent of the country, the *taliban* regime is recognised by only a few states, including Pakistan, Saudi Arabia and the UAE. In Central Asia, the Afghan conflict is regarded as potentially the most dangerous strategic issue facing the region. A further complication is the development of petroleum in the Caspian Sea Basin and the need to construct a pipeline network. A major pipeline through Afghanistan would not only benefit that country but would support economic expansion in Pakistan and possibly India. Apart from the security of such a pipeline, the other fear is that its construction would necessitate collusion with a *taliban* administration, partially condemned worldwide for its human rights record and imposition of extreme religious observances. In its present approach to government, the *taliban* regime is incompatible with international norms.

As sporadic fighting continues within the country, the fear of contamination from religious extremism will remain in the countries beyond Afghanistan's boundaries. Thus, Afghanistan will continue to be a regional and potentially global flashpoint for the foreseeable future.

Reading ■ International Institute for Strategic Studies (IISS) (1998) Pakistan's growing crisis in the shadow of Afghanistan, *Strategic Comments*, 4(8)
Keating, M. (1998) Principles clash in Afghanistan, *The World Today*, 54(5), pp. 31–2
Magnus, R. (1998) Afghanistan in 1997, *Asian Survey*, 38(2), pp. 109–15
Marley, W. (1998) The perils of pipelines, *The World Today*, 54(8–9), pp. 231–2
Saikal, A. (1998) Afghanistan's ethnic conflict, *Survival*, 40(2), pp. 114–26

4

ALBANIA

Other than the micro-states, Albania is regarded as the smallest and least developed state in Europe. With the disintegration of the Soviet Union and Yugoslavia, Estonia, Slovenia, Macedonia and Latvia have smaller populations, while Slovenia and Macedonia comprise smaller areas. Albania has an area of 28,748 km^2 and a population of approximately 3.6 million. With regard to development, it has the second lowest gross domestic product (GDP) per capita in Europe (Moldova is lower). To this lack of natural endowment can be added a highly vulnerable location. Albania is situated near the entry to the Adriatic Sea and has boundaries with Montenegro, Kosovo (both constituent elements of Yugoslavia), Macedonia and Greece. Only the last of these boundaries can be considered stable and, following the conflict over Kosovo (see p. 180), the Balkan Peninsula must be characterised as volatile.

■ *Situation*

The mountainous nature of the country has tended to inhibit development and the population is split between two main ethno-linguistic groups, separated by the Shkumbin River. To the north are the Ghegs and to the south, the Tosks. The country has its own language and is the only predominantly Muslim state in Europe.

Following the occupation of the country by Italy in 1939 and the departure of King Zog, a power struggle ensued between communist and non-communist resistance groups. In 1945, Enva Hoxha, the leader of the Albanian Communist Party, took power and remained in place until 1985. Through the secret police, the army and the Communist Party, he followed hard-line Stalinist policies well after they had been repudiated elsewhere in the 1960s. He resisted incorporation into Yugoslavia following the Soviet–Yugoslav dispute of 1948 and combated Soviet pressures by developing a close relationship with China.

■ *Issue*

Following the demise of the Warsaw Pact countries after 1989, Ramiz Alia, Hoxha's successor, introduced a series of reforms which culminated in the first Albanian election of March 1991. However, the return of land to peasant ownership resulted in excessive fragmentation and other economic measures produced high inflation, massive unemployment and a large budget deficit. Nevertheless, the economy recovered strongly in the mid-1990s, only to collapse again in 1997 following the 'pyramid' financial schemes in which agency rights are sold to more and more distributors at increasingly lower levels. Even more than the replacement of the former socialist system, this event brought the country to the edge of anarchy. Rebels seized control of the southern third

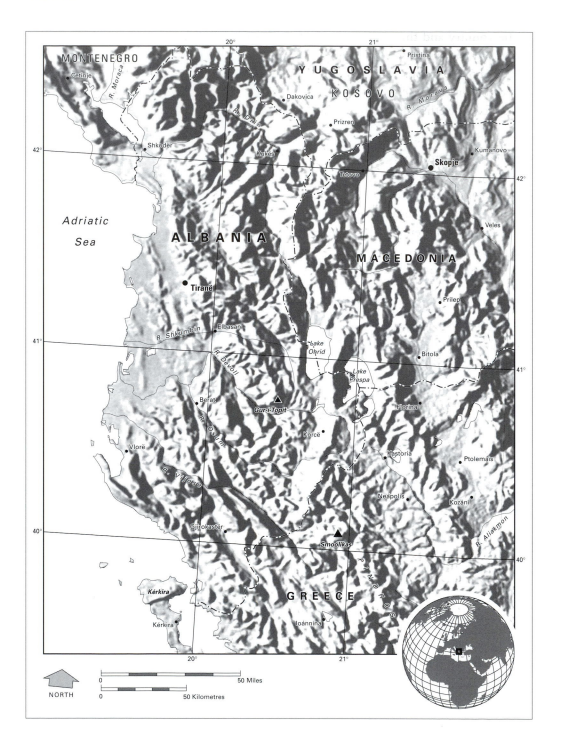

MONTENEGRO

Cetinje

R. Moraca

Shkodër

Adriatic

Sea

ALBANIA

Tiranë

R. Shkumbin

Elbasan

R. Devoll

R. Osüm

Berat

Gur-i-Topit

R. Vijose

Vlorë

Gjirokastër

Kérkira

Kérkira

YUGOSLAVIA

KOSOVO

Pristina

Dakovica

R. Drin

Prizren

R. Morava

Kukes

Skopje

Tetovo

Kumanovo

Veles

MACEDONIA

Prilep

Lake
Ohrid

Bitola

Lake
Prespa

Florina

Korcë

Kastoria

Ptolemaïs

Neápolis

Kozáni

R. Aliakmon

Smoólikas

P I N D H O S

GREECE

Ioánnina

20°   21°

42°   42°

41°   41°

40°   40°

NORTH

0   50 Miles

0   50 Kilometres

of the country and the government called for external support. This was forthcoming from eight nations which feared a further torrent of refugees and an overspill of conflict. A total of 5,900 troops were despatched under 'Operation Alba'. The southern rebellion ended and, in early 1998, national attention turned to Kosovo, the population of which was, before the ethnic cleansing in the first half of 1999, predominantly Albanian.

In the 1990s, Albania has been implicated in illegal interstate and transnational activities, ranging from arms smuggling to drug trafficking and international prostitution. The economy has yet to show signs of recovery from past problems and there is widespread unemployment and poverty. With the expulsion of ethnic Albanians from Kosovo there is the added issue of refugees, not only in Albania but also in Macedonia and Bosnia. All three states are potentially unstable, while the future of Kosovo itself, and indeed of Yugoslavia, is very much in the balance. Thus, Albania is more than ever a focal point for potential geopolitical activity in the Balkans.

■ *Status*

Hibbert, R. (1998) Quiet after the storm? *The World Today*, 54(1), pp. 24–5
Schmidt, F. (1998) Upheaval in Albania, *Current History*, 97(617), pp. 127–31
Thomas, R. (1998) Choosing the warpath, *The World Today*, 54(5), pp. 118–20

■ *Reading*

5

ALGERIA

Situation ■ Algeria is the central state in the Maghreb or Far West of the Arab world and has an area of 2,381,740 km^2. It is the largest Arab state, some one-fifth larger than Saudi Arabia, and its population of more than 30 million comprises 12 per cent of the total Arab world population. Algeria extends from the Mediterranean southwards well into the Sahel and completely dwarfs its neighbours, being the second largest country in Africa. More than the other countries of the Maghreb, Algeria is involved in African affairs.

More important has been the fact that Algeria is part of the Mediterranean world and has close ties with the European Union (EU) and particularly France. With the decline in trans-Saharan trade apparent in the modern era, the southern areas of Algeria are chiefly significant for oil, the state's major resource and the basis of its GDP.

Geopolitically, the direct links with France in particular have distinguished the Maghreb from the Mashreq, the Middle East proper. Algeria is in the centre of the littoral of the western Mediterranean basin in the approaches to the Strait of Gibraltar. The survival of Berber dialects provides a clear indication of Algeria's eccentric position in the Arab world, while the importance of French as a language illustrates the strong European connections.

Issue ■ Algeria occupied a large part of the fluctuating area between the ancient kingdoms of Morocco and Egypt and only became a sovereign state during the colonial period. It was occupied by France in 1844 and gained independence in 1962 after a long and very bloody war which lasted for eight years and accounted for 1 million lives. The resulting hostility overshadowed French anxiety to maintain access to oil and its Saharan nuclear testing sites and, with the signing of the Evian Accords, most of the settler population, the *Colons* or *pieds noirs*, left the country. The Front de Liberation Nationale (FLN) had won the war, but fighting continued in both Algeria and France.

The FLN therefore inherited a chaotic situation which was greatly exacerbated by in-fighting within its own factions. Eventually, in 1963 Ahmed Ben Bella, released from gaol in France specifically for negotiations, was confirmed as president. A mere two years later, following an army coup, he was replaced by his erstwhile colleague, Houari Boumedienne, leader of a separate faction, the Armée de Liberation Nationale (ALN). Under the new government, the economy pursued an erratic course over the next 13 years. Oil nationalisation in 1971 allowed the benefits of the oil price rises of 1973–74 and 1979–80 to be enjoyed, but there were great problems in the agricultural sector.

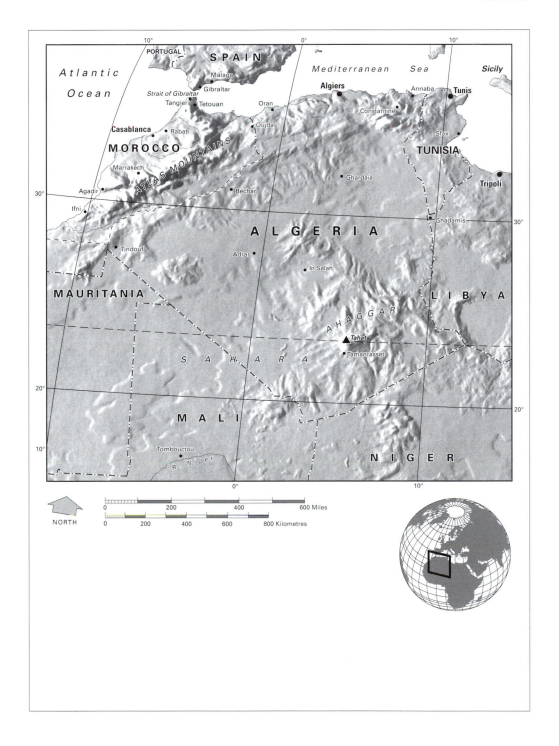

Atlantic
Ocean

PORTUGAL
SPAIN
Malaga
Gibraltar
Strait of Gibraltar
Tangier • Tetouan
Oran
Oujda
Casablanca
• Rabat
MOROCCO
Marrakech
ATLAS MOUNTAINS
Agadir •
Ifni •
Bechar •
Tindouf •

Mediterranean   Sea

Sicily

Algiers
Constantine
Annaba •
Tunis
Sfax •
TUNISIA
Ghardaia •
Tripoli
Ghadamis

ALGERIA

Adrar •
In Salah •

MAURITANIA

LIBYA

AHAGGAR
S A H A R A
▲ Tahat
• Tamanrasset

MALI

Tombouctou •
R. Niger

NIGER

10°   0°   10°
30°   30°
20°   20°
10°
0°   10°

NORTH

0   200   400   600 Miles

0   200   400   600   800 Kilometres

On the death of the president, the army again took over and the presidency of Chadli Ben Jedid was confirmed by national elections in 1979, 1984 and 1988. Over this period further problems arose, particularly over the imposed conformity to the Arabic language and Islam. Nonetheless, Algeria appeared on the world stage as a mediator in the USA–Iran Tehran hostages crisis and tempered its support for the Polisario Front engaged in its war with Morocco over Western Sahara (see p. 364). However, plunging oil prices during the mid–1980s severely weakened the economy and a number of country-wide riots ensued. The beneficiaries were the Front Islamique de Salut (FIS), the fast-growing Islamic fundamentalist movement. In the liberalisation that followed the riots, they and other groups thrived and, although it was formerly disbanded, the FIS won 44 per cent of the seats in the National Assembly during the first round of the electoral process, the president resigned and Mohammed Boudiaf took over. Some five months later, amid growing problems, the new president was assassinated, thereby ending any attempt to develop a political movement separate from both the FLN and FIS. Conflict between the FIS and the military-supported government ensued, neither side enjoying popular support.

By 1993, the underground movement had developed into the Group Islamique Armé (GIA), which was dominant in the central and northern areas, including the capital, Algiers, and the Mouvement Islamique Armé (MIA) which controlled large areas of the east and west. Only in the south, in the area of the oil and gas fields, was government control unhampered by the threat of Islamic fundamentalism.

As during the later stages of the colonial period, the government was divided between the *Conciliateurs* and the *Eradicateurs*. The latter's lack of success brought to power in 1994 a representative of the former Liamine Zerouel with the intention of negotiating with the FIS. However, the level of extremism on both sides always made the possibility of compromise unlikely.

Violence, often extreme, continued. So complex was the situation, with so many potential sources of violence, that outside influence had little effect and reports of atrocities have appeared in the media regularly up to the present time. Meanwhile, Zerouel has endeavoured to legitimise the dominance of his military-political group, thereby preventing any possible repeat of the 1991 Islamist victory. The organ for effecting this has been the National Democratic Rally (RND), founded in 1997, which has worked with the FLN and the Movement for a Peaceful Society (MSP), a non-extreme Islamist group.

Despite these shrewd political moves, many consider the changes to be merely cosmetic. ■ *Status*
Following the dominance of the RND in the 1997 elections, the government was
accused of fraud and the slaughter in the villages continued. Indeed, there are allegations
that the military has been implicated in the brutality. Others have suggested that the GIA
is taking revenge on formerly supportive villages, that former landowners are seeking to
reclaim their land and that various militias, overtly supported by the government, are
indulging in violence. Claims and counter-claims abound, but the stark fact remains that
between January 1992 and the early part of 1998 more than 60,000 lives had been lost
through bombings, assassinations and what can only be described as wanton brutality.

Given the disparate elements involved in the situation, the fact that it is impossible to
identify the combatants and that motives remain opaque, it is extremely difficult to see
how Algeria will not remain a flashpoint for the medium term. Furthermore, there must
be great anxiety that the violence will spill over into Tunisia and Morocco, both of which
appear to have overcome their own internal problems.

Boyd, A. (1998) *An Atlas of World Affairs*, London: Routledge ■ *Reading*
Central Intelligence Agency (CIA) (1997) *The World Fact Book*, Washington, DC:
   Central Intelligence Agency
IISS (1998) *Strategic Survey 1997/98*, Oxford: Oxford University Press
Sluglett, P. and Farouk-Sluglett, M. (1996) *The Times Guide to the Middle East*, London:
   Times Books

6

ANGOLA

Situation ■ Located on the south-west coast of Africa, Angola, large and well endowed with minerals, includes a small but important enclave, Cabinda (see p. 63). Boundaries are shared with Congo, Democratic Republic of the Congo (formerly Zaire), Zambia and Namibia. The Caprivi Strip (see p. 71) is a panhandle which separates Angola from Botswana. With an area of 1,246,700 km^2 and a population of just over 11 million, population density is low. Despite its immense potential wealth, the GDP per capita of Angola is only just over half that of Albania. Since independence from Portugal in 1975 there has been almost continuous conflict.

Issue ■ During the last part of the colonial period, liberation forces gathered momentum, but by the early 1960s had split into three main movements:

a) the Popular Movement for the Liberation of Angola (MPLA), which was Soviet backed and controlled most of Cabinda, together with most of the centre of Angola;

b) the National Front for the Liberation of Angola (FNLA), which controlled most of the north; and

c) the National Union for the Total Independence of Angola (UNITA), which controlled most of the south and east under the leadership of Jonas Savimbi.

Even before the official proclamation of independence on 11 November 1975, the FNLA had entered into an alliance with UNITA against the MPLA. Under the auspices of MPLA, the People's Republic of Angola was declared, but 12 days later the FNLA–UNITA announced the establishment of the Democratic People's Republic of Angola.

The country descended into civil war, with the MPLA supported by extensive Soviet aid and some 18,000 Cuban troops in the field. The FNLA received US finance and direct military support from up to 5,000 South African troops. By 1984, the FNLA had been largely beaten in the north and the confrontation with UNITA became locked into a vicious and continuing stalemate. Basically, the MPLA controlled the urban areas and UNITA the rural.

In 1992 the leadership of both groups finally agreed to post-election unity but in the subsequent election, Savimbi would not accept defeat. Widespread violence ensued, with the result that the USA withdrew support from UNITA; on 2 June 1993, the UN Security Council declared UNITA responsible for the breakdown of peace negotiations.

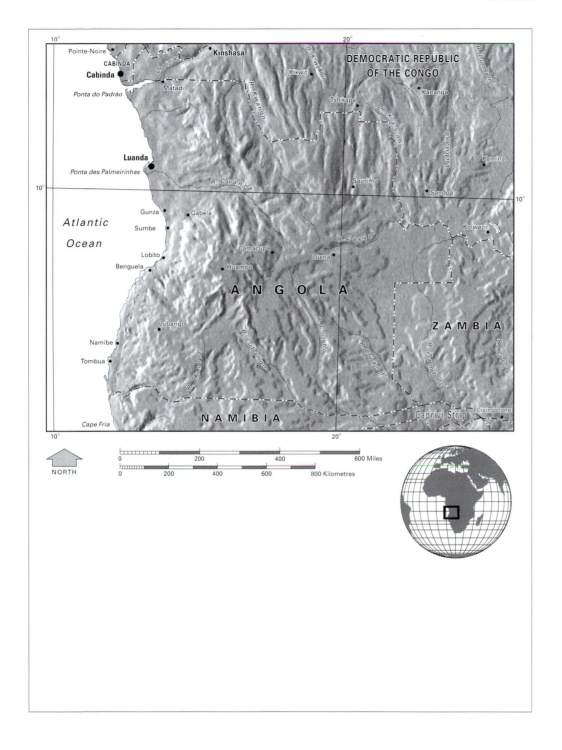

10°
Pointe-Noire
CABINDA
Cabinda
Ponta do Padrão

Kinshasa

Matadi

Kikwit

20°

R. Kwilu

R. Kwango

**DEMOCRATIC REPUBLIC
OF THE CONGO**

Tshikapa

R. Kasai

Kananga

R. Lomami

R. Lubilash

Kamina

Luanda
Ponta des Palmeirinhas

R. Cuanza

Saurimo

Sandoa

Kolwezi

10°

10°

*Atlantic
Ocean*

Gunza
Gabela
Sumbe

Camacupa
Lobito
Benguela
Huambo

R. Cassai

Luena

A N G O L A

R. Cuito

R. Cuando

Z A M B I A

R. Zambezi

R. Kafue

Lubango

R. Cunene

R. Cubango

Namibe

Tombua

Cape Fria

N A M I B I A

Capriví Strip

Livingstone

10°

20°

NORTH

0   200   400   600 Miles

0   200   400   600   800 Kilometres

19

In 1994, a final agreement on peace was reached in Lusaka, but the transfer of UNITA-held territory to government control did not begin until 1997. In July 1997 the UN Security Council imposed sanctions on UNITA. However, earlier in the same year, Angolan troops became involved in the conflict in the Democratic Republic of the Congo (see p. 86), thus re-establishing a long-standing connection.

Status ■ Throughout 1998 there was little progress towards the fulfilment of the Lusaka Agreement and fighting continued, reportedly linked at times with that in the Democratic Republic of the Congo. UNITA supports the Tutsi-led Congolese rebels and retains control over areas of southern Angola. Savimbi is relying upon the fact that, in the long term, the advantage will swing towards him. Therefore, Angola is unlikely to attain political stability in the near term. Furthermore, the conflict will remain enmeshed in those of neighbouring states.

Reading ■ Anstee, M. (1998) The fight goes on, *The World Today*, 54(10), pp. 256–8

Brittain, V. (1998) *Death of Dignity: Angola's Civil War*, London: Pluto Press

Guimaraes, F.A. (1998) *The Origins of the Angolan Civil War: Foreign Intervention and Domestic Political Conflict*, Basingstoke: Macmillan

IISS (1998) Renewed war in Angola: a threat of regional conflict, *Strategic Comments*, 4(7), p. 2

7

AZERBAIJAN

Located in the Transcaucasus on the Caspian Sea, Azerbaijan has an area of $86,600$ km^2 and is landlocked with regard to the world's oceans. It shares boundaries with the Russian Federation, Georgia, Armenia and Iran, all four of which have witnessed instability in its immediate neighbourhood. It includes an enclave, Nagorno-Karabakh (see p. 236), which has witnessed continuing conflict, and an exclave, Nakhichevan, in the south-western border area of Armenia. To the south, Azerbaijan borders on the Kurdish areas, the major parts of which are in Turkey, Iraq and Iran. As one of the world's oldest oil-producing regions, the country was at the hub of the Soviet petroleum industry. With such a strategic position and a key resource, Azerbaijan is at the point of convergence of many geopolitical issues.

■ *Situation*

The population of Azerbaijan is just over 7.5 million, but a further 9 million Azerbaijanis live across the boundary in Iran. The Azeri language is Turkik, but the population is predominantly Shi'a Muslim and natural religious ties are therefore with Iran.

■ *Issue*

During the last years of the Soviet Union, tensions between central governments and minorities escalated throughout the Transcaucasus and at independence these became full-scale wars in the Abkhazian republic of Georgia (see p. 120) and in Nagorno-Karabakh. Thus, well before 1991 there was already anti-Soviet protest, but with independence in that year, the Communist Party was transformed into the Democratic Party of Azerbaijan.

Apart from the economy, which like those of other former Soviet states went into sharp decline, the major issue was the war with Armenia over Nagorno-Karabakh, which itself absorbed almost a quarter of the national budget. The main pressure on successive governments resulted from their inability to either protect Azeris from ethnic cleansing by Armenian troops or to evict Armenian forces from Nagorno-Karabakh.

In 1994, Azerbaijan signed a Caspian Sea oil exploitation agreement with a consortium of companies led by British Petroleum and this clearly displeased the Russian Federation. Further complications followed over the proposed routes of pipelines from the Caspian Basin. However, in October 1995 the consortium, which included Lukoil of Russia, agreed that there should be two pipelines: one an upgraded version of the current pipeline which passed through Russia to the Black Sea and the other would run through

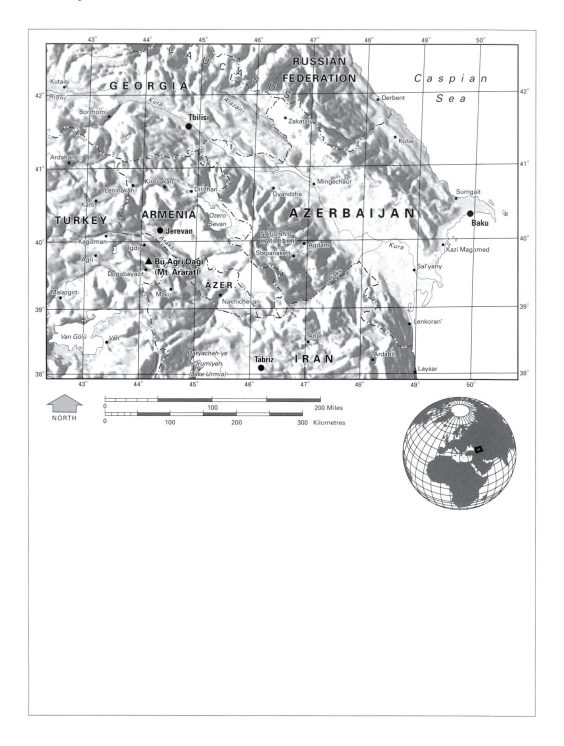

NORTH

0   100   200 Miles

0   100   200   300 Kilometres

Georgia and then possibly Turkey. Under pressure from the USA, Iran was excluded from the deal but was granted a share in the next phase of development.

Meanwhile, attempts at settlement of the Nagorno-Karabakh question with the help of the Organisation for Security and Co-operation in Europe (OSCE) had foundered and, in 1996, the Armenians of Nagorno-Karabakh declared independence unilaterally. Although it had achieved less prominence, the Nakhichevan had also been a source of military confrontation since 1990. In 1994 Azerbaijan was pressured into joining the Commonwealth of Independent States (CIS) but, unlike Georgia, managed to resist the placement of permanent Russian troops on its soil.

International pressure is likely to mount for the settlement of the conflict in Azerbaijan so that the Caspian Basin oilfields can be developed. However, unrest among Azeri refugees is growing and for various reasons the situation in Azerbaijan is more critical than that in Georgia. Russia is less of a constraining influence and, with the expected oil revenues, Azerbaijan may well act independently to solve its own problems. In this context, the Azerbaijan army has been restructured with foreign, especially Turkish, assistance. While such action may potentially frighten foreign conglomerates, once there has been substantial investment it is likely that Azerbaijan would receive Western support. Relations with Russia, which has been accused of sponsoring separatist movements working towards the unification of parts of Dagestan and Azerbaijan, remain strained. With internal and external disputes, oil reserves estimated at 0.7 per cent of the world total, pipeline routing problems and a division of Caspian oil resources yet to be resolved, Azerbaijan is likely to remain a major flashpoint.

■ *Status*

Cornell, S. (1997) The unruly Caucasus, *Current History*, 96(612), pp. 341–7

Croissant, M.P. (1998) *Armenia–Azerbaijan Conflict: Causes and Implications*, Westport, CT: Praeger

Ebel, R. (1997) The oil rush in the Caucasus, *Current History*, 96(612), pp. 344–5

Halbach, U. (1998) The Caucasus as a region of conflict, *Aussenpolitik*, 48(4)

Harvard University (1998) *Future Prospects for the Eurasian Corridor: a Series of Round-table Discussions*, Cambridge, MA: Harvard University (pamphlet)

Leeun, C. (1998) *Storm over the Caucasus: in the Wake of Independence*, Richmond: Curzon Press

■ *Reading*

8

BAB EL MANDEB

Situation ■ Bab el Mandeb is the strait controlling the entrance to the Red Sea from the Gulf of Aden and is considered one of the major choke points of the world. Choke points are locations, frequently straits, in which there is a convergence of sea-lines of communication and a concentration of shipping, and which are therefore vulnerable to attack. Perim Island, which measures 8 km^2, divides Bab el Mandeb into a small strait on the eastern side and the main strait on the western side. The shipping lane is approximately 6 km wide and up to 200 metres (m) deep. The northern side is occupied by Yemen and the southern is shared between Eritrea and Djibouti.

Issue ■ Britain occupied Perim Island in 1799 and annexed the port area of Aden in 1839. Aden was considered a major coaling station and naval base to protect the important route to India. As a protection for Aden, accord was reached with neighbouring sheikhdoms and the Aden Protectorate was set up. Aden was considered even more important following the short war which resulted in the loss of the Suez Canal in 1956 (see p. 318). In 1962, the Federation of South Arabia was established but, in the face of national liberation forces, Britain withdrew in November 1967.

To illustrate the strategic significance of Bab el Mandeb, two incidents can be cited. On 11 June 1971, the *Coral Sea* a Liberian-flag tanker chartered by Israel, was attacked in the Strait of Tiran (at the head of the Red Sea) by rockets from a gunboat positioned in the vicinity of Perim Island. During the October 1973 war with Israel, Egypt blockaded the Red Sea and, to reinforce this measure, used Perim Island from the then People's Democratic Republic of Yemen (PDRY) in October 1974. During July and August 1984, some 18 vessels were damaged by mines laid in the Red Sea, predominantly at the southern end.

Bab el Mandeb is important for global trade between Asia and Europe, including oil exports from the Persian/Arabian Gulf. However, its significance is not only related to traffic through the Suez Canal since Red Sea ports, particularly of countries like Sudan and Eritrea with no other coastline, are dependent upon it for trade with Asia. To an extent, trade has been undermined by the construction of the Saudi Petroline across the Arabian Peninsula, but this factor has been partly counteracted by the increase in the capacity of the Suez Canal and the further development of the Suez–Mediterranean (SUMED) pipeline built through Egypt to circumvent the canal. As with almost all straits in the world, other than Dover, there are no accurate statistics kept on ship transits. It is

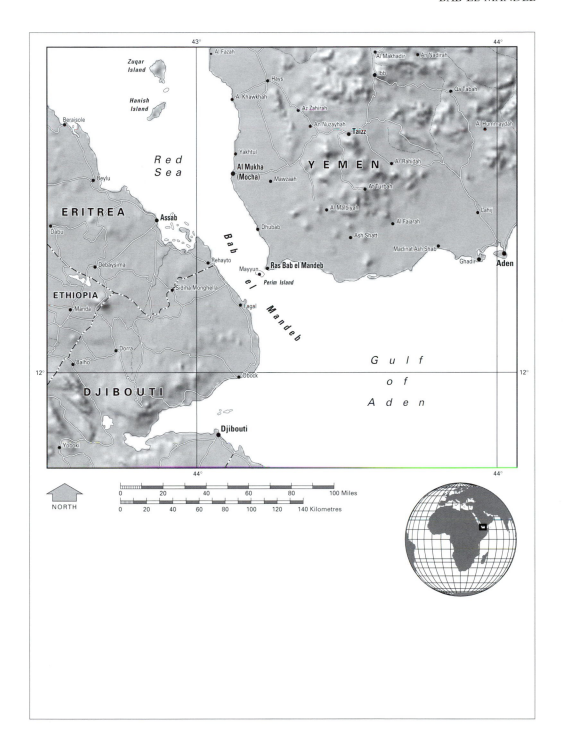

43°

44°

Al Fazah

Al Makhadir
An Nadirah

Hays

Ibb

Al Khawkhah

Qa Tabah

Zuqar
Island

Az Zahirah

Al Hummaydah

Hanish
Island

An Nuzayhah

Beraisole

Taizz

Red
Sea

Yakhtul

Y E M E N

Beylu

Al Mukha
(Mocha)

Ar Rahidah

Mawzaah

At Turbah

ERITREA

Al Malbiyah

Lahij

Assab

Al Fajarah

Dabu

Dhubab

Ash Shatt

Debaysima

Madinat Ash Shab

Ghadir

Aden

Rehayto

Ras Bab el Mandeb

Sidiha Monghella

Mayyun

Perim Island

ETHIOPIA

Manda

Fagal

Dorra

Balho

Gulf

Obock

12°

12°

of

DJIBOUTI

Aden

Djibouti

Yoboki

44°

44°

NORTH

0   20   40   60   80   100 Miles

0   20   40   60   80   100   120   140 Kilometres

25

reasonable to assume that Bab el Mandeb is transited by approximately 55 ships a day, making a total of 20,000 a year. This is considerably less than Dover, or the Malacca straits, but is only slightly less than Hormuz and places Bab el Mandeb among the most heavily used sea routes is the world.

Closely linked to traffic through the strait is Hanish Island, which is virtually on the median line of the Red Sea. In December 1995, Eritrean and Yemeni forces clashed on the island which is of strategic significance, but also potentially important for fishing, tourism and possibly petroleum exploitation. In October 1998, a tribunal ruled in favour of Yemen and the Hanish Islands were formally handed over to Yemeni sovereignty on 1 November 1998. Having agreed on sovereignty, the delimitation of the maritime boundary between the two states was completed in December 1999. This is the first maritime delimitation in the Red Sea and may sensitise the region to the need for maritime boundaries.

Status ■ Bab el Mandeb is vital for world maritime trade and remains a key strategic location. This point can be illustrated by the fact that the USA has opened discussions with Yemen on the use of both Mocha and a rejuvenated Aden by its fleet. Furthermore, on the northern side there remains the boundary dispute between Saudi Arabia and Yemen (see p. 367) and on the southern side, the increasingly bitter war between Eritrea and Ethiopia (see pp. 109–13). Bab el Mandeb therefore lies in an unstable region.

Reading ■ Anderson, E.W. (1985) Dire straits, *Defense and Diplomacy*, 3(9), pp. 16–20
Dzurek, D. (1996) *Eritrea–Yemen Dispute over the Hanish Islands*, Durham: Boundary and Security Bulletin 4(1), pp. 70–7
Hildesley, W. (1994) *Boundary and Security Bulletin*, 2(2)
Plant, M. (1996) A clash for control in the shipping lanes, *The World Today*, 2(6), pp. 46–7
Rais, R.B. (1986) *The Indian Ocean and the Superpowers*, London: Croom Helm

9

THE BALTIC REPUBLICS

The Baltic Republics are three small, independent states which have much in common, but there are major differences between them. They have common political, economic and social concerns, but each guards jealously its own distinctive language and heritage. The basic statistics are:

■ *Situation*

	Area (km^2)	Population (millions)
Estonia	45,100	1.5
Latvia	63,700	2.5
Lithuania	65,200	3.7

Key problems concern internal ethnic issues, boundary disputes and, above all, relations with the rest of Europe.

Throughout their history, the Baltic Republics have been dependent upon their more powerful neighbours, in particular Russia, Germany and Poland. They were independent between the two world wars but were incorporated into the Soviet Union in 1940. During the Cold War they were strategically significant in providing bases for the Soviet Union, most notably the ice-free ports of Tallin and Riga. However, several states, including the USA and the UK, never accepted the Soviet sovereignty, despite the plebiscite in 1944 which apparently supported it.

■ *Issue*

All three states declared independence in 1990, Lithuania in March and the other two in May, and all received international recognition. Nevertheless, there remain disputes between them. Estonia and Latvia have a problem over a maritime boundary and fishing rights, while the dispute between Latvia and Lithuania concerns oil exploration on the continental shelf. There are also boundary disputes with Russia, although a Lithuanian–Russian border agreement of maritime delimitation was signed in October 1997. Estonia and Latvia still have unsettled land boundary concerns with Russia.

Potentially more important are the ethnic problems which concern the future of Russian speakers, who make up the following percentages of the population: Estonia 29, Latvia 30 and Lithuania 8.5. The rights of these minorities have been constantly raised by Russia. The other key Russian problem concerns Kaliningrad *oblast* (province), which remains a major military centre, and part of the Russian Federation, but is completely

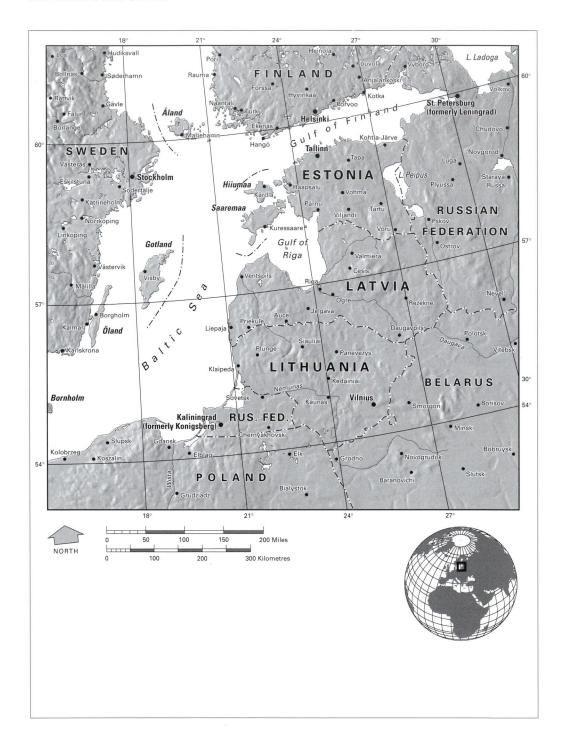

detached from it (see p. 159). Issues include the route connecting Kaliningrad to Russia through Lithuania, oil exploitation in the boundary zone and pollution.

In the decade since independence, the Baltic Republics have made far more advancement towards a market economy than any of the other states of the FSU. Accordingly, the question of NATO membership has arisen and this has caused a major problem in relations with Russia. Whichever, if any, state is admitted, it would be the first FSU state to join NATO. Since the accession of Poland, in particular, pressure for membership has increased. In January 1998, the republics signed a Charter of Partnership with the USA and the potential for NATO membership was reiterated. Russia remains fiercely opposed and the practicality of defence guarantees by NATO must be in question. ■ *Status*

In December 1997, Estonia was selected to begin accession talks with the EU. Russia had far fewer qualms about the eastward extension of economic influence than it had about NATO. The question raised a point about the Baltic states acting in concert as opposed to individually and what the reaction of Latvia and Lithuania might be. It seems that the Baltic Republics will only constitute a flashpoint if NATO's eastwards extension proceeds to include them.

Asmus, R. (1996) NATO enlargement and the Baltic states, *Survival*, 38(2), pp. 121–42 ■ *Reading*
Baev, P. (1998) Bear hug for the Baltic, *The World Today*, 54(3), pp. 78–9
Lejins, A. (1997) *Small States in a Turbulent Environment: the Baltic Perspective,* Riga: Latvian Institute of International Affairs (pamphlet)
Lieven, A. (1996) Baltic iceberg dead ahead: NATO beware, *The World Today*, 52(7), pp. 175–9
Lucas, H. (1997) The Baltic states in Europe – problems and prospects, *Aussenpolitik*, 47(42), pp. 127–36
Mauritzen, H. (1998) *Bordering Russia: Theory and Prospect for Europe's Baltic Rim,* Aldershot: Ashgate Publishing
Osterlund, B. (1996) *The Baltic Sea of Changes*, Helsinki: National Defence College of Helsinki (pamphlet)
Sergounin, A. (1997) *Russia and Evolving Security Environment in the Baltic Sea Area,* Nizhny Novgorod: University of Nizhny Novgorod (pamphlet)

10

THE BARENTS SEA

Situation ■ The Barents Sea is a marginal sea of the Arctic Ocean, bordered by the three island groups of Spitzbergen, Franz Josef Land and Novaya Zemlya, a stretch of the Russian coastline, including the Kola Peninsula, and a short length of the Norwegian coastline. Apart from a narrow deep close to the mainland, it is relatively shallow and, owing to the North Atlantic Drift, ice-free as far east as Murmansk. During the Cold War, with the presence nearby of the Soviet Northern Fleet, it was one of the most critical areas of water in the world. Now, the problems are different, but the maritime boundary issue between Norway and Russia has yet to be settled.

Issue ■ Militarily, the Barents Sea has been closely associated with the Kola Penninsula (see p. 174) and the Soviet ballistic missile submarine fleet. This is based primarily at Polyarny and Murmansk and is controlled from Severomorsk, located together on the Tuloma River. The inshore deep helped protect the submarines from Western surveillance as they moved round the North Cape into the Greenland Sea. For further protection, there were some 40 airfields and many other military bases on the Kola Peninsula. The peninsula remains one of the most heavily armed areas in the world, but the state of the equipment and the morale of the troops is open to question. There is some evidence that the major components of the Northern Fleet are still fully operational. The other problem concerning the region is the decommissioning of nuclear submarines which has resulted in an extreme risk of radioactive pollution.

Apart from its military significance, which, with changes in Russia, might be at least partially re-activated, the Barents Sea is also important economically. On 11 January 1993, a declaration was signed by Russia, Norway, Sweden, Finland, Denmark, Iceland and the EU to establish the Barents Euro-Arctic Council (BEAC). The priority areas were identified as: environment, economic development and infrastructure, science and technology, education, culture, tourism and the welfare of native peoples. However, it does not cover co-operation at sea in fisheries and resource extraction as long as the Norway–Russian maritime boundary remains undelimited. This was the only active territorial dispute between the countries of NATO and the Warsaw Pact during the Cold War. The claim line of Russia is constructed due north from the Russia–Norway land boundary terminus, while the Norwegian claim is based on a median line constructed between Spitzbergen and Novaya Zemlya. As a result, there are two disputed areas which in total cover 180,000 km^2. In 1978, these areas were designated a common 'Grey Zone'.

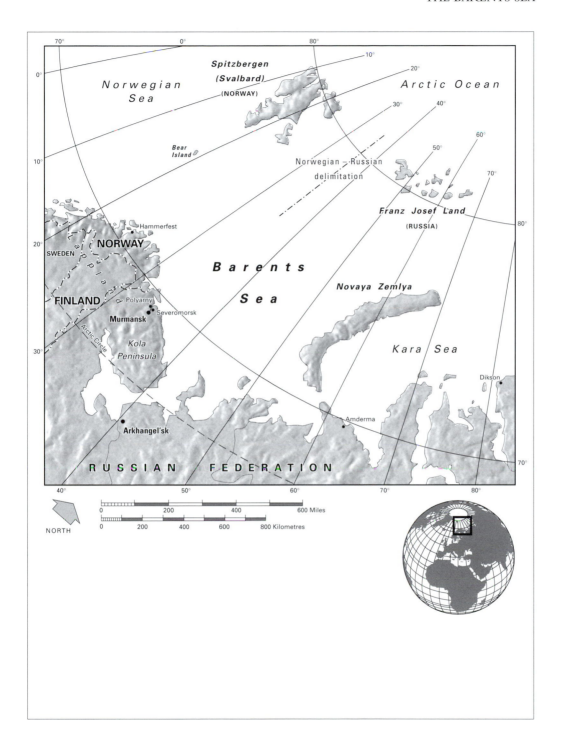

70° 0° 80°
10°

Norwegian Sea   **Spitzbergen (Svalbard)**   *Arctic Ocean*
0°   (NORWAY)   20°

30°   40°

Bear Island   50°   60°
10°

Norwegian – Russian   70°
delimitation

Franz Josef Land   80°
(RUSSIA)

20°   •Hammerfest
NORWAY
SWEDEN

B a r e n t s
S e a

FINLAND   •Polyarny   **Novaya Zemlya**
Murmansk •Severomorsk

30°   *Kola Peninsula*   *K a r a   S e a*

•Dikson
80°

•Amderma

70°

•**Arkhangel'sk**

R U S S I A N   F E D E R A T I O N

40°   50°   60°   70°   80°

0   200   400   600 Miles
0   200   400   600   800 Kilometres

NORTH

Also in the region, dispute over Spitzbergen continues and that is considered elsewhere in this volume (see p. 308). Franz Josef Land was disputed as late as 1930, but is now accepted as Russian.

Status ■ With the end of the Cold War, concerns over the Barents Sea have been transformed and there is a far higher degree of co-operation between all the parties concerned. However, the viable remaining portion of the Northern Fleet still represents a major global force. Nevertheless, the accent is on co-operation and development, which is in the interests of both Scandinavia and Russia. Norway is anxious to re-launch the northern or 'Pomor' trade route from Scandinavia to Russia. The large Russian population, having lost its defence-based employment, is in need of work. There is the possibility of opening a North-East Passage which would offer more rapid delivery from north-east Asia to Western Europe. Meanwhile, the question of actual and potential pollution on a massive scale, including the need for safety measures at the Polyarny Zori nuclear power plant, remains the key issue. For a variety of reasons, the Barents Sea must be considered a dormant flashpoint.

Reading ■ Leighton, M.K. (1979), *The Soviet Threat to NATO's Northern Flank,* Agenda Paper No. 10, New York: National Strategy Information Center

Luton, G. (1986) Strategic issues in the Arctic region, in E.M. Borgese and N. Ginsburg (eds), *Ocean Yearbook 6*, Chicago, IL: University of Chicago Press, pp. 399–416

Royal Institute of International Affairs (RIIA) (1993) Cooperation in Europe's High North: the Barents region, *The World Today*, 49(3), pp. 46–7

11

THE BASQUE COUNTRY

The Basques live in the coastal area that straddles the Franco–Spanish boundary at the eastern end of the Pyrenees. The people themselves have preserved a distinctive identity based on language and heritage. While there have been no obvious problems in France, the Spanish Basque country has been politically tense for more than a hundred years. The Basque country has a total area of 17,700 km^2 and a population of approximately 2.5 million, giving it geographical parity with many of the smaller countries of Europe. It consists of four provinces: Alava, Guipuzcoa, Vizcaya and Navarra. Only the first three of these are in the autonomous region which was recognised in 1980. This reduced the size to 7,260 km^2 and the population to about 2 million. From the 1980s, the call for independence has been more muted.

■ *Situation*

One result of the political centralisation and rapid industrialisation of Spain in the latter part of the 19th century was the development of Basque nationalism. This situation merely mirrored many others that have resulted from the centrifugal forces in many peripheral areas which have remained powerful since Spanish unification in 1715.

■ *Issue*

The Basques had their own legal-administrative system, including common ownership of some natural resources, and a separate taxation system, which included the operation of their own tariff barriers. Standardisation occurred under the central government which led to many of these local structures being destroyed. By the end of the 19th century, the Basques had lost their main distinguishing autonomous factors and the language was in decline. In parallel with this, rapid industrialisation occurred and there was a large influx of Spanish-speaking workers. The iron industry in particular produced appalling industrial pollution and this, together with the loss of traditional practices and the influx of Spanish workers, resulted in enhanced Basque nationalism. The first nationalist newspaper appeared in 1893 and in 1895 the Partido Nacionalista Vasco (PNV) was founded.

During the Spanish Civil War, one critical event occurred which completed the alienation of the Basques from the central government. On behalf of General Franco, Guernica, the ancient capital and cultural symbol of Basque autonomy, was bombed by the German Luftwaffe and more than 15,000 people were killed. The event was immortalised in a painting by Picasso which remained such a potent symbol of resistance throughout the Franco regime that it could only be returned to the country on the resumption of the monarchy, following Franco's death.

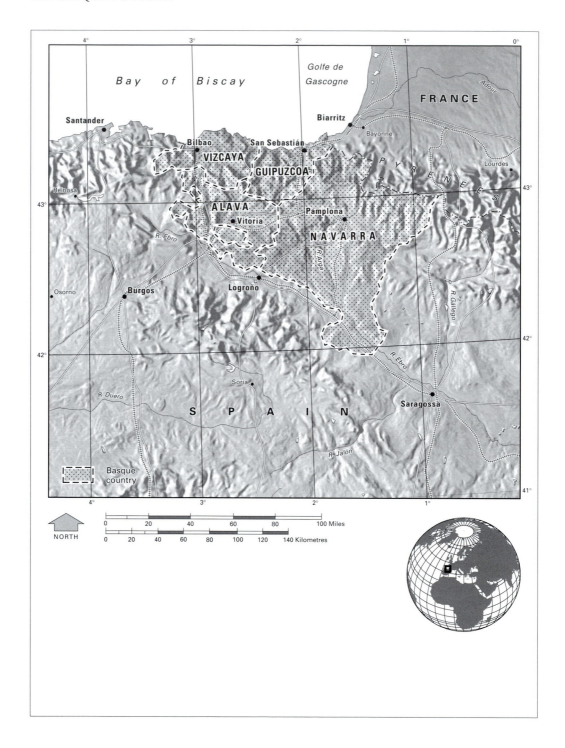

After the Civil War, repression of Basque culture increased. Language and folklore were outlawed. The PNV had become moribund and a far more militant and separatist Euzkadi ta Askatasuna (ETA) was formed from it in 1959. This radical movement combined Basque nationalism with guerrilla operations during the Franco period and completely transformed the political situation. In 1970, trials of ETA activists focused global attention on Spain, which was renewed in 1973 when ETA guerrillas assassinated Franco's chosen successor and thereby enhanced the pace of democratic transition. Franco died on 23 November 1975 and the return of Spain to democracy deprived ETA of much of its impetus. This declined further with autonomy and throughout the 1980s ETA became increasingly isolated, even within the Basque nationalist community. Furthermore, the socialist government reversed the previously centralised structure of the Spanish state. With virtual internal self-government, including their own police force, many Basques now question the need for independence.

The objective of ETA is that Basques should be able to choose whether or not they want independence. To coincide with the multi-party peace agreement in Northern Ireland in April 1998, a Basque ceasefire was announced. It appeared that the movement did not want to be isolated as the only significant armed insurgent group operating in Western Europe. On 16 September 1998, ETA announced an indefinite and total unilateral truce. With increasing centralisation in Europe, peripheral groups will continue to produce limited local flashpoints – for example, although ETA as a force has largely disintegrated, there was renewed Basque nationalist activity in 1999.

■ *Status*

Bonnefous, M. (1998) Euzkadi, *Defense Nationale*, January, pp. 95–100
Chisholm, M. and Smith, D.M. (eds) (1990) *Shared Space: Divided Space*, London: Unwin Hyman
Convers, D. (1997) *The Basques, the Catalans and Spain,* London: C. Hurst & Co.
Von Targer Page, M. (1998) *Prisons, Peace and Terrorism*, Basingstoke: Macmillan

■ *Reading*

12

THE BEAGLE CHANNEL

Situation ■ Apart from the Panama Canal or the route round Cape Horn, the only other maritime passages linking the Atlantic and the Pacific both occur near the southern tip of South America. The Beagle Channel is the southerly of these two passages and is named after *HMS Beagle*, the British survey ship in which Charles Darwin made his famous voyage in the 1830s. The channel is narrow and sinuous and although it is sheltered, meteorological and sea conditions are likely to be unfavourable. The western half is through the territory of Chile and the eastern half defines the boundary between Argentina and Chile.

Although the territorial dispute between Argentina and Chile is known as the 'Beagle Channel dispute', it is not the channel itself that is contested but three small islands at its eastern end: Lennox, Nueva and Picton.

Issue ■ The dispute, although it has now been settled, illustrates a number of interesting points. The international boundaries in the area were recognised by 1810 but, following disputes in the 1870s, there was a new Boundary Treaty of 23 July 1881. This assigned all islands east of Tierra del Fuego to Argentina and all islands south of the Beagle Channel, as far as Cape Horn and west of Tierra del Fuego, to Chile. There were, however, differences over this delimitation and in 1896 the British government, which had been in charge of executing the 1881 treaty, was asked to arbitrate. Owing to the fact that in the 1890s there was an arms race in both Chile and Argentina, there appeared at the time a distinct possibility of war over the issue in 1898. However, in 1902 both governments subscribed to a General Treaty of Arbitration, the solution by friendly means of any bilateral problems, and the British Crown was made responsible for arbitration.

The dispute resurfaced in 1904 and then on a further six occasions before, on 7 December 1967, Chile lodged an appeal based on the 1902 General Treaty of Arbitration. Britain took up the responsibility and co-opted France, Nigeria, Sweden and the USA to set up an Arbitration Court. The Arbitration Court's decision, which was formally accepted by Britain in early 1977 and delivered to Chile and Argentina on 2 May 1977, was that Chile should retain the three islands, together with other islands further south, including that on which Cape Horn is situated. Chile accepted the terms but, on 25 January 1978, Argentina rejected them, issuing a 'nullity declaration'. The dispute rumbled on in the latter part of 1978 and war seemed a possibility as both countries built up their forces in the region. In fact, conflict was forestalled when it was agreed to refer the dispute to the Pope.

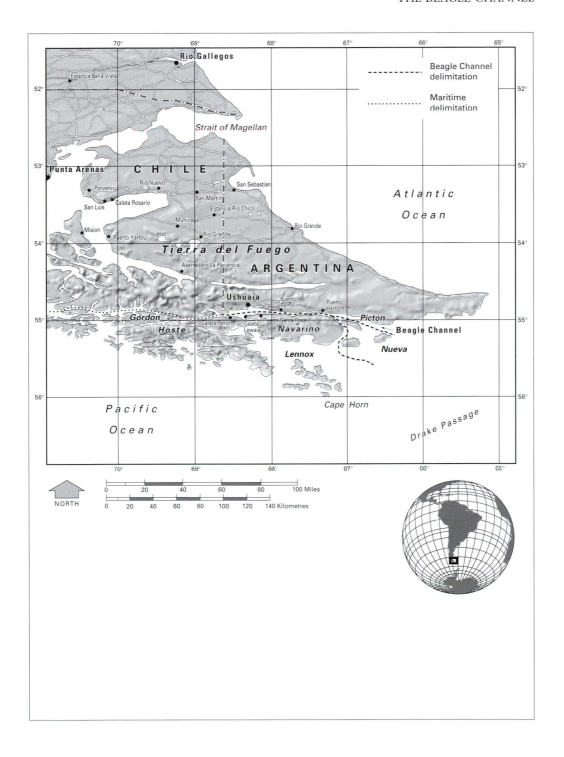

Beagle Channel delimitation

Maritime delimitation

Rio Gallegos

Estancia Bella Vista

Strait of Magellan

52°

53°

Punta Arenas

C H I L E

Rio Nuevo

Porvenir

San Sebastian

Caleta Rosario

San Martin

San Luis

Estancia Rio Chico

Munizaga

Mision

Rio Grande

Puerto Yartou

Rio Grande

Atlantic

Ocean

Tierra del Fuego

Aserradero La Paciencia

ARGENTINA

54°

Ushuaia

Puerto Remolino

Puerto Harberton

Gordon

Picton

Puerto Santa Rosa

Hoste

Caleta Peron

Caleta Lewaia

Navarino

Beagle Channel

Nueva

Lennox

Pacific

Ocean

Cape Horn

Drake Passage

NORTH

0 20 40 60 80 100 Miles

0 20 40 60 80 100 120 140 Kilometres

Status ■ During the long-running dispute, the relative importance of any decision changed. Originally, disagreement was over territory and strategic issues, but with the introduction of the EEZ the problem attained far greater significance. Possession of the islands would determine the control of large areas of ocean with their attendant fish stocks and sea-floor minerals. In the event, the proposals made by Pope John Paul II in 1980 closely resembled those of the Arbitration Court and were again refused by Argentina. In 1982, Argentina seized the Malvinas (Falkland Islands) and South Georgia and was repelled in a short and bloody conflict by the UK (see p. 116). The war highlighted the importance of resources but Argentina's defeat, together with Chile's desire to avoid a full-scale war, led to compromise and agreement on the Peace and Friendship Treaty (1984–5). With a slight modification, the terms remained much the same. Chile was to keep the islands and a boundary running due south from Cape Horn was accepted. There were sufficient adjustments with regard to navigation and access that Argentina's political and maritime aspirations were probably satisfied. However, given relations in the region between Chile, Argentina and the UK, together with overlapping claims on Antarctica, this part of the South Atlantic will remain of geopolitical interest.

Reading ■
Child, J. (1985) *Geopolitics and Conflict in South America*, Stanford, CA: Praeger/Hoover Institution Press

Hunter, W. (1997) Continuity or change? Civil–military relations in democratic Argentina, Chile and Peru, *Political Science Quarterly*, 112(3), pp. 453–75

Morris, M.A. (1986) EEZ policy in South America's southern cone, in E.M. Borgese and N. Ginsburg (eds), *Ocean Yearbook 6*, Chicago, IL: University of Chicago Press, pp. 417–37

Morris, M.A. (1988) South American Antarctic policies, in E.M. Borgese and N. Ginsburg (eds), *Ocean Yearbook 7*, Chicago, IL: University of Chicago Press, pp. 356–71

Santis-Arenas, H. (1989) The nature of maritime boundary conflict resolution between Argentina and Chile, 1984, in *International Boundaries and Boundary Conflict Resolution*, Conference Proceedings, Durham: IBRU, University of Durham, pp. 301–22

13

BELARUS

Belarus, the former Soviet republic of Byelorussia, is a landlocked state sharing boundaries with Latvia, Lithuania, Poland, Ukraine and the Russian Federation. It has an area of 207,600 km^2 and a population of just over 10.1 million. It has an economy which is well balanced between agriculture and industry but, of all the former Soviet states, it is the one which has developed the closest relations with the Russian Federation. The geopolitical issue concerns the influence these strengthening ties may have on the other former Soviet states in the region and the long-term effects on the eastward extension of NATO.

■ *Situation*

Following a declaration of independence in 1918, the country was reconquered by the Red Army and in 1922, became a constituent republic of the Soviet Union. In 1939 the Byelorussian Soviet Socialist Republic (SSR) regained the western sector of its territory, which had been awarded to Poland in 1921. On 27 July 1990, Byelorussia made a declaration of sovereignty and on 25 August 1991 proclaimed independence. Within a month, the name of the state had been changed to Belarus. In the same year, Minsk, the capital of Belarus, became the headquarters of the CIS.

■ *Issue*

Following independence, the entire infrastructure developed during the Soviet era remained in place and, despite disputes with the non-communist opposition, a pro-Russian policy has been pursued. This can be clearly illustrated by the four referendums of 1995 which all attracted large, affirmative votes:
1. The Russian language to have equal status with Belarussian.
2. There should be a new state flag and emblem based on those of the Soviet era.
3. There should be economic integration with the Russian Federation.
4. Constitutional changes should be made to give the president the right of parliamentary dissolution.

With lack of progress in the development of the CIS, in 1995 Russia and Belarus signed a treaty specifically aimed at further bilateral re-integration. Agreement was reached for joint border protection and, eventually, the creation of a single administration for economic and monetary union.

Prior to this, Belarus had renounced its nuclear weapons and, with assistance from the USA, some 80 SS-25 missiles were dismantled. Belarus joined the Partnership for Peace (PfP) in January 1995 and the last nuclear missiles were removed from its soil in late 1996.

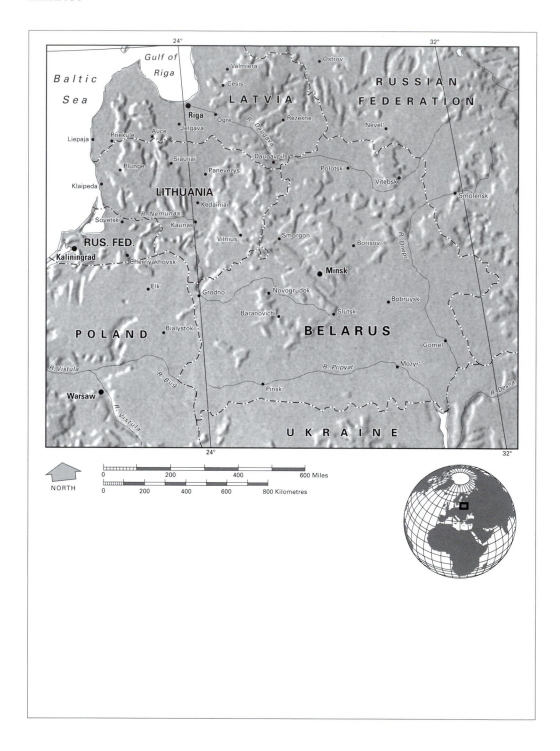

24°   32°

Baltic
Sea

Gulf of
Riga

Valmiera   • Ostrov

• Cesis

LATVIA   RUSSIAN
FEDERATION

Riga   Ogre   R. Daugava   • Rezekne   • Nevel'

Liepaja •   • Priekule   Auce   • Jelgava
Siauliai   Daugavpils

• Plunge   • Panevezys   Polotsk •   • Vitebsk

Klaipeda •

LITHUANIA   • Kedainiai   • Smolensk

R. Nemunas

• Sovetsk   Kaunas   R. Dnepr

RUS. FED.   • Vilnius   • Smorgon   • Borisov

Kaliningrad   • Chernyakhovsk   **Minsk**

• Elk   Grodno   • Novogrudok   • Bobruysk

• Baranovichi   • Slutsk

POLAND   Bialystok   **BELARUS**

    Gomel •

R. Vistula   R. Bug   R. Pripyat   • Mozyr'

R. Desna

Warsaw •   • Pinsk

R. Vistula

UKRAINE

24°   32°

NORTH

0   200   400   600 Miles

0   200   400   600   800 Kilometres

Meanwhile, amidst growing international isolation, Belarus pursued authoritarian policies and its major policy thrust remained the development of closer re-integration with Russia.

Varying interpretations have been placed upon the efforts by Belarus towards re-integration. In Russia, it is reported that there are fears that such a union might worsen the economic situation and also that the general lack of respect for human rights in Belarus might harm the emergent Russian democracy. In the other CIS states, re-integration is seen at best as a threat to the CIS itself and, at worst, as a harbinger to the restoration of Soviet hegemony. In the West, union is seen as a counter to the eastward expansion of NATO. However, on this last point in particular there is dispute.

■ *Status*

Already, military re-integration is, to all intents and purposes, being effected. Nevertheless, from the Russian viewpoint, it might appear that a degree of separation needs to be maintained if other states of the FSU are to be discouraged from opting for NATO membership. A likely outcome is, therefore, that there will be no significant Russian presence in Belarus and that full political unification will be put off, if not avoided completely.

Dawisha, K. (1997) *Democratic Change and Authoritarian Reactions in Russia, Ukraine, Belarus, Moldova*, Cambridge: Cambridge University Press

Kennaway, A. (1996) *Prospects for Research and Development in Belarus*, Camberley: Royal Military Academy Sandhurst (pamphlet)

Main, S. (1996) *Belarus: Back to the Past?*, Camberley: Royal Military Academy Sandhurst (pamphlet)

Main, S. (1998) *Belarus–Russian Military Relations (91–98)*, Camberley: Royal Military Academy Sandhurst (pamphlet)

Rich, V. (1994) Why Belarus matters, *The World Today*, 50(3), pp. 43–4

Sanford, G. (1996) Belarus on the road to nationhood, *Survival*, 38(1), pp. 131–53

■ *Reading*

14

THE BENGUELA AND TANZAM RAILWAYS

Situation ■ The mineral-rich areas of central southern Africa, particularly the copper belt in Shaba Province and the adjacent parts of Zambia, are located far from the coast. Both Zambia and Zimbabwe are landlocked, while the infrastructure of the Democratic Republic of the Congo is such that Shaba Province is also effectively cut off. Although copper is vital for the economy, the key minerals at issue are cobalt in Zaire Province and chromium in Zimbabwe. Both are among the most strategic minerals and the only economic means of transport can be by railway, but all possible routes involve transboundary movements. To the south is the South African railway network leading to the principal export port of East London. To the west is the Benguela Railway and to the east the Tanzam Railway.

Issue ■ The need for mineral transport from this part of Africa was foreseen early in the 20th century, but it was not until 1931 that the Benguela Railway opened, linking the ports of Lobito and Benguela on the coast of Angola, with Shaba Province in the then Belgian Congo and Ndola in the then Northern Rhodesia. The railway is some 2,500 km in length and forms the western half of the Trans-African Railway from Lobito to Beira, Mozambique, in the south and Dar es Salaam, Tanzania, in the north. The Tanzam Railway forms the eastern part of the network, linking the copper belt with Dar-es-Salaam. The line is more than 1,680 km in length and was completed by the Chinese in 1975.

Following independence from Portugal on 11 November 1975, Angola dissolved into civil war between three rival movements. The Popular Movement for the Liberation of Angola (MPLA), supported by Soviet aid and the Cuban military, was located broadly in the central area. In the north was the National Front for the Liberation of Angola (FNLA) and in the south, the National Union for the Total Independence of Angola (UNITA). Eventually, the FNLA merged into the MPLA, and gained control of the central government. However, UNITA carried on a long and effective campaign, directed by Savimbi. One objective was the continuous dislocation of the Benguela Railway, which was first severed in 1975, at which time it was carrying over half the copper exports of Zambia (formerly Northern Rhodesia).

In December 1988, following US mediation, agreement was reached between Angola, Cuba and South Africa under which there would be a South African military withdrawal from Namibia in 1989 and a phased departure of Cuban troops from Angola by

42 ■

NORTH

0	500	1000 Miles
0	500 1000	1500 Kilometres

mid–1991. The result was that, although fighting continued in Angola, the MPLA had lost its Cuban support and UNITA its backing from the Namibia-based South African troops. There followed a ceasefire in May 1991. However, as discussed in the entry on Angola in this volume (see p. 18), agreement still has to be finally reached as Savimbi and UNITA have still not accepted central government.

During the 1970s and 1980s, first Zambia and then Zimbabwe, as frontline states, made every effort to support opposition to white racist regimes in Southern Rhodesia and the Republic of South Africa. One approach was to attempt to divert mineral trade from the South African rail network to either the west or the east coast. Therefore, while nationalists in Angola sought to keep the Benguela line closed, nationalists and governments elsewhere made every attempt to reopen it. The Benguela line became part of the South African issue. In the event, the only line that remained open and provided guaranteed transport was that to the south, ending at East London, South Africa.

As the Benguela Railway ceased operating in 1975, so the Chinese, following Western disinclination to participate, had constructed the Tanzania–Zambia (Tanzam or Tanzara) Railway. With problems in both Angola and Rhodesia, this provided what was potentially a key lifeline, but for a variety of reasons, mainly technical, it was rarely fully operational.

Status ■ It has been reported that the western half of the Benguela Railway is now open to traffic and restoration is being continued on the remainder of the line. However, with the civil war continuing in Angola, there can be no guarantee of successful long-term transit for the minerals of Central Africa. The utility of the Tanzam Railway has been hampered by port congestion, limited load carrying capacity and a variety of technical difficulties. It remains a strategic option, but faces a potential decline as the Benguela Railway comes more into use. At the same time, the need to avoid the South African rail network has ended.

Reading ■ Anderson, E.W. (1988) *Strategic Minerals: The Geopolitical Problem for the United States*, New York: Praeger

Anderson, E.W. (1988) *The Structure and Dynamics of United States Government Policy Making: The Case of Strategic Minerals*, New York: Praeger

Griffiths, I.L.-L. (1985) *An Atlas of African Affairs*, London: Methuen

15

BESSARABIA

Bessarabia was part of the autonomous principality of Moldova under the Ottoman Empire, but in 1812 it was ceded to the Russian Empire. At that time, Moldova comprised the area from the Dniester River westwards – across the River Prut, which now forms the boundary with Romania – to the Carpathians. In taking over the territory in 1812, the Russians annexed Bessarabia, the area between the rivers Prut and Dniester. With the removal of areas to the north and south, but with the addition of a strip of land to the east of the Dniester, this became the Moldovan SSR with a territory of some 33,700 km^2. This of course remains the stated size of the independent state of Moldova, considered elsewhere in this volume (see p. 224).

(see p. 224)

■ *Situation*

The Congress of Berlin in 1878 formally recognised Wallachia and the remains of Moldova as the independent state of Romania, but the whole of Bessarabia was declared to be Russian. This accounts for the continuing irredentist campaign and general dissatisfaction in Romania.

■ *Issue*

In November 1918, a council set up by anti-Bolshevik forces reached agreement on unconditional union with Romania and this was recognised in the Treaty of St Germain. However, the transfer was not agreed by the Soviet Union which, in October 1924, established the 'autonomous Moldovan' SSR in a strip of Ukrainian land on the east bank of the Dniester, as a prelude to taking over the whole of Bessarabia. An ultimatum was issued to the government of Romania on 26 June 1940 and Bessarabia was secured for the Soviet Union. Most of the area was then added to the strip on the east bank of the Dniester, to become the Moldovan SSR. Nevertheless, the Black Sea coastal area to the south, a territory of some 15,000 km^2, was incorporated into Ukraine. In June 1941, Romania declared war on the Soviet Union and recaptured Bessarabia, which it held until the Soviet advance on 29 August 1944. The legality of the Soviet annexation in 1940 was later confirmed by the Soviet–Romanian Peace Treaty of 1947.

This extremely contorted history illustrates the geopolitical importance of the 'Bessarabian question' in relations between Romania, Russia, Ukraine and Moldova. The issue continues, but the focus is now upon Transdniester. The current view from Moldova is that the territory of the state is indivisible, while that from Transdniester is that the state is part of a confederation of equal partners. Separatists are particularly wary of reunification with Romania and this is a major reason for the pursuit of independence. The ethnic Russians in Transdniester number only some 170,000 and are therefore fewer

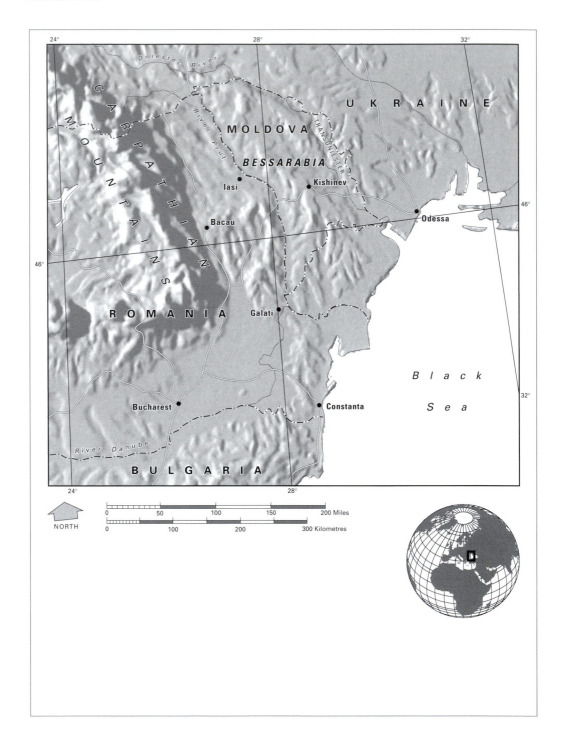

than the Moldovans and the Ukrainians, but they have the advantage of military backing. This raises the spectre that in the event of the emergence of some form of reconstituted Russia and a renewed East–West confrontation, Moldova could again become the springboard for operations against the Balkans, the Black Sea region and the eastern Mediterranean.

The question of Transdniester remains unresolved. The future constitutional status of the region has not been specified, although various levels of autonomy have been considered. These range from the provision of its own constitution, flag and anthems, to the right of self-determination should Moldova lose its independence, presumably to Romania. Joint Moldovan, Russian and Transdniesterian peacekeeping forces have been operating along the Dniester security zone since late 1992 and it is clear that whatever the final decision about the territory, Bessarabia/Transdniester will remain a potential flashpoint.

■ *Status*

Baleanu, V. (1997) *Republic of Moldova's Acrobatic Diplomacy*, Camberley: Royal Military Academy Sandhurst (pamphlet)

King, C. (1993) Moldova and the new Bessarabian questions, *The World Today*, 49(7), pp. 135–9

Waters, T. (1997) *Moldova 97*, Camberley: Royal Military Academy Sandhurst (pamphlet)

Waters, T. (1997) Problems, progress and prospects in post-Soviet borderland: the Republic of Moldova, *Boundary and Security Bulletin*, 5(1), pp. 71–9

■ *Reading*

16

THE BLACK SEA

Situation ■ Until the disintegration of the Soviet Union, the Black Sea was effectively a Soviet preserve. Apart from the Soviet Union, the other littoral states, Romania and Bulgaria, were both staunch members of the Warsaw Pact, and Turkey alone was not under Soviet control. As a result of its position on the Turkish Straits, and abutting onto the Warsaw Pact countries, Turkey became a member of NATO in 1952. Since 1991, Ukraine and, to a lesser extent, Georgia have become significant littoral states. The status of the Black Sea has thus changed considerably and, given developments in the Caspian Basin, it has become of great geopolitical importance. It has been transformed from a potential battle site for naval warfare into a key hub for trade. Black Sea geopolitics depend upon the interrelations of the three major states: the Russian Federation, Ukraine and Turkey (see also pp. 276, 352 and 345).

Issue ■ The end of the Cold War converted the Black Sea into an open system. The effect of this was seen with the inauguration of the Black Sea Economic Co-operation (BSEC) initiative put forward by Turkey in 1991. In 1994, the Bucharest Convention for the Protection of the Black Sea against Pollution was initiated and this was followed by a Strategic Action Plan to achieve the same objectives which resulted from the Istanbul Summit of 31 October 1996.

In contrast to these developments, continuing tensions in all of the former Soviet territories threatened the co-operation. Relations between Russia and the Ukraine were strained over the future of the former Black Sea Fleet but on 28 May 1997, agreement was reached on the fleet's future. This normalisation of relations also emphasised the immutability of existing borders and is likely to move the Ukraine rather closer to Russia. In late 1997, the Ukrainian and Russian navies held joint exercises, following exercises off the coast of Crimea earlier in the year which had included the USA, Bulgaria, Romania, Georgia and Turkey. Long-term questions that remain include the future of Ukrainian nationality and the potential for further integration within the CIS.

In the interests of preserving the new geopolitical situation in the Black Sea Basin, Ukraine and Turkey have enjoyed cordial relations, following the disintegration of the Soviet Union. There has been co-operation over both political and security issues and Ukraine supported Turkey's concerns over the environmental and safety problems of the Turkish Straits.

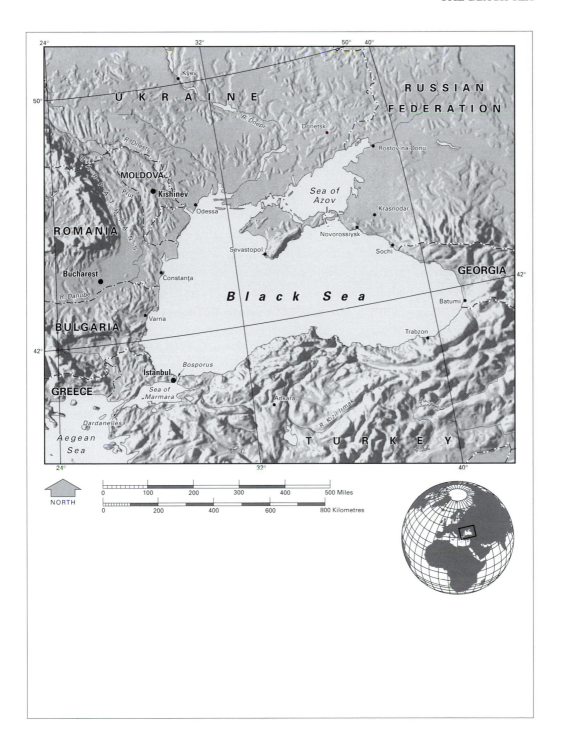

NORTH

| 0 | 100 | 200 | 300 | 400 | 500 Miles |
| 0 | 200 | 400 | 600 | 800 Kilometres |

Relations between Turkey and Russia had for centuries focused upon rivalry over the Black Sea but, with the disintegration of the Soviet Union, there was no longer a shared boundary. Thus, Turkey's security was enhanced, particularly with regard to the Turkish Straits. Relations have been strained by Russian perceptions of Turkey's political incursions into Central Asia and the Transcaucasus and by minority secessionist movements. Given its long-term membership of NATO, Turkey is also seen as a potential military threat, in collusion with the West. In response, Russia has developed relations with Greece, Iran and Armenia in a long-term effort to isolate Turkey.

Status ■ The geopolitical transformation of the Black Sea following the demise of the Soviet Union has resulted in several examples of co-operation but has also led to new sets of tensions. The region is considerably less stable than it was and its future will depend greatly upon the relationships Russia establishes with Ukraine and Turkey. Problems can only be exacerbated by the economic potential of the region and the need to export Caspian Basin oil through it.

Reading ■ Cottey, A. (1998) *Subregional Cooperation in the New Europe*, Basingstoke: Macmillan

Sezer, D. (1997) From hegemony to pluralism: the changing politics of the Black Sea, *SAIS Review*, 17(1), pp. 1–30

Sherr, J. (1997) Russian–Ukraine rapprochement? The Black Sea Fleet Accords, *Survival*, 39(3), pp. 33–50

17

BOLIVIA

With an area of 1,098,581 km^2 and a population of 7.4 million, Bolivia is a landlocked state between Brazil, Paraguay, Argentina, Chile and Peru. It therefore borders most of the major states of South America. Geographically, it is divided between the lowlands, predominantly of the Amazon Basin, to the east and the high Andes, including the Altiplano, to the west. The Bolivian GDP per capita is similar to that of Suriname and, apart from that of Guyana, is the lowest in South America. Some 75 per cent of Bolivians live in poverty; 40 per cent are underemployed and 25 per cent are unemployed. The major geopolitical issue has been the question of access to a Pacific port.

As a result of the War of the Pacific (1879–84) in which Chile defeated the combined forces of Peru and Bolivia, Bolivia became a landlocked state. At the same time, it became a major world exporter of tin, an important strategic metal. The tin era and effective rule by the tin barons continued until well after World War II.

However, on 9 April 1952, workers and peasants led by the Nationalist Revolutionary Movement (MNR) took power and introduced what was effectively a social revolution. Agricultural reform and universal suffrage were introduced and the tin industry was nationalised. This period ended with a military coup in 1964 and a series of military governments which lasted until 1982. Since the end of military rule there has been a proliferation of political parties and changing coalitions. Throughout, the military have continued to play an active role. A key factor in Bolivian life has been the drug trade and the production of coca in the Bolivian lowlands. In combating this, the military have raised fears that it may return to a central role in politics.

Throughout most of the modern era, Bolivia's relations with Chile and Peru have been strongly influenced by the desire to regain access to the Pacific which was lost to Chile as a result of the War of the Pacific. In 1975, it appeared that an agreement had been reached with Chile, but negotiations proved complicated and it was not until January 1992, at the Peruvian port of Ilo, that a treaty was concluded granting Bolivia unrestricted access along a route from the border town of Desaguadero to small free zones in the neighbourhood of Ilo.

BOLIVIA

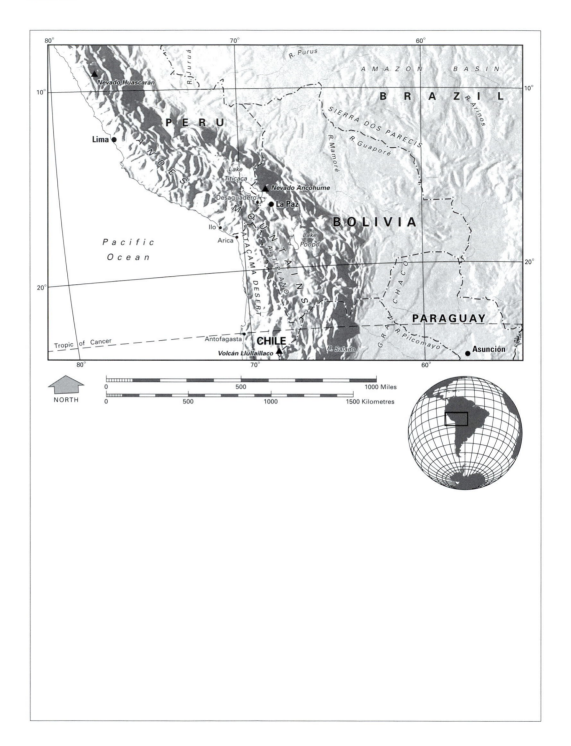

52

With the apparent solution of its major geopolitical problem, a measure of stability should characterise Bolivia's foreign relations. The coca eradication programme continues to cause conflict and there were violent protests in 1998. Nonetheless, for one of the most politically volatile states in the world, the era of coup and counter-coup seems to have passed. Improved regional relationships and national confidence are illustrated by Bolivia's application to join MERCOSUR, the Common Market of the Southern Cone.

■ *Status*

Arenas, H. (1994) *The Bolivian Maritime Aspiration to Chilean Political Space: Towards a Non-territorial Solution*, London: Routledge

Mettenheim, K. (1998) *Deepening Democracy in Latin America*, Pittsburgh, PA: University of Pittsburgh Press

■ *Reading*

18

BOSNIA

Situation ■ With less than 13 km of coastline, Bosnia-Herzegovina is a virtually landlocked Balkan state which shares boundaries with Croatia and Yugoslavia (Serbia and Montenegro). Its area is 51,129 km^2 and its population is just under 4.5 million. However, the key factor is the ethnic make-up of the population, 34 per cent of whom are Muslim Slavs. The remaining 66 per cent is made up of 70 per cent Serbs and 30 per cent Croats. The country is therefore located on the fracture zone between the Roman Catholic and the Eastern Orthodox churches. After a conflict that included mass killings, ethnic cleansing and destruction on a wide scale, and involved the first offensive ever mounted by NATO, the problem remains the prevention of the state's disintegration.

Issue ■ The area of the Balkans has long been associated with conflict. The assassination of the heir to the imperial throne of the Austro-Hungarian Empire in Sarajevo in June 1914 by a Serbian nationalist resulted directly in the outbreak of World War I. At the end of that war, Bosnia became part of the kingdom of the Serbs, Croats and Slovenes, a country that was officially named Yugoslavia in 1929. After World War II, Bosnia-Herzegovina became one of the six republics of the Federal People's Republic of Yugoslavia (FPRY), established and ruled as a communist state by Tito. Apart from that between Slovenia and Croatia, the internal boundaries delimited in 1946 did not follow ethnic divisions.

With the breakdown of the Warsaw Pact, the instability of Yugoslavia increased and fighting broke out initially over minority groups along the Bosnian boundaries in August 1990. At the end of that year, in the country's first multi-party election since World War II, the three major nationalist parties (Muslim, Serb and Croat) won a collective majority.

The communists had therefore been routed but a crisis occurred on 26 June 1991, when Croatia and Slovenia both made unilateral declarations of independence. This event precipitated action by the Serb-dominated federal army and by September fighting had spread to Bosnia. On 3 March 1992, following the recognition of Slovenian and Croatian independence by Germany, the independence of Bosnia-Herzegovina was proclaimed. Agreement was reached at Sarajevo between the leaders of the three main ethnic groups that facilitated the division of the country into three autonomous units. However, Serbs still pressed for the inclusion of the republic in Yugoslavia, while Muslims proved unable to accept the ethnic divisions. The situation was brought to a head on 27 March 1992 when Bosnian Serbs proclaimed the Serb republic of Bosnia and Herzegovina.

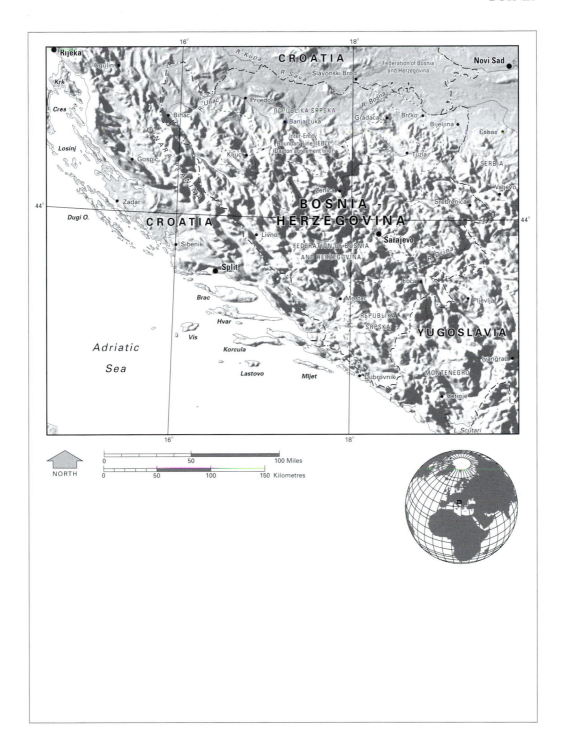

Adriatic
Sea

NORTH

| 0 | | 50 | | 100 Miles |
| 0 | 50 | | 100 | 150 Kilometres |

Ethnic conflict mounted and in April 1992 the UN Security Council agreed to the deployment of a UN Protection Force (UNPROFOR). By the end of 1992, Serbian forces controlled approximately 70 per cent of Bosnia and Croatian forces much of the remainder. Amid the continued fighting, interspersed with acts that plumbed the depths of barbarity, several plans for the division of Bosnia were advanced. The Vance–Owen plan of early 1993 envisaged a decentralised state divided into 10 semi-autonomous provinces. In the meantime, following the pattern established after the Gulf War, the UN Security Council recognised six Muslim safe areas. The next suggested solution, the Owen–Stoltenberg plan which would have resulted in the division of Bosnia into three ethnically based states under a federal constitution, appeared to have been accepted when on 28 August 1993, Bosnian Croats proclaimed a Croatian republic of Herzeg-Bosna.

Fighting continued within and between the three ethnic groups but on 18 March 1994 a US-brokered plan for a federation of the Bosnian, Muslim and Croat populations was put forward. Although this was rejected in its initial form, it was effectively taken up by the international contact group comprising France, the UK, Germany, Russia and the USA.

After a four-month ceasefire in early 1995, the conflict escalated when, following a UN/ NATO air strike, the Bosnian Serbs took 400 UN peacekeepers as hostages. France and the UK despatched rapid-reaction troops in response. Subsequent to a further atrocity, NATO launched Operation Deliberate Force, a series of air strikes against the Serbs. Large-scale hostilities were eventually ended by the Dayton Accord which specified that, under international law, Bosnia-Herzegovina would remain a single state but would be partitioned into Muslim-Croat and Serb entities that would enjoy substantial autonomy. The former would have 51 per cent of the territory and the latter 49 per cent. An Implementation Force (IFOR) under NATO command but with NATO authority and contingents from non-NATO countries was promptly deployed to safeguard the agreement. On 14 September 1996 there followed an election of extreme complexity which confirmed the dominance of the three ethnic groups. In June 1997, IFOR was replaced by a new NATO-run Dissuasion Force (DFOR) comprising, as did its predecessor, some 30,000 troops.

Status ■ Progress is hinted at by the name of the current peacekeeping body, the Stabilisation Force (SFOR), and by the gradual retreat of hardline nationalists. A common flag and coat of arms has been accepted by both the Bosnjak Croat Federation and by the Republic of Srpska. However, issues that remain to be resolved are the plight of refugees, the arrest of those indicted for war crimes and crimes against humanity, and the eventual political and constitutional integration of Bosnia. The stability of Bosnia is still far from guaranteed although, with the lessons of Kosovo in mind (see no. 60), there are major incentives to make the present system work.

Barschdorff, P. (1998) Can NATO deliver?, *SAIS Review*, 18(2), pp. 185–206

Bass, W. (1998) The triangle of Dayton, *Foreign Affairs*, 77(5), pp. 95–108

Gow, J. (1998) Ready for the long haul, *The World Today*, 54(5), pp. 121–2

Holbrooke, R. (1998) *To End a War,* New York: Random House

Partos, G. (1998) Persistence pays, *The World Today*, 54(8–9), pp. 210–11

Rosengarten, U. (1998) The Geneva Conference on the former Yugoslavia, *Aussenpolitik*, 49(1), pp. 32–9

Williams, M. (1998) The folly of partition, *Survival*, 40(2), pp. 181–3

■ *Reading*

19

BURKINA FASO

Situation ■ A landlocked state in the Sahel, Burkina Faso has an area of 274,000 km^2 and a population of 10.2 million. Access to the sea lies through Côte d'Ivoire or Togo and there are no navigable rivers. With few natural resources, the country is largely dependent upon agriculture and is therefore at the mercy of the recurrent regional droughts.

Issue ■ Following independence from France on 5 August 1960 as the state of Upper Volta, there ensued a series of military coups punctuated by civilian rule by the Rassemblement Démocratique Africain (RDA). The coup of 1980 finally ended the dominance of the RDA in the politics of Upper Volta. However, there followed further coups in 1980, 1983 and 1987. The last of these removed extreme left political factions and brought Blaise Compaore to power. Despite being confronted by an increasingly vital opposition, Compaore won presidential elections in 1991 and 1998.

Apart from Côte d'Ivoire and Togo, Burkina Faso also has boundaries with Ghana, Benin, Niger and Mali. Initially, Upper Volta adopted Ghana and Libya as models for its development as it rid the country of its colonial past and changed the name to Burkina Faso. At various stages there were fears that it might become a Libyan satellite or might enter into union with Ghana.

Boundary problems with Mali and Ghana have been settled. Continuing problems include the presence of Touareg refugees from Mali (see p. 218) and Niger and relations with Liberia. In 1993, Burkina Faso sent troops to join the Economic Community of West African States Monitoring Group (ECOMOG) forces in Liberia (see p. 203).

Status ■ After the extraordinary political volatility of the past 40 years, Burkina Faso now appears to be more stable than at any time since independence. In 1997, joint military exercises were held with Benin, Togo and France and few obvious disputes remain with neighbours. The long-term potential peril remains the agricultural situation and in 1998 the government was forced to make an international appeal to donors for grain. Geopolitically, therefore, Burkina Faso can be characterised as at best stable, at worst quiescent.

Reading ■ Clapham, C. (1998) *African Guerrillas*, Oxford: James Currey
European Commission (1997) *The European Union, the Countries of W. Africa and the AEMU*, Brussels: European Commission (pamphlet)

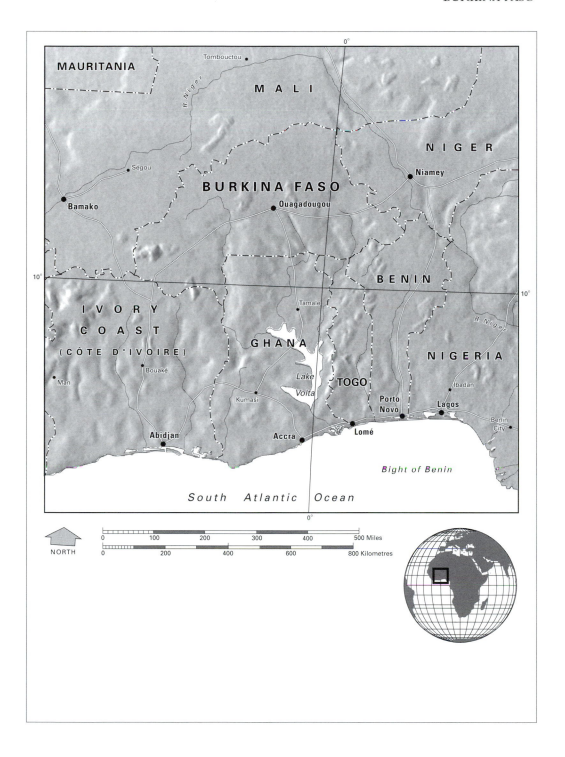

20

BURUNDI

Situation ■ A small landlocked republic in the Great Lakes region of Africa, Burundi is bordered to the north by Rwanda and to the west and east by powerful neighbours – the Democratic Republic of the Congo and Tanzania respectively. With an area of only 27,834 km^2 and a population of almost 6 million, Burundi is one of the world's more densely populated countries. Apart from the problems of a rapidly expanding population and an enclaved economy, the major recent issue has been a high-profile civil war conducted between ethnic groups: the Hutu constitute 84 per cent of the population and the Tutsi 15 per cent. Burundi is among the world's least developed countries with a declining GDP per capita which is already among the lowest in the world.

Issue ■ Ethnic conflict in Burundi only appeared in the post-colonial era. Indeed, the ethnic nationalism considered so characteristic of the country results from the effects of European occupation rather than any long-standing hatred. Since independence in 1962, rivalry between the Tutsis and the Hutus has erupted on several occasions, although there had previously been few violent confrontations. Independence resulted in a struggle for power which, in a country like Burundi, over-populated with two radically different populations with different social statuses, proved more conflictual than elsewhere, with the exception of Rwanda (see p. 285). However, the rise of Hutu power in independent Rwanda led to the displacement of a large part of the Tutsi population.

In 1965, the Tutsis appeared to be in control but an attempted political coup resulted in the liquidation of most of the Hutu political leaders and the beginning of a long series of military governments. Such repression generated extreme resistance movements and the cleavage was along ethnic lines. Rivalry for power became enmeshed with selective genocide and fears of group extinction.

Following further mass killings and the well-publicised Rwandan genocide, the UN special representative helped the political parties produce a series of power-sharing agreements. These were aimed at ensuring stability for the 1998 elections but failed, principally because they focused more on the distribution of government positions than on the real problems of the country. Arms imports to both sides burgeoned and the conflict spread through the neighbouring porous boundaries of Tanzania and (the then) Zaire (Democratic Republic of the Congo).

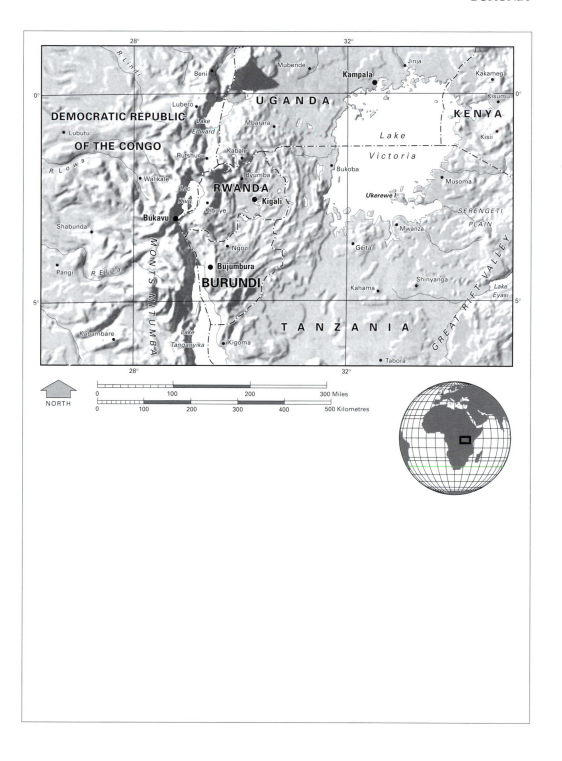

NORTH

| 0 | 100 | 200 | 300 Miles |

| 0 | 100 | 200 | 300 | 400 | 500 Kilometres |

Throughout 1998 the displacement of population, retaliatory massacres and failed peace talks continued. Eventually, in early 1999, the sanctions imposed upon Burundi in 1996 were lifted.

Status ■ The basis for future civil war and genocide still exists and no compromise political settlement appears likely. Partition is not possible as there are no traditional homelands of either the Hutu or the Tutsi and any such division might also upset the balance of power in Rwanda. Over the past 40 years Burundi and Rwanda have become bywords for ethnic violence and there seems little prospect of long-term peace. Furthermore, many of the neighbouring states are either unstable or potentially unstable and therefore the small state of Burundi, located in the centre of the African land mass, is likely to remain a global flashpoint.

Reading ■ Lund, M. (1998) *Democratization and Violence in Burundi: the Failure of Preventative Action*, New York: Twentieth Century Fund
Weissman, S. (1998) *Preventing Genocide in Burundi*, Washington, DC: US Institute of Peace Press

21

CABINDA

Cabinda is an enclave of Angola, from which it is separated by some 40 km of coastline, including the mouth of the Congo/Zaire River. The area of Cabinda is 7,270 km^2 and the population is 150,000. It has boundaries with the Republic of Congo to the north and the Democratic Republic of the Congo (formerly Zaire) to the south. Its geopolitical importance is based upon its petroleum resources.

Situation

Portugal had claimed Angola since the late 15th century. It did not occupy Cabinda until 1783 and was then ejected by France within 11 months. Later, in a convention to the Angolo-Portuguese Treaty of 22 January 1815, Portugal laid claim to Cabinda but it was not until 1884, in a version of the same treaty, that Portuguese claims were acknowledged. In the Angolo-Portuguese Treaty of 26 February 1884, Portugal's claims were recognised to the whole of the Atlantic coast of Africa between latitudes 5° 12′S and 8°S.

Issue

At the Berlin Conference of 1884–5, Portuguese interests north of the Congo were recognised. On 14 February 1885, Portugal and the International Association of the Congo (subsequently renamed the Belgian Congo, Republic of Congo, Zaire, Democratic Republic of the Congo) signed a treaty delimiting the Cabinda–Congo boundary, recognising Portuguese sovereignty in the area and guaranteeing the International Association a narrow corridor to the sea. It is of course this corridor that prevents the Democratic Republic of the Congo from being landlocked. The boundary between Cabinda and Congo (Republic of Congo) was agreed at the Franco-Portuguese Convention of 12 May 1886.

The key date for Angola was 1966, when petroleum was discovered in the coastal waters. As a result, the enclave became crucial, first for the Portuguese and then the Angolans. There has been a continuing fear of any attempt towards independence. After Angola became independent on 11 November 1975, Cabinda did have its own short insurgency and both Zaire and Congo considered the idea of demanding a referendum. However, support by Zaire for separatism was always likely to be tempered by the fact that Shabam secessionist groups (see p. 86) operate from Angola. The Front for the Liberation of Cabinda (FLEC), under its leader Captain Bonga Bonga, is active and Cabindans base their independence claim on the Treaty of Simulambuco (1885), which first linked Cabinda to Angola but recognised its special status.

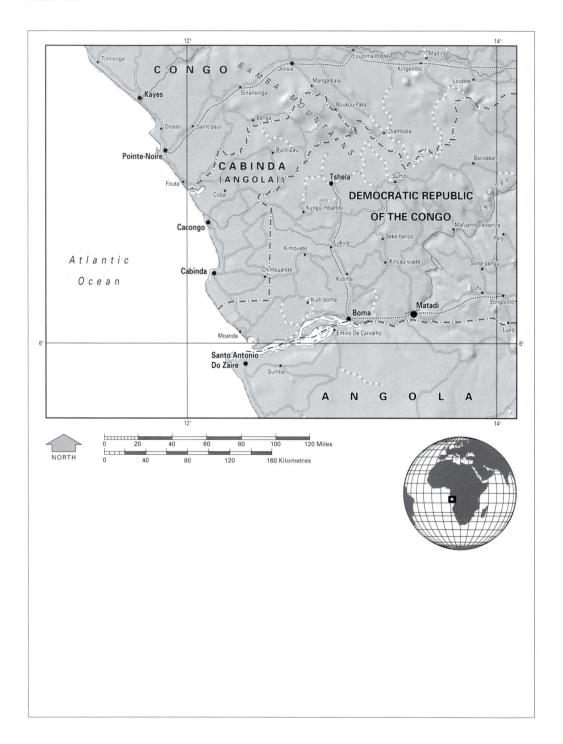

NORTH

0 20 40 60 80 100 120 Miles

0 40 80 120 160 Kilometres

Cabinda remains extremely important for Angola, for which it produces over half the foreign exchange earnings. However, at present only 1 per cent of the oil revenues are spent on Cabinda, which remains among the poorer parts of Angola. To prevent UNITA from disrupting the petroleum infrastructure, Angola had normally kept a large military force in Cabinda, but in August 1998 this was relocated to support Lauent Kabila in the Democratic Republic of the Congo. The 'Cabinda question' remains dormant, but given its strategic location with regard to the Democratic Republic of the Congo and its petroleum resources, it is an obvious potential flashpoint.

■ *Status*

Griffiths, I.L.-L. (1985) *An Atlas of African Affairs*, London: Methuen

Maier, R. (1996) *Angola: Promises and Lies*, London: Serif

US Department of State (1970) *Angola–Congo (Brazzaville) Boundary*, International Boundary Study No. 105, 15 October, Washington, DC: Office of the Geographer, Bureau of Intelligence and Research

US Department of State (1974) *Angola–Zaire*, International Boundary Study No. 144, 4 April, Washington, DC: Office of the Geographer, Bureau of Intelligence and Research

■ *Reading*

22

CAMBODIA

Situation ■ Cambodia is a small state in South-East Asia occupying the middle drainage basin of the Mekong River. It has boundaries with Thailand, Laos and Vietnam and a short coastline on the Gulf of Thailand. Its area is 181,035 km^2 and the population 9.8 million. The state gained universal notoriety through the 'Killing Fields' of the then dictator, Pol Pot.

Issue ■ Both before and after World War II Cambodia was a protectorate of France. In November 1953, when nearing defeat in Vietnam, France granted independence to Cambodia under the government of King Sihanouk. Following victory in the 1955 election, Sihanouk won successive single-party elections until 1970. In that year, he was deposed and the Khmer republic, which had little rural support and was fatally implicated in the Vietnam War, was proclaimed. In 1975, the Khmer Rouge and its leader Pol Pot established the government of Democratic Kampuchea.

There followed one of the most brutal and oppressive regimes of the post-World War II period. The boundaries were closed and all traces of Western influence were removed in a complete urban and rural reorganisation. There was horrendous loss of life – possibly a figure as high as 10 million – and alienation of the population. Attacks on Vietnam resulted in an invasion from that country and a change of regime in 1979.

The new People's Republic of Kampuchea continued with one-party rule until a peace agreement in 1991 provided for political party pluralism and UN-supervised elections in 1993. Until 1990, the year after it was renamed Cambodia, the country's seat at the UN was occupied by Democratic Kampuchea and among the non-communist states only India recognised the government in Phnom Penh. However, the Khmer Rouge boycotted the election and sporadic fighting between its members and the government continued until the arms struggle was abandoned in 1997. Later that year, the continuing threat of the Khmer Rouge and the opposition resulted in civil war which ended in a Japan-brokered peace treaty in January 1998. Pol Pot died after a heart attack on 17 April 1998 and it now appears that other Khmer Rouge leaders will escape trial for human rights abuses.

Status ■ When the last vestiges of the Khmer Rouge forces surrendered to the government on 7 December 1998, 30 years of civil war effectively ended. Elections on 26 July 1998 confirmed in power the government of Hun Sen and subsequently Cambodia, with a new coalition government, joined the Association of South-East Asian Nations

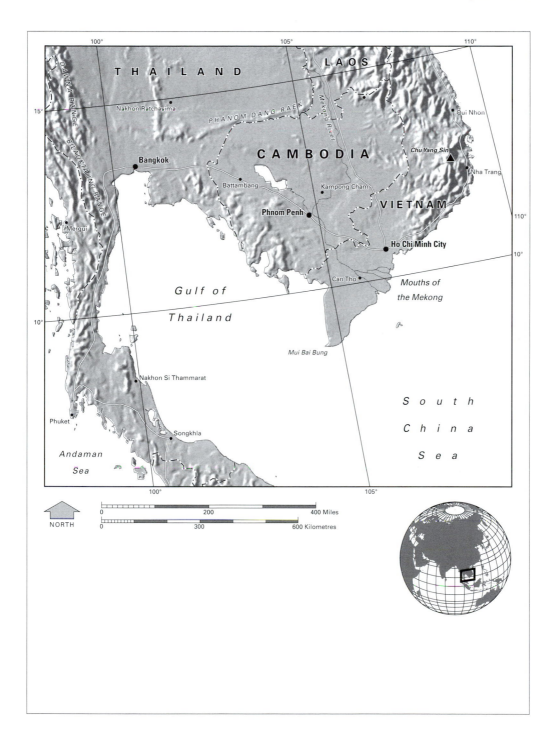

THAILAND

LAOS

DAWNA RANGE

BILAUKTAUNG RANGE

Nakhon Ratchasima

PHANOM DANG RAEK

Mekong River

Qui Nhon

CAMBODIA

Chu Yang Sin

Bangkok

Battambang

Kampong Cham

Nha Trang

Phnom Penh

VIETNAM

Ho Chi Minh City

Mergui

Can Tho

Mouths of
the Mekong

Gulf of

Thailand

Mui Bai Bung

South

China

Sea

Nakhon Si Thammarat

Phuket

Songkhla

Andaman

Sea

100°   105°   110°

15°

110°

10°

10°

100°   105°

NORTH

0   200   400 Miles

0   300   600 Kilometres

(ASEAN). Two main geopolitical issues remain. First, given the long history of violence, it must be asked whether long-term stability is a possibility. The other concern is over boundaries. The main issue involves Vietnam and the maritime, including continental shelf, areas in the Gulf of Thailand where complex boundary problems have yet to be settled. These are complicated problems and, given its restricted length of coastline, they are critical for the future of Cambodia.

Reading ■   Amer, R. (1997) Border conflicts between Cambodia and Vietnam, *Boundary and Security Bulletin*, 5(2), pp. 80–91

Eng, P. (1998) Cambodian democracy: in a bleak landscape, strong signs of hope, *Washington Quarterly*, 21(3), pp. 71–91

Ott, M. (1997) Cambodia between hope and despair, *Current History*, 96(614), pp. 431–6

23

CAMEROON

Cameroon is a large equatorial country of 475,442 km^2, with a population of 13 million, located at the head of the Gulf of Guinea. It gained full independence in October 1961 as the result of a merger between the former French and British Cameroon trust territories. The state became the United Republic of Cameroon in 1972 and the Republic of Cameroon in 1984. There are more than 200 ethnic groups, 24 major languages and 3 main religious groupings (Christian, traditional African and Muslim). However, the most important cleavage is between the Anglophones who make up 20 per cent of the population and the Francophones who comprise the other 80 per cent. Cameroon is the only country in Africa with both English and French as official languages.

■ *Situation*

With so many potential political cleavages, the government has striven to suppress a division between the north and the south which would coincide with historical, cultural and religious distinctions. The one-party system which had been established on independence continued until 1991, when opposition groups were formally recognised. President Paul Biya, in power since 1982, has survived many anti-government clashes and, largely as a result of boycotts, has won many elections; the most recent was on 12 October 1997.

■ *Issue*

The relationship between Cameroon and its neighbours, particularly Nigeria, has at times been troubled. Diplomatic relations with Nigeria were severed from 1981 to 1987 and conflict erupted again in 1993. A particular flashpoint was caused by two islands off the Bakassi Peninsula, claimed by Cameroon but allegedly occupied by Nigerian troops. The underlying problem concerns the substantial oil reserves which are located along the boundary between the two countries. Violence erupted again in early 1996 and continues.

The boundary dispute has been referred to the International Court of Justice (ICJ) which, in 1995, announced a timetable for the receipt of documents. However, with settlement required for not only part of the land boundary but also the whole maritime boundary, these procedures are likely to be lengthy. Meanwhile, clashes continue on the disputed Bakassi Peninsula. Given the tensions in both Nigeria and Cameroon, it seems unlikely that this boundary dispute will escalate into anything greater than, at most, a regional concern.

■ *Status*

Walle, N. (1993) *The Politics of Nonreform in Cameroon*, New York: Columbia University Press

■ *Reading*

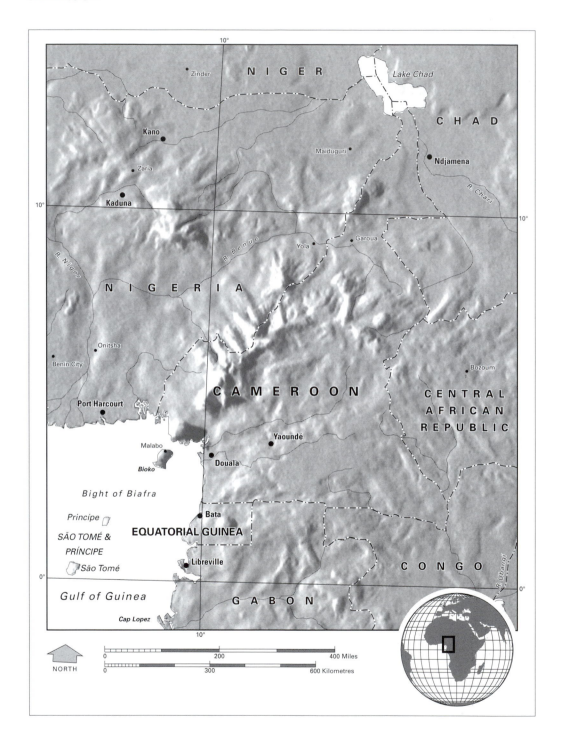

NORTH

0   200   400 Miles
0   300   600 Kilometres

24

THE CAPRIVI STRIP

The Caprivi Strip is a classic example of a panhandle, a narrow strip of land either providing or denying access. The Wakhan Panhandle (see p. 360) from north-eastern Afghanistan was constructed to prevent access to the Indian subcontinent. The Caprivi Strip, extending 450 km eastwards from the north-east corner of Namibia, was designed to provide access to the River Zambezi and, in doing so, to the quadripoint with Zimbabwe.

(see p. 360)

■ *Situation*

The Caprivi Strip takes its name from the German foreign minister of the time and was ceded to Germany by Britain in 1893 to give German South-West Africa (Namibia) access to and an outlet through the Zambezi River corridor. However, although it was originally transferred for strategic reasons, the intent was later found to be impracticable.

■ *Issue*

Until their withdrawal in 1989, the strip served as an important base for the intervention of South African troops in the Angolan civil war against the Soviet-backed MPLA. Local Caprivi Baragwena Basarwa were recruited as trackers for the South African Defence Forces (SADF) and formed, under white officers, the 201 (Bushmen) Batallions. Furthermore, as it provided access to the unique international quadripoint, the strip also offered South Africa a route into the heart of the frontline states. For example, the ferry route from Zambia to Botswana which crossed the Zambezi at Kazungula, the farthest extremity of Caprivi, was regarded by both South Africa and Rhodesia (Zimbabwe) as an infiltration route for insurgents and was attacked from the Caprivi Strip on several occasions. Thus, the strip was of strategic importance during the main part of the Angolan civil war.

Since Namibia became independent in 1990, there has been no military conflict in the Caprivi Strip and there are no territorial or boundary disputes. However, the Basarwa people, less than 5 per cent of the state population, are remote from the centre of the country and have a strong and distinct cultural identity. The withdrawal of SADF's financial and medical support has left them largely destitute and disaffected. In November 1998, government officials claimed to have uncovered a plot led by a former leader of the opposition to launch a secessionist rebellion in the Caprivi Strip. Given its unique location, the other potential problem concerns smuggling, and in 1991 the government established a border post near Manbora. The Caprivi Strip provides access to four countries, but any potential problems are likely to be merely local.

■ *Status*

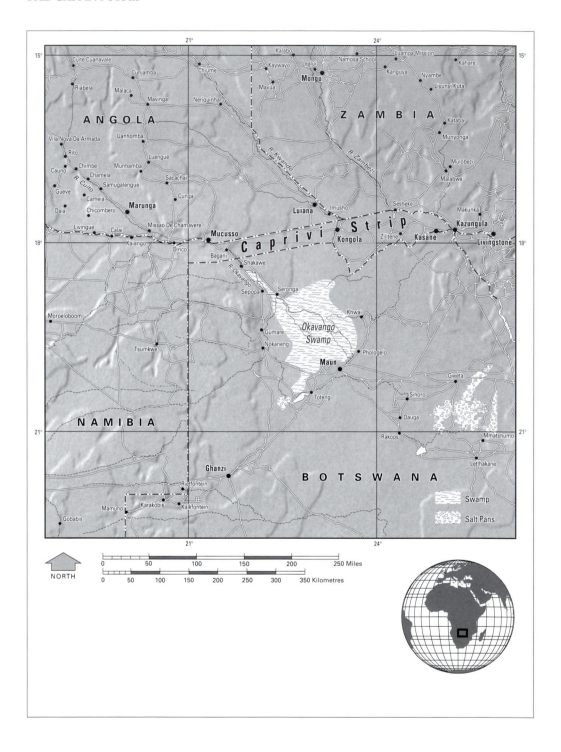

Brownlie, I. (1979) *African Boundaries: A Legal and Diplomatic Encyclopaedia*, London: Royal Institute of International Affairs

Pankhurst, D. (1996) *A Resolvable Conflict? The Politics of Land in Namibia*, Bradford: School of Peace Studies, University of Bradford (pamphlet)

Solomon, H. (1998) *Security, Development and Gender in South Africa*, Pretoria: South African Institute for Security Studies

■ *Reading*

25

THE CASPIAN SEA

Located at the boundary of Europe and Asia, the Caspian Sea is the largest inland water body in the world. Owing to climatic factors its dimensions change but its surface area is approximately 371,000 km^2 with a north–south length of some 1,200 km and an average width of about 300 km. Prior to 1991, it was effectively a Russo-Iranian lake, important for largely internal transport. The littoral is now shared by five states: the Russian Federation, Azerbaijan, Iran, Turkmenistan and Kazakstan. The Caspian has become more obviously of international concern and the situation has been exacerbated by successful large-scale prospecting for oil and natural gas.

Issue ■ With the effective change in status of the Caspian Sea and the requirement to share its resources among the five littoral states, the problem of boundary delimitation has arisen. If the Caspian is a lake, then an agreement based on sharing the resources between all the states concerned might be appropriate. This would follow precedents set by other boundary lakes although, in most cases, these involve only bilateral negotiations. If the Caspian is a sea, then delimitation can be carried out according to the procedures established by the UN Convention on the Law of the Sea (UNCLOS). If a sea is defined as having natural connections with the world's oceans, then the Caspian is a lake. However, a sea might be defined according to size or longevity. Lakes are taken to be temporary features of the earth's surface and the Caspian has been extant for the order of 25 million years. Some agreement has already been reached in the northern part of the sea but as yet there is no consensus on a general procedure.

Apart from the legal aspects, there have been various agreements between the co-littorals, particularly on environmental issues, fishing and the importance of maintaining the water level of the Caspian. It is obviously vital in this unique environment that the exploitation of oil and natural gas should not destroy the ecology. Thus, modes of transporting oil across the Caspian either by pipeline or by barges have both come under close scrutiny. It must also be remembered that the Caspian is the home of the Caspian sturgeon which provides the main global source of high-quality caviar. The life cycle of the fish involves migration between fresh and salt water and environmental change could prove fatal.

The Caspian Basin is also the meeting place of the major north–south route through the Caucasus and the east–west route linking Central Asia and Europe. Politically, therefore, it is a highly sensitive area. Of critical importance is the policy adopted by Russia towards its former republics. Russia still provides border guards for most of the states and is closely

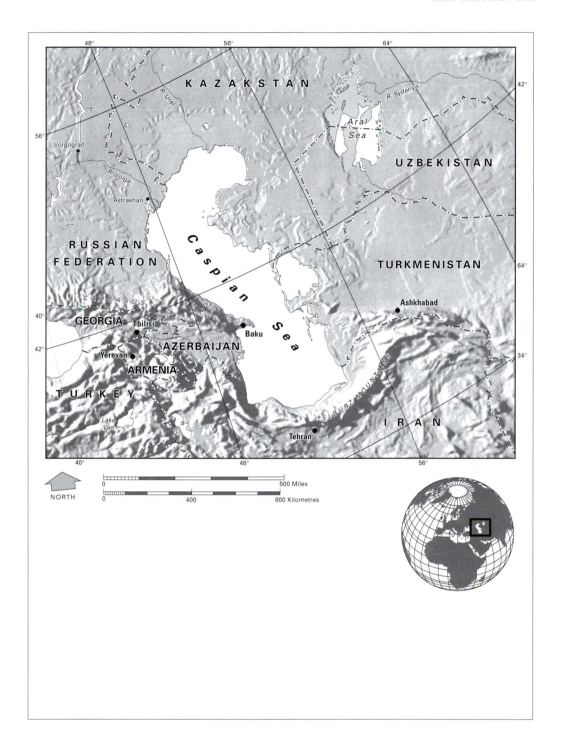

NORTH

0   500 Miles

0   400   800 Kilometres

involved in their development. Therefore, it is important that progress towards democracy and a market economy in Russia is maintained. If the state implodes, or there is a military takeover, the political, economic and social effects upon the region could be severe. The latest proposals suggest that the Caspian should be divided into three regions – upper, middle and lower – with subdivisions ensuring that no part is owned by more than one state.

The other influential regional powers are Turkey and Iran. Beyond these, China has a developing interest in the region, as does the West, particularly through the PfP developed by NATO. Further Western influence is of course commercial and is concerned principally with the development of the petroleum industry.

Status ■ The Caspian Basin is emerging as a geopolitical focus. The states of the Transcaucaus all have their own flashpoints, while those of Central Asia, particularly Tajikistan (see p. 330), are affected by the continuing conflict in Afghanistan. All the states of the region have boundary problems, often including questions of settlement, surveillance and control. The issue of the boundary delimitation of the Caspian itself remains, as does the pipeline conundrum. In May 1998, Iran issued a tender for a pipeline from the port of Neka to Tehran, while there are plans for other pipelines from Turkmenistan and Kazakstan to Azerbaijan (see p. 21) and thence through Georgia to Turkey. Any routes through Iran are not favoured by the USA, while Turkey is anxious to maintain a reasonable limit to traffic through the Turkish Straits. However, perhaps the most salient point to arise is that many experts consider the reserves of oil and natural gas to have been greatly exaggerated. At a time of low petroleum prices, there is less impetus to develop resources. Furthermore, in becoming fully involved in the region, the West might be drawn into a complex web of ethnic conflicts in what has been characterised as the 'Eurasian Balkans'. Whatever happens, the region is bound to be highly geopolitically significant over the next few years.

Reading ■ Blandy, C. (1998) *The Caspian Sea: A Sea of Troubles*, Camberley: Royal Military Academy Sandhurst (pamphlet)

Blandy, C. (1998) *The Caucasus Region and the Caspian Basin: 'Change, Complication and Challenge'*, Camberley: Royal Military Academy Sandhurst (pamphlet)

Dion, R. (1998) Cutting up the Caspian, *The World Today*, 54(3), pp. 80–2

Olcott, M. (1998) The Caspian's false promise, *Foreign Policy*, Summer, pp. 95–113

26

CEUTA

Enclaves are particularly prone to become flashpoints and there is no greater concentration of enclaves than on either side of the Strait of Gibraltar. In the immediate environs of the strait are Gibraltar, a British enclave in Spain on the northern side, and, on the south, Ceuta, a Spanish enclave in Morocco. Ceuta has an area of 19 km^2, a sea coast 20 km long and a land boundary of 8 km. Its population, predominantly Spanish, is about 67,000. Spain possesses a further series of enclaves in Morocco, the largest being Melilla, located east of Ceuta, near Nador. Melilla has an area of 12 km^2, a sea coast of 3.9 km and a land boundary of 10 km. It too has a predominantly Spanish population of about 65,000. In these two main enclaves there are approximately 19,000 Spanish troops.

Spain also controls the Rock of Velez (Penon de Velez de la Gomera), the Rock of Alhucema (Penoes de Alhucemas) – both of the small groups of islands just off the Moroccan coast between Ceuta and Melilla – as well as the Chafarinas Islands, which lie 23 nml east of Melilla. Each of the Penones has a civilian and military population of about 100 and the Chafarinas a population of approximately 200.

On the opposite side of the strait is Gibraltar, a British-controlled enclave which has developed as a strategic military base and port city. It is considered elsewhere in this volume (p. 123), but to provide a comparison with the Spanish enclaves, it can be noted that Gibraltar has an area of 6 km^2 and a population of 28,000, making it the fifth most densely populated political entity after Macao, Monaco, Hong Kong and Singapore.

The Strait of Gibraltar is approximately 58 km long and 12.5 km wide at its narrowest point. Shipping is in lanes and, in the main channels, depths vary from 320 to 935 m. For international shipping, it is the second most important international strait after the Strait of Dover, although if vessels of all sizes are included, the Strait of Malacca is also more important. Taking 1,000 gross tonnes as the minimum load, approximately 150 vessels a day (55,000 a year) transit the strait. Since the capacities of both the Suez Canal and the SUMED pipeline – which skirts the canal – were increased, there has been a significant growth in the oil trade and approximately one-third of these vessels are oil tankers.

The dates of occupation of the Spanish enclaves were as follows: Melilla 1497, the Rock of Velez 1508, Ceuta 1580, the Rock of Alhucema 1673 and the Chafarinas 1848. Gibraltar was occupied by the Moors between 711 and 1462 and was then held by the Spanish until 1704. It was captured by the Anglo-Dutch fleet on 4 August 1704 and

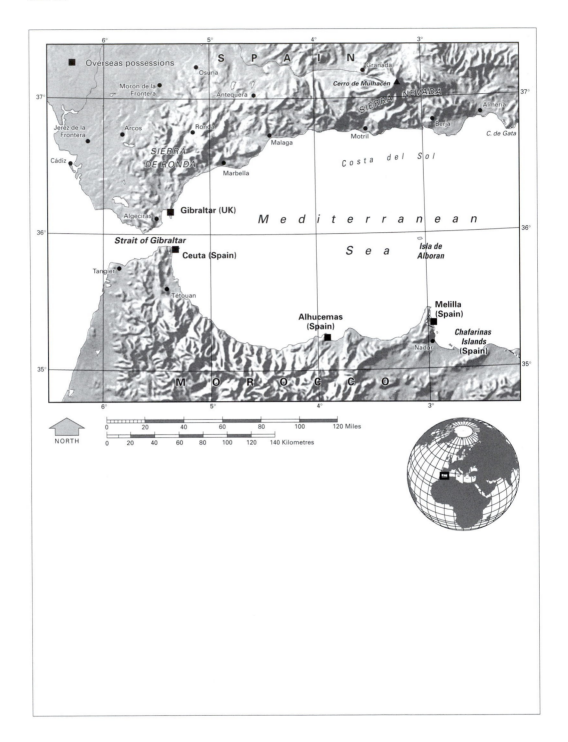

acquired by Britain following the Treaty of Utrecht on 17 July 1713. Morocco became independent in 1956 and since then has pressed for the return of Ceuta and the other enclaves. Spain has demanded the return of Gibraltar since the end of World War II, but the strength of its claim has always been limited by the fact that it controlled its own enclaves in Morocco.

In 1961, Morocco appealed to the UN to recognise its rights with regard to Ceuta and the other enclaves, but Spain merely reinforced their borders. On 29 June 1962, Morocco reasserted its claim and the next day extended its own territorial waters from 6 to 10 nml. On 27 January 1975, Morocco formally requested the UN Decolonisation Committee to put the Ceuta case on its agenda – where it remains – and, in 1978 and 1979, the Moroccan Patriotic Front carried out several bomb attacks in Ceuta and Melilla. In September 1979, the Spanish government announced a plan to construct a security zone round Ceuta to keep out illegal immigrants, a similar zone around Melilla having been completed. In April 1998, the newly appointed prime minister of Morocco pledged to resolve the state's territorial issues, including the restatement of its claim to the Spanish enclaves. Morocco has in fact always stated that it would raise the question of the two 'presidios', as both Ceuta and Melilla are known in Morocco, together with the other enclaves, if Gibraltar were to be transferred to Spanish control.

The Strait of Gibraltar is a vital choke point and therefore the enclaves on either side have strategic significance. Further current issues include illegal transnational movements and the relative ease with which small enclaves can be used for smuggling, drug trafficking and money laundering. In the case of the enclaves on either side of the Strait of Gibraltar, there is also the issue of maritime boundaries. With its enclaves, together with the strategically placed island of Alboran, Spain is technically in a position to virtually close off entry to the Mediterranean. If Spain were to retain its own enclaves and regain Gibraltar, it would possess, in the words of the late King Hassan of Morocco, 'both keys to the same straits'. In October 1991, Spain categorically rejected the idea that Gibraltar could become a self-governing dependency of the European Community (EC). Whatever the final decisions, it is difficult to believe that the futures of the enclaves on either side of the strait will not be linked. However, it seems unlikely that their existence would cause the western end of the Mediterranean to become a flashpoint.

■ *Status*

Boyd, A. (1991) *An Atlas of World Affairs*, London: Routledge
The Observer (1990) Gibraltar: rock seeks home rule within Europe, *The Observer*, 2 December, p. 14
Prescott, J.R.V. (1985) *The Maritime Political Boundaries of the World*, London: Methuen

■ *Reading*

79

27

THE CHAGOS ARCHIPELAGO (DIEGO GARCIA)

Situation ■ The Chagos Archipelago consists of six major islands, located centrally in the Indian Ocean. The largest of the islands, an atoll some 21 km long and 6 km wide, is Diego Garcia. It is located at 6° 34′S 7° 24′E, approximately 1,000 nml south of India, 2,000 nml south-east of the Persian/Arabian Gulf and 1,200 nml north-east of Mauritius. The issues are the use of such an island as a major military base by Western powers and the depopulation of the island, which made the establishment of such a base possible. When the island became a joint US–UK base in 1966, more than 1,000 people were immediately removed from Diego Garcia to Mauritius. In the period 1965–71, 508 families were forcibly resettled, the remainder leaving between 1971 and 1973. In 1981, a survey reported that the total number of Chagos refugees in Mauritius after these periods of expulsion was 2,800.

Issue ■ Diego Garcia passed from French to British control at the end of the Napoleonic Wars. Its importance was first realised during World War II when it was used for ship repairs and refuelling. From the late 1950s, to secure its interests in the Indian Ocean, the USA needed a naval replenishment base and airfield. For this purpose, a centrally placed island was obviously ideal. On 8 November 1965, the British Indian Ocean Territory (BIOT) was established. This comprised the Chagos Archipelago, formerly administered with Mauritius, and three islands belonging to the Seychelles, which were returned upon the independence of the Seychelles on 29 June 1976.

In December 1966, one year after it had been established, the UK signed a defence agreement leasing the BIOT to the USA for 50 years, with an option of an extra 20 years. A major development programme followed, including the construction of a 4,000 m runway, allowing accommodation for B52 bombers. These developments gained particular impetus after the Iranian revolution of 1979, when facilities at Bandar Abbas and Chah Bahar were lost. In the same year, the Soviet Union invaded Afghanistan and this put added pressure upon the Indian Ocean region. On 4 January 1980, the USA announced that facilities on Diego Garcia were to be upgraded to maintain a permanent presence of up to 4,500 troops. From then until 1986, there was large-scale investment which allowed the prepositioning of 17 vessels with a marine amphibious brigade of 12,000 men.

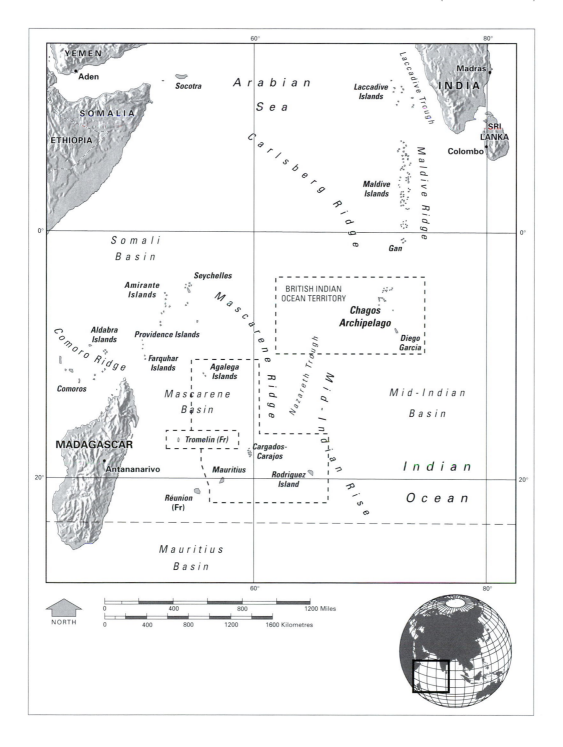

YEMEN

Aden

SOMALIA

ETHIOPIA

Socotra

Arabian

Sea

Laccadive
Islands

Madras

INDIA

SRI
LANKA

Colombo

C a r l s b e r g   R i d g e

Maldive
Islands

Maldive Ridge

Laccadive Trough

Gan

0°   0°

*S o m a l i
B a s i n*

Seychelles

Amirante
Islands

M a s c a r e n e   R i d g e

BRITISH INDIAN
OCEAN TERRITORY

*Chagos
Archipelago*

Diego
Garcia

C o m o r o   R i d g e

Aldabra
Islands

Providence Islands

Farquhar
Islands

Agalega
Islands

Comoros

*M a s c a r e n e
B a s i n*

Nazareth Trough

*M i d - I n d i a n
B a s i n*

Mid-Indian Rise

MADAGASCAR

Antananarivo

Tromelin (Fr)

Cargados-
Carajos

Mauritius

Rodriguez
Island

I n d i a n

20°   20°

Réunion
(Fr)

O c e a n

*M a u r i t i u s
B a s i n*

60°   80°

NORTH

0   400   800   1200 Miles

0   400   800   1200   1600 Kilometres

Diego Garcia provides a major facility for the region since it is remote, secure and centrally placed. It is relatively immune from land-based attack and, since the local population was moved to Mauritius, from any serious local political conflict. It has a deep anchorage, refuelling facilities, a repair capability and a major airbase. It can support a full carrier task force.

The political issue of Diego Garcia was revived in 1989 when, following a US–Soviet *détente*, its strategic significance seemed to have declined. This fact, together with the accidental dropping of a bomb by a US fighter plane, provided encouragement for those supporting demilitarisation. However, in 1991 the installation proved of major value to US forces during the Gulf War. It was used again during the 1998 stand-off between the USA, the UK and Iraq. In 1996, Mauritius demanded a share of the proceeds from fishing permits, while still not accepting use of the island as a US base.

Status ■ Despite the end of the Cold War, the value of Diego Garcia as a military base has been clearly illustrated by its use during operations in the Persian/Arabian Gulf. As a result, the political position of the UK towards the island has hardened. Since 1980, the Organisation of African Unity (OAU) has called for the return of the atoll to its former inhabitants and its demilitarisation. There is also the question of the morality of forcible resettlement. All of these issues ensure that Diego Garcia will remain a geopolitical focus.

Reading ■ Anderson, E.W. (1988) *Strategic Minerals: the Geopolitical Problem for the United States*, New York: Praeger

Cottrell, A.J. and Hahn, W.F. (1978) *Naval Race or Arms Control in the Indian Ocean*, Agenda Paper No. 8, New York: National Strategy Information Center

Rais, R.B. (1986) *The Indian Ocean and the Superpowers*, London: Croom Helm

28

COLOMBIA

Colombia is a large country with an area of 1,138,914 km^2 and a population of 35 million, which places it third in Latin America after Brazil and Mexico. Like all of the Andean states, there is a sharp contrast between the coastal plains, the mountains (which, in Colombia's case, includes three ranges of the Andes) and the eastern lowlands. Contrasts in relief are reflected in a society which is highly stratified and where many in the rural areas live in absolute poverty. The country gained independence as Gran Colombia in 1830 and by the 1850s the two major political parties which still predominate today – the Partido Liberal and Partido Conservador – were established. The subsequent history of Colombia comprises periods of one-party rule, coalition and civil war. Located in the north-east corner of South America, with coastlines on both the Caribbean and the Pacific, Colombia is a link with Central America. The key issue is the maintenance and development of a democratic state in the face of a rising tide of violence.

Since the 1980s there has been some level of civil war in Colombia and this has posed the most serious long-term security threat to the region. The chief opposition to the government has been provided by the leftist Revolutionary Armed Forces of Colombia (FARC) which has grown increasingly powerful. Both it and the anti-communist forces are closely involved with the drug trade. In December 1993, the head of the Medellin drug cartel was killed and in 1995 the leaders of the more sophisticated Cali cartel were apprehended. Progress was, however, hampered by the fact that key members of the government also appeared to be implicated in narcotics.

The power of the guerrillas has been checked to an extent by the growth of paramilitary groups and there must be a danger that the country could fragment between the different warlords, each linked to the drug trade. The fear of overspill has already produced responses in neighbouring Panama and Venezuela.

The outlook appears dire as assessments indicate that the balance of power has shifted away from the Colombian armed forces to the insurgents. FARC now operates across 70 per cent of rural Colombia and the National Liberation Army (ELN) has also expanded. FARC effectively administers the southern half of Colombia and exacts taxes, particularly on coca transactions. The potential wealth from this source is illustrated by 1998 US statistics that give an overview of international narcotics and law enforcement which show that the estimated area of coca cultivation increased from 38,000 hectares

Caribbean Sea

Pta. Gallinas

Netherlands
Antilles

Aruba

Curaçao
Bonaire

Gulf of
Venezuela

Barranquilla

Maracaibo

Caracas

Barquisimeto

Valencia

Panama

PANAMA

Lake
Maracaibo

VENEZUELA

Gulf of
Panama

Pacific

Ocean

Cabo Corrientes

Medellin

R. Cauca

R. Magdalena

Manizales

Pereira

Nevado del Tolima

Bogotá

Armenia

Ibagué

COLOMBIA

R. Meta

LLANOS

R. Gauviare

Buenaventura

Cali

Nevado del Huila

Neiva

Punta Galera

ANDES MOUNTAINS

Quito

ECUADOR

R. Caqueta

BRAZIL

Chimborazo

Guayaquil

Gulf of
Guayaquil

PERU

R. Juruá

NORTH

0   500 Miles

0   400   800 Kilometres

(ha) in 1992 to 98,500 ha in 1997. Although the accent is upon the US market, the trade is now international, with markets throughout Europe and the FSU and established linkages with the mafias of both Italy and Russia.

The drug and guerrilla problems are interlinked. The counter-narcotics policy of the government, strongly supported by the USA, is aerial crops spraying – but this forces peasants who are growing coca to seek protection from FARC. Furthermore, the Colombian armed forces are known to have connections with the paramilitaries and the narcotics trade. During 1998, there were various attempts to bring the warring groups together and on 7 January 1999 milestone peace talks took place between the government of Colombia and FARC. However, later in the same month FARC suspended the talks until there was a government crackdown on the militia men who provide protection for wealthy landowners.

■ *Status*

With the Colombian armed forces, FARC, other guerrilla groups and paramilitaries, the civil war is highly complex and multi-polar. The key is the narcotics industry which has, at times, provided the necessary funding to all the combatants and the government of Colombia itself. The drug problem brings Colombia into direct conflict with the USA and increasingly with other Western countries. The scale and violence of the continuing conflict has implicated neighbouring states and highlighted both land and maritime boundary problems. While Colombia remains a focus of the international drug trade, it must be considered a major geopolitical flashpoint.

■ *Reading*

IISS (1998) Growing conflict in Colombia: a widening and brutal 'dirty' war, *Strategic Comments*, 4(5)

Tickner, A. (1998) Colombia: chronicle of a crisis foretold, *Current History*, 97(616), pp. 61–5

Watson, C. (1998) Colombian contagion, *The World Today*, 54(2), pp. 49–50

29

DEMOCRATIC REPUBLIC OF THE CONGO

Situation ■ With an area of 2,344,858 km^2, the Democratic Republic of the Congo is approximately the size of Western Europe and is the third largest state in Africa. It is strategically located in the centre of the continent and has boundaries with nine states: Congo, Central African Republic, Sudan, Uganda, Rwanda, Burundi, Tanzania, Zambia and Angola. If the number of contiguous neighbours can be correlated with the potential for conflict, the significance of this location is obvious. The population of 44 million places it behind only Nigeria, Egypt and Ethiopia in the continent of Africa. Its strategic location allied to its vast mineral wealth has ensured that the country has maintained a high profile in African affairs.

Issue ■ Following anti-colonial riots, the Democratic Republic of the Congo became independent on 30 June 1960. The first republic, which lasted until 1965, was characterised by large-scale Western (particularly Belgian) interference, together with pressure from the USA. Mutiny in the army was followed by a secessionist movement in Katanga (Shaba Province) with its rich mineral deposits. The UN offered no assistance, the prime minister was assassinated and the country was plunged into popular insurrections which were ended on 24 November 1965 by Sese Seko Mobutu with a CIA-assisted coup.

Mobutu's republic lasted from 1965 until 1990 and involved one-party dictatorship and extreme authoritarian control. In 1967, the country was renamed Zaire and corruption and violation of human rights followed. By 1990, the country's economic and social structure had been largely destroyed but the end of the Cold War and the rise of democracy elsewhere influenced Mobutu towards moderate liberalisation. By 1992 Mobutu's rule had all but collapsed but it took until 1997 before liberation occurred and the government of Laurent Kabila took power. In 32 years, Mobutu had reduced one of the most richly endowed countries in Africa to abject penury.

However, Kabila's hold on power has been at best tenuous and what was essentially a long-running internal conflict has been transformed into a regional war. At one stage, troops from Rwanda and Uganda almost ousted the government, which was saved only by support from Angola, Zimbabwe and Namibia. More recently, Chad and Sudan have also sent troops to support Kabila.

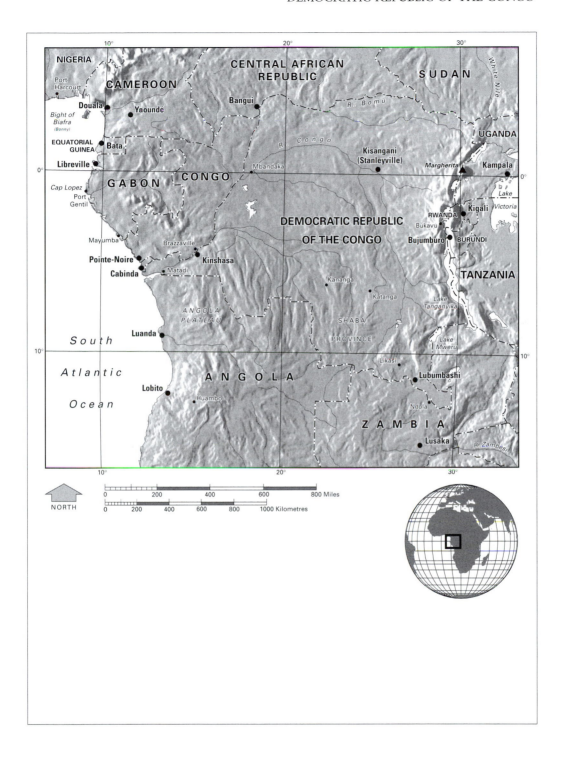

Status ■ The forecast must be that events will descend further into chaos and there must be a serious danger that the country will disintegrate. The lack of even a rudimentary infrastructure, particularly for transport, militates against long-term co-operation and stability. Furthermore, there are problems in many of the neighbouring states and each leader offering assistance to the Democratic Republic of the Congo has his own agenda. Shaba Province is likely to remain a particular flashpoint with its vital mineral deposits. Among them, cobalt is one of the most strategic of minerals.

Reading ■ IISS (1998) Renewed danger in the Congo: a year of Laurent Kabila's rule, *Strategic Comments*, 4(6)
IISS (1998) Renewed war in Angola: a threat of regional conflict, *Strategic Comments*, 4(7)
Shearer, D. (1998) Lines on a map, *The World Today*, 54(11), pp. 294–5

30

CROATIA

Croatia is a small, crescent-shaped state bordered by Hungary, Slovenia, Bosnia-Herzegovina and Serbia (Vojvodina). Its eastern boundary, considered by many to coincide with one of the major global cultural fracture zones, that between the Roman and the Orthodox churches, almost encircles Bosnia and ensures that for its size Croatia has an extensive coastline. At independence, 78 per cent of the population was Croat and 12 per cent Serb, but this latter figure has been reduced to perhaps 2 or 3 per cent, following ethnic cleansing in 1995. As the most industrialised republic, Croatia shared with Serbia the power base in the former Federal People's Republic of Yugoslavia (FPRY). It is an irony of history that, after World War II, Croatian atrocities were highlighted and Serbia received Western support, while the position has been reversed since 1990. With an area of 88,117 km^2 Croatia is rather smaller than the current Federal Republic of Yugoslavia and its population of 4.5 million is under half the size.

■ *Situation*

In 1918, Croatia became part of the Kingdom of the Serbs, Croats and Slovenes, renamed Yugoslavia in 1929. With the German invasion in 1941, the Ustase, a far-right movement responsible for the massacre of thousands of Serbs, proclaimed an Independent State of Croatia. In November 1945, Croatia became one of the six republics of the FPRY.

■ *Issue*

In the spring of 1990, the first multi-party elections since World War II were won by the Croatian Democratic Union (HDZ) and Franjo Tudjman became president. The leaders of Serb groups in Croatia promptly proclaimed their own sovereignty and autonomy in three separate regions. In early 1991, following a defence pact between Croatia and Slovenia, the Serbian Autonomous Region of Krajina was declared. On joining adjacent Serb areas of Bosnia, the name Republic of Serbian Krajina was assumed. On 25 June 1991, Croatia and Slovenia declared independence and the long-forecast civil war began. The Yugoslav National Army, dominated by Serbs, allied with Serb insurgents and took control of almost a third of Croatia. The UN Protection Force (UNPROFOR) was despatched and hostilities subsided.

At the second attempt, Croatia recovered most of the territory which had been under Serb control by late 1995. In January 1998, the last remaining area, Eastern Slavonia, returned to Croatian control.

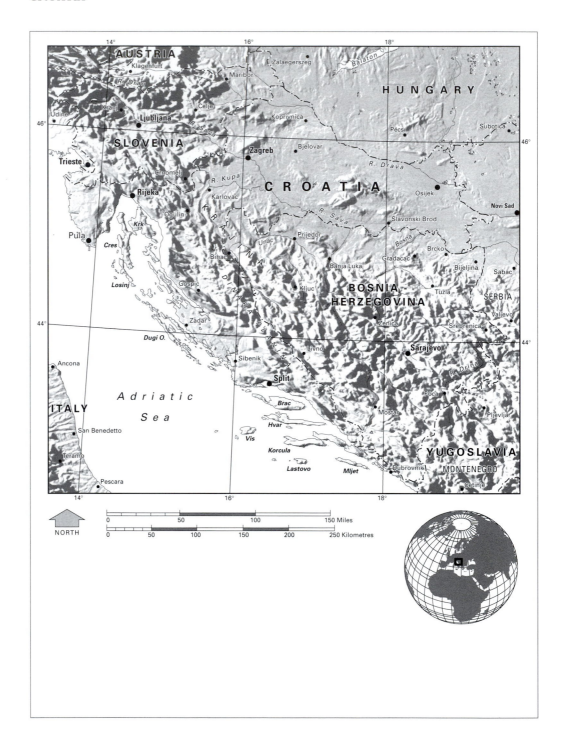

Until the events in Kosovo in 1999 (see p. 180), the records of Serbia and Croatia appeared similar, with the former just ahead in terms of democratic development. There were long delays in arresting Croatian war criminals, a key condition of the Dayton Accord, the agreement reached to end the fighting. However, Croatia now appears stable and likely to receive strong Western support as efforts are made to rebuild the shattered economy of much of the Balkans. The country looks set to join the PfP but Balkan memories are long and Krajina is likely to remain an emotive issue. ■ *Status*

Cushman, T. (1997) *Critical Theory and the War in Croatia and Bosnia*, Seattle: University of Washington ■ *Reading*

Cviic, C. (1997) *Plus ça change* in former Yugoslavia, *The World Today*, 53(10), pp. 247–9

Dyker, D. (1997) *Yugoslavia and After: a Study in Fragmentation, Despair and Rebirth*, Harlow: Addison Wesley Longman

31

CUBA

Situation ■ Cuba, with an area of 110,861 km^2, is a large island 78 nml from the US coast. With a population of more than 11 million, it is easily the most highly populated island state in the Caribbean. It is strategically located between choke points, with the Florida Strait to the north-west and the Windward Passage to the south-east. However, the main issue of concern has been its relationship with the USA over the past 40 years.

Issue ■ As a result of the Spanish–American War, Cuba gained independence in 1898 but was effectively an American protectorate until 1933. The legal justification for this status was the Platt Amendment, which authorised the USA to safeguard Cuban independence, but the underlying intention was to protect US economic interests.

Owing to alleged communist tendencies in the Cuban government, the USA backed a coup in 1934 by Fulgencio Batista, and helped him to regain power by a further coup in 1952. This latter action was opposed by a group of left-wing Cubans, among them Fidel Castro. From 1956 until 1958, Castro and his revolutionary supporters opposed the Batista army throughout the country. Finally, on 1 January 1959, Batista fled and Castro marched into Havana as a national hero.

Although the Cuban revolution was initially nationalist rather than socialist, US corporations feared nationalisation and a trade embargo was imposed. There followed the USA's abortive 'Bay of Pigs' invasion of April 1961 and Castro turned to the Soviet Union for survival. On 15 October 1962, US intelligence identified the first of six Soviet nuclear missile bases under construction in Cuba. The Cuban missile crisis, which ended with Soviet agreement to withdraw the missiles 13 days later, is still regarded by many analysts as the nearest the Cold War approached to nuclear war.

Over the years, the Cuban economy has maintained respectability, while on the social front there have been major advances in literacy, employment and health care. Foreign policy has been guided by the desire to support socialist regimes, and aid programmes have been established in 17 African countries, the most important in Angola and Ethiopia. Initially, support was also provided for revolutionaries in several Latin American countries – in Bolivia, for example, through the fabled 'Che' Guevara.

Following the demise of the Soviet Union, the government had severe economic adjustment problems but in February 1998 Castro was confirmed as president for a further five years. Meanwhile, US hostility continues, if in a somewhat muted form. In

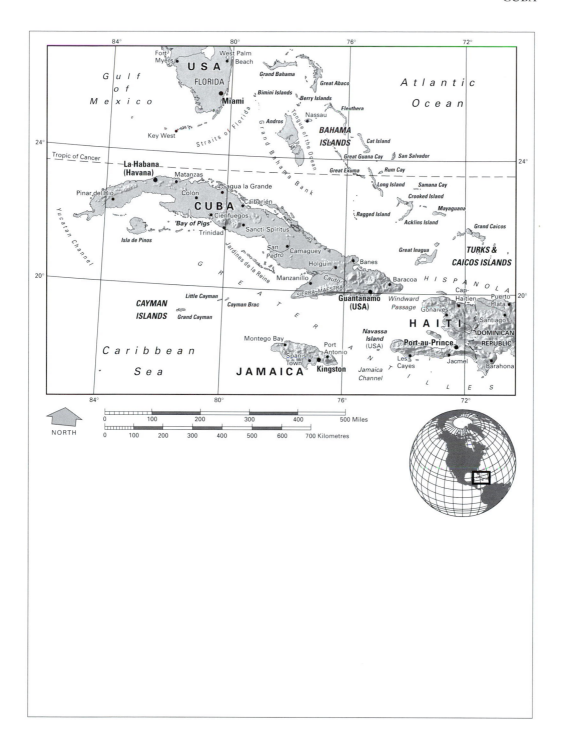

NORTH

0 100 200 300 400 500 Miles

0 100 200 300 400 500 600 700 Kilometres

1992, President George Bush had tightened the economic embargo and the result was the large-scale exodus of Cuban 'boat people'. In 1996, the US government passed the Helms–Burton Act, mandating sanctions against foreign companies doing business in Cuba. In October 1998, for the seventh consecutive year, the UN passed a resolution calling for an end to the US economic embargo.

Status ■   The Cuban government under Castro remains loyal to communism, despite the demise of its main sponsor. This is presumably a major factor in attempting to explain the continuing hostility of the USA. While FSU states and members of the Warsaw Pact received investments and loans, despite in many cases retaining the same people in power, the needs of Cuba have been disregarded. Cuba's government is no more extreme than that of China where the USA began constructive engagement in 1973. Nonetheless, the Cuban economy has recovered at least as effectively as any in the former communist world and relations with neighbouring states have improved. The US base at Guantanamo Bay remains a memorial to the Cold War. It is difficult to envisage Cuba as a flashpoint but it remains a continual irritant to the one remaining superpower.

Reading ■   Falcoff, M. (1998) Reflections on a dying revolution, *Orbis*, 42(4), pp. 565–74
McGuinness, E. (1998) Castro's leap of faith, *The World Today*, 54(1), pp. 16–17
Shipman, A. (1998) Polishing the long spoon, *The World Today*, 54(8–9), pp. 233–5

32

THE CURZON LINE

Situation

The Curzon Line is the eastern boundary of Poland with Lithuania, Belarus and Ukraine. Following the Russian Civil War, the repulse of the first Polish invasion of Russia and the subsequent Soviet invasion of Poland, the alignment of the boundary was proposed by the Western powers at the Spa Diplomatic Conference in July 1920. In October 1920, the boundary was finally settled some 100–150 km east of the Curzon Line by the Treaty of Riga. This gave Poland large population minorities from White Russia (Belarus) and Ukraine.

Issue

During the Yalta Agreement of 4–10 February 1945, the main allied governments – the USA, the UK and the Soviet Union – agreed that the eastern frontier of Poland should follow the Curzon Line, apart from certain digressions of between 5 and 8 km from it, in favour of Poland. Poland was effectively moved bodily westwards and the Danzig Corridor was eliminated. The Curzon Line, together with the Oder–Neisse Line, thus became two of the key boundaries in post-World War II Europe. The Curzon Line was subsequently declared inviolable by the Final Act of the Conference on Security and Co-operation in Europe, signed in Helsinki on 1 August 1975. In the immediate post-World War II period, the Soviet Union was able to use a continuation of the Curzon Line southwards to remove part of Slovakia, thereby giving itself access through Ukraine to both Czechoslovakia and Hungary. This proved highly significant during the Cold War period.

Status

The Curzon Line divides East Central Europe from the FSU, but Polish fears in the early 1990s about refugees from the FSU states proved largely unfounded. The more significant event was the accession of Poland to NATO in 1999, which resulted in the Curzon Line becoming the eastern boundary of NATO. Should Belarus integrate with the Russian Federation (see p. 39), the northern part of the Curzon Line would become the only boundary of direct contact between NATO and Russia. Thus, throughout much of the 20th century, the Curzon Line was a critical geopolitical feature in the landscape of Europe. It could yet again become a flashpoint.

Reading

Boundary Bulletin, No. 1 (1991)
Boundary Bulletin, No 2 (1991)
Day, A.J. (ed.) (1984) *Border and Territorial Disputes*, Harlow: Longman

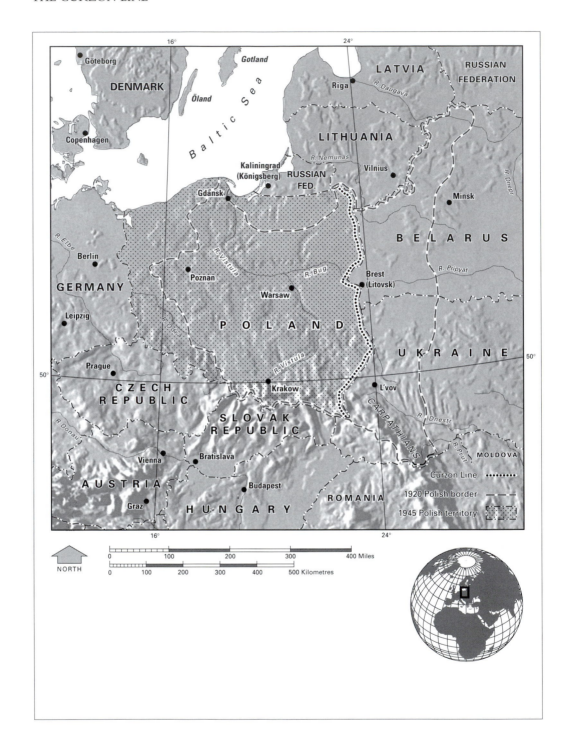

33

CYPRUS

After 80 years as a British colony, Cyprus became independent in 1960, following a decade of unrest. The island, 9,251 km^2 in area, is located at the far eastern end of the Mediterranean and is geographically part of the Middle East although, owing to strong Greek connections, it is predominantly culturally European. The population of just under 800,000 is divided in the ratio 3:1 between Greek Cypriots and Turkish Cypriots, the latter group having increased through a deliberate policy of resettlement from Turkey. ■ *Situation*

The rise of ethnicity as a governing force resulted directly from colonial rule and, since the 1950s, Cyprus has remained an almost continuous flashpoint. It is no exaggeration to suggest that Greek–Turkish relations and the security of the eastern Mediterranean depend crucially upon a settlement of the Cyprus issue.

In the period before independence, both Greek and Turkish Cypriots developed nationalist movements, each with a guerrilla arm: the National Organisation of Cypriot Fighters (EOKA) for the Greeks and the Turkish Resistance Organisation (TMT) for the Turks. Segregation was re-enforced and the best-known movement against the island's president Archbishop Makarios was that calling for *enosis* (union) with Greece. A multi-party democracy was eventually agreed but the balance between the two communities was so complex and requirements were so stringent that there was, in effect, stalemate. ■ *Issue*

When Makarios was overthrown in 1974 by Greek Cypriot elements seeking *enosis*, Turkish troops from the mainland invaded and the island was divided by a 'green line'. The Greek Cypriot government controls the southern 70 per cent of the island and the northern third now forms the Turkish republic of Northern Cyprus. The southern area, which also contains two British sovereign bases, has prospered more than the north, which has adopted various measures aimed at closer integration with Turkey. Through Operation Medusa, potable water is supplied from the mainland.

Broadly speaking, the Greeks are adamant that Cyprus should be a unitary state, while the Turks favour a federation. As a result, there have been long, drawn-out talks but little progress. The issue has effectively become a function of relations between Greece and Turkey.

The two most significant events since 1974 have been the decision of the Greek Cypriots, revealed in January 1997, to purchase Russian S-300 surface-to-air missiles and ■ *Status*

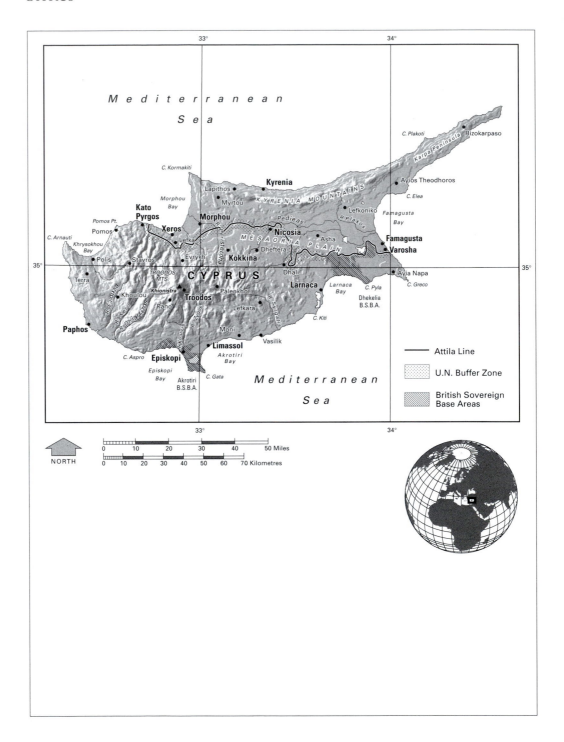

the decision in 1997 at the EU summit in Luxembourg to include Cyprus among the countries with whom membership negotiations would be launched in early 1998.

The situation remains fraught. Greece and Turkey, both NATO members, have been locked in dispute over the delimitation of the maritime boundary in the Aegean (see p. 5). The latest clash occurred over an islet, known as Imia (Greek) or Kardak (Turkish), in January 1996. It has been hoped that the possibility of EU membership would pressurise the two sides in Cyprus into settling their differences and would thereby remove the main obstacle to full Turkish membership. Furthermore, improved relations between Greece and Turkey would bring stability to the southern flank of NATO. Another key issue is the importance of Turkey in the development of the Black Sea and the Caspian Basin (see pp. 48 and 69). The Cyprus problem is therefore multi-layered and far reaching. At present, it appears intractable.

■ *Reading*

Athanassopaulou, E. (1997) Blessing in disguise? The Imia crisis and Turkish–Greek relations, *Mediterranean Politics*, 2(3), pp. 76–101

Gordon, P. (1998) Storms in the Med blow towards Europe, *The World Today*, 54(2), pp. 42–3

IISS (1998) Missiles and the Eastern Mediterranean, *Strategic Comments*, 4(5)

Olgun, E. (1998) Recognising 2 states in Cyprus would facilitate co-existence and stability, *Survival*, 40(3), pp. 35–42

34

EAST TIMOR

Situation ■ Timor is a large island – approximately 33,900 km^2 – north of Australia, within the Indonesian Archipelago. The population is about 650,000 and, like all the peripheral areas of Indonesia, incomes are low. The heartland of Indonesia – Java, Bali and Madura – contains two-thirds of the population but the periphery, with its resources of oil, gas and other commodities, produces the bulk of the foreign exchange earnings. The predatory relationship between the core and the periphery helps to explain the development of resistance movements in the outer islands such as East Timor. In addition, in the case of East Timor, the question of history makes it contested territory.

Issue ■ In 1520, the Portuguese became established on the island of Timor, but in 1680 West Timor was taken over by the Dutch. This division, laid down so early in modern history, has resulted in continuing conflict until the present day. In 1702, East Timor became a Portuguese colony and in 1926 it was granted self-government.

In 1949, West Timor became part of the Republic of Indonesia along with the remainder of the Dutch East Indies. East Timor remained a Portuguese colony until April 1974, when it was agreed by Indonesia and Australia that the best interests of the Timorese lay in Indonesian annexation. In May 1974, Portugal promised a referendum on decolonisation but this failed to take place.

On 21 August 1975, Portugal finally lost control of East Timor and a full-scale civil war broke out between the Revolutionary Front for Independence (FRETELIN) and other movements and parties. On 8 September, FRETELIN claimed complete control of East Timor, while on 3 November, a memorandum of understanding between Portugal and Indonesia identified Portugal as the legitimate authority. On 28 November 1975, FRETELIN announced the independence of the Democratic Republic of East Timor. This act was claimed by pro-Indonesian parties to have removed the last vestiges of Portuguese sovereignty, thus legitimising the union with Indonesia. In support of its case, Portugal requested UN assistance but, on 7 December, 1,000 Indonesian troops entered East Timor and Portugal broke off diplomatic relations with Indonesia. By the end of the year, various parts of East Timor had been annexed.

UN condemnation followed, but on 21 March 1976 Indonesia announced the formation of a parliament in East Timor to sanction integration. In August 1976, East Timor was declared Indonesia's 27th province, to be known as Loro Sae. The war in East Timor had

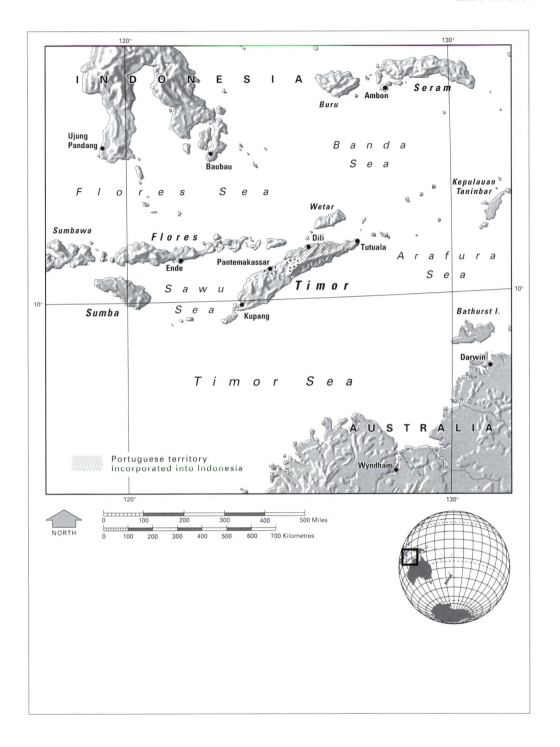

120°   130°

I   N   D   O   N   E   S   I   A

Seram

Buru   Ambon

Ujung
Pandang   B a n d a
                                          S e a
                                                           Kepulauan
Baubau   Taninbar

F l o r e s   S e a

Wetar

Sumbawa
          F l o r e s   Dili
                                              Tutuala
          Ende   Pantemakassar   A r a f u r a
                            Timor   S e a
          S a w u
10°   Sumba   S e a   10°
                         Kupang   Bathurst I.

          T i m o r   S e a   Darwin

                                                       R. Daly

                              A U S T R A L I A

          Portuguese territory
          incorporated into Indonesia

                                              Wyndham

120°   130°

NORTH

0   100   200   300   400   500 Miles
0 100 200 300 400 500 600 700 Kilometres

101

cost 100,000 lives and a further 300,000 people were imprisoned. In the wake of communist victories in Vietnam and Cambodia, the events in East Timor received little attention in the West. Indonesia was considered a key bulwark against communism and there was little analysis of its internal affairs.

In January 1978, Australia recognised the annexation, but in 1979 the Non-Aligned Movement adopted a resolution reaffirming the right of the Timorese to self-determination. Since that time, Indonesia has attracted criticism for the violation of human rights and armed resistance by FRETELIN has continued. In August 1998, Indonesia and Portugal agreed to hold talks on autonomy for East Timor. This followed an announcement by Indonesia which offered special status for East Timor in exchange for international recognition of Indonesian sovereignty. Meanwhile, during 1998, various groups within the resistance were brought together under one movement, the National Council for Timorese Resistance (CNTR).

A UN-sponsored referendum on 30 August 1999 resulted in an overwhelming vote for the independence of East Timor from Indonesia. Violence immediately flared up, initiated by Indonesian militias opposed to the self-determination of East Timor. Chaos mounted, and by 9 September agreement had been reached for the despatch of a UN task force, headed by Australia, to Dili, the capital of East Timor. Within days some semblance of order had been restored, but feelings still ran high.

Status ■ East Timor is important because of the key issue of self-determination which seems to be an increasingly dominant theme of the post-Cold War era. Furthermore, there are large, proven oil reserves in the Timor Sea. However, there are growing concerns over the possible further fragmentation of Indonesia. As the most powerful state in South-East Asia, the stability of Indonesia is seen as critical for the continuing development of the entire region. Given the local and regional events that have followed the referendum, it seems unlikely that East Timor will not remain a flashpoint for the foreseeable future.

Reading ■ Carey, P. (1998) Will the centre hold?, *The World Today*, 54(7), pp. 176–7

Krieger, H. (ed.) (1997) *East Timor and the International Community*, Cambridge: Cambridge University Press

Roy, J. S. (1997) Letter from Jakarta, *SAIS Review*, 17(2), pp. 77–92

Suter, R. (1997) *East Timor, West Papua, Iran and Indonesia*, London: Minority Rights Group (pamphlet)

35

ECUADOR

Among the smaller republics of South America, Ecuador is located on the east coast, astride the Equator after which it is named. It has an area of 283,561 km^2 and a population of just under 11.5 million. While there have been significant internal problems, the major issue remains the boundary dispute with Peru.

■ *Situation*

Initially within the Federation of Gran Colombia, Ecuador became an independent republic in 1830. However, there has been little national integration and politics have been dominated by individuals rather than parties. The key fragmenting factor has been geography since the country comprises four distinct regions: the Pacific coastal plain, the highlands of the Andes, the eastern lowlands of the Amazon Basin, and, offshore, the Galapagos Islands. Development has been restricted by environmental problems, including climate, seismic activity and recurrent natural disasters.

■ *Issue*

Two key regions have been the Andean area – which includes the capital city – which had remained largely rural until the advent of oil to the east, and the coastal area with the cosmopolitan coastal port of Guayaquil. Dependence upon primary agricultural exports has left the economy vulnerable and weak and politics have been correspondingly unstable. The oil boom of the 1980s aided development but failed to provide the expected funding because of the drop in oil prices. The enduring problem is the boundary dispute with Peru which dates back to the 16th century. At issue is an area of approximately 323,700 km^2 between the Putumayo and Maranon rivers, both tributaries of the upper Amazon. There have been a number of agreements but the problem has never been permanently resolved. Fighting occurred in 1981 and 1991, while in January 1994 forces again massed on both sides of the border. A month later, under the Itamaraty Declaration, demilitarisation was accepted but there was still no settlement with regard to delimitation. In late 1995, there were further border incidents, and on 19 January 1998 agreement was reached in Rio de Janeiro on a timetable leading to a peace treaty.

Ecuador faces a range of domestic, economic, political and social issues but the outstanding problem remains the boundary dispute. The 1942 treaty, following the 1941 war between the two countries – which Ecuador lost – gave Peru approximately half the land area of Ecuador, including probable mineral resources and direct access to the Amazon river. For Ecuador, the territorial issue is crucial, both economically and psychologically. However, the dispute is likely to remain a local flashpoint.

■ *Status*

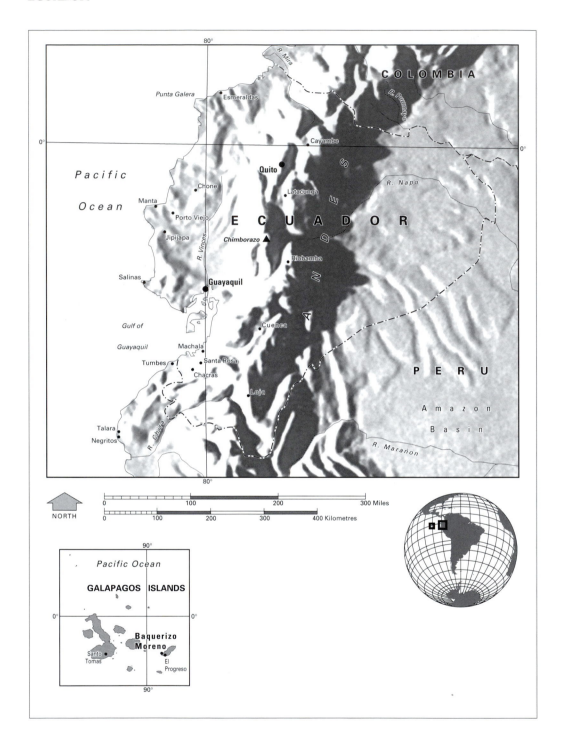

Egan, K. (1996) Forging new alliances in Ecuador's Amazon, *SAIS Review*, 16(2), pp. 123–42

Larrea, C. (1997) Ecuador: adjustment policy impact on truncated development and democratisation, *Third World Quarterly*, 18(5), pp. 913–34

Writer, R. (1996) Ecuador settling a new presidency, *Defense and Foreign Affairs*, August, pp. 16–17

■ *Reading*

36

EPIRUS

Epirus is the mountainous region that straggles the 280 km-long Greek–Albanian border. Immediately before World War II, the Greek population in southern Albania (northern Epirus) was estimated to be about 300,000, or 20 per cent of the population of Albania. After World War II many Greeks left and in 1981 the estimated Greek population was 200,000. The history of Epirus reflects the very complex political history and geography of the region.

On 12 November 1912, Albania proclaimed its independence and this was recognised by the European powers. The boundaries were agreed in principle the following summer by the ambassadors of the Great Powers. However, in October 1914 Greece occupied southern Albania and from 1915 Austro-Hungarian forces occupied the centre and north.

In 1915, in a secret treaty designed to bring Italy into the war on the Allied side, Greece was promised the south of Albania, Serbia the north and Italy the central part. In 1920, the Albanians again declared their independence and this was recognised by the Italians, who withdrew. Albania was then admitted to the League of Nations. By 1926, the British, Italian and French Boundary Commission had completed its work and the final Demarcation Act was signed by Greece and Yugoslavia on 30 July 1926 in Paris. This was followed in November 1926 by a Treaty of Friendship and Security between Italy and Albania.

On 17 April 1939, Albania was occupied by Italy and in October 1940 Italy attacked Greece from Albania. However, the Italians were repulsed and Greece occupied about half of Albania. In April 1941, Germany overran Yugoslavia and Greece but was resisted in Albania by a National Front of Communists and Nationalists. In 1945, the National Front was recognised by the Allies, but on 10 November 1945, the Greek government protested, demanding the union of north Epirus with Greece. In July 1946, the US Senate passed the 'Pepper Resolution', favouring the ceding of north Epirus to Greece. However, after protests from Albania, the Epirus issue was struck off the agenda of the Paris meeting of Allied foreign ministers in August and September 1946. In this way, the Allies gave *de facto* recognition to the 1913 boundaries. In 1958, Greece reiterated its claim, which was rejected by Albania. In 1971, a peace treaty was signed which implied recognition of Albania's boundaries.

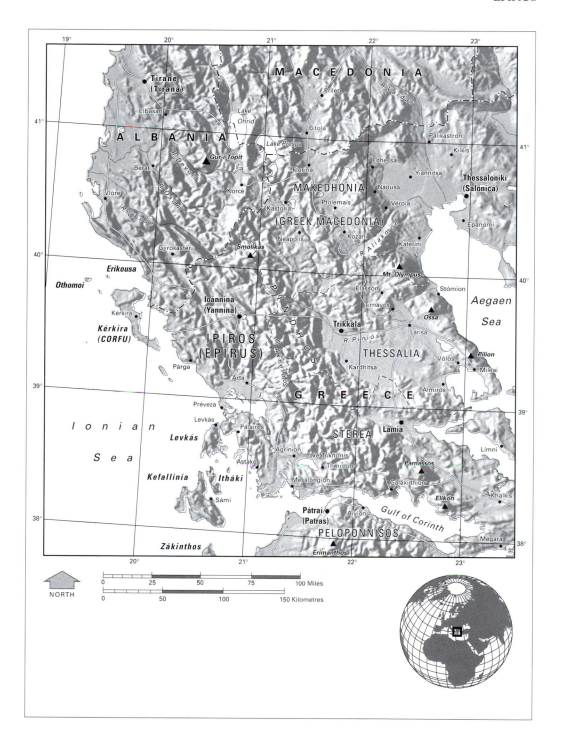

NORTH

0   25   50   75   100 Miles

0   50   100   150 Kilometres

It had been assumed that the Greeks living in southern Albania would become integrated, but inter-communal tension and violence persist. The situation is exacerbated by illegal Albanian immigration into Greece. There is also small-scale breakdown of law and order near the boundary, and in April 1994 two Albanian soldiers were killed in a border attack, claimed in Albania to be by Greek terrorists from the Northern Epirus Liberation Front. In 1997, during widespread rebellion in Albania, there was a fear that the Greek minority might press for the secession of the south.

Status ■ Although the issue of north Epirus now appears to be settled, it has remained as an underlying factor in Greek–Albanian relations. Given the present problems in Albania (see p. 11) and the surrounding states, there is always a possibility that the ethnic Greeks in southern Albania may wish to leave, or at least to seek Greek protection. A further issue affecting Greek–Albanian relations is that of maritime boundaries. The position of the Greek islands of Corfu, Erikousa and Othomoi off the coast of Albania will seriously complicate negotiations.

Reading ■ Day, A.J. (ed.) (1984) *Border and Territorial Disputes*, Harlow: Longman

Pettifer, J. (1994) Albania, Greece and the Vorio Epirus question, *The World Today*, 50(8–9), pp. 147–9

Prescott, J.R.V. (1985) *The Maritime Political Boundaries of the World*, London: Methuen

US Department of State (1971) *Albania–Greece*, International Boundary Study No. 113, 18 August, Washington, DC: Office of the Geographer, Bureau of Intelligence and Research

37

ERITREA

Formerly a province of Ethiopia, Eritrea is an independent state bordering the southern end of the Red Sea, with an area of 117,600 km ^{2} and a population of just over 3.5 million. As a result of Eritrea's independence, Ethiopia became a landlocked state. Being adjacent to Bab el Mandeb, Eritrea is a strategic location, illustrated by the Hanish Island dispute, settled in Yemen's favour in 1998 (see p. 24). Eritrea has boundaries with Sudan, Ethiopia and Djibouti and has had boundary disputes with all three. With Sudan and Ethiopia, Eritrea has one of the lowest figures for GDP per capita in the world. With regard to ethnicity and religion, the state is very mixed, but approximately half of the population consists of Tigrinya speakers who share their language with the neighbouring Tigre province of Ethiopia.

■ *Situation*

By 1890, following the establishment of earlier colonies at Assab and Massawa, Italy controlled the entire coast, from the boundary with Sudan to that with French Somaliland (Djibouti). In 1896, a protectorate over Ethiopia was declared, but the Italians were defeated at the battle of Adowa and it was only in 1936 that they were able to control the country. From 1936 until 1941 Ethiopia and Eritrea were governed together as part of the Italian East African Empire. However, in 1941, Eritrea was placed under British military administration which lasted for nine years. Meanwhile, a Four Powers Commission failed to agree on the future for Eritrea, but finally passed Resolution 390A in December 1950, which favoured close association with Ethiopia. In September 1951, Eritrea became an autonomous territory federated with Ethiopia.

■ *Issue*

As a result of its strategic location, a Defence Pact was signed between Ethiopia and the USA in 1953. It was of course the coastline that was vital and therefore this pact was posited upon the retention of Eritrea by Ethiopia. Subversion by Ethiopia in Eritrea was overlooked and on 14 November 1962, direct control was imposed unilaterally. This immediately led to the formation of the Eritrean Liberation Front, which became the Eritrean People's Liberation Front (EPLF) in 1970. The year 1962 marked the beginning of a 30-year civil war.

In 1974, as a result of the Ethiopian revolution, the emperor Haile Selassie was overthrown and a neo-Marxist government, the *Dergue*, installed. In December 1976, this government signed a military assistance pact with the Soviet Union and Ethiopia became one of the few states to change sides during the Cold War. Meanwhile, with the

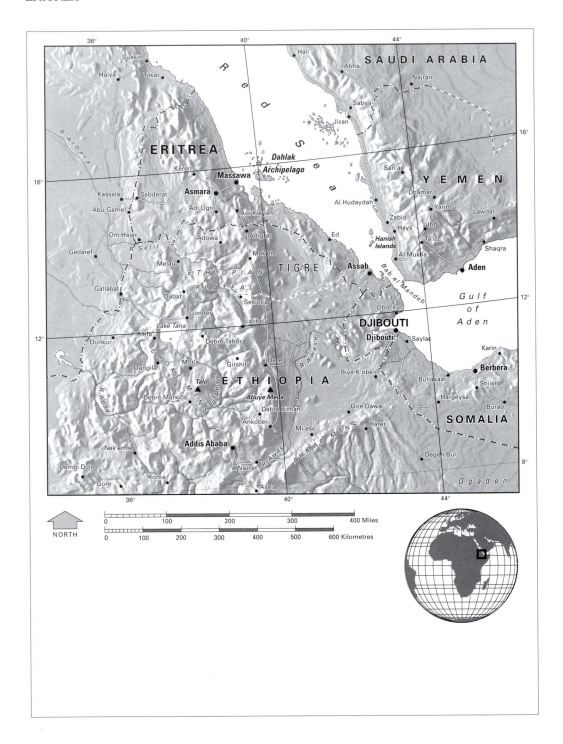

NORTH

0   100   200   300   400 Miles

0   100   200   300   400   500   600 Kilometres

Ogaden War of 1977 (see p. 251), the EPLF was able to gain control of much of Eritrea, but in 1978, backed by Cuba, Ethiopia recaptured most of the territory.

During the period 1983–5, severe drought and famine afflicted the country, bringing it and the events within it to worldwide attention. By 1987, the EPLF had gained effective control of northern Eritrea, together with the port of Massawa, and within a year Ethiopia had been largely defeated and was denied access to the Red Sea coast. In 1991, the *Dergue* collapsed and a coalition government based essentially on the Tigre People's Liberation Front (TPLF) came to power in Ethiopia. In the later stages of the civil war, the EPLF and the TPLF had worked in close co-operation and the new government recognised Eritrea's right to secede. However, in the agreement was a guarantee to access to Assab for Ethiopia.

Whereas Ethiopia had set up a federal administration, Eritrea became a unitary state. Almost immediately there were problems, first over the expulsion from Eritrea of large numbers of Ethiopians, secondly over the introduction of a new Eritrean currency, the nakfa, and thirdly over the issue of their joint boundary. Ethiopia had been administering an area known as a *Yirga* triangle, but when a map of the boundary was produced, it showed a boundary different from the Eritrean interpretation. By June 1998, the confrontation had turned to conflict, particularly around the area of Badme and Zela Ambesa near Assab. The war has been ascribed to trade problems, to territorial rivalry and to Ethiopia's use of Assab.

Amid acts of brutality, the war has settled into something of a stalemate although, given the far greater size of its armed forces, Ethiopia is likely to prevail. Eritrea, already poor, has lost transit trade to Ethiopia, and in 1998 lost the maritime arbitration with Yemen over the Hanish Islands. Previously, it had severed diplomatic relations with Sudan in July 1994, and in 1996 produced a confrontation with Djibouti by moving their mutual boundary some 7 km eastwards. Ethiopia is now concentrating its imports on Djibouti and Somalia, where its infrastructure is already stretched and further drought and famine are looming. With regard to the boundary, evidence can be produced for both sides and the question arises as to whether the dispute was the cause or merely the excuse for the war. As a result of the continuing war, the threatening drought and the poverty of both countries, this region will remain a flashpoint for the foreseeable future.

■ *Status*

Anderson, E.W. (1991) Making waves on the Nile, *Geographical Magazine*, 63(4), pp. 10–13

Griffiths, I.L.-L. (1985) *An Atlas of African Affairs*, London: Methuen

■ *Reading*

Ottaway, M. (1998) Africa's 'new leaders': African solution or African problem?, *Current History*, 97(619), pp. 209–13

Plant, M. (1998) On the map, *The World Today*, 54(7), pp. 191–2

38

ETHIOPIA

Ethiopia is the dominant country in the Horn of Africa and, with an area of 1,104,300 km^2 and a population of 56.6 million, the third largest in Africa. Its origin goes back into the mists of time but it emerged as a modern state under Menelik II.

■ *Situation*

An Italian invasion was beaten in 1896 and Abyssinia was expanded to become the heterogeneous state of Ethiopia. Haile Selassie, regent in 1917, king in 1928 and emperor in 1930, ruled Ethiopia until 1974 and modernised the state. However, opposition grew among the disparate groups, particularly those in Eritrea, the former Italian colony which had been deprived of self-government when its federal link with Ethiopia was dissolved in 1962. There was discontent among Muslims, as numerous as the Christians in a Christian state, and problems arose with the newly educated elite and the developing working class.

■ *Issue*

The key factor bringing these problems to a head was the severe famine of 1972–4. A junior group from the military seized power, adopted Marxism and became known as the *Dergue* (Committee). In the face of military suppression, a variety of military movements arose and there was a Somali invasion of Eritrea. The Ethiopian army was now fighting on all fronts while the economy stagnated. Eventually, a drought of biblical proportions occurred in the north and east of the country in the early 1980s, which resulted in Ethiopia being beholden to international charity for a time.

From 1987, the government re-fashioned itself, granting self-government to a number of regional units, and the military leader, Haile Mariam Mengistu, became president. However, opposition continued from the Eritrean People's Liberation Front (EPLF), the Tigre People's Liberation Front (TPLF), a coalition established by the TPLF known as the Ethiopian People's Revolutionary Democratic Front (EPRDF), and the Oromo Liberation Front (OLF), which represented the largest ethnic group in the country.

After the TPLF had reportedly accepted a post-victory referendum on self-determination in Eritrea, the EPRDF and the EPLF, together with the OLF, formed an alliance and on 21 May 1991 Mengistu fled to Zimbabwe. The EPRDF took control of the government and endorsed the results of the referendum in Eritrea, which became independent on 24 May 1993. The support for Eritrea was contingent upon continued access for Ethiopia to the Red Sea port of Assab.

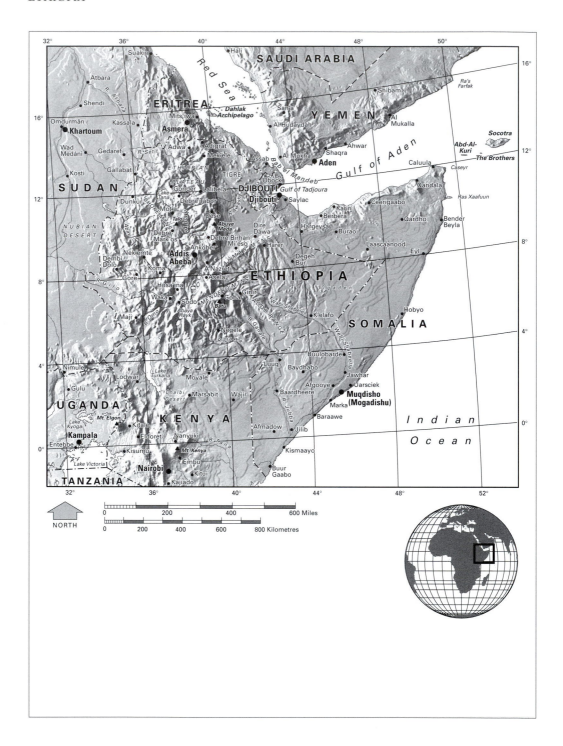

NORTH

0   200   400   600 Miles

0   200   400   600   800 Kilometres

During the 1980s there had been tensions with Somalia and Sudan and in 1997 there was a border clash with Kenya. However, the worst violence began in 1998 and reached a peak in 1999 in a renewed dispute with Eritrea.

The major internal problem for Ethiopia is that the government is drawn largely from the Tigre region and is therefore unrepresentative of much of the population. There is now a border war with Eritrea and there remain boundary disputes with Sudan, Kenya and Somalia. A further crucial geopolitical issue concerns the waters of the Nile, the chief source of which is the Blue Nile, which rises in Lake Tana in the Ethiopian highlands. Ethiopia desperately needs to develop irrigation but any significant depletion of the Nile discharge would undoubtedly cause conflict with Egypt. As a background to these issues, there is a recurrent concern over drought and food security. Ethiopia already has a greater concentration of aid agencies than any other country and, for any of several reasons, is likely to remain a key flashpoint.

■ *Status*

Ottaway, M. (1998) Africa's 'new leaders': African solution or African problem?, *Current History*, 97(619), pp. 209–13

Young, J. (1998) Regionalism and democracy in Ethiopia, *Third World Quarterly*, 19(2), pp. 191–204

■ *Reading*

39

THE FALKLAND ISLANDS (MALVINAS)

Situation ■ In the far south of the Atlantic Ocean, the Falkland Islands are located some 260 nml east of Argentina. There are two main and approximately 200 smaller islands, with a total area of 12,173 km^2 and a population of about 2,000. This population is in fact only marginally larger than the number of troops stationed on the islands in the late 1980s. South Georgia, a dependency of the Falkland Islands and involved in the early stages of the Falklands War (1982), lies some 694 nml east-south-east from the main group, has an area of 3,750 km^2 and is uninhabited. The Falkland Islands are among a number of territories that remain, from their imperial past, UK Overseas Territories. The present UK government is considering extending citizenship rights to all the remaining dependencies.

Issue ■ The early history of the Falklands involved the Dutch, the British, the French and the Spanish. In 1765, the British had established a settlement, Port Egmont, and claimed the entire island group. In 1774, they withdrew the garrison from Port Egmont and in 1811 Spain also abandoned the Falkland Islands. In 1816, the province of Buenos Aires declared its independence from Spain and, in 1820, a Falklands claim was lodged on its behalf. In 1823, the United Provinces of La Plata were recognised by the USA and one year later by the UK which, in 1825, signed a Treaty of Amity, Trade and Navigation. When in June 1829 the Buenos Aires government claimed sovereignty over the Islands of the Malvinas and those adjacent to Cape Horn in the Atlantic Ocean, Britain protested, basing its case on the fact that its withdrawal in 1774 did not terminate its claim.

Eventually, in 1832–3, the UK took possession of both West and East Falkland and settlers from the UK arrived to develop sheep farming and to establish a port for the Cape Horn route. The Falkland Islands Company, a British-based trading company, was established. In 1908, the UK extended its sovereignty to South Georgia and the South Sandwich Islands. Later, both were claimed by Argentina and the case was submitted by the UK to the ICJ.

In 1966, the UN initiated talks between the UK and Argentina over the Falkland Islands and in 1972 an air link was established to Comodoro Rivadavia, Argentina. The talks proved inconsequential and, as the UK was considering withdrawing the patrol ship *HMS Endurance* from the area, the flag of Argentina was raised on South Georgia and on 2 April 1982 the Argentinian forces captured East Falkland.

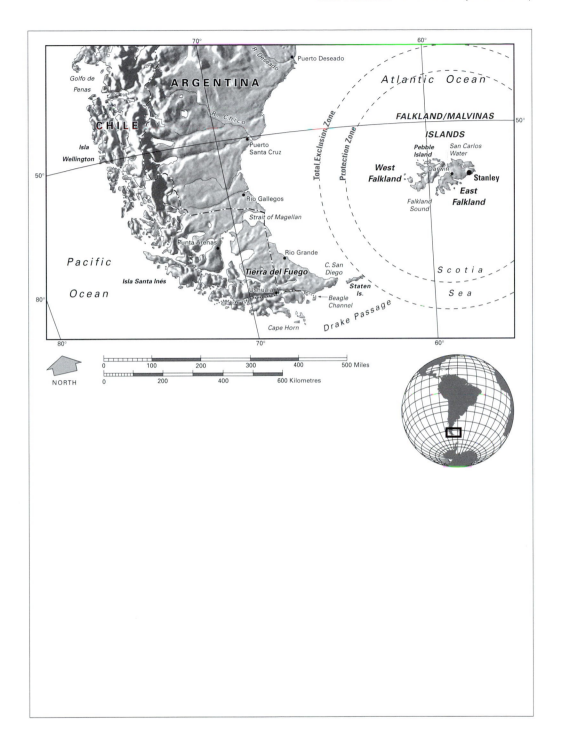

NORTH

| 0 | 100 | 200 | 300 | 400 | 500 Miles |
| 0 | 200 | 400 | 600 Kilometres |

Argentina refused to withdraw despite a UN Security Council Resolution, and the UK dispatched a naval task force. On 25 April, South Georgia was taken and on 14 June the Argentinian forces in the Falklands surrendered. The war was short, but it cost at least a thousand lives and the loss of an Argentinian battle-cruiser, the *General Belgrano,* and a number of British warships, including *HMS Sheffield*. On 22 July, the 200-nml Total Exclusion Zone, established during the war, was replaced by a 150-nml Protection Zone. Before the end of 1982, the UK had established the Falkland Islands Development Agency and had agreed to provide, over six years, a sum of £31 million for development. Central to this was the construction at Mount Pleasant of a military airport, which was completed in 1985. In October 1989, a formal end to hostilities was declared and, on 15 February 1990, full diplomatic relations were re-established between Argentina and the UK. The cause of the war was ostensibly the issue of self-determination, but important considerations were that valuable fishing grounds and petroleum deposits existed within the EEZ. There were the added questions of the UK claim to Antarctica and the strategic location of the islands with regard to inter-ocean passages to the Pacific.

Status ■ On 28 November 1990, a joint agreement was reached on fishing rights and, most importantly, in September 1995 there was a joint declaration which offered a structure for future Anglo-Argentinian co-operation over resource exploitation. The fact that the issue of sovereignty was set aside made this agreement possible.

Apart from the Anglo-Argentinian co-operation, the other factor that keeps the Falkland Islands in the geopolitical focus is that the economic situation in the islands was transformed during the late 1990s. As a result of fishing revenue and the potential of oil, the people of the islands might in future be in a position to consider full independence or self-governance in association with an external nation. For Argentina, the Malvinas remain a major concern. In September 1997, the USA offered Argentina the status of a special partner of NATO, and on 29 October 1998 the UK and Argentina signed a defence agreement. There are a number of options: Argentina might renounce its sovereignty claim in exchange for a largely symbolic presence on the islands, but it is more likely that there will be permanent co-operative arrangements over fishing, oil and communications, combined with a degree of self-governance.

Reading ■ Beck, P. (1991) Fisheries conservation: a basis for a special Anglo-Argentine relationship, *Boundary Bulletin*, No. 2, pp. 29–36

Child, J. (1985) *Geopolitics and Conflict in South America*, Stanford, CA: Praeger/Hoover Institution Press

Dodds, K. (1998) Towards rapprochement? Anglo-Argentine relations and the
    Falklands/Malvinas in the late 90s, *International Affairs*, 74(3), pp. 617–30
Monaghan, D. (1998) *The Falklands War: Myth and Countermyth*, Basingstoke: Macmillan

40

GEORGIA

Situation ■ Georgia is a mountainous state in the Transcaucasus, bordering the Black Sea. It has boundaries with the Russian Federation, Azerbaijan, Armenia and Turkey. With an area of 69,700 km^2 and a population of just under 5.5 million, Georgia is smaller in these respects than Azerbaijan but considerably larger than Armenia. In 1918, Georgia became a republic but was invaded in 1921 and incorporated into the Transcaucasian Federation, a constituent republic of the Soviet Union. It became a union republic in 1936 but there were regular uprisings throughout the period of Soviet rule. In the 1950s, particular objection was taken to de-Stalinisation since Josef Stalin himself was a Georgian. Eventually, following further secessionist movements, independence was declared in April 1991. Since then, there has been almost unremitting violence and the long-term survival of the state must be in question.

Issue ■ Following multi-party elections in October 1990, a coalition came to power but its authoritarian policies, which included the imposition of martial law, resulted in an uprising in December 1991. The Georgian National Guard set up a State Council to run the country and in March 1992 Eduard Shevardnaze, the former Soviet foreign minister, returned as its head.

The key source of conflict has been the inclusion within the state of three Muslim-dominated areas: the autonomous Republic of Abkhazia, the autonomous Republic of Adzhira, and the autonomous region of South Ossetia. Georgia has a strategic location and, potentially, a balanced economy, but the issue of these three areas has dominated the 1990s.

In September 1990, South Ossetia proclaimed itself a fully independent union republic. A mini civil war ensued and, despite a referendum which showed overwhelming support for integration with its Russian counterpart North Ossetia, this move was rejected by both Georgia and Russia.

On 23 July 1992, Abkhazia proclaimed state sovereignty, although the area was only 17.8 per cent Abkhaz against 45.7 per cent Georgian. Elements of the Russian forces supported Abkhazia and the conflict dragged on until agreement was finally reached on 4 April 1994 that Abkhazia should be an autonomous republic within Georgia. However, despite the intervention of the UN, unrest continued. Georgia proposed an international peacekeeping operation for Abkhazia, the leadership of which considered the CIS to be

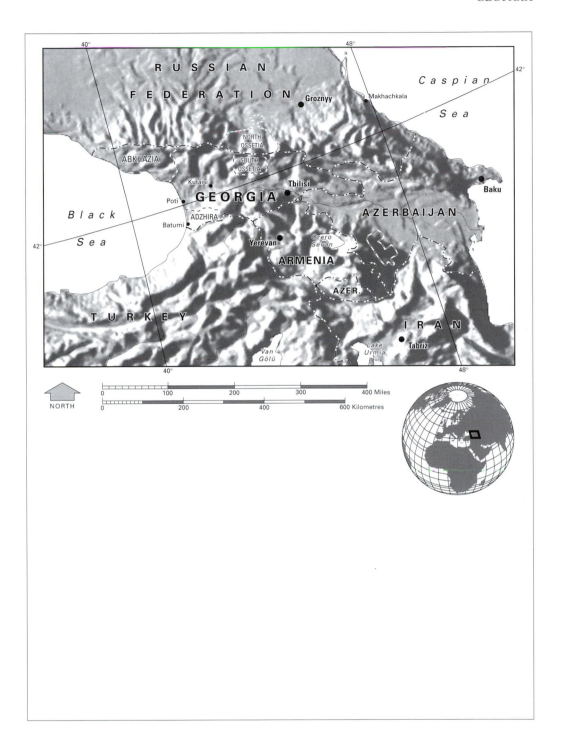

NORTH

| 0 | 100 | 200 | 300 | 400 Miles |

| 0 | 200 | 400 | 600 Kilometres |

the only acceptable body for mediation. Meanwhile, problems continued with South Ossetia, but an agreement reached in March 1997 which preserved Georgia's territorial integrity while giving South Ossetia 'special powers of self-determination' appears to be holding.

Status ■ Its location at the interchange of global routes, together with the problems of its Muslim-dominated areas, makes it very unlikely that stability will return to Georgia in the near future. In addition, there is the question of relations with Russia, which has four military bases in the state. An informal alliance with Azerbaijan and Ukraine has gradually taken shape and this is decidedly Western in orientation. Georgia is also closely involved in plans for pipelines from the Caspian Basin and in the development of the Transcaucasus Corridor. There are clearly great opportunities but, as the several attempts on Shevardnaze's life show, the prerequisite is political stability.

Reading ■ Coppieters, B. (1998) *Georgians and Abkhazians: the Search for Peace and Settlement,* Köln: Bundesinstitut für östwissenschaftliche und internationale Studien

IISS (1998) Another defeat for Georgia: reopened wounds in the Caucasus, *Strategic Comments*, 4(6)

Kaldor, M. (1997) *New Wars*, London: Pinter

41

GIBRALTAR

Gibraltar, with an area of 6 km^2 and a population of 28,000, is a rocky headland located on the northern side of the entry to the Mediterranean. Owing to the importance of the Strait of Gibraltar (see p. 77), it has always been regarded as a strategic point.

■ *Situation*

Gibraltar is a crown colony captured by the British in 1704 and ceded to the UK by Spain as a result of the Treaty of Utrecht in 1713. Since World War II it has been the subject of a dispute between Britain and Spain. Spain has brought pressure to bear on the UN for decolonisation of the territory and has, at times, impeded access to it by land and air. In 1968, the UN upheld the Spanish position, but the 1969 constitution guaranteed Gibraltar that the colony would never have to accept Spanish rule unless the majority of Gibraltarians desired it. As a result, Spain closed its land frontier with Gibraltar. The blockade continued until there was a qualified re-opening in 1982. The border only fully re-opened in February 1985, when an agreement granting equal rights for Spaniards in Gibraltar and Gibraltarians in Spain was reached. At the same time, the UK agreed to enter discussions on sovereignty while stating that the paramount factor would be the wishes of the inhabitants.

■ *Issue*

Gibraltar briefly re-entered the news in March 1988 when it was the scene of the killing of three members of the Irish Republican Army (IRA) by members of Britain's Special Air Services (SAS) regiment. Meanwhile, discussions over the future of Gibraltar continued, heightened by Spanish concern over drug trafficking and money laundering.

In June 1997, the Chief Minister proposed that the status of Gibraltar be changed from that of a dependent territory to a crown dependency.

The situation over Gibraltar appears to be deadlocked. Gibraltarians demand the right of self-determination, while Spain insists on its right of first refusal of sovereignty, enshrined in the 1713 Treaty of Utrecht. In the broader sphere, Gibraltar has proved an irritant in relations between Britain and Spain and has, to an extent, prejudiced European integration in several aspects. For Spain, the issue is rather larger in that it continues to hold enclaves in Morocco, most notably Ceuta and Melilla (see p. 77). Furthermore, among its own constituents are some units with a strong desire for autonomy, including the Basque provinces (see p. 33). In global affairs, it can be concluded that Gibraltar will remain an irritant rather than a potential flashpoint.

■ *Status*

123

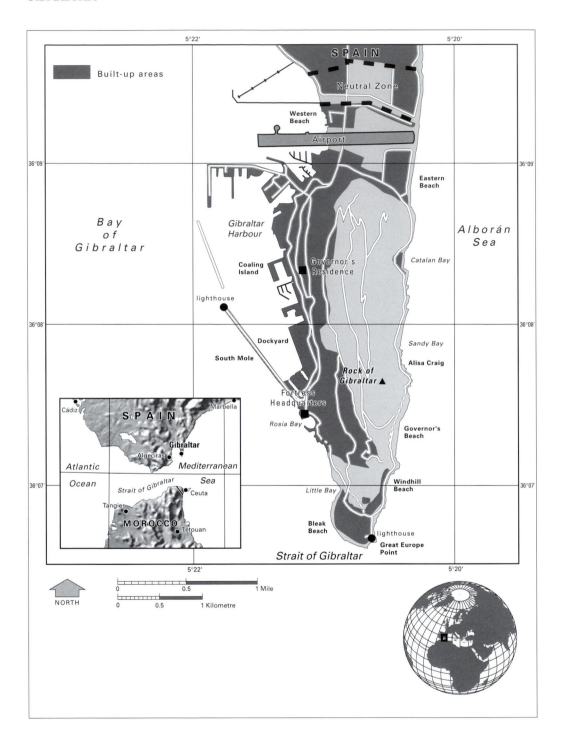

Groom, A. (1997) Gibraltar: a pebble in the EU's shoe, *Mediterranean Politics*, 2(3), pp. 20–52 ■ *Reading*

42

GOLAN HEIGHTS

Situation ■ The Golan Heights comprise an upland area which provides a natural boundary between Israel and Syria. After 1948, the international boundary was along the foot of the Golan and this represented the most vulnerable section of the boundaries of the new state. During the 1967 war with its Arab neighbours, Israel occupied a part of the Golan Heights, effectively moving the boundary some 20 km eastwards.

Issue ■ The interim status of the occupied strip of Golan was established in a disengagement agreement made with Syria in May 1974. However, on 14 December 1981, in an action that was almost universally condemned, the area under Israeli military control was made formally subject to the 'law, jurisdiction and administration' of Israel.

The inclusion of the Golan Heights in the Occupied Territories has provided Israel with a military buffer zone against Syria and a location from which to control the headwaters of the River Jordan. Additionally, Israeli settlements have been established and a number of reservoirs have been built. Nevertheless, the fact remains that the inhabitants are largely Druse and the Jewish settlers are a minority among the population of approximately 26,000.

The importance of the Golan Heights is that, with agreements already having been reached with Egypt and Jordan, this small territory provides the major constraint on some sort of settlement with Syria. Between 1992 and 1996, Israel tried to transform Israeli-Syrian relations and find an accommodation. However, the advent of Benjamin Netanyahu to the Israeli premiership in 1996 brought negotiations to an end. In the same year, the threat of an Israeli-Syrian military confrontation came to the fore as Syria redeployed some units to the Bekaa Valley.

In July 1998, the Israeli Parliament, the Knesset, gave preliminary approval to a bill that would make Israeli withdrawal from the Golan Heights subject to a national referendum. One month later, the government announced a plan to expand the number of Jewish settlements in the area. Meanwhile, Syria moved two Scud-C missile units to bring Israel's nuclear research centre at Dimona within range for the first time.

In early 1999, the Israeli Parliament made it mandatory that a national referendum should be held before any withdrawal from the Golan Heights.

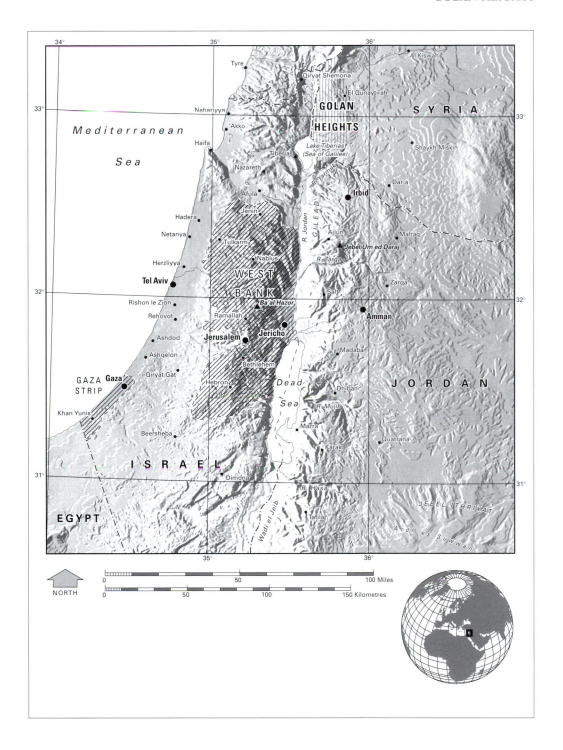

NORTH

0   50   100 Miles

0   50   100   150 Kilometres

Status ■ The new Israeli government of Ehud Barak seems set to withdraw troops from South Lebanon and some movement may be possible over the Golan Heights. Syria remains highly influential in its control over Hezbollah, an Islamic guerrilla group which has periodically caused chaos in Israel. Therefore, Israel needs a settlement with Syria but this is unlikely without terms being agreed over Golan. It is difficult to envisage what form such an agreement might take. Thus, the Golan Heights must be designated a currently dormant flashpoint.

Reading ■ Anderson, E.W. (1988) Water: the next strategic resource, in J.R. Starr and D.S. Stoll, *The Politics of Security*, Boulder, CO: Westview, pp. 1–21

Anderson, E.W. (1991) The Middle East and hydropolitics, *World Energy Council Journal*, December, pp. 35–8

Rabinovitch, I. (1998) *The Brink of Peace: the Israeli-Syrian Negotiations*, Princeton, N J: Princeton University Press

43

GUATEMALA

Guatemala is a small state located in the middle of Central America, with coastlines on both the Caribbean and the Pacific. It has boundaries with Mexico, Belize, Honduras and El Salvador, making it part of an extremely unstable region. Guatemala has an area of 108,889 km^2 and a population of 10.6 million, far greater than that of any other Central American state other than Mexico. Under a series of prolonged dictatorships, the country has undergone continuous upheaval. The civil war, apparently concluded in 1996, had lasted for 36 years. The issue for Guatemala concerns the possibility of continuing instability.

In Guatemala, the roots of turbulence lie deep. With the Spanish conquest, Guatemalan Indians were forcibly integrated into Spanish culture and then into the capitalist world. The result, still felt, was the concentration of land ownership, the focus on cash crops for export and forced Indian labour.

Guatemala became independent in 1821, but this only served to replace the external power of Spain with, eventually, that of the USA. Between 1944 and 1954, there was a period of modernisation and democracy, but land reform in particular and the expropriation of land owned by US multinationals prompted a CIA-inspired overthrow of the government. Notwithstanding, many of the social reforms could not be overturned and, based on the export of agricultural products, the economy flourished. However, economic inequality within Guatemala among the people became even more extreme and with the slump of the 1980s, almost 90 per cent of the population were living below the poverty line.

Since 1954, the Guatemalan regimes have been either military or military dominated and the repression has generated the longest civil war in the Western hemisphere. Initially, there were two guerrilla groups: the Rebel Armed Forces (FAR) and the 13th November Movement (M-13). In 1981 the left-wing groups united to form the Guatemalan National Revolutionary Unity (URNG), which has continued as the main opposition party in negotiations with the government ever since. Finally, after six years of negotiations, the 36-year war officially ended on 8 December 1996 and the URNG was legalised.

Gulf of
Mexico

Yucatan Channel

Cancun

Mérida

Isla
Cozumel

Yucatan

Peninsula

Campeche

Bahia
de
Campeche

Chetumal

Caribbean

Sea

Laguna de
Terminos

Villahermosa

Belize City

MEXICO

Belmopan

BELIZE

Islas de
La Bahia

Flores

Gulf
of
Honduras

Tuxtla
Gutiérrez

Puerto
Lempira

Puerto
Barrios

La Ceiba

San Pedro Sula

GUATEMALA

HONDURAS

Golfo
de
Tehuantepec

Quezaltenango

Tegucigalpa

Guatemala

Santa
Ana

EL
SALVADOR

Choluteca

NICARAGUA

San
Salvador

San
Miguel

Pacific   Ocean

Managua

NORTH

0   100   200   300   400 Miles

0   200   400   600 Kilometres

The post-World War II history of Guatemala has been a classic of the Cold War period, during which the USA gave vast military support to oppose actual or supposed Marxist rebellions. The nearness of Guatemala to the USA merely exacerbated the situation. During this whole catalogue of violence, virtually nothing serious was done to address the underlying political, economic and social problems of the country. Violence remains, in effect, a way of life; on 26 April 1998, the auxiliary bishop of Guatemala City was bludgeoned to death. While it is possible that a more enlightened approach may be taken and that external forces may exercise a benevolent influence in the interests of Guatemala, the chances must be that the country will remain on the edge of a crisis that is locally containable.

■ *Status*

Calvert, P. (1998) *The Democratic Transition in Central America*, London: Research Institute for the Study of Conflict and Terrorism (pamphlet)

Cameron, M. (1998) Latin American autoglopes, *Third World Quarterly*, 19(2), pp. 219–39

Holiday, D. (1997) Guatemala's long road to peace, *Current History*, 96(604), pp. 68–74

■ *Reading*

44

GUYANA

Situation ■ Guyana, officially styled the Co-operative Republic of Guyana, is located on the north-east coast of South America, the westernmost of the three former colonial Guianas. It has an area of 214,969 km^2 and a population of 835,000. The population is ethnically divided, but the main groups are those of East Indian origin, predominantly engaged in agriculture, who make up 50 per cent of the population, and the African group, including most civil servants, who amount to 35 per cent. Approximately 90 per cent of the population live in the coastal strip on some 500 km by 16 km, which is the only suitable area for intensive agriculture. Guyana has been considered a flashpoint not only as a result of ethnic tensions during its political development, but more importantly because of its long-standing boundary problems.

Issue ■ Formerly British Guiana, Guyana became independent in 1966 under the People's National Congress (PNC), the African-backed party. In 1964, the PNC had replaced the people's communist-led, East Indian-supported People's Progressive Party (PPP). Despite economic and political turbulence, the PNC continued in power until 1992, when the PPP returned to government.

The boundary dispute with Venezuela, the Essequibo dispute, concerns the territory between the Essequibo and the Cuyuni–Amakura rivers which constitute Guyana's western boundary. The area in question is some 140,000 km^2, or 65 per cent of Guyana. Furthermore, the Essequibo Basin is important for resources and the generation of hydro-electric power.

Following the Spanish–Dutch wars, the Spanish provinces of Essequibo and Berbice were recognised as Dutch. However, Venezuela, as the successor state to Spain, considered the Essequibo to constitute its 'natural' eastern boundary and claimed the area. In the early 19th century, the UK acquired Guiana from the Dutch and later extended its influence west of the Essequibo to borders defined as the 'Schonburgh Line'. Finally, there was disagreement between the UK and Venezuela, the case went to arbitration and in 1899 the majority of the territory was awarded to the UK, but Venezuela was given 13,000 km^2, including the mouth of the Orinoco River and much of the Cuyuni Basin.

This appeared to have ended the problem, but in 1962 Venezuela unilaterally declared the 1899 decision to be null and void and an agreement was reached with the UK on 16

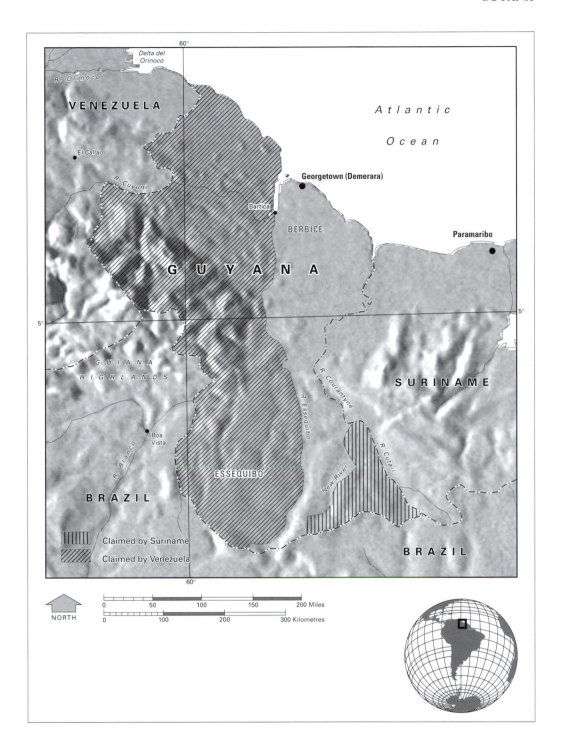

Delta del
Orinoco

R. Orinoco

VENEZUELA

El Callao

R. Cuyuni

Atlantic

Ocean

Georgetown (Demerara)

Bartica

BERBICE

Paramaribo

G U Y A N A

SURINAME

GUIANA
HIGHLANDS

R. Courantyne

R. Essequibo

R. Cutari

Boa
Vista

R. Branco

ESSEQUIBO

New River

BRAZIL

Claimed by Suriname
Claimed by Venezuela

BRAZIL

NORTH

| 0 | 50 | 100 | 150 | 200 Miles |

| 0 | 100 | 200 | 300 Kilometres |

133

February 1966 to seek a settlement. Later that year, British Guiana became independent and joined the UN but, owing to its ambivalent attitude, did not join the Organisation of American States (OAS) until January 1991. The dispute remains unresolved.

On Guyana's border with Suriname there is the New River Triangle, a disputed area of approximately 14,500 km^2 between the Courantyne–Cutari rivers, the New River and Guyana's boundary with Brazil. Both the Cutari and the New rivers are tributaries of the Courantyne and the dispute concerns which of them should be the boundary. In the 1840s, the boundary was surveyed and defined as the main course of the Courantyne–Cutari. In 1871, when the New River was discovered, it was believed to be a larger tributary than the Cutari. Accordingly, in 1899 the Dutch, who controlled Suriname, claimed the New River as the source of the Courantyne and therefore their territory's boundary with Guyana. On 4 August 1930, the Dutch offered to accept the Courantyne–Cutari boundary and the UK agreed, but the final draft of the agreement was not signed owing to the onset of World War II. After the war, the Dutch position changed in favour of the New River. In November 1975, Suriname became independent and maintained the claims.

Status ■ While these boundary disputes lacked global significance, they have remained unresolved for so long that they have engendered certain instability. Furthermore, the area of Guyana in dispute is so large that a favourable settlement is fundamental to its survival as an independent state.

Reading ■ Child, J. (1985) *Geopolitics and Conflict in South America*, Stanford, CA: Praeger/Hoover Institution Press

The Economist (1989) *The Economist Atlas*, London: Economist Books and Hutchinson

Hintzen, P. (1989) *The Costs of Regime Survival: Racial Mobilization, Elite Domination and Control of the State in Guyana and Trinidad*, Cambridge: Cambridge University Press

45

HATAY

Hatay, or the Sanjak of Alexandretta, is a southern appendage of Turkey and the only part of the state's territory that is within the Levant. It measures some 120 km from north to south and about 90 km at its widest from east to west. It has a population of approximately 750,000. Geographically, the main elements are a coastal range and the lowlands around Lake Amik Golü but, most importantly, it also includes the lower course and mouth of the Orontes River.

Under the terms of the Sykes–Picot Agreement of 16 May 1916, and with the subsequent agreement of the Allies at the San Remo Conference in April 1920, France was given the mandate over Syria, including Hatay. On 24 July 1923, the Treaty of Lausanne confirmed French control and it also stated that Turkey had relinquished all territory outside its current frontiers.

On 9 September 1936, Syria became independent and its territorial integrity was confirmed in a treaty with France. Later in 1936, a Turkish press campaign began alleging that of the 300,000 people in the Hatay, 240,000 were Turkish. French statistics of the time showed a total population of 220,000, with just 85,000 Turks. However, in the period leading up to World War II, France needed Turkey's support and, in attempting appeasement, proposed to give Alexandretta separate administration. On 29 May 1937, a treaty was promulgated under which only the economic and foreign affairs of the area were to be under Syrian jurisdiction. An International Commission of the League of Nations reported that the Turkish population constituted less than 50 per cent of the total population. Nevertheless, following the exodus of non-Turks, especially Armenians, the Turks gained a majority in the elections of 1938. Accordingly, on 4 July 1938, France agreed to the establishment of an autonomous republic of Hatay and permitted French troops to enter. Elections two months later were won by Turkey and, following pressure for union with Turkey, this was accepted by the new Parliament. After a plebiscite later in the year, the incorporation of the district within the republic of Turkey was proclaimed. Finally, on 23 June 1939, France recognised the transfer of the territory in exchange for a non-aggression pact that ensured Turkish neutrality during World War II. Thus, essentially as a result of political manoeuvring and military pressure, Hatay was moved from Syrian to Turkish control. This reduced the length of the Syrian coastline by almost 50 per cent and removed the important agricultural area along the lower course of the Orontes.

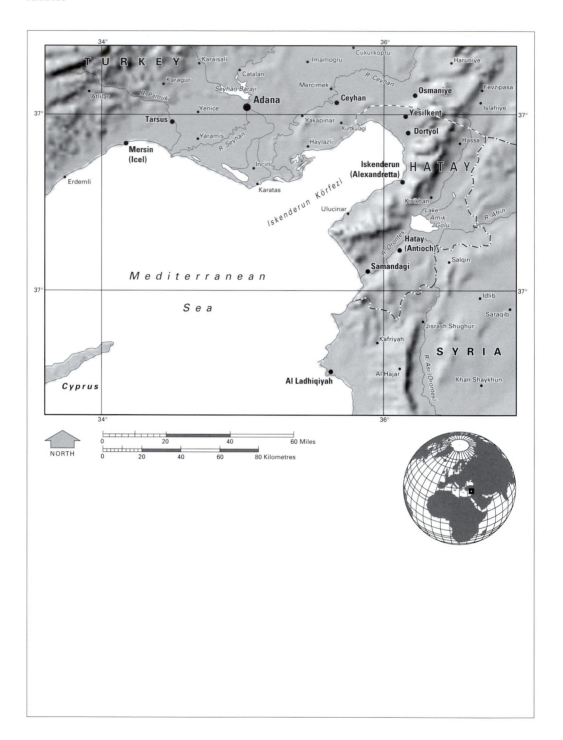

Hatay is now fully integrated into the Turkish state but Syria has never accepted its detachment. The issue has now become a factor in Syrian–Turkish relations. The major Turkish grievance is about alleged Syrian support for the Kurdish Workers' Party (PKK), while Syria is worried about Turkey's plans for large-scale irrigation and hydro-electric power projects which will reduce the flow of the Tigris and, particularly, the Euphrates. In addition to these two issues, Syrian territorial claims to Hatay are recognised as being of serious concern. In September 1998, Turkey threatened military action against Syria over its continuing support for the PKK. On 29 October 1998, the two countries agreed that in return for Syria's acceptance that the PKK issue should be treated in isolation, Turkey would drop its requirement that Syria no longer press historic demands on Hatay. The Hatay issue therefore is not dead, but it is only likely to become a flashpoint in the context of the full range of Syrian–Turkish relations.

■ *Status*

Arnakis, G.G. and Vucinich, W.S. (1972) *The Near East in Modern Times*, Vol. 2, Austin, TX and New York: Jenkins

Aroian, L.A. and Mitchell, R.P. (1984) *The Modern Middle East and North Africa*, Basingstoke and New York: Macmillan

■ *Reading*

46

THE HAWAR ISLANDS

Situation ■ Hawar is by far the largest of a group of 16 barren islands and reefs in the Gulf of Bahrain. It lies less than 2 km from the west coast of Qatar and the major oilfield at Dukhan. It has been reported that the island may be reached on foot at low tide. The Hawar group is uninhabited apart from the occasional presence of Bahraini military forces.

Issue ■ The Hawar issue dates back to the 1930s and a disagreement over oil concessions between the Bahrain Petroleum Company and Petroleum Concessions Ltd in Qatar. In 1936, the ruler of Bahrain set up a small military post on Hawar Island and the ruler of Qatar complained to the British political agent in Bahrain. Subsequently, both rulers presented their claims to the British political resident in the Persian Gulf, who awarded the islands to Bahrain in 1939.

This award was not accepted by Qatar, which continued to pursue its claims, but talks on the Bahrain–Qatar maritime boundaries became deadlocked in 1967. The issue resurfaced in 1976 when the foreign ministers of both countries restated their claims. Then in March 1978, following Bahraini military manoeuvres near the islands, Qatar detained some Bahraini fishermen. The dispute then became relatively heated.

However, in February 1981, Qatar and Bahrain, together with Kuwait, Oman, Saudi Arabia and the UAE, formed the Gulf Co-operation Council (GCC). One of its stated functions was to settle disputes between member states. Membership did exercise a calming influence and from 1982 the two countries agreed to freeze their differences and accept Saudi Arabian mediation. Nevertheless, this did not stop Qatar objecting in March 1982 when Bahrain named its new warship *Hawar*.

The dispute erupted again in 1986 and, despite Saudi attempts at diplomacy, Qatari forces seized 29 foreign workers building a coastguard station for Bahrain on one of the islands. In July 1991 tensions again rose and affected attendance at GCC meetings. As a result, Oman, which supports the case of Qatar, proposed that there should be international arbitration.

On 8 July 1991, a communiqué from the International Court of Justice (ICJ) reported that Qatar had filed a case against Bahrain over the Hawar Islands. Bahrain maintained that the ICJ was not entitled to deal with the dispute, which ought to be resolved through bilateral talks or through mediation by other GCC states, probably Saudi Arabia. In February 1995, the ICJ ruled that it did have the jurisdiction to adjudicate on this dispute;

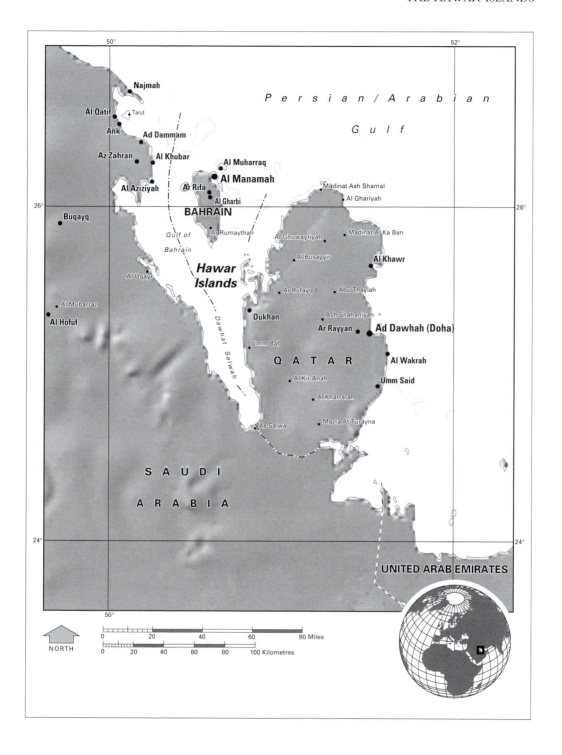

Najmah

Al Qatif Tarut

Ank Ad Dammam

Az Zahran Al Khubar

Al Aziziyah Ar Rifa Al Muharraq

Al Manamah

Al Gharbi

BAHRAIN

Buqayq

Madinat Ash Shamal

Al Ghariyah

Gulf of
Bahrain

Ar Rumaythan

Al Ghuwayriyah Madinat Al Ka Ban

*Hawar
Islands*

Al Busayyir **Al Khawr**

Al Uqayr

Al Mubarraz

Ar Rufayq Abu Thaylah

Dukhan

Ash Shahaniyah

Al Hofuf

Ar Rayyan **Ad Dawhah (Doha)**

Umm Bab

Dawhat Salwah

Q A T A R Al Wakrah

Al Kir Anah Umm Said

Al Kharrarah

As Salwa Mazra At Turayna

P e r s i a n / A r a b i a n

G u l f

S A U D I

A R A B I A

UNITED ARAB EMIRATES

50°

52°

26° 26°

24° 24°

50°

NORTH

0   20   40   60   80 Miles

0   20   40   60   80   100 Kilometres

a ruling that was welcomed by Qatar, which had unilaterally submitted the case in November 1994. The result of this activity was that Bahrain boycotted the GCC meeting of November 1996, but relations were restored by March 1997 when the two countries agreed to open embassies in each other's territories.

Status ■   Apart from any question of territorial integrity, the islands, and particularly Hawar itself, are important as a result of the hydrocarbon resource potential of the area. For example, there are proved reserves of 150 million cubic feet of gas in the North Dome gasfield, some 15 km from the disputed coral reef of Fasht-al-Dibal. Bahrain has only minimal petroleum resources remaining, while Qatar, although a major producer of gas, has only modest amounts of oil. Therefore, the dispute is, economically, of great importance to both states and both have had teams working on the maritime boundary issue throughout the latter part of the 1990s. Given other problems in the Persian/Arabian Gulf, Hawar is unlikely to become a major flashpoint, but will remain a severe irritant in the context of GCC development.

Reading ■   Peterson, J.E. (1985) The islands of Arabia: their recent history and strategic importance, *Arabian Studies*, VII(3), pp. 23–35

Prescott, J.R.V. (1985) *The Maritime Political Boundaries of the World*, London: Methuen

Swearingen, W.D. (1981) Sources of conflict over oil in the Persian/Arabian Gulf, *The Middle East Journal*, 35(3), pp. 314–30

47

THE STRAIT OF HORMUZ

Arguably the best-known choke point in the world, the Strait of Hormuz is the narrow curved channel connecting the Persian/Arabian Gulf with the Gulf of Oman. It is approximately 100 nml long and just 24 nml wide at its narrowest point between Larak Island (Iran) and the Quoin Islands (Oman). Oman is thus involved as a result of its ownership of the Musandam Peninsula, a detached part of its territory. Both Iran and Oman claim territorial waters of 12 nml and therefore the centre line of the strait follows approximately the median line between the two states. There is a shipping lane in either direction, with a separation lane between them, and the main channels are 70–90 m deep. Although exact records are difficult to obtain, it is reliably reported that between 70 and 80 ships transit the strait each day. As these ships include a high proportion of tankers transporting oil to the industrialised world, the continuing importance of Hormuz is obvious.

■ *Situation*

The Persian/Arabian Gulf region and its oil resources have achieved increasing geopolitical significance since World War II. Together, the Gulf countries have 63 per cent of the world oil reserves. In 1973–4 the first major oil price hike occurred. The second hike, in 1979, made less impact but, owing to the fact that the Iranian revolution and the Soviet invasion of Afghanistan occurred in the same year, this was the time when the Strait of Hormuz first impinged on public awareness. From 1979 until 1988, the strait acquired an even higher profile as a result of threats, mainly Iranian, to close it. Indeed, during the Iran–Iraq war (1980–8), Iranian threats to close Hormuz in response to Iraqi attacks on third-party shipping loading at Iranian oil installations were defused only by joint American–European action.

■ *Issue*

During the Iran–Iraq war large numbers of ships were damaged. In 1984, Iraq made a series of air attacks on Kharg Island, a major Iranian oil loading terminal, and Iran retaliated against ships using Kuwaiti and Saudi Arabian ports. This phase of the Iran–Iraq war was known as the 'tanker war' and became steadily more dangerous to shipping. In 1984, 51 ships were attacked and by 1987 the figure had risen to 178. Damage was caused by mines, by Iranian missiles and by direct attack from fast patrol boats manned by Iranian Revolutionary Guards. As the damage escalated, the USA reflagged some Kuwaiti tankers in 1987 and escorted them through the Gulf in convoy. However, one of the first tankers, the *Bridgetown*, was struck by a mine on 4 July 1987. To defend the convoys,

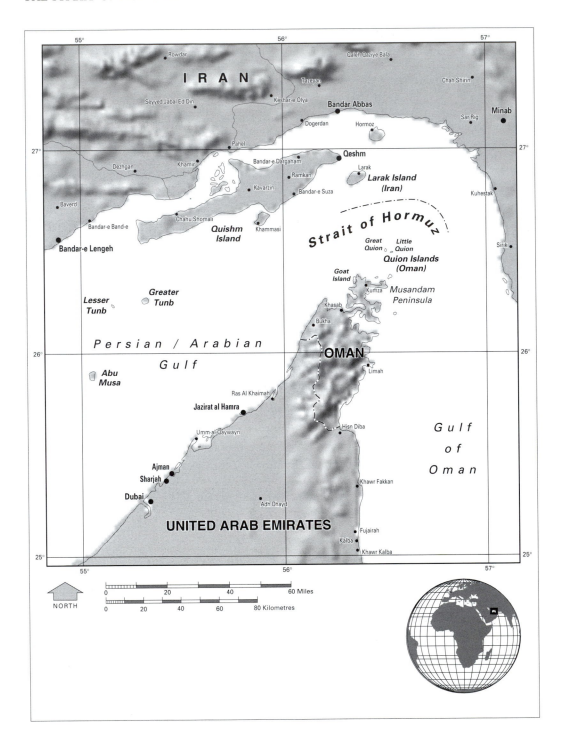

patrols were initiated, using a fleet of 75 warships. Minesweeping operations were also carried out, mainly using British and French minesweepers.

Given the depth of the strait, the methods of attack upon ships gives some indication of the way in which Iran might have intended to close Hormuz. In 1982, a 'wall of fire' was provided by 130 mm guns on islands in the strait and air-to-air missiles, and the sinking of large tankers was threatened. Towards the end of the Iran–Iraq war, Iran renewed threats against Hormuz and warned that it would use land-based Silkworm missiles, which have an 80 km range and a 450 kg warhead. The effects of such threats were to increase insurance rates and, more significantly in the long term, to solidify Western support behind Iraq. Despite the erroneous attack by an Iraqi fighter aircraft on the *USS Stark* on 17 May 1987, this wholehearted support continued until the war ended abruptly in August 1990.

■ Status

The Strait of Hormuz remains critical for Iran, Kuwait, Bahrain and Qatar as it provides their main or only exit to the world sea lanes. For Saudi Arabia and Iraq, the 'Hormuz factor' has been at least partially overcome by the construction of pipelines, notably the Petroline across the Arabian Peninsula to the Red Sea and the two Dortyol pipelines from Iraq to the Mediterranean via Turkey. Iran has increasingly developed links with Central Asia and the Russian Federation and has plans for a pipeline along the northern side of the Persian/Arabian Gulf to beyond Hormuz. Additional pipelines have been mooted from Saudi Arabia and the UAE through Oman, and from Saudi Arabia through Yemen, but there have yet to be political agreements for such constructions. Furthermore, as illustrated by events during Operation Desert Storm in the Gulf War, transnational pipelines can be switched off. While the critical nature of the Strait of Hormuz has been reduced by the development of a pipeline network, it remains crucial as a global oil transport artery. Therefore, Hormuz must remain a key flashpoint.

■ Reading

Anderson, E.W. (1985) Dire straits, *Defense and Diplomacy*, 3(9), pp. 16–20

Blake, G.H., Dewdney, J. and Mitchell, J. (1987) *The Cambridge Atlas of the Middle East and North Africa*, Cambridge: Cambridge University Press

Rais, R.B. (1986) The Indian Ocean and the Superpowers. London: Croom Helm

48

INDIA

Situation ■   With an area of 3,278,590 km^2, India is so large in area and, with a population of over 1 billion, so populous that it cannot be considered in the same context as most flashpoints. Acknowledged areas of geopolitical instability such as Kashmir and the China–India boundary are considered elsewhere in this volume (see pp. 165 and 209 respectively). India is the world's largest democracy but it is riven with cleavages which are becoming increasingly politicised. The most persistent cleavage remains that between the Hindu and Muslim populations which provided the basis for partition and the establishment of Pakistan in 1948. Hindus account for 80 per cent of the population and Muslims for 11.4 per cent. However, the Muslims number some 120 million and, although a minority in India, nonetheless constitute the third-largest Muslim population in the world. The key issue for India as a whole is its long-term relations with Pakistan (see also p. 254).

Issue ■   The long-standing dispute over Jammu and Kashmir has poisoned relations between India and Pakistan since partition. Following conflict in 1947–8, Kashmir was divided and there have been several occurrences of armed conflict, notably in 1965, 1971 and 1998–9. In 1971, Indian intervention resulted in the independence of Bangladesh, much against the wishes of Pakistan.

The election of the Hindu nationalist Bharatiya Janata Party (BJP), which eventually led to power in coalition, have raised a number of issues. Internally, the question must be asked as to what effect this will have upon the social threads that bind Hindus and Muslims in Indian society. Externally, the main issue is the effect on the relations with Pakistan and the signal that this electoral success sends. Although the BJP seems unlikely to adopt a confrontational stance in the near future, it may not be able to control extremists and some have hinted at a hidden long-term agenda.

However, the main focus must be upon the nuclear tests conducted by both India and Pakistan during May 1998. According to the Institute for Science and International Security, in 1998 India had 78 weapons and Pakistan approximately 30. For India, the tests were designed to complete weaponisation, the process by which a nuclear explosive is incorporated into a deliverable warhead or bomb. For Pakistan, the objectives are less clear, although it is thought the purpose may have been to reduce the size of weapons, while increasing their yield and storage life.

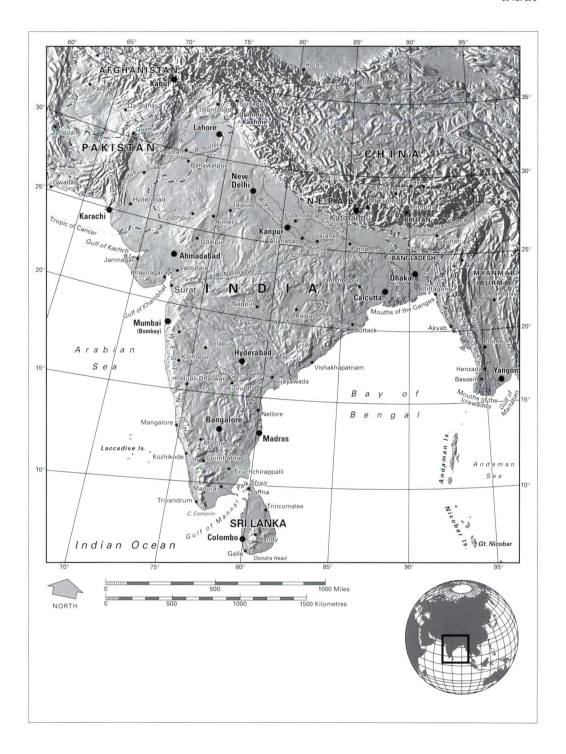

While India also has disputes internally in Assam and externally with both Bangladesh and Sri Lanka, it is the relationship with Pakistan that dominates.

Status ■ Nuclear testing by India and Pakistan has implications that are both regional and global. India has signed neither the Non-Proliferation Treaty (NPT) nor the Comprehensive Test Ban Treaty (CTBT) and has indeed been an opponent of nuclear disarmament. The incentives for the nuclear tests undoubtedly concern security, but more obviously resulted from internal politics and a concern for global status. However, one result must be that, for the foreseeable future, India is unlikely to become a permanent member of the UN Security Council. To offset criticism, India announced on 20 January 1999 that it would conduct no further nuclear tests and would sign the CTBT. Meanwhile, Russia is said to be seeking a strategic triangle partnership, comprising itself, China and India. Such a partnership obviously has the potential to completely reorientate international relations.

Reading ■ Bouton, M. (1998) India's problem is not politics, *Foreign Affairs*, 77(3), pp. 80–93
Chellaney, B. (1998) After the tests: India's options, *Survival*, 40(4), pp. 93–111
Hopkinson, W. (1998) Testing times, *The World Today*, 54(6), p. 165
IISS (1998) The BJP: chauvinists or pragmatists? *Strategic Comments*, 4(4)
IISS (1998) India and Pakistan's nuclear tests: a new arms race? *Strategic Comments*, 4(5)

49

INDONESIA

As with India, Indonesia's size means that it cannot be considered one flashpoint; nonetheless, recent social and political unrest and economic turbulence have been widespread. With an area of 19,044,569 km^2 and a population of some 194 million, Indonesia is a megastate. It comprises at least 16,500 islands, of which approximately 6,000 are inhabited. With more than 250 distinct languages and four of the world's major religions, Indonesia is multi-ethnic and multi-religious. Culturally, it is more diverse than any other state in Asia except India. However, despite this wide-ranging diversity, there is unity in that Java is in every sense the predominant island. The archipelago as a whole stretches some 5,100 km east to west and includes the flashpoint of East Timor. It provides a bridge from South-East Asia to Oceania and Australasia.

■ *Situation*

At the end of World War II, after the withdrawal of the Japanese forces, nationalists proclaimed the independent Republic of Indonesia in August 1945. There followed a four-year period during which the Dutch attempted to re-colonise the islands, but the Dutch government was forced to recognise the independence of Indonesia on 27 December 1949. At the same time, it relinquished claims to all its former East Indian possessions except the Irian Jaya, the western part of New Guinea, which was only included fully within Indonesia in 1963. In December 1975, Indonesian troops occupied the Portuguese territory of East Timor, an island within the main Indonesian chain, and incorporated the territory on 17 July 1976. East Timor continues as the most high-profile problem of Indonesia and is considered separately in this volume (see p. 100).

■ *Issue*

The revolutionary hero had been Achmed Sukarno, who became president in 1949. His rule became increasingly repressive and was guided by the Indonesian Communist Party (PKI). Following a mass uprising, he was replaced by General T.N.J. Suharto in 1968. Suharto effectively turned the clock back and adopted a non-aligned posture, but in fact moved closer to the West. Indonesia played a leading part in the foundation of the ASEAN and improved relations with its neighbours.

However, problems with East Timor continued and the question of the independence of the South Moluccan Islands resurfaced in August 1989. Relations with Australia have fluctuated, but in 1997 agreement was reached on the maritime boundaries between the two states. Nevertheless, turbulence returned with the virtual economic meltdown during the latter part of 1997. Major loans were negotiated, but reform was not undertaken and Suharto faced the most serious problems of his 30-year rule.

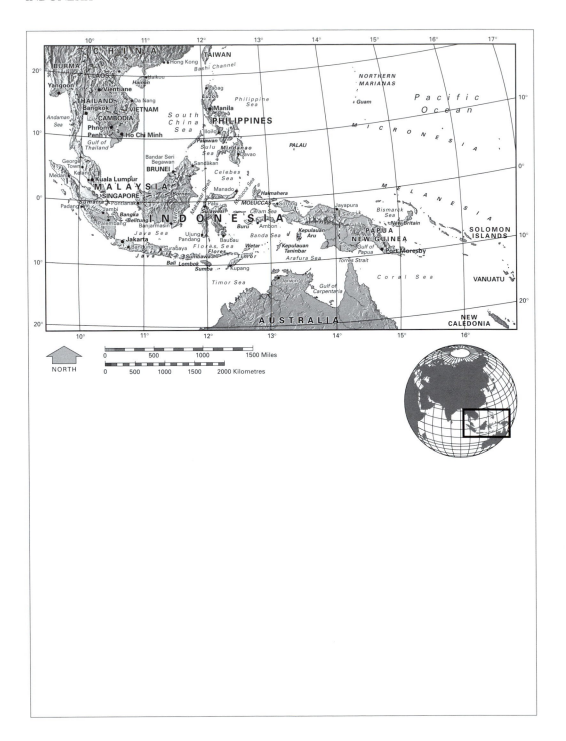

During 1998, there was large-scale rioting and the situation was exacerbated by environmental problems attendant upon the *El Niño* effect. Food imports were required and the Chinese, the main entrepreneurial group in the country, lost confidence. Nonetheless, on 10 March 1998 Suharto was re-elected for a seventh term. This resulted in even greater unrest, and in May 1998 he resigned to be succeeded by B.J. Habibic. However, rioting continued into 1999.

In less than a year, what had been one of the most stable regimes in the world collapsed.   ■ *Status*
With its strategic location controlling the South-East Asian Straits, its natural wealth and its large population, Indonesia is a crucial element in the security of South Asia, East Asia and Australasia. By reducing the obvious influence of the military in political life and by moving tentatively towards increased democracy, the new president has produced what may be a temporary calm. However, key problems remain, including independence movements and the overall stark contrast between Java and the remainder of the country. Conflict has already erupted over the independence of East Timor and this is likely to affect Indonesia in general. Given Indonesia's geographical position, there is a severe danger of overspill elsewhere.

Friend, T. (1998) Indonesia in flames, *Orbis*, 42(3), pp. 387–407   ■ *Reading*
Howard, S. (1998) The burning season, *The World Today*, 54(7), pp. 172–5
Jones, D. (1998) Miracle turns into nightmare, *The World Today*, 54(11), pp. 279–81
Leifer, M. (1998) So far, so good?, *The World Today*, 54(3), pp. 69–71

50

IRAN

Situation ■ With an area of 1,633,188 km^2 and a population of 67.3 million, Iran is one of the three megastates in the Middle East. Its population is higher than that of either Turkey or Egypt and its area is second only to that of Saudi Arabia. Iran has boundaries with Iraq, Turkey, Armenia, Azerbaijan, Turkmenistan, Afghanistan and Pakistan, all of which have exhibited instability in the recent past. When delimitation is agreed, it will have maritime boundaries in the Persian/Arabian Gulf and the Gulf of Oman and with a further six states. Its coastline in the south embraces approximately half of the Persian/Arabian Gulf and, with Oman, it controls the Strait of Hormuz (see p. 141). Iran therefore lies between the countries with the major petroleum resources in the world and the Caspian Basin, which is also set to become a significant producer. Iran itself has approximately 9 per cent of global reserves.

Issue ■ Located between the spheres of influence of a changing pattern of superpowers, and possessing major resources, Iran has long suffered from external interference. In the post-World War II period it became one of the earliest settings for the bipolar struggle.

Initially, attempts to nationalise its oil failed, but following other developments in the industry, the producer states achieved parity, if not ascendency, over the multinationals. Having been removed during internal conflict, the Shah was restored to power in August 1953, following a Western-supported coup, but his autocratic rule was ended in February 1979 when the monarchy was overthrown and a theocratic republic under Ayatollah Khomeini was established. Later in the same year, the US embassy in Tehran was occupied and 66 hostages were seized. Thus began the American hostage crisis which only ended with the inauguration of US president Ronald Reagan on 20 January 1981.

During this time, Iraq, sensing a weakness in the new theocracy, invaded Iran, ostensibly in the hope of re-adjustment to the Shatt al Arab boundary, an issue which is discussed separately in this volume (see p. 285). The war lasted from 1980 until 18 July 1988 and, despite vicious interludes, comprised a series of stalemates. The Arab world and the West supported Iraq, even when it deployed chemical weapons. The minor gains made by Iraq were returned to Iran during the early stages of the Gulf War. The invasion by Iraq had mobilised popular support for the revolution within Iran, but the theocracy was severely restricted by the uneasy relationship between the secular and the religious.

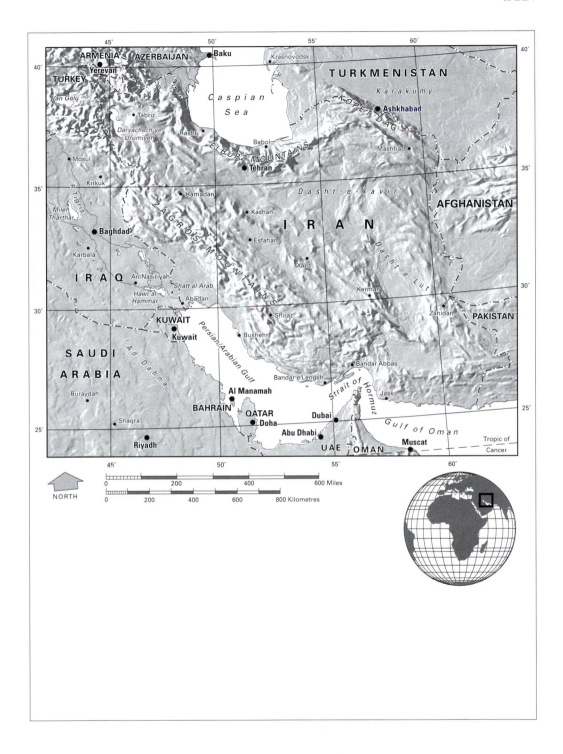

NORTH

| 0 | 200 | 400 | 600 Miles |

| 0 | 200 | 400 | 600 | 800 Kilometres |

During the 1980s, Iran achieved prominence on two other counts. First, in 1986 came the revelation of the Iran–Contra Affair, whereby the sale of military equipment to Iran was used to finance forces opposed to the Sandinista National Liberation Front, a left-wing organisation in Nicaragua. Relations with the West sank again when British authorities refused to ban the publication of *The Satanic Verses* by Salman Rushdie, a work considered deeply offensive to Muslims. In response, Khomeini issued a *fatwah*, or death sentence.

Status ■ Both internally and externally, Iran now appears more stable than at any time during the past 20 years. The new leader, Ayatollah Khatami, has improved foreign relations, even with Iran's long-term opponent, Saudi Arabia and, although US sanctions remain, there are signs that relations are warming. However, many issues remain unsettled. The question of Abu Musa and the Tunbs, already considered in this volume (see p. 1), remains to be solved. Iran has successfully test fired the Shehab-3 missile with a range of 1,300 km. Iran remains one of the three states mainly involved in the Kurdish problem (see p. 184). At the same time, it has its own Azeri minority issue. Iran is a key state in the Middle East and also in the development of Central Asia, but it also maintains contact with terrorist groups. Few countries are as deeply involved with key global geopolitical events, while also having so many problems internally and within their immediate neighbourhood. It is difficult to see how Iran will not remain a major flashpoint.

Reading ■ Chubin, S. (1998) Engaging Iran: a US strategy, *Survival*, 40(3), pp. 153–61

Hunter, S. (1998) Is Iranian *perestrioka* possible without fundamental change?, *Washington Quarterly*, 21(4), pp. 23–41

IISS (1998) Iran's conservatives and reformers: a struggle for power, *Strategic Comments*, 4(7)

Olson, R. (1998) *The Kurdish Question and Turkish–Iranian Relations*, Costa Mesa, CA: Mazda Publishers

51

IRAQ

With a population of 20.5 million, Iraq is the third most populous Arab state after Egypt and Algeria. It has an area of 437,072 km^2 and is located at the head of the Persian/Arabian Gulf and occupies most of what was Mesopotamia, the flood plains of the Tigris and Euphrates rivers. Iraq has boundaries with Saudi Arabia, Jordan, Syria, Turkey and Iran and is greatly handicapped by having a coastline of just 40 km on the Gulf. Thus, Iraq, militarily the most powerful among the Arab states before the Gulf War, is located at the border between the Arab world and the two most powerful non-Arab states in the Middle East: Turkey and Iran. Geopolitically, the situation is exacerbated by the fact that Iraq has about 10 per cent of the global petroleum reserves, placing it with Iran, Kuwait and the UAE, second to Saudi Arabia.

■ *Situation*

Iraq emerged in 1920 as an artificial construct from parts of the former Ottoman Empire, with the UK as mandatory power. The state became independent in 1932, after which the development of the oil industry and the various tensions, at least in part generated by oil production, occupied the state until 1958. The revolution of 1958 ended the monarchy and saw the establishment of a military government which began reforms. However, unrest continued as other political groupings, in particular the communists, the Kurds and the Pan-Arab nationalists, became increasingly important. The communists were the main force and also opposed the demand by the nationalists that Iraq should join the new United Arab Republic, alongside Egypt and Syria. In the north, the Kurdish National Movement is divided into factions to produce the problems that still exist today.

■ *Issue*

The Ba'athists, a Pan-Arab socialist movement, thwarted a coup in 1963, but came to power themselves in another coup in July 1968. In 1979, Saddam Hussein became president, concentrated power in his own hands and immediately launched the war against Iran. Given the lack of international sympathy for the new theocracy in Iran, Iraq was almost universally and uncritically supported. This situation only ended with the attack on Kuwait in August 1990.

Whether Saddam was in some sense encouraged by the USA to enter Kuwait remains a question of debate, but the immediate result was Operation Desert Shield in which a vast array of forces, including those from many Middle Eastern states, was built up to supplement the 500,000 US troops which had been transported to Saudi Arabia. On 17 January 1991, Operation Desert Storm began. The alliance commenced a bombing

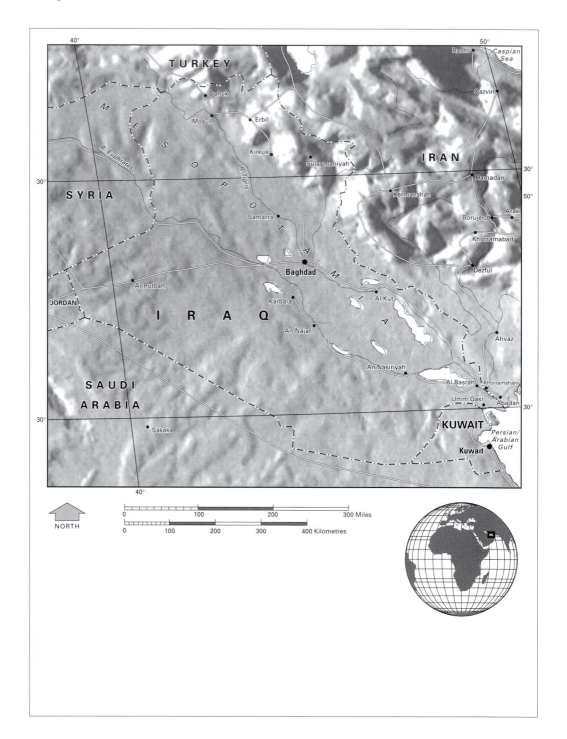

NORTH

0   100   200   300 Miles

0   100   200   300   400 Kilometres

offensive and the ground war was launched on 23 February. It ended 100 hours later on 27 February, after the destruction of much of the Iraqi force.

Following the war, unrest broke out in the Kurdish area in the north of Iraq and also in the region of the 'Marsh' Arabs in the south. This generated some 2.5 million refugees and effectively forced the West to set up safe havens or 'no-fly zones' (27 August 1992) in both the north and south of the country.

Sanctions imposed in 1990 remain in force, but UN Security Council Resolution 986 permits the sale of oil for food and other humanitarian needs. The boundary with Kuwait has been delimited under the auspices of the UN, but a small part of the Rumaila oilfield remains in Kuwait and as such, while the boundary is internationally agreed, its long-term stability must be uncertain. Indeed, it has already been called into question by Iraq. The other major internal issue remains the search for and annihilation of the weapons of mass destruction by the UN. Non-compliance with this resulted in a second round of bombing of Iraq in December 1998, since when inspection has not been resumed. In 1999, the Kosovo problem (see p. 180) removed the spotlight from Iraq, but reports suggest that regular attacks are maintained from US aircraft.

■ *Status*

Saddam is still in power and there is an obvious international unwillingness to see the dismemberment of the state. Assailed by problems and wreathed in disinformation, Iraq is a current and future mega-flashpoint.

Adebajo, A. (1998) Saddam's bazaar, *The World Today*, 54(3), pp. 60–3
Alkadiri, R. (1999) Saddam's survival strategy, *The World Today*, 55(1), pp. 7–9
IISS (1998) A new challenge for Saddam Hussein, *Strategic Comments*, 4(8)
Kemp, G. (1998) The Persian Gulf remains the strategic prize, *Survival*, 40(4), pp. 132–49

■ *Reading*

52

JAN MAYEN ISLAND

Situation ■ Jan Mayen Island is located on the Jan Mayen Ridge, in the Norwegian Sea. It is 55 km long, has an area of approximately 380 km^2 and is positioned 310 nml north-east of Iceland. The island is an extinct volcano which rises to 2,277 m and is covered in glaciers. There are no native inhabitants but the island has periodically been populated by small groups of scientists and, since 1921, has been the site of a Norwegian weather station. Jan Mayen was formally annexed by Norway on 8 May 1929. As the only island in a vast area of sea, Jan Mayen has obvious continuing strategic importance but, in the post-Cold War environment, its potential control over resources within its EEZ is probably of greater importance.

Issue ■ During the Cold War period, Jan Mayen was considered vital as a centre for the NATO surveillance of Soviet ship movements, particularly those involving the Northern Fleet. It was part of a network that allowed the dispersion of the ballistic missile submarines to be closely monitored. Indeed, there is evidence that key elements of the Northern Fleet remain operational and Jan Mayen will therefore have continuing strategic potential.

Of more obvious current relevance is the location of Jan Mayen in the centre of very rich fishing grounds. On 22 December 1976, Denmark declared a 200-nml fishing zone around Greenland, although this terminated at latitude 67°N on the east coast, approximately the location of northern Iceland. On 29 May 1980, Norway declared a 200-nml fishing zone around Jan Mayen. Three days later, Denmark replied with a proclamation extending Greenland's fishing zone north of 67°N.

If, as stated by Denmark in 1981, the fishery zone of Greenland is 200 nml in the area of Jan Mayen, then the island would be left with no fishing zone. The special circumstances advanced by Denmark in support of its claim included Greenland's dependence on fishing, Jan Mayen's remoteness from Norway and the small size and non-indigenous nature of the population. Countering these arguments, it can be said that Greenland had previously shown little interest in the area. Furthermore, Jan Mayen is by any definition an island and therefore warrants entitlements under the UN Convention on the Law of the Sea (UNCLOS).

A further complication occurred in 1981 when Iceland and Norway established a Conciliation Commission which concluded that the sea-bed was a 'micro-continent' and therefore could not be regarded as the natural prolongation of either Jan Mayen or

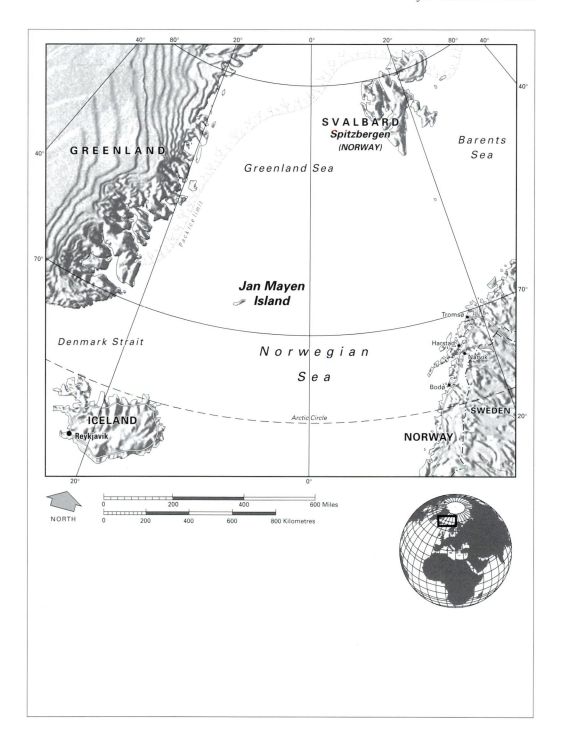

GREENLAND

SVALBARD
Spitzbergen
(NORWAY)

*Barents
Sea*

Greenland Sea

**Jan Mayen
Island**

Denmark Strait

Norwegian

Sea

Tromsø

Harstad

Narvik

Bodø

Arctic Circle

SWEDEN

ICELAND

Reykjavik

NORWAY

NORTH

0   200   400   600 Miles

0   200   400   600   800 Kilometres

Iceland. It therefore recommended joint exploitation in an area three-quarters on the Jan Mayen side of Iceland's 200-nml EEZ and one-quarter within Iceland's claim. In the latter area, Norway would acquire a 25 per cent stake in any venture, while Iceland would receive 25 per cent in the former area.

The dispute between Denmark and Norway was settled by the ICJ for an area of some 25,000 nml^2. This specifically excluded the area between Jan Mayen Island, Greenland and Iceland. However, in November 1997, the maritime boundary dispute between Norway, Greenland (as a self-governing overseas administrative division of Denmark since 1979) and Iceland was settled with the three countries signing an agreement which fixed the extent of their territorial waters in a sea area of approximately 750 nml^2 of water which is particularly rich in fish.

Status ■ For economic considerations, Jan Mayen can no longer be considered a flashpoint. However, given the volatility of post-Cold War politics, its strategic importance remains.

Reading ■ Armstrong, T., Rogers, G. and Rowley, G. (1978) *The Circumpolar North*, London: Methuen
Leighton, M.K. (1979) *The Soviet Threat to NATO's Northern Flank*, Agenda Paper No. 10, New York: National Strategy Information Center
Prescott, J.R.V. (1985) *The Maritime Political Boundaries of the World*, London: Methuen

53

KALININGRAD

Kaliningrad is a completely detached small administrative region or *oblast* of Russia. It has an area of 15,500 km^2 and a population of 900,000, supplemented by up to 400,000 members and ex-members of the armed forces. It has boundaries only with Lithuania and Poland and, for its size, a lengthy Baltic coastline. The *oblast* comprises an area of flat north European plain around the city of Kaliningrad; the area was originally part of Prussia and then of Germany, until it was captured by the Red Army. At the Potsdsam Conference of 17 August 1945, it was transferred to the Soviet Union and in 1946 its name was changed from Königsberg to Kaliningrad.

Following the transfer to Soviet ownership, the Germans were expelled from Kaliningrad and there was mass immigration from the Soviet Union. Kaliningrad's port became the centre of the Soviet Baltic Fleet operations and, as a result, the whole area was declared a military zone. As one of the most heavily militarised areas in the Soviet Union, it was sealed off from the West. The military presence is still large, comprising several army and aviation units as well as the navy. The Baltic Fleet headquarters are located at Baltisk.

As a major receiving area for redundant former Soviet military personnel, the *oblast* has become the focus for illegal arms transactions. To ease the economic situation, Kaliningrad was granted the status of a free economic zone by Russia in November 1991. This attracted a number of joint ventures, particularly with Germany.

The major concern must focus on the future of the *oblast* as a detached part of the Russian Federation, as an independent state or as a territory linked in some way with Lithuania or Poland, or both. Evidence seems to support the view that Kaliningrad will remain part of Russia, given its importance militarily and, potentially, economically. Furthermore, its population is 78 per cent Russian.

Not only is Kaliningrad the headquarters of the Baltic Fleet and the 11th Independent Guards Army, but it is an ice-free port and has been a frontline state with NATO since the accession of Poland in 1999.

Apart from weapons smuggling, there is strong evidence of drugs trafficking and an increase in crime. The *oblast* is also reported to have the highest number of AIDS victims in the Russian Federation.

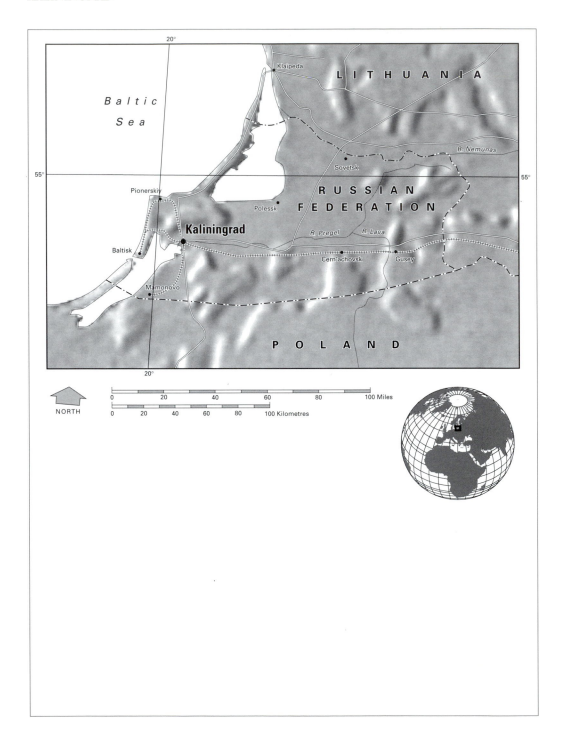

NORTH

0   20   40   60   80   100 Miles

0   20   40   60   80   100 Kilometres

The future of Kaliningrad is uncertain. It has advantages of location but considerable **■** *Status*
disadvantages of recent history. It would seem unlikely that either Poland or Lithuania
would be keen to absorb a territory with such a high proportion of Russian citizens. The
possibility of independence as the fourth Baltic state has attractions, particularly as its
economic prosperity seems set to increase. Realistically, it is likely that the Kaliningrad
oblast will remain part of the Russian Federation and, despite problems of communication
with Russia, will not become a flashpoint.

Main, S.J. (1997) *The Problems Posed by the Kaliningrad Oblast and Possible Solutions for the* **■** *Reading*
   Future, Sandhurst: Conflict Studies Research Centre (pamphlet)
Sharp, T. (1977–8) The Russian annexation of the Königsberg Area, 1941–1945, *Survey*,
   23(4), pp. 156–62
Smith, A. R. (1992) The status of the Kaliningrad *oblast* under international law, *Baltic
   Studies*, 38(1), pp. 7–52

54

KARELIA

Situation ■ Karelia is an autonomous republic of Russia which has long acted as a buffer zone between Finland and the Russian Federation/Soviet Union. To the south is Leningrad *oblast* which includes the southern half of Lake Ladoga and the city of St Petersburg, while to the north is the Kola Peninsula (see p. 174). Karelia therefore lies between two areas of great military and strategic significance.

Issue ■ For approximately 400 years, the whole of what is now Finland was a buffer zone between two great powers: Russia and Sweden. By the early 1300s, the Swedes had begun to colonise lower Finland and eventually, during the 15th and 16th centuries, a loose Swedish–Finnish confederation was formed. In 1617, following a successful campaign, Sweden was able to annex the Karelian districts of Kakisalmi and Inkeri. However, the Great Northern War (1700–21) and subsequent disastrous campaigns later led to their return to Russia. Eventually, the Russian–Swedish conflict of 1807–9, which followed Napoleon's Truce of Tilsit, ended with the Treaty of Hamina and the complete cession of Finland to Russia.

On 6 December 1917, Finland declared itself independent and, on 4 January 1918, Russia, France, Germany and Sweden recognised its independence. In the 1920 Treaty of Dorpat, the boundary was renegotiated and delimited and Finland abandoned claims for Russian Karelia in exchange for Petsamo (Pechenga) and a corridor to the Barents Sea. The border was surveyed and demarcated from 1920 onwards and the final protocol signed in 1938.

In 1939, the Soviet Union demanded a pact of mutual assistance, together with territorial concessions in Karelia and the north and the lease of the naval base at Hango. When the Finns refused, the 'Winter War' broke out on 30 November 1939. On 12 March 1940, Finland signed an armistice which led to the loss of eastern Karelia, Salla and Petsamo and the lease of Hango, located at the mouth of the Gulf of Finland. The territory lost included 10 per cent of the Finnish population as well as a major port, Vyborg (Viipuri).

With Soviet attention directed elsewhere during World War II, Finland was able to regain its former boundaries, but on the defeat of Germany it was forced to sue for peace and to return to the 1940 boundaries. Concessions after World War II included one-eighth of its territory to the Soviet Union. A further treaty in 1948 committed Finland to help defend the Soviet Union if it were attacked across Finnish territory. In 1956,

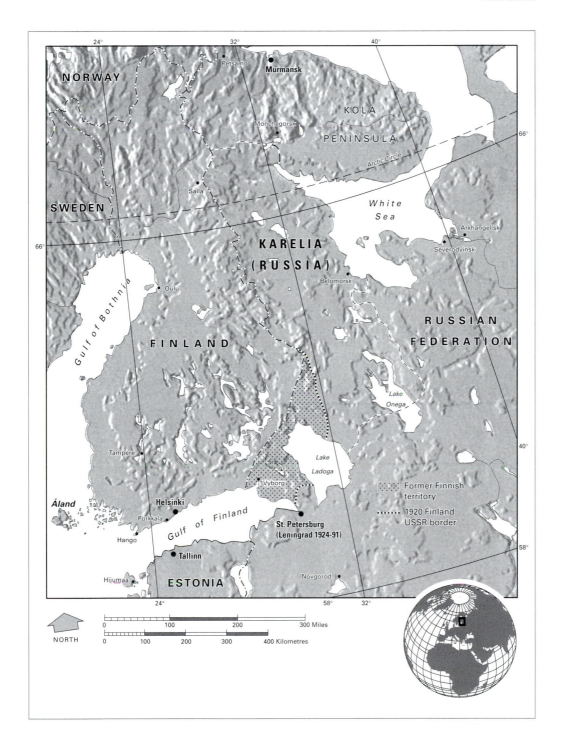

NORWAY

Petsamo
Murmansk

KOLA

Monchegorsk

PENINSULA

Arctic Circle

66°

Salla

White
Sea

SWEDEN

Arkhangel'sk

Severodvinsk

66°

KARELIA
(RUSSIA)

Gulf of Bothnia

Oulu

Belomorsk

RUSSIAN

FINLAND

FEDERATION

Lake
Onega

40°

Tampere

Lake
Ladoga

Vyborg

Former Finnish
territory

1920 Finland
USSR border

Åland

Helsinki

Porkkala

Gulf of Finland

St. Petersburg
(Leningrad 1924-91)

58°

Hango

Tallinn

Hijumaa

ESTONIA

Novgorod

24°

58°

32°

NORTH

0   100   200   300 Miles

0   100   200   300   400 Kilometres

Porkkala, the naval base near Helsinki which had been occupied in 1944, was handed back to Finland.

Karelia is a classic buffer zone, the whole or part of it having changed hands many times over the past 600 years. Its importance to the Soviet Union was indicated by the fact that some 1.5 million Soviet troops were sacrificed in the Finnish campaign.

Status ■ On 10 August 1990, the Republic of Karelia issued a declaration of sovereignty, but remains within the Russian Federation. The importance of the area as a gateway to Russia can be seen by the development of three cross-border contact groups between neighbouring Finnish and Russian regions. These include the provinces of Oulu and north Karelia with the Russian Republic of Karelia. The possible reunification of Karelia seems unlikely but, depending on developments in Russia itself, could yet become an issue.

Reading ■ Austin, D. (1996) *Finland as a Gateway to Russia: Issues in European Security*, Aldershot: Ashgate Publishing

Leighton, M.K. (1979) *The Soviet Threat to NATO's Northern Flank*, Agenda Paper No. 10, New York: National Strategy Information Center

Tiilikainer, T. (1998) *Europe and Finland: Defining the Political Identity of Finland in W. Europe*, Aldershot: Ashgate Publishing

US Department of State (1967) *Finland–USSR Boundary*, International Boundary Study No. 74, February, Washington, DC: Office of the Geographer, Bureau of Intelligence and Research

55

KASHMIR

Before 1947, the state of Jammu and Kashmir had an area of 220,000 km^2 and a population of just over 4 million (1941 census). The population comprised 77 per cent Muslims and 20 per cent Hindus, with small numbers of Sikhs and Buddhists. The Vale of Kashmir around the capital, Srinagar, was overwhelmingly Muslim, while the Hindu majority were located around Jammu in the south-west. Almost since their independence from the UK in 1947, India and Pakistan have disputed the right to Kashmir. Three wars have been fought over the issue: two directly on Kashmir and one in the context of Bangladeshi emancipation from Pakistan. Despite the obvious advantages in all forms of co-operation within the subcontinent, Kashmir is an issue that provides continuing antagonism between India and Pakistan.

■ *Situation*

In the period before independence, a permanent separation between Muslims and Hindus became policy after it had been endorsed by the Muslim League in 1940. In 1947 the Congress Party (predominantly Hindu) and the Muslim League proved unable to agree on the terms for a draft constitution for an independent India. As a result, in June 1947 the British government declared its intention to grant dominion status to what would be two separate countries: India and Pakistan. To achieve this, the districts with Muslim majorities – British India, Bengal and the Punjab – would be partitioned. The remaining princely states would be offered the chance to accede either to India or Pakistan. In 1947, independence within the Commonwealth was granted to both countries.

■ *Issue*

In Kashmir, despite the overwhelming Muslim majority, the Maharajah of Jammu and Kashmir could not decide which way to accede and eventually, in October 1947, was forced to join India. As a result, Pakistan immediately invaded, while Indian forces occupied the eastern portions of Kashmir, including the Vale of Kashmir and Srinagar. Hostilities were halted by a ceasefire in January 1949 and a line of control between the two countries was established in the Karachi Agreement. Under this agreement, India had control of the south and east, including the Vale of Kashmir, while Pakistan exercised authority over the north and west. Despite constant hostility during the 1950s, the two countries were able to agree in 1960 to the equitable distribution of the surface flow of Kashmir under the terms of the Indus Water Treaty, mediated by the World Bank.

The situation became even more complex in 1962 when China made a number of territorial claims along the Kashmir boundary. On 3 May 1962, Pakistan and China

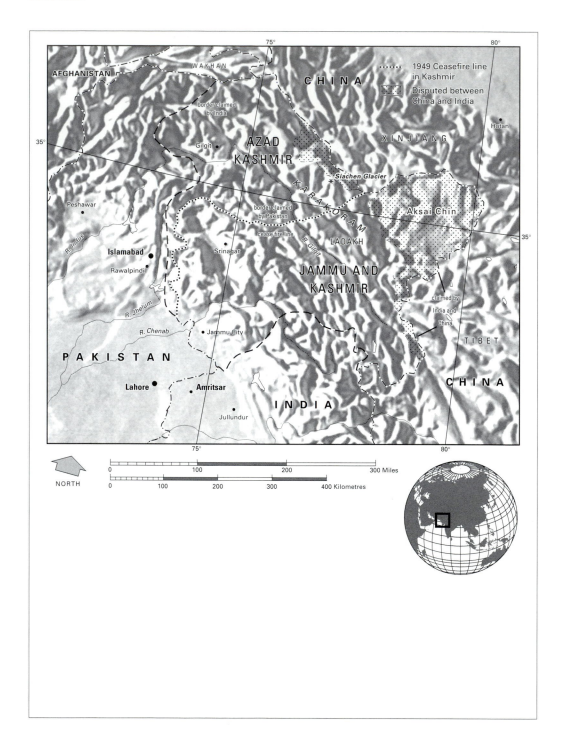

AFGHANISTAN

WAKHAN

CHINA

.... 1949 Ceasefire line
in Kashmir

Disputed between
China and India

border claimed
by India

Gilgit

AZAD
KASHMIR

XINJIANG

Hotan

Siachen Glacier

Aksai Chin

KARAKORAM

Peshawar

border claimed
by Pakistan

cease fire line

LADAKH

R. Gilgit

R. Indus

Islamabad

Srinagar

JAMMU AND
KASHMIR

35°

claimed by
India and
China

Rawalpindi

R. Jhelum

TIBET

R. Chenab

Jammu City

PAKISTAN

CHINA

Lahore

Amritsar

INDIA

Jullundur

NORTH

0   100   200   300 Miles

0   100   200   300   400 Kilometres

signed an agreement delimiting the boundary between the part of Kashmir held by Pakistan and Xinjiang Province. This action, in which Pakistan abandoned its claim to some 34,000 km^2 of territory, was disputed by India. As a result, in July 1962 fighting broke out between Indian and Chinese forces in the Karakoram mountains. The area of Azad Kashmir (Pakistan) remains disputed, as does the far larger area of Aksai Chin in Jammu and Kashmir (India).

Conflict again erupted in 1964 and 1966 between India and Pakistan but, following the Tashkent Declaration (January 1966), troops were withdrawn from the line of control. In 1971, further fighting accompanied the break-up of Pakistan and, in 1972, a new line of control between India and Pakistan was delineated by the Simla Agreement.

Throughout the 1980s the conflict simmered with the focus on the mountainous areas of Kashmir and the Siachen Glacier in particular. Violence escalated again in 1990 and towards the end of the 1990s. In 1995, there was a hostage crisis involving five Western nationals taken by the militant separatist group Al-Faran. Further violence and repeated exchanges of fire across the line of control continued in 1996, and in 1998 more than 150 people were killed. By September 1998, it was calculated that almost 20,000 people had been killed in military-related violence in Kashmir in the 1990s. In late 1998, exchanges of fire began in the area of the Siachen Glacier and these continue. The Siachen Glacier has been described as the world's highest and most inhospitable battleground.

Conflict for more than half a century indicates the importance of Kashmir to both India and Pakistan. The two countries have mutually exclusive positions, with no solution in sight. Following nuclear weapons tests by both sides in 1998, dispute between the two countries would seem to have increasing criticality (see p. 144). For Pakistan, Kashmir is the core issue, whereas for India it is one of many problems in its relationship with Pakistan. Kashmir does not seem to have been a motivating factor in the initiation of military tests and, in military terms, the area is not of fundamental concern. Therefore, the prospect for Kashmir must be that there will be continued low-level insurgency and that Kashmir will remain a key geopolitical flashpoint.

■ *Status*

Biringer, K. (1998) *Siachen Science Center*, New Mexico: Sandia National Laboratories
Krishnan, M. (1998) Paradise lost, *The World Today*, 54(4), pp. 104–5
Lodhi, M. (1998) Still a Cold War, *The World Today*, 54(5), pp. 133–6
Osmaston, H. (1990) The Kashmir problem, *Geographical Magazine*, June, pp. 16–19

■ *Reading*

56

KAZAKSTAN

Situation ■ Kazakstan is an immense country, the largest landlocked state in the world and the major state in terms of area, apart from Russia itself, in the FSU. With an area of 2,717,300 km^2 it is almost 30 per cent of the size of the USA and its population of 16.6 million is third in size after those of Ukraine and Uzbekistan among the states of the FSU. Kazakstan has boundaries with the Russian Federation, China, Kyrgyzstan, Uzbekistan and Turkmenistan. It is distinguished by being more ethnically diverse than its neighbours.

Issue ■ Kazakstan became an autonomous Russian republic in 1920 and in 1936 a full union republic. Of all the FSU states, it was the most cautious in its approach to the changes of the early 1990s. Its declaration of sovereignty was made only in October 1991 and it declared its independence on 16 December, five days before the initiation of the CIS.

The key issue in its severance from the Soviet Union was, as in the other two nuclear republics, Belarus and Ukraine, the question of nuclear arms. Both the Non-Proliferation Treaty (NPT) and the Strategic Nuclear Arms Reduction Treaty (START) were signed in December 1993, and on 24 May 1995, it was announced that all nuclear weapons formerly deployed in Kazakstan would either be destroyed or transferred to Russia.

As a littoral state of the Caspian Sea, Kazakstan has been closely involved in plans for the exploitation of petroleum resources. Highly publicised contracts were initiated in 1989 and 1993 with the Chevron Oil Company. In September 1997, an agreement was signed with China, which thereby joined the USA and Russia as predominant states in the exploitation of Caspian petroleum. However, current prices are relatively low and there is no global oil shortage. Furthermore, it seems that the potential of the Caspian Basin has been, if anything, exaggerated.

Nevertheless, Kazakstan is rich in minerals, particularly chromium, and these provide obvious potential for development. However, with both oil and minerals, approaches to the global market are restricted by the landlocked location of the country. The question of petroleum pipelines has already generated its own branch of geopolitics.

The main minority problem concerns the Muslim Uighurs who inhabit an area overlapping eastern Kazakstan and western China. China, in particular, is apprehensive about separatism in the Xinjiang Uighur autonomous region. With this in mind, agreement was reached in February 1996 to demarcate the Syno–Kazak boundary. There are other boundary issues, but the only one to receive attention so far has been that

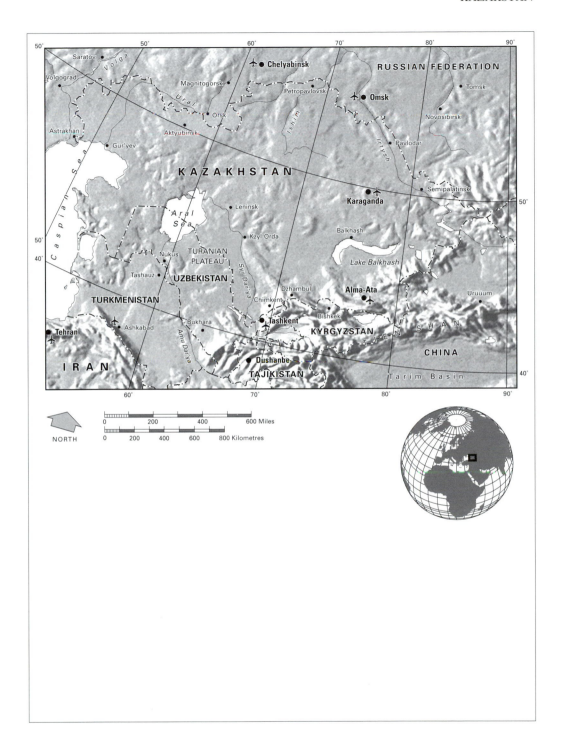

NORTH

| 0 | 200 | 400 | 600 Miles |
| 0 | 200 | 400 | 600 | 800 Kilometres |

connected with the Caspian. In July 1998, a bilateral agreement was signed with Russia on the demarcation of the northern sector of the Caspian. However, objections were raised by Iran, which considers that all five littoral states should share the resources of the sea.

Status ■ Despite the problems of its economy, Kazakstan has made progress since independence. In 1994, it helped establish the Central Asian Economic Union (CAEU) and joined the PfP. In 1995, it signed a partnership and co-operation accord with the EU.

Although there may have been little progress towards democracy, there has been a focus on the market economy and stability. Major problems that remain include all the issues connected with the desiccation of the Aral Sea, together with extensive radioactive pollution, particularly around Semipalatinsk. Relationships have been strengthened, not only with the West, but also with Russia.

Reading ■ Curtis, G. (1997) *Kazakstan, Kyrgyzstan, Tajikistan, Turkmenistan and Uzbekistan*, Country Studies, Washington, DC: US Library of Congress
Open Society Institute (1998) *Kazakstan: Forced Migration and Nation Building*, New York: Open Society Institute

57

KENYA

Kenya lies astride the Equator and is, by African standards, a medium-sized country. It has boundaries with Somalia, Ethiopia, Uganda and Tanzania, a coastline on the Indian Ocean and a small share of Lake Victoria. It is therefore a key element in East Africa and the African lakes region, while also being included among the states of the Horn. It has an area of 580,367 km^2 and a population of 30.5 million, with what has consistently been one of the highest growth rates in the world.

■ *Situation*

From 1895, Kenya was under direct British colonial administration and one key aspect of this was the leasing of land to white settlers. This possession of land particularly affected the main tribe, the Kikuyu, who instigated and led a guerrilla war against the UK from 1952 until 1956. The Mau Mau rebellion was defeated, but independence was granted in December 1963. The state became a republic on 12 December 1964 with Jomo Kenyatta, leader of the Kenya African National Union (KANU) as president; party rule through KANU has been continuous since that date. The current president, Daniel arap Moi, succeeded Kenyatta and in June 1982 made KANU the only legal political party. However, by the early 1990s there were moves for democracy and unrest continued throughout the decade. Following World Bank pressure, Moi legalised opposition parties for the election of 1992 but took measures to guarantee the success of KANU. In 1991, advocates from the various parties regrouped to establish the Forum for the Restoration of Democracy (FORD).

■ *Issue*

In June 1967 Kenya had joined with Uganda and Tanzania to form the East African Community (EAC), but this was disbanded 10 years later. In 1978, the states of Eastern and Southern Africa established a preferential trade area. The main geopolitical issues concern the boundaries and the relations of Kenya with Somalia and Ethiopia. In the disputed north-east, there is a large Somali ethnic population and the virtual collapse of Somalia in the early 1990s (see p. 301) resulted in large influxes of refugees. Closely associated are relations with Ethiopia, since Somalia also claims large areas of the Ogaden (see p. 251). There have also been cross-border incidents involving the Oromo Liberation Front (OLF) in search of Kenyan support for their liberation movement in Ethiopia. Relations with Uganda have been uneven, not least when the two states recently supported opposing factions in the Rwanda/Burundi catastrophe (see pp. 285 and 60). The long-standing border dispute with Sudan over the ownership of the Elemi Triangle, a potentially petroleum-rich territory, also remains unresolved.

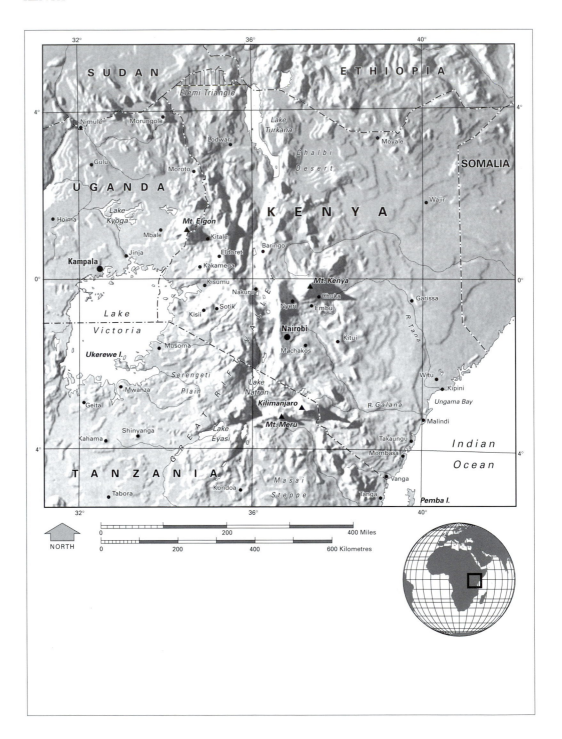

SUDAN

ETHIOPIA

Elemi Triangle

Nimule

Morungole

Lodwar

Lake Turkana

Moyale

SOMALIA

Gulu

Moroto

Chalbi Desert

U G A N D A

K E N Y A

Wajir

Hoima

Lake Kyoga

▲ **Mt. Elgon**

Mbale

Kitale

Baringo

Jinja

Eldoret

Kampala

Kakamega

Kisumu

Nakuru

▲ **Mt. Kenya**

Chuka

Garissa

Kisii

Sotik

Nyeri

Embu

R. Tana

Lake Victoria

Nairobi

Kitui

G R E A T   R I F T   V A L L E Y

Musoma

Machakos

Ukerewe I.

Witu

Serengeti Plain

Kipini

Mwanza

Lake Natron

R. Galana

Ungama Bay

Geita

Kilimanjaro ▲

Malindi

Shinyanga

Lake Eyasi

▲ **Mt. Meru**

Takaungu

Indian

Kahama

Mombasa

Ocean

T A N Z A N I A

Masai Steppe

Vanga

Tabora

Kondoa

Tanga

Pemba I.

NORTH

0   200   400 Miles

0   200   400   600 Kilometres

Despite allegations of widespread fraud and gerrymandering, Moi won the presidential   ■ *Status*
election of December 1997, but there were disturbances in the country throughout 1998.
It is estimated that during the elections more than 2,000 people were displaced by
violence. At times, Kenya has appeared to be on the brink of civil war, but order has been
restored on each occasion. On 7 August 1998, there were co-ordinated bomb attacks on
the US embassies in Nairobi and Dar es Salaam. In Nairobi, 253 people were killed and at
least 5,000 injured. This led to reprisals on Sudan and Afghanistan, both said by the USA
to have been involved in the atrocities. There would appear to be a fundamental stability
about Kenya but this may be eroded unless there is increased democracy.

Baynham, S. (1997) Kenya: prospects for peace and stability, *Conflict Studies*, 297   ■ *Reading*
Kahl, C. (1998) Population growth, environmental degradation and state-sponsored
    violence: the case of Kenya, *International Security*, 23(2), pp. 80–119
Makinda, S. (1997) Hiding corruption and division, *The World Today*, 54(10), pp. 263–5

58

THE KOLA PENINSULA

Situation ■ During the Cold War, the Kola Peninsula was considered to be the most important military area in the Soviet Union. For its size, it was probably the most heavily armed territory in the world. Since the demise of the Soviet Union, the area has been beset with problems of pollution, radioactive contamination and unemployment. The reduction of the armed forces of Russia has had particularly serious economic and social consequences in this area. Nonetheless, there is evidence that key elements of the military structure remain operational and it is reasonable to conclude that the Kola Peninsula remains a vital military strongpoint for Russia.

Located at the far north-western extremity of the Russian Federation, the peninsula measures approximately 600 by 300 km. It is bounded to the north by the Barents Sea and to the south and east by the White Sea. To the west, beyond the main military concentrations, is the land boundary with Finland and Norway. The population of the peninsula is approximately 1 million and the region is linked to St Petersburg by rail. Apart from the many military-related activities, the Kola Peninsula is significant for fish products, timber and a variety of ores.

Issue ■ Under the terms of the armistice of 17 March 1940, which ended the 'Winter War', Finland was forced to cede to the Soviet Union part of the Rybachi Peninsula in the Petsamo (Pechenga) region. At the end of World War II, the whole of the Pechenga region was ceded, the transfer confirmed by the 1947 final Treaty of Peace between the two countries. Pechenga was of particular importance as an ice-free port with the potential to become a major military base. However, the more important bases for the Northern Fleet are located to the east in the area of Polyarnyy and Severomorsk. The great strategic advantage of this region for the Soviet Union, and later for Russia, is that it is ice-free and allows access to deep-water channels, facilitating penetration to the Barents Sea and the Atlantic Ocean. Since the break-up of the Soviet Union, the Kola Peninsula bases, untouched by political change, have become relatively more significant. In the Baltic, the loss of bases in Estonia and Latvia has considerably restricted the potential of the Russian Fleet, while in the Black Sea, an accommodation over the fleet has been reached with Ukraine. For both these fleets, the constraints of narrow straits and relatively easy NATO surveillance remain.

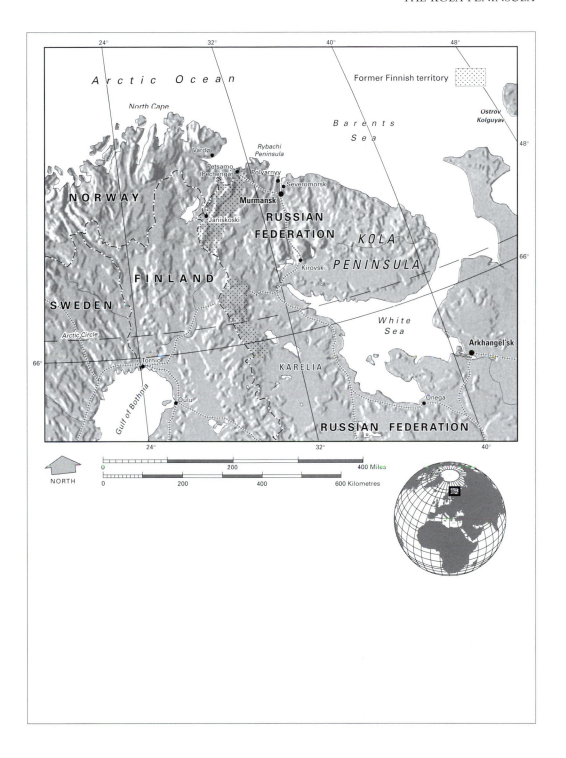

Former Finnish territory

Arctic Ocean

North Cape

Barents Sea

Ostrov Kolguyav

Vardø

Rybachi Peninsula

Petsamo (Pechenga)

Polyarnyy

Severomorsk

Murmansk

NORWAY

Janiskoski

RUSSIAN FEDERATION

KOLA PENINSULA

Kirovsk

FINLAND

White Sea

SWEDEN

Arkhangel'sk

Arctic Circle

Tornio

KARELIA

Gulf of Bothnia

Oulu

Onega

RUSSIAN FEDERATION

NORTH

0   200   400 Miles

0   200   400   600 Kilometres

The Northern Fleet was already the most powerful of the three fleets located on the western side of the Soviet Union and it is reasonable to suppose that this predominance has, if anything, been enhanced by the Russian Federation.

Status ■   Despite having environmental, economic and social problems, the Kola Peninsula remains of vital strategic importance to the Russian Federation. Indeed, notwithstanding general reports of military run-down, there is evidence that key elements of the Northern Fleet have been sustained. The advantages of the region, particularly for the operation of ballistic-missile submarines, remain.

Reading ■   Leighton, M.K. (1979) *The Soviet Threat to NATO's Northern Flank*, Agenda Paper No. 10, New York: National Strategy Information Center

Luton, G. (1986) Strategic issues in the Arctic region, in E.M. Borgese and N. Ginsburg (eds), *Ocean Yearbook 6*, Chicago, IL: University of Chicago Press, pp. 319–416

59

DEMOCRATIC PEOPLE'S REPUBLIC OF KOREA

The Democratic People's Republic of Korea (DPRK) occupies the northern part of the Korean peninsula and has boundaries with China, South Korea and, for about 20 km, with Russia. There is still a sufficient level of confrontation with South Korea along the demilitarised zone to warrant the constant attention of the USA. Therefore, the DPRK is effectively in the unique geopolitical position of having three boundaries shared with the three global military superpowers. With an area of 120,538 km^2 the DPRK is infinitely larger than its southern neighbour, but its population of 23.9 million is barely half that of South Korea.

■ *Situation*

The DPRK was formally claimed on 9 September 1948, under the auspices of the Soviet Union. With more natural resources than South Korea and a substantial industrial base inherited from the Japanese occupation, prospects for development appeared promising. However, the Korean War of 1950–3 destroyed much of the economic infrastructure.

■ *Issue*

The DPRK is one of the most secretive states and it is therefore difficult to obtain statistics, but it has been estimated that the gross national product (GNP) is probably less than one-tenth of South Korea's.

Both the government and the ruling Korean Workers' Party (KWP) were led by Kim Il Sung until his death in 1994. His regimes were rigid and spartan, following the thoughts of China's Chairman Mao, with occasional recourse to Soviet doctrine. Self-reliance was proclaimed, although the country depended on both the Soviet Union and China for aid.

On 17 September 1991, both Koreas were admitted to UN membership and on 13 December there was a historic North–South accord. In September 1992, a North–South Joint Reconciliation Commission was announced, dealing with a series of agreements on non-aggression and cross-border exchange. However, during 1993 and 1994, the issue of the DPRK's non-compliance with the Non-Proliferation Treaty (NPT) was then raised by the International Atomic Energy Agency (IAEA). By the end of 1994, agreement had been reached on inspection of all the key sites and the freezing of its current nuclear activities.

While in some senses the DPRK has returned to mainstream global politics, it remains a maverick. On 31 August 1998, there was an unannounced satellite launch which

■ *Status*

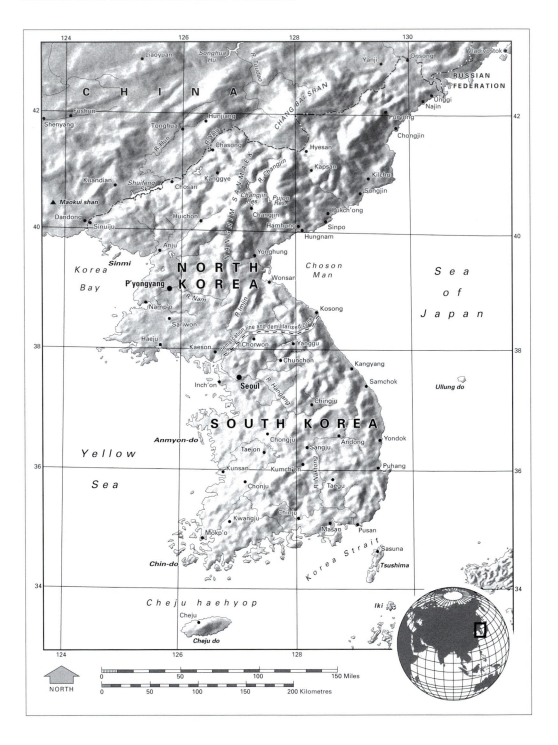

illustrated the point that the country had long-range missile technology capable of adaptation for ballistic missiles. Four years after the death of his father, Kim Jong-Il was moved to the post of effective head of state. There is evidence that the economy, which required food aid in 1997, is still in a parlous situation. While relations with the USA have improved, there is pressure for the DPRK to end its missile programme and, in particular, the export of equipment and technology to the Middle East. As the new president seeks to consolidate his policies in the face of a worsening economic crisis, the DPRK could again become a major flashpoint. During 1998, there was a further serious food crisis, while at the same time there was a warning that the nuclear programme might be resumed. Meanwhile, talks continue with South Korea, but were there to be unification in the style achieved by Germany, it is estimated that it would cost the South more than $400 billion.

■ *Reading*

IISS (1998) North Korea's anniversary fireworks: a troubled fiftieth birthday, *Strategic Comments*, 4(8)

Jordan, A. (1998) Coping with North Korea, *Washington Quarterly*, 21(1), pp. 33–46

Reese, D. (1998) The Prospects for North Korea's Survival, *Adelphi Paper* 323, Oxford: Oxford University Press

60

KOSOVO

Situation ■ Kosovo, an area of approximately 5,000 km^2, is located between the major components of the Yugoslav state, Serbia and Montenegro, and the independent states of Albania and Macedonia. It is a mountainous, economically very backward area which has received much development assistance but remains poor. It had the highest birth and death rates in the former Yugoslavia and the highest population density.

Kosovo has an estimated population of just over 2 million, of whom approximately 90 per cent are Albanian. Under the Yugoslav constitution (1974), Kosovo was made an autonomous province within Serbia, of which it has always been part. However, since 1989, autonomy has been withdrawn and the population has been mostly under martial law with a strong Yugoslav police and army presence. In 1999, for what were listed as humanitarian reasons, NATO initiated the aerial bombardment of Kosovo which lasted for more than two months.

Kosovo continues to be a central flashpoint in the Balkans – a region including a high density of flashpoints. Locally, it is also a flashpoint since it is considered the birthplace of the Serb nation.

Issue ■ Since the demise of the Yugoslav Federation (FPRY), Serbia has effectively taken over the government of this Albanian-dominated region which has, throughout a large part of its history, seen the struggle of Albanian irredentism and Serbian expansionism. However, since at least the 14th century the history of Kosovo has been intimately associated with all the major events of the region. For example, in 1389 the Turks defeated a coalition of Serbs, Albanians, Bosnians and Walluchians at the Battle of Kosovo.

Nevertheless, the focus must be upon modern times – particularly the period since 1929 when the word 'Yugoslavia' first appeared on the world map. In 1939, Italy annexed Albania and in 1941 the Axis powers (Germany, Bulgaria, Italy and Hungary) invaded Yugoslavia. In November of that year, the Yugoslav communists established the resistance movement, the Partisans, and helped set up a Communist Party in Albania. At the same time, the region of Kosovo–Metohija, formerly part of Serbia, was integrated with Albania and placed under Italian administration.

In 1944, Partisans under the leadership of Marshal Tito liberated Albania and Yugoslavia, with the result that communist regimes took power in both countries and the Kosovo–

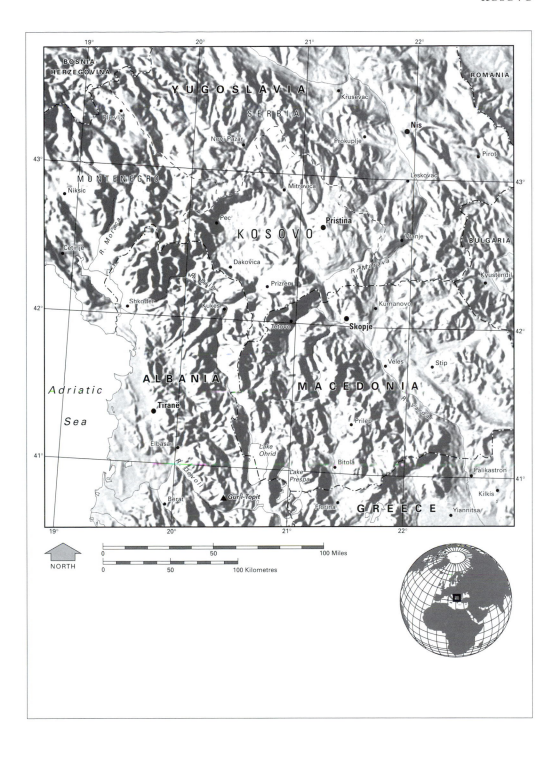

NORTH

0   50   100 Miles

0   50   100 Kilometres

181

Metohija region was returned to Serbia. However, the close relationship between Albania and Yugoslavia was short-lived, terminated by the latter upon Stalin's expulsion of Yugoslavia from the Cominform – the Soviet-led alliance of communist states – in 1948. There followed a number of border incidents, but in 1953 relations between the two countries were normalised and the boundary was demarcated. This was but a temporary lull and several incidents, and rumours of incidents, occurred during the remainder of the 1950s.

In 1963, Kosovo–Metohija was given the status of an autonomous province within Serbia. In 1968, the region changed its name to Kosovo and further unrest took place, with demands that the republic become autonomous and that it should be largely governed by Albanians. During the 1970s, nationalist feelings spread throughout the provinces of Yugoslavia, leading to further clashes between Albanian and Serbian loyalists. However, in 1978, when Chinese support for Albania ended, attempts were made to develop closer economic contact between Albania and Yugoslavia.

In May 1980, President Tito died and the potential for the fragmentation of Yugoslavia increased. It seems probable that for the remainder of the 1980s, only the threat of the Soviet Union maintained the integrity of Yugoslavia. However, during this period there was continuing unrest in Kosovo and martial law was imposed in 1987. In 1989, a decision of the Serbian Republican Assembly to extend its control over Kosovo led to further large-scale protests and strikes, but in March of that year the Kosovo provincial assembly endorsed the measures extending Serbian control over the internal affairs of Kosovo and Vojvodina. This action resulted in another crescendo of violence and in July 1990 the Kosovo Parliament was suspended when delegates proclaimed independence from Serbia.

The problem of Kosovo is clearly more than a mere territorial dispute. In the 12th century the Serbian state originated in Kosovo, which is therefore considered an integral part of Serbia despite its majority Albanian population. This view is overwhelmingly supported in Serbia. However, the Albanian population do not wish to live under Serb rule and desire full independence.

The latest round of violence began in February 1998 when the Serbian leadership in Belgrade initiated a policy to crush Albanian resistance in Kosovo by force. The extreme violence led to large-scale Albanian protests in Pristina, the capital of Kosovo, and violence has intensified since then. The Kosovo Liberation Army (KLA) appears to receive support from Albania in the form of both fighters and equipment. Meanwhile, refugees leave the province bound for Albania and Macedonia, both of which are desperate to remain separate from the conflict. After only a few months' deployment, in March 1999, the international peace verifiers were withdrawn from Kosovo and on 24

March the secretary general of NATO ordered air strikes. On 8 June, the president of Yugoslavia, Slobodan Milosevic, accepted NATO's terms for the end of the bombing. The short aerial war proved to be globally highly controversial; lawyers considered that it contravened international law and certainly it was initiated without the direct support of the UN. It has subsequently been claimed by Western leaders that international law should be rewritten to allow intervention in the internal affairs of nation states. Nevertheless, by late September 1999, a situation in some ways similar to that in Kosovo had arisen in Chechnya and NATO was notably silent about the possibilities of bombing Russia.

Kosovo is now occupied by NATO, together with a contingent of Russian soldiers ■ *Status* which, in an unexpected move, occupied the area of Pristina airport. Humanitarian agencies are involved in attempting to rebuild the country, but any return of refugees is likely to be very slow. Kosovo remains recognised as part of the republic of Yugoslavia by all states, although the KLA appears intent on forcing the issue of self-determination. Given the huge mismatches between the interested parties and the potential for continuing violence in the neighbouring states, particularly Albania and Macedonia (see pp. 11 and 206), Kosovo is likely to remain a major flashpoint for the foreseeable future.

Allin, D. (1998) Facing realities in Kosovo, *The World Today*, 54(11), pp. 286–8 ■ *Reading*
Amnesty International (1998) *Kosovo: The Evidence*, London: Amnesty International
Anderson, E.W. (1993) *An Atlas of World Political Flashpoints*, London: Pinter
Caplan, R. (1999) Christopher Hill's road show, *The World Today*, 55(1), pp. 13–14
IISS (1998) War suspended in Kosovo: Serbian retreat, Albanian defiance, *Strategic Comments*, 4(9)

61

KURDISTAN

Situation ■ Kurdistan is neither a state nor a defined political entity. It is an area of some 191,600 km² which straddles the boundaries of several countries, notably Turkey, Iran and Iraq. Its population of 3.6 million is principally composed of ethnic Kurds, the fourth most numerous people in the Middle East. Globally, there are approximately 20 million Kurds, with 10 million in Turkey, 5 million in Iran, 4 million in Iraq, 400,000 in Syria and about 200,000 in the neighbouring states of the FSU. Together, Kurds probably form the largest nation in the world to have been denied an independent state.

The boundaries of Kurdistan represent the approximate limits of Kurdish settlement, but include several other minorities. The whole area is located across a global transport junction between the north–south Caucasus route and the east–west Europe–Central Asia route. The area is essentially mountainous and the Kurds are mountain people. In each of the states in which they live – particularly Turkey, Iraq and Iran – there have been problems with the people of the surrounding plains, compounded by little unanimity of purpose between themselves.

For most of the 20th century, the Kurds have fought to obtain greater autonomy within their various states, while retaining the ultimate vision of an independent Kurdistan. However, the problems of the Kurds differ from state to state – and even within individual states – so they have been unable to develop a cohesive approach. The states of the region have frequently used the Kurds as pawns and there has been little in the way of support from any major power.

Issue ■ The Kurds are descendants of an Indo-European tribe which settled south-west of the Caspian Sea some 4,000 years ago. They were thus located between the Arabs, the Persians and the Turks and, despite the cultural and political influences of these powerful neighbours, they have developed and retained a distinctive identity. The majority are Sunni Muslims and they have their own language, Kurdish, although the different regional dialect groups are not able to communicate freely with each other.

Politically squeezed between the Ottoman and Persian empires, the relationship between the Kurds and their neighbours has been one of almost continuous confrontation, particularly since the early 19th century. There were notable rebellions against their Turkish rulers in 1826, 1834 and 1853 and, following World War I and the disintegration of the Ottoman Empire, it did seem that self-determination might be possible. Indeed,

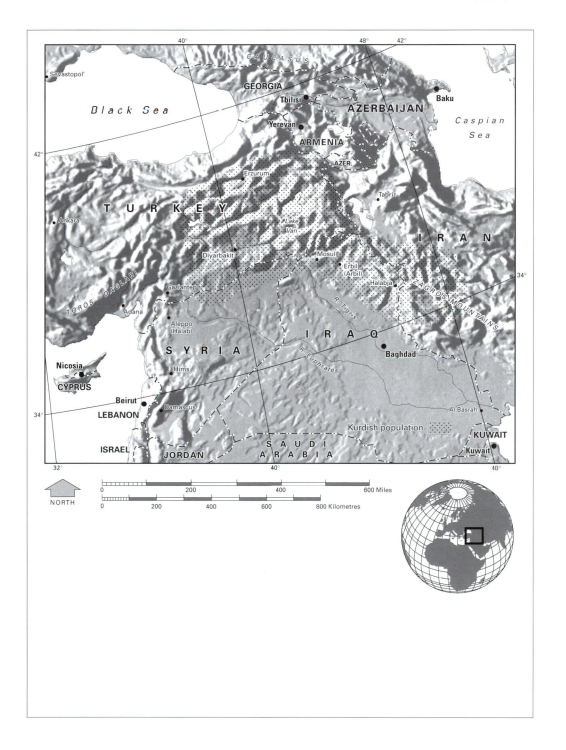

NORTH

0   200   400   600 Miles

0   200   400   600   800 Kilometres

the Treaty of Sèvres in 1920 not only established the British and French mandates in the Middle East but also envisaged local autonomy in Kurdish areas and the possible creation of a Kurdish state. However, with the rise of Kemalism, a cult which developed following the success of Kemal Ataturk in Turkey, the treaty was revised. In 1923 it was effectively replaced by the Treaty of Lausanne, which made no mention of an independent Kurdistan.

Kurdish revolts continued in the 1920s and 1930s. Following the British and Soviet occupation of Iran during World War II, the Kurdish Republic of Mahabad was created in December 1945. However, by May 1946 the Soviet troops had withdrawn and the Iranian army had crushed and removed the new republic.

Since World War II, Turkey, Iraq and Iran have all pursued essentially anti-Kurdish policies. There was a ferocious campaign by Iraq against the Kurds in 1961–2 and a similar onslaught followed the Iranian revolution of 1979. Clashes in Turkey also continued and in 1984 martial law was introduced in the Kurdish areas. In 1988, Iraq responded to Kurdish advances by bombing the town of Halabja with chemical weapons, resulting in the death of 5,000 people.

As a result of these conflicts, the Kurdish question was brought to global attention and in October 1989 the leaders of the main Kurdish separatist movements met in Paris. World opinion again focused on the Kurds after Operation Desert Storm (1991) and during the Kosovo conflict (1999).

Status ■ At present, the main focus of attention is upon the plight of the Kurds in eastern Turkey and the Kurdish Workers' Party (PKK). Syria's support for the PKK has soured its relations with Turkey, but Turkey's own increasingly close military alliance with Israel has emboldened it to take ever more extreme measures. In Iraq, the Kurdish area is effectively autonomous and is protected by NATO over-flights from any attack by the Iraq army. A joint administration between the two main parties, the Kurdistan Democratic Party (KDP) and Patriotic Union of Kurdistan (PUK), has been set up in preparation for elections, originally planned for June 1999.

Turkey, Iraq and Iran all fear Kurdish autonomy, while the Kurds themselves, despite conflicts with the armies of all three states and massive refugee problems, are still faced with their age-old dilemma of whether to settle for autonomy or whether to push further for complete independence. Whichever they choose, Kurdistan will remain a major global flashpoint.

Anderson, E.W. and Rashidian, K. (1991) *Iraq and the Continuing Middle East Crisis*, London: Pinter

IISS (1998) Tougher Turkey: growing cooperation with Israel, *Strategic Comments*, 4(9)

Olson, R. (1998) *The Turkish Question and Turkish–Iranian Relations: From World War I to 1998*, Costa Mesa, CA: Mazda Publishing

Randall, J.C. (1999) *After Such Knowledge, What Forgiveness? My Encounters with Kurdistan*, Boulder, CO: Westview

■ *Reading*

62

THE KURILE ISLANDS

Situation ■ The Kurile Islands form a chain linking the Kamchatka Peninsula (Russia) with Hokkaido, the most northerly island of Japan. The islands divide the Sea of Okhotsk from the main basin of the Pacific Ocean and have a population of 25,000 civilians and perhaps as many as 10,000 Russians. In the chain are 160 volcanoes, of which 41 are active.

The islands in dispute between Japan and Russia are located at the southern end of the chain and comprise three main islands – Etorofu, Kunashiri and Shikotan – together with the Habomai group. The areas of these are respectively 3,139 km^2, 1,500 km^2, 255 km^2 and 102 km^2, giving a total of 4,966 km^2. Legally, all the Kurile Islands are part of Russia despite the fact that Suisho, one of the Habomais, is only 2.7 nml from Hokkaido.

Issue ■ The history of the islands is complex and contradictory, and is viewed quite differently in Japan and Russia. A further complexity is added by the fact that the island of Sakhalin, which has a closely related history, is usually included in the discussion. The 1855 Treaty of Simoda (or Treaty of Commerce, Navigation and Delimitation) confirmed that the Kuriles south of and including Etorofu were Japanese, while those to the north were Russian. This was further reinforced by the Treaty of St Petersburg (1875) in which Japan also renounced claims to Sakhalin Island to the west. However, it is the view of Russia that, as a consequence of the Russo–Japanese war (1905) and the Portsmouth Treaty of the same year, the treaties of 1855 and 1875 are no longer valid.

In April 1941, the Soviet Union and Japan signed a neutrality pact, but in August 1945 the Soviet Union declared war on Japan. Under the terms of the Yalta Agreement, made in February 1945 between the Soviet Union, the USA and the UK, the islands were given to the Soviet Union. However, Japan was not a party to the agreement and, what is more, it was stated in both the Cairo Declaration (1943) and the Potsdam Declaration (1945) that the Allies were not fighting for territorial gain. In addition, the Russians based their arguments on the Yalta Agreement, while the Japanese considered that their claims to the southern islands were covered by the treaties of 1855 and 1875. On 8 September 1951, Japan signed the San Francisco Peace Treaty and, according to the Soviet Union, thereby gave up its claim to the disputed islands. In contrast, Japan insists that the Kurile Islands are not part of the northern territories which it gave up in 1951 and, furthermore, that the Soviet Union's failure to sign the San Francisco Treaty means that it cannot pursue claims under it.

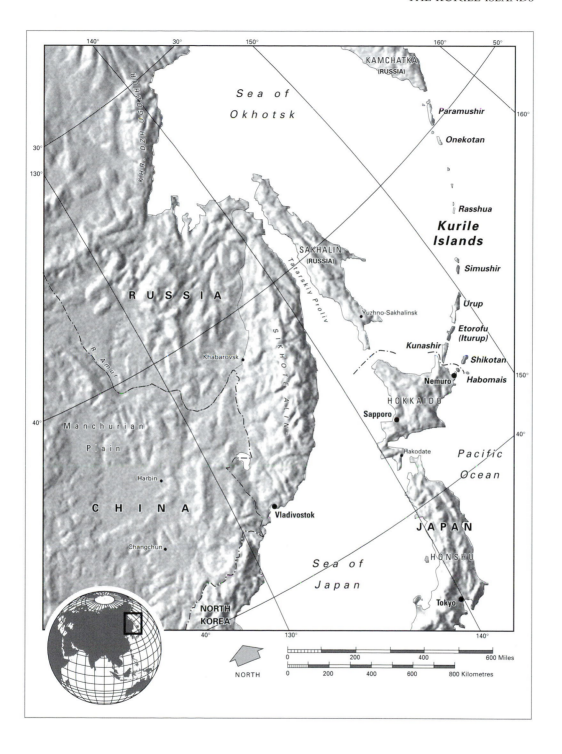

140°   30°   150°   160°   50°

KAMCHATKA
(RUSSIA)

Sea of Okhotsk

Paramushir

Onekotan

160°

KHR. DZH UGDZHUR

30°

130°

Rasshua

Kurile Islands

SAKHALIN
(RUSSIA)

Simushir

Taltarskiy Proliv

Urup

Yuzhno-Sakhalinsk

Etorofu (Iturup)

R U S S I A

Kunashir

Shikotan

150°

S I K H O T E   A L I N'

Khabarovsk

Habomais

Nemuro

HOKKAIDO

40°

M a n c h u r i a n
P l a i n

Sapporo

40°

Harbin

Hakodate

Pacific Ocean

C H I N A

Vladivostok

J A P A N

Changchun

H O N S H U

Sea of Japan

Tokyo

R. Amur

NORTH
KOREA

40°   130°   140°

NORTH

0   200   400   600 Miles

0   200   400   600   800 Kilometres

189

Finally, in 1956, under a Japan–Soviet Joint Declaration, the Soviets agreed to return Shikotan and the Habomais, but not until all foreign troops had been removed from Japan. The United States–Japan Mutual Co-operation Security Treaty, signed in January 1960, served to harden the Soviet position.

The islands at the southern end of the Kurile chain are of great strategic and economic importance. Between them lie the choke points that control the movements of the Russian Pacific Fleet, based at Vladivostok, and they provide access to one of the three most productive fishing grounds in the world. Indeed, on 10 December 1976, the Soviet Union declared a 200-nml fishing zone around the islands and on 26 January 1977 Japan responded in kind. By 27 May a fisheries agreement had been reached, but this was suspended in August 1978 when Japan signed a Treaty of Peace and Friendship with China.

Status ■ With the collapse of the Soviet Union, relations between Russia and Japan, particularly in the economic sphere, have greatly improved. In February 1998, a landmark fishing agreement was signed covering fishing quotas for Japan in the waters around the disputed islands. Both states reaffirmed their commitment to signing a peace treaty before the year 2000. In July 1998, two Japanese naval vessels took part in the first joint naval exercises with Russia in the history of relations between the two countries. Meanwhile, for Russia the islands represent territorial integrity, and for Japan, their historic rights. Given the *rapprochement* between the two countries, it is difficult to see the southern Kurile Islands becoming an international flashpoint.

Reading ■ Alexander, L.M. (1988) Choke points of the world ocean: a geographic and military assessment, in E.M. Borgese, N. Ginsburg and J.R. Morgan (eds), *Ocean Yearbook 7*, Chicago, IL: University of Chicago Press, pp. 340–55

Falkenheim, P.L. (1987) Japan, the Soviet Union and the Northern Territories: prospects for accommodation, in L.E. Grinter and Y.W. Kihl (eds), *East Asian Conflict Zones*, Basingstoke: Macmillan, pp. 47–69

Hara, K. (1991) Kuriles quandary: the Soviet/Japanese territorial dispute, *Boundary Bulletin*, No. 2, pp. 14–16

Stephenson, M. (1998) *The Kurile Islands*, Camberley: Royal Military Academy Sandhurst (pamphlet)

63

KYRGYZSTAN

Kyrgyzstan is the most mountainous and isolated of the Central Asian FSU republics. It has boundaries with Kazakstan, China, Tajikistan and Uzbekistan. The boundary with the latter two states is highly convoluted in the area of the Fergana Valley, acknowledged to be a global flashpoint. With an area of 198,500 km^2 and a population of only 4.7 million, the mean density of population is low. However, relief has effectively divided the country into two concentrations of population, one in the north around the capital Bishkek and the other in the south on the edge of the Fergana Valley. Geopolitically, this division is critical for Kyrgyzstan, the population of which comprises three groups: the indigenous Kyrgyz, Russians and Uzbeks. The Russians are predominantly in the north, and in the south there is a high concentration of Uzbeks. Foreign relations in the north are dominated by Kazakstan and in the south by Uzbekistan.

■ *Situation*

Having originally been conquered by Russia, Kyrgyzia was incorporated into the Russian Soviet Federated Socialist Republic (RSFSR) as an autonomous *oblast* (province) in 1924. It then became an autonomous republic in 1926 and a constituent republic in 1936.

■ *Issue*

During the Soviet period, it was integrated economically and socially into the region and ethnic problems were suppressed. With the demise of the Soviet Union, ethnic problems appeared in the form of violent clashes between the Kyrgyz and Uzbeks in which at least 300 people are reported to have been killed. Following the declaration of independence on 31 August 1991, problems resulting from the economic break-up gradually became apparent. In particular, Kyrgyzstan had been reliant upon Kazakstan and, especially, Uzbekistan for resources, including natural gas and oil, while supplying them with water. With the independence of the states, Kyrgyzstan was forced to pay for its imports of petroleum, but there was no obvious way of levying reciprocal charges on Uzbekistan for water.

However, as in the Middle East, water is the ultimate resource in Central Asia. Over-use of the major rivers – the Amudarya and the Syrdarya – has resulted in the desiccation of the Aral Sea, but water planning and management is required for the entire region. The three major states – Kazakstan, Uzbekistan and Turkmenistan – all have major desert areas and desertification is an increasingly important issue. Bodies have been set up to save the Aral Sea, but the major requirement must be the production of an agreed water

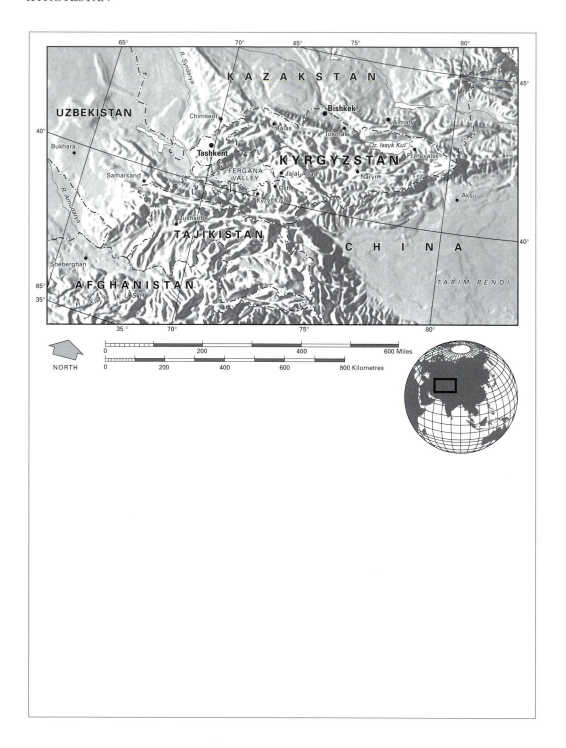

NORTH

0   200   400   600 Miles

0   200   400   600   800 Kilometres

balance, and in this Kyrgyzstan is the key. This would follow as a natural development of the Central Asian Economic Union (CAEU), which has already instituted plans for an improved communications network, including pipelines, and has attracted the interest of Western and Asia–Pacific investors. In January 1997, Kyrgyzstan announced that it was considering stationing its own peacekeeping force on the border with Tajikistan as a safeguard against the possible transboundary movements of *taliban* forces from Aghanistan.

While the civil war in Tajikistan is probably the overriding problem (see p. 330), there are potential difficulties with the Uighur population near the Chinese border, while the Fergana Valley presents a complex of actual and potential geopolitical issues. Kazakstan and Uzbekistan have both recognised their existing borders with Kyrgyzstan; Tajikistan has yet to do so. There are also a few remaining difficulties with the Chinese boundary. ■ *Status*

Of all the Central Asian states, Kyrgyzstan has demonstrated the most obvious advance towards democracy. However, it is a relatively small state with only one key resource and it is beset with potential problems. Relations with Uzbekistan, given the large minority living within its borders, will be critical. The future management of water will be vital for the entire region. Nevertheless, it is the town of Osh and the region of the Fergana Valley, with transnational smuggling of all kinds in evidence, which provide the strongest indication that Kyrgyzstan will remain a potential flashpoint.

Chukin, A. (1994) Free Kyrgyzstan: problems and solutions, *Current History*, 93(582), pp. 169–72
Curtis, G. (1997) *Kazakstan, Kyrgyzstan, Tajikistan, Turkmenistan and Uzbekistan*, Country Studies, Washington, DC: US Library of Congress ■ *Reading*

64

LAOS

Situation ■ Located centrally in the former Indo-China, Laos has an area of 236,800 km^2 and a population of 5.2 million. It is a landlocked state which has boundaries with China, Vietnam, Cambodia, Thailand and Myanmar (Burma). It is thus central in what has been one of the least stable regions since World War II. The country is mainly mountainous, but there is a sharp division between the uplands and the lowlands of the Mekong River, where some 40 per cent of the population lives. The remaining 60 per cent are classified into mountainside Lao, tribal Lao and mountaintop Lao. Laos is one of the world's poorest countries.

Issue ■ The country became a French protectorate in 1893 and was recognised as a sovereign state on 23 October 1953. With independence came civil war, in which the revolutionary Marxist Pathet Lao overcame the forces of the Royal Lao government and the 600-year-old monarchy ended. The Lao People's Democratic Republic (LPDR) was proclaimed on 2 December 1975 as an orthodox Marxist-Leninist state, run by the Lao People's Revolutionary Party (LPRP). Political power remains the monopoly of the governing party, as promulgated in the constitution of 1991. While there have been changes, the party remains overtly devoted to the proletariat, but covertly the key to success has been ethnicity rather than class or ideology.

During the struggle for power, close relations were established with Vietnam and a 25-year Treaty of Friendship and Co-operation was signed. In 1979, with the advent of the People's Republic of Kampuchea (Cambodia), the three states of Vietnam, Laos and Cambodia formed a solidarity bloc in opposition to ASEAN. With the demise of the socialist bloc, aid was reduced and Laos accelerated its policy of economic reform and improved relations with its neighbours and the West. It became a member of ASEAN in June 1997. Earlier, in 1995, with Cambodia, Thailand and Vietnam, it had helped in the establishment of the Mekong River Commission.

Status ■ After its long sojourn in the socialist bloc, Laos has now re-integrated into the global mainstream. Unfortunately, its reappearance coincided with a major downturn in the South-East Asian economies and this damaged its efforts at modernisation. There remains stability without political liberalisation. In February 1996, Laos and Vietnam signed an agreement on transborder transport and during the 1990s relations with its neighbours had improved sufficiently for boundary demarcation with China, Myanmar and Thailand. There remain boundary problems, but these are unlikely to constitute flashpoints.

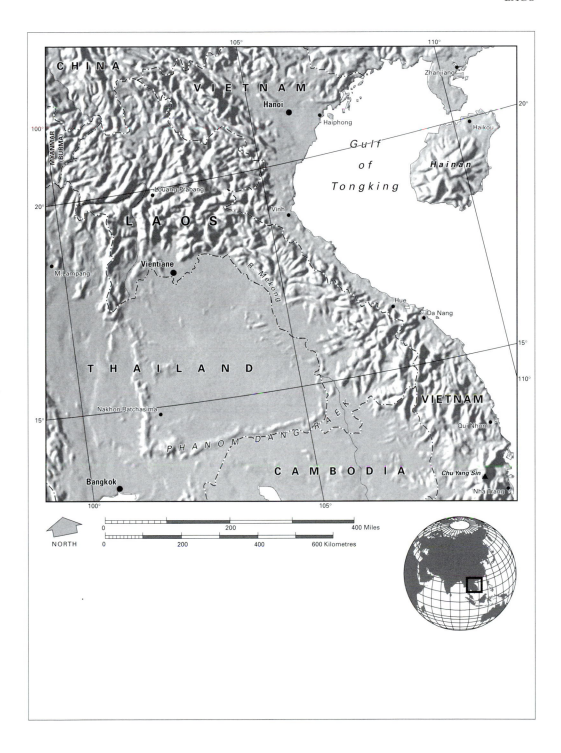

NORTH

| 0 | | 200 | | 400 Miles |

| 0 | 200 | 400 | 600 Kilometres |

Reading ■   Bourdet, Y. (1998) The dynamics of regional disparities in Laos: the poor and the rich, *Asian Survey*, 38(7), pp. 629–52

St John, R. (1998) *The Land Boundaries of Indochina: Cambodia, Laos and Vietnam*, Durham: IBRU, University of Durham (pamphlet)

Stuart-Fox, M. (1998) Laos in 1997, *Asian Survey*, 38(1), pp. 75–9

65

LESOTHO

Said to be the highest state in the world, Lesotho is a micro-state in the Drakensberg Range, completely surrounded by South Africa. It is the only state of any size with only one international boundary, and it is not only landlocked but is totally dependent upon South Africa. It is 30,355 km^2 in area and has a population of just over 2 million. There are effectively no ethnic divisions, but the state is distinguished by having one of the highest crime rates in the world.

■ *Situation*

Formerly the British High Commission Territory of Basutoland, the state came under British protection in 1868. Independence within the Commonwealth was granted in 1966 and Moshoeshoe II became king of the state. There then followed a series of confrontations between the king and the prime minister as both struggled for the upper hand in policy-making.

■ *Issue*

From 1966, the Basutoland National Party (BNP) took power which, by various means, it was able to retain until removed by the previously outlawed Basotho Congress Party (BCP) in the elections of 1993. In the meantime, there were coups, dismissals and departures by the king on 'sabbaticals'. In 1990, the king was dethroned and replaced by his son, who was sworn in as Letsie III. Later, Moshoeshoe returned as head of the royal family, but not as monarch. However, on 17 January 1994, there was a monarchial transfer with the return of Moshoeshoe II to the throne. In early 1996, the king was killed in an accident and Letsie III ascended the throne for the second time. In 1998, conflict between the monarch and the ruling party continued. In May of that year, the Lesotho Congress for Democracy (LCD) won the election, but protests continued throughout the remainder of the year and, in September, forces from the Southern African Development Community (SADC) were brought in to restore order. The violence resulted in the departure of some 4,000 refugees to South Africa.

The series of changes throughout Lesotho's independence illustrate well the effects of internal and external pressures for liberalisation that have engulfed Africa. Liberalisation increases demands and raises expectations which the state is unable to meet leading to relations between state and society becoming fraught. In the case of Lesotho, the problems are particularly acute because of the vital nature of its relationship with South Africa, which itself has witnessed perhaps the most extreme change of any country since the end of the Cold War. Co-operation with South Africa remains crucial and this has been underpinned by a major water project. As democracy takes a firmer hold in South

■ *Status*

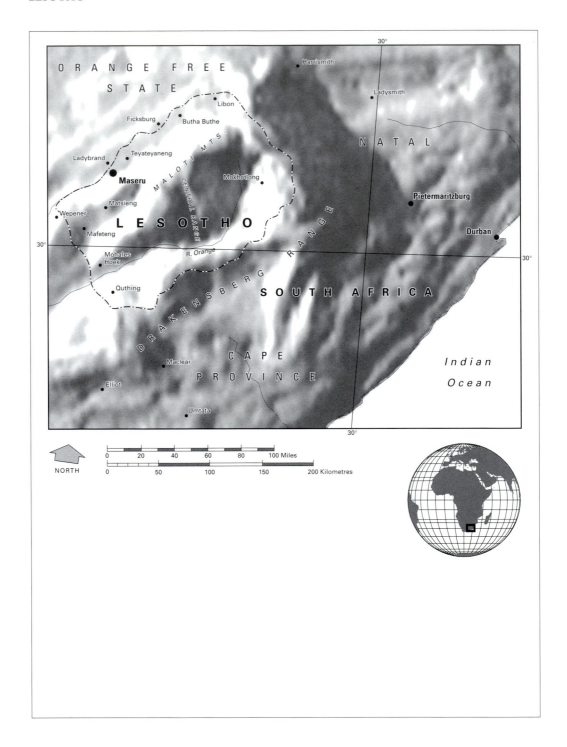

NORTH

| 0 | 20 | 40 | 60 | 80 | 100 Miles |
| 0 | 50 | 100 | 150 | 200 Kilometres |

Africa, it is possible that Lesotho will be absorbed. As it is, the recent history of the country presents an amazing picture of violence which rarely makes the world's headlines.

Ferguson, J. (1990) *The Anti-politics Machine: Development, Depoliticization and Bureaucratic Power in Lesotho*, Cambridge: Cambridge University Press

Matlosa, K. (1998) Democracy and conflict in post-apartheid Southern Africa: dilemmas of social change in small states, *International Affairs*, 74(2), pp. 319–37

■ *Reading*

66

THE LIANCOURT ROCKS

Situation ■ The Liancourt Rocks are a small island group known as Tak-do by South Korea and Takeshima by Japan. They are in several ways typical of many small islands worldwide that lie in the middle of large water bodies and have both strategic and economic importance. The Liancourt Rocks are located at the southern end of the Sea of Japan, almost equidistant (approximately 130 nml) from the two disputants, South Korea and Japan.

Issue ■ Until 1952, the potential importance of such isolated islets had not been considered, but then the dispute between South Korea and Japan began. In 1954, South Korea occupied the rocks and subsequently refused international arbitration.

The Sea of Japan lies between Russia, Japan, North Korea and South Korea and, with easy access from China, is one of the world's most strategic water bodies. Furthermore, with the exception of the Korea Strait, it is virtually landlocked. The Liancourt Rocks are particularly well positioned to provide surveillance over entry to the sea through the Korea Strait.

During the Cold War, the Sea of Japan was a potential area of confrontation between the superpowers. The Soviet Union had its Pacific Fleet based at Vladivistok, while the USA had a variety of bases in Japan. With the demise of the Soviet Union, the situation has become, if anything, more complex. There is a potential vacuum in naval power within the region, which could be filled by Japan or China with smaller-scale assistance from a variety of other states. Whatever happens, the location of Liancourt Rocks will make ownership of the islets important.

At present, the accent is on economic factors and ownership of the rocks would allow claims to some 16,600 nml^2 of sea and seabed. There are important fisheries in the region and prospects for petroleum exploitation also look promising. In November 1996, Japan made a formal protest when South Korea began the development of a harbour facility on the islands. In January 1998, Japan unilaterally terminated a bilateral fishing agreement with South Korea after attempts to update the agreement foundered on the islands dispute. Negotiations finally collapsed over the issue of fishing rights in the vicinity of the Liancourt Rocks. However, by October 1998 the two states had agreed to implement a new fisheries policy as soon as possible. This implied some compromise on both sides on the contentious issue of island ownership.

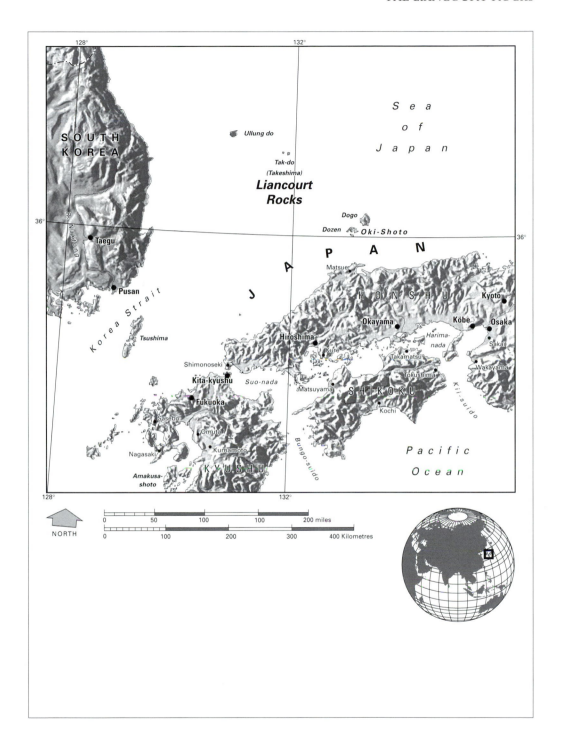

Status ■ With the improved relationship between South Korea and Japan, there appear to be a number of possibilities for the Liancourt Rocks, currently held by South Korea. One obvious possibility is joint development, similar to that which has occurred at the southern end of the Korea Strait. Another option is for one side to withdraw its claim in return for major concessions in the demarcation of maritime boundaries. Given the potential naval problems in the region, the possibility that the Liancourt Rocks will become a flashpoint cannot be discounted.

Reading ■ Downing, D. (1980) *An Atlas of Territorial and Border Disputes*, London: New English Library

Olsen, E.A. (1987) Stability and instability in the Sea of Japan, in L.E. Grinter and Y.W. Kihl (eds), *East Asian Conflict Zones*, Basingstoke: Macmillan, pp. 70–96

Prescott, J.R.V. (1985) *The Maritime Political Boundaries of the World*, London: Methuen

67

LIBERIA

Liberia is located on the coast of West Africa and has boundaries with Sierra Leone, Guinea and Côte d'Ivoire. It is one of the smaller countries of the region with an area of 111,369 km ^{2} and a population of 2.8 million. It achieved prominence initially as a result of its unique origins and, recently, because of the continuous and violent fighting over many years. Its chief exports are iron ore, rubber and cocoa, and it was in the exploitation of these that the seeds of its problems were sown.

Liberia originated through a charter granted by the US Congress in 1816 to the American Colonisation Society to establish a settlement for freed slaves on the west coast of Africa. In 1822 the first settlers arrived and by 1847 Liberia had become an independent republic with an American-style constitution.

There was early interference from European powers, but the main economic and social problems resulted from the hegemony established by the Americo-Liberian elite and the intervention of US multinational corporations (MNCs). Firestone Corporation signed an agreement with Liberia in 1927 and established the world's largest rubber plantation at Harbel. Despite the problems, there was relative stability under the True Whig Party (TWP), which came to power in 1878 and ruled for more than a century. However, under its last two leaders, William Tubman and William Tolbert, fiscal mismanagement, nepotism and corruption gradually generated strong domestic opposition. On 12 April 1980, Tolbert was overthrown and a People's Redemption Council chaired by Samuel Doe took over with a civilian–military cabinet. The new regime immediately became repressive and there were several coup attempts before Doe, with his newly launched National Democratic Party of Liberia (NDPL), won the election of 1985 in highly dubious circumstances.

Coup attempts continued and the major event occurred in 1989 when a group of rebels, known as the National Patriotic Front of Liberia (NPFL), began a successful insurrection in the north-east border zone. By the middle of 1990 the rebel troops were advancing on Monrovia, which descended into total chaos. Meanwhile a third force, the Independent NPFL (INPFL) under Prince Yormic Johnson, took control of central Monrovia on 23 July 1990. The violence reached such a crescendo that the Economic Community of West African States (ECOWAS) sent a 4,000-man peacekeeping force, ECOMOG, in an effort to end the state of anarchy. On 11 September 1990, Doe was killed and four individuals, including Charles Taylor, subsequently proclaimed themselves president.

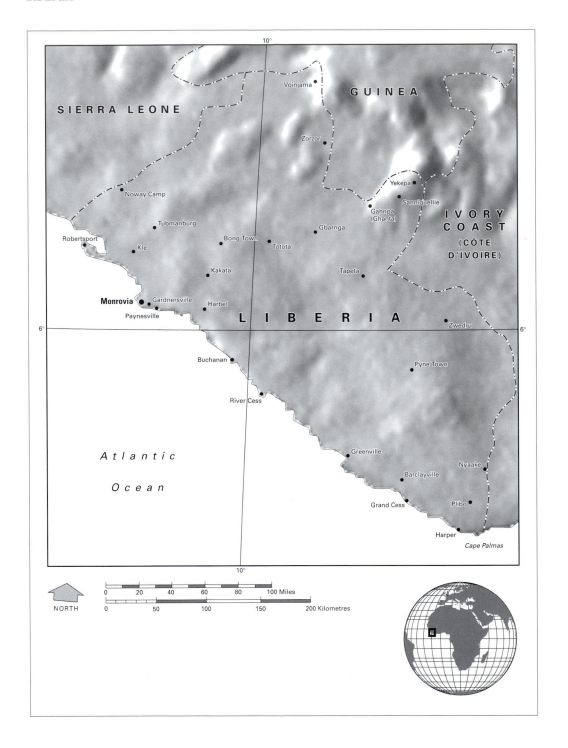

SIERRA LEONE

GUINEA

Voinjama

Zorzor

Yekepa
Sanniquellie
IVORY
COAST
(CÔTE
D'IVOIRE)

Noway Camp

Gahnpa
(Ghanta)

Tubmanburg

Gbarnga

Robertsport

Bong Town
Totota

Kle

Kakata

Tapeta

Monrovia
Gardnersville
Harbel

Paynesville

L I B E R I A

Zwedru

6°

6°

Buchanan

Pyne Town

River Cess

Atlantic

Ocean

Greenville

Nyaake

Barclayville

Grand Cess
Plibo

Harper
Cape Palmas

10°

NORTH

0   20   40   60   80   100 Miles

0   50   100   150   200 Kilometres

After many summits involving, among others, the OAU, the UN and several neighbouring states, and regular bouts of conflict and violence, peace was agreed in August 1996. At the election of 19 July 1997, Taylor, who had transformed the NPFL into the National Patriotic Party (NPP), was overwhelmingly elected to lead the government. In January 1998, ECOMOG completed its departure from Liberia. During 1998 however, there were allegations of Liberian interference in Sierra Leone and the border between the two countries had been closed by the end of the year.

During the late 1980s and half the 1990s, Liberia was a byword for anarchy. By the end of the conflict it was estimated that 10 per cent of the population had died, 30 per cent had become refugees and most of the rest had become displaced at some stage. Following the peace agreement of 1990, the capital region was governed by an interim government, while the remainder of the country was controlled by Taylor. It seems miraculous that any sort of government has arisen from this and some credit must be given to ECOMOG. However, Liberia illustrates the depths of deprivation and depravity reached when there is no effective government. Liberia drew back from the abyss, but several states remain poised on the edge.

■ *Status*

Lyons, T. (1998) Liberia's path from anarchy to elections, *Current History*, 97(619), pp. 229–33

Lyons, T. (1998) *Voting for Peace: Post-conflict Elections in Liberia*, Washington, DC: The Brookings Institution

Reno, W. (1996) The business of war in Liberia, *Current History*, 95(601), pp. 211–15

■ *Reading*

68

MACEDONIA

The current state of Macedonia comprises the component of the historic Macedonia that formed the poorest of the republics of the former Yugoslavia. It is a small, landlocked country which has boundaries with Yugoslavia (including Kosovo), Bulgaria, Greece and Albania. It has an area of 25,713 km^2 and a population of just under 2.2 million. The population is mixed, with two-thirds ethnic Macedonians and 23 per cent Albanians, with the remainder comprising Romanies, Serbs, Turks and Vlachs.

Issue ■ The Macedonia of Alexander the Great, having been ruled by the Ottomans for 500 years, was divided into three components as a result of the Treaty of Bucharest (1913). Greece was awarded Aegean Macedonia, Serbia was given Vardar Macedonia and a much smaller section, Pirin Macedonia, went to Bulgaria. At the end of World War I, Vardar Macedonia became part of the Kingdom of the Serbs, Croats and Slovenes, renamed Yugoslavia in October 1929. After World War II, Macedonia became a constituent republic of the Federal People's Republic of Yugoslavia (FPRY).

On 25 January 1991, sovereignty and secession from Yugoslavia were declared. This was followed by a referendum, from which most Albanians abstained, which endorsed independence. In early January 1992, Albanians reacted by demanding political autonomy for their community. Initially, independence remained unrecognised internationally, as a result of a Greek protest over the country's name. Indeed, not only did Greece have strong feelings, but Bulgaria had territorial claims on Macedonia. However, the main underlying tensions which restricted the development of the state were over the Albanian minority who were accused of planning separatism and the creation of a greater Albania. In Albania, the alleged plot was portrayed as Serbian provocation to destabilise the country before annexing it.

In December 1993, the leading EU states recognised Macedonia but early in 1994 Athens imposed a trade embargo by cutting access to part of Thessaloniki. Following UN mediation, the dispute with Greece was settled on 15 October 1995 and Macedonia was admitted to full membership of the Organisation for Security and Co-operation in Europe (OSCE). However, security problems remained and Macedonia, fearing the Yugoslav–Greek axis and expecting no support from Albania, turned to Turkey.

Unrest in Albania following the pyramid financial scandal (see p. 11) and the increasing problems of Kosovo (see p. 180), combined with internal rising ethnic tensions and

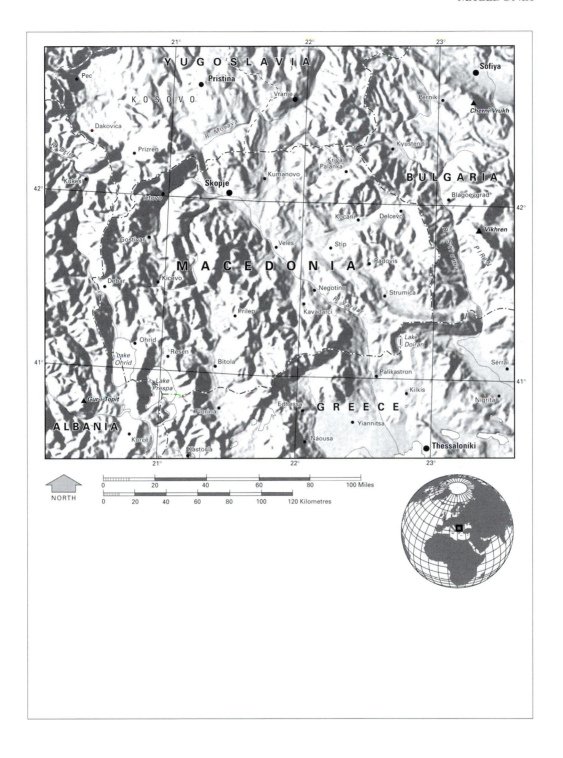

NORTH

0 20 40 60 80 100 Miles

0 20 40 60 80 100 120 Kilometres

207

rioting from early 1997, produced a measure of chaos during 1998, including bombings for which the Kosovo Liberation Army (KLA) claimed responsibility. In March 1998, the UN Protection Force increased its presence along the border with Yugoslavia. As the war in Kosovo escalated in ferocity, Macedonia assumed a key role. Actions towards the end of 1998 saw victory for the nationalist Internal Macedonian Revolutionary Organisation – Democratic Party for Macedonian National Unity (VMRO–DPMNE). A government with close links to Bulgaria had replaced one that was largely pro-Serb. There was immediate agreement that NATO could deploy a force of 1,700 to protect the OSCE monitors in Kosovo.

Status ■ The early development of Macedonia as an independent state could scarcely have occurred in more traumatic circumstances. The major powers in the region, with all of which it has boundaries, were opposed to it for one reason or another. As a result of the war in Kosovo, the region became largely dysfunctional in economic terms and Macedonia received a large number of Albanian refugees. It is therefore difficult to believe that the Albanian issue will not be resurrected and it seems likely that the Macedonian question will remain upon the global geopolitical agenda for some while.

Reading ■ Cappelli, V. (1998) The Macedonia question ... again, *Washington Quarterly*, 21(3), pp. 129–35
Pettifer, J. (1999) Macedonia rejects Milosevic, *The World Today*, 55(1), pp. 15–16

69

THE McMAHON LINE

The McMahon Line is the *de facto* boundary line extending from the tripoint between Myanmar (Burma), China and India to the tripoint between Pakistan (Azad Kashmir), Afghanistan and China. It was originally proposed at the Simla Conference (1913–14) on the status of Tibet. It was proposed that the line, which follows the watershed of the Himalayas, should be the boundary between Tibet and India, but no agreement was reached. As a result, the entire length of the Sino-Indian boundary, some 14,000 km, is still unsettled. However, it is only the sectors between India and China, including the whole of Kashmir, that are in dispute. These can be distinguished as the eastern, central and western sections.

■ *Situation*

In 1939, the McMahon Line appeared as the boundary on the official Survey of India maps. However, when Chinese troops occupied Tibet in 1950, Chinese maps showed that the boundary extended to the south, to the Brahmaputra River. There appeared to be some agreement when, in 1954, the Sino-Indian agreement on respect for territorial integrity and sovereignty, non-aggression and non-interference was signed, and in 1956 China stated that although the McMahon Line was unfair, it would not be challenged in the interests of maintaining friendly relations. Nevertheless, Chinese maps continued to show the boundary well to the south of the McMahon Line.

■ *Issue*

While there were border incidents, it was not until 1959, with the uprising in Tibet and the departure of some 12,000 Tibetan refugees, that relations between the two countries deteriorated. The area claimed by China south of the line amounted to 83,000 km^2. There was one concession in 1960–1 when China dropped its claim to the Kachin Hills area of northern Burma and accepted the Burmese part of the McMahon Line.

However, on 20 October 1962 a Chinese offensive began at both ends of the eastern section of the McMahon Line. Troops advanced at the western end of this section, some 160 km to the south, and at the eastern end, some 50 km southwards. On 21 November, China announced a ceasefire and withdrawal to 20 km north of the line. In the central section of the McMahon Line there have only been minor disagreements and the boundary between Nepal and China was agreed in 1960–1.

In the western (or Ladakh) sector, respect for current boundaries was included in peace treaties of 1684 and 1842, but neither treaty defined the location of the boundary and no survey was made until 1864. Following the Chinese occupation of Tibet in 1950, the

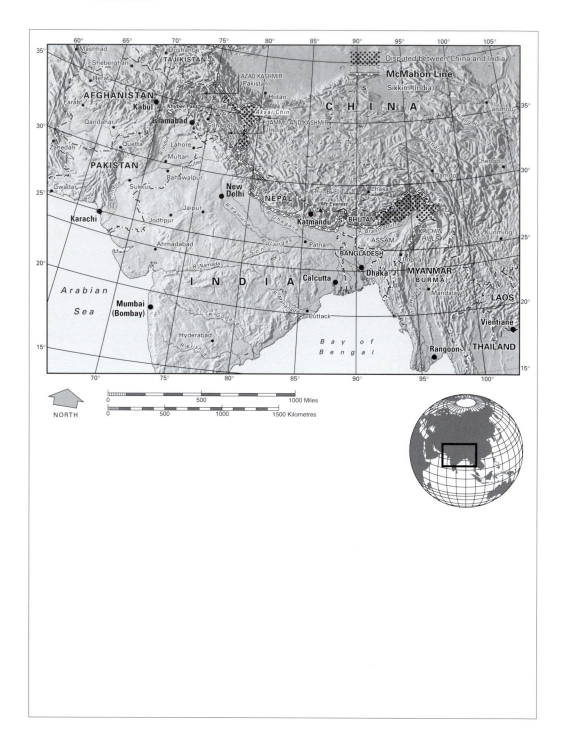

Ladakh frontier (Jammu and Kashmir) became part of the Sino–Indian boundary. British maps had indicated that the boundary followed the crest of the Karakoram mountains, but in July 1954 a new Indian government map showed the Kuenlun Crest as the boundary and the whole of the Aksai Chin (36,000 km^2) as Indian. In fact, the area had been under Chinese control since 1950 as the Aksai Chin is particularly strategic in providing the link between Tibet and Xinjiang Province. Following an offensive on 20 October 1962, India announced that Chinese troops had occupied 15,500 km^2 of the disputed area. The Aksai Chin remains under Chinese control.

On 3 May 1962, China and Pakistan announced an agreement to demarcate their common boundary, Azad Kashmir, but India strongly protested. A delimitation agreement was signed on 2 March 1962 and, of the 8,800 km^2 in dispute, Pakistan obtained approximately 3,300 km^2 and China 5,500 km^2. Thus, the China–Pakistan (Azad Kashmir) boundary has been agreed, but that between China and India, which involves an area of 119,000 km^2, is still in dispute.

Boundary talks between India and China were held in September 1993, February 1994 and August 1995, but the major concern was troop reductions along the Line of Actual Control. In May 1998, following the nuclear tests by Pakistan, India specifically linked China with Pakistan's nuclear technology and identified China as the greatest potential security threat to India.

Given the growing global importance of China and the great potential for Indian development in the 21st century, the boundary between the two states is of great geopolitical importance. There are major discrepancies between the claims of the two states in the eastern and the western sectors, while in the west, the dispute overlaps with that of India and Pakistan over Kashmir (see p. 165). In such difficult terrain, it is hard to believe that the McMahon Line will become a live flashpoint, but it could well constitute more than an irritant in the long-term relations between China and India.

■ *Status*

■ *Reading*

Bradnock, R.W. (1990) South Asia: the frontiers of uncertainty, in N. Beschorner, St-J.B. Gould and K. McLachlan (eds), *Sovereignty, Territoriality and International Boundaries in South Asia, South West Asia and the Mediterranean Basin*, Proceedings of a seminar held at the School of Oriental and African Studies, University of London, pp. 1–8

Day, A.J. (ed.) (1984) *Border and Territorial Disputes*, Harlow: Longman

70

THE MAGELLAN STRAIT

Situation ■ The Magellan Strait is located near the southern tip of South America, to the north of the Beagle Channel. Although longer than the Beagle Channel, it is wider and considerably less tortuous and provides an alternative inter-oceanic link. It lies between the South American mainland and Tierra del Fuego and, apart from its entrance, is wholly within the territory of Chile. It is relatively sheltered and can be navigated by comparatively large ships so that it provides a far safer route than that around Cape Horn.

Issue ■ Since 1847 Argentina has claimed historical and judicial rights to the Magellan oceanic connection between the Atlantic and the Pacific. The dispute with Chile was apparently settled by the Boundary Treaty of 23 July 1881, as a result of which Chile maintained control over the Magellan Strait, but the strait itself remained international for shipping.

While the definition of the nautical sea was limited to 3 nml, there was no problem with the sea area fronting the eastern entrance to the strait. However, with the expansion of state jurisdiction to a 12-nml territorial sea, claimed by both Argentina and Chile, and a 200 nml EEZ, the position changed. An EEZ of 200 nml from the eastern entrance to the strait would be almost contiguous with the EEZ of the Falkland Islands.

As discussed in the section on the Beagle Channel (see p. 39), in 1978 it proved impossible to reach an agreement on a number of issues, including the Magellan Strait. At that time, conflict between Chile and Argentina seemed likely, but intervention by the Papacy defused the situation.

The Magellan Strait is of great importance for maritime boundaries and thereby control over resources, but it is also significant geopolitically. There is a strong Argentinian perception that Chilean ownership of territory on the Atlantic seaboard would threaten Patagonia, the southern islands of South America and Argentina's claims to Antarctica. The policy of Chile is governed by an absolute desire to keep Argentina out of the Pacific. In pursuing this, the Magellan Strait has been useful in keeping the dividing line between the two countries as far east as possible. Thus, the dispute over the strait is an aspect of the Chilean–Argentinian bi-oceanic principle: Chile in the Pacific, Argentina in the Atlantic.

Status ■ The issue of the Magellan Strait has been complicated by the 'Beagle Channel dispute', since resolution of the latter, alone, would lead to the re-opening of the former. A comprehensive, simultaneous approach to both disputes was therefore necessary and this

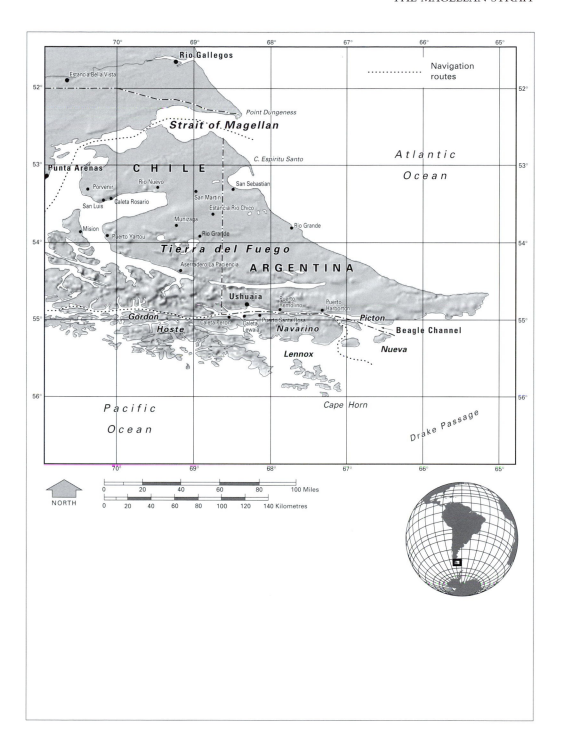

contributed to the complex and lengthy negotiations for the Peace and Friendship Treaty of 1985. Future relations between Chile and Argentina are likely to depend on other issues, such as concerns over Antarctica, but the Magellan Strait could still be considered a potential flashpoint.

Reading ■ Child, J. (1985) *Geopolitics and Conflict in South America*, Stanford, CA: Praeger/Hoover Institution Press

Morris, M.A. (1986) EEZ Policy in South America's southern cone, in E.M. Borgese and N. Ginsburg (eds), *Ocean Yearbook 6*, Chicago, IL: University of Chicago Press, pp. 417–37

Morris, M.A. (1988) South American Antarctic policies, in E.M. Borgese and N. Ginsburg (eds), *Ocean Yearbook 7*, Chicago, IL: University of Chicago Press, pp. 356–71

Santis-Arenas, H. (1989) The nature of maritime boundary conflict resolution between Argentina and Chile, 1984, in *International Boundaries and Boundary Conflict Resolution*, Conference Proceedings, Durham: IBRU, University of Durham.

71

THE MALACCA STRAIT

Lying between the Malay Peninsula and Sumatra (Indonesia), the Malacca Strait is one of the most important choke points in the world. It links the Indian Ocean with the Pacific Ocean via the South China Sea and is particularly important for the movement of petroleum from the Middle East to Asia Pacific. The strait is 500 nml long and varies in width from 200 to 31 nml. However, at its southern end, the navigable channel is only 7.5 nml wide in places. Completion of the passage from west to east then requires a sharp turn through the narrow Singapore Strait. Throughout the strait, but particularly at its southern end, there are numerous navigational hazards, including fishing boats, ferries and wrecks. There are also many small islands and the increasing threat of piracy. According to different authorities, the daily ship count varies between anything from 230 to 600. These statistics indicate that in terms of tonnage transiting it, the Malacca Strait is second only to Dover.

■ *Situation*

Portugal took control of the strait in 1513 but was evicted by the Dutch in 1641. In 1824, British merchants founded Singapore at the eastern entrance to the strait, and by the end of the 19th century the whole Malay Peninsula had come under British protection. During World War II, the Japanese captured the strait, but since then control has been left to the three riparian states: Malaysia, Singapore and Indonesia.

■ *Issue*

Indonesia declared a 12 nml territorial sea in August 1957 and Malaysia followed suit in August 1969. Given the dimensions at the southern end of the strait, the entire width was therefore territorial sea and international concern was expressed over the freedom of navigation. This issue was taken up on 16 November 1971 when, at a meeting in Kuala Lumpur, the three states confirmed that they were solely responsible for navigation and that safety and internationalisation of the Malacca Strait would be considered as separate issues. Indonesia and Malaysia agreed that the strait was not international although they recognised the 'rights of innocent passage'. Singapore expressed reservations about this and the Kuala Lumpur Declaration provoked strong international protest. Later, Indonesia and Malaysia declared that tankers over 200,000 tonnes and warships were prohibited from transiting this strait. As a result, such ships were required to take the circuitous route through the Lombok Strait. The issue was finally defused in 1974 by the start of the UN Convention on the Law of the Sea (UNCLOS) III negotiations which, by 1982, had reached broad agreement on many of the issues concerning straits.

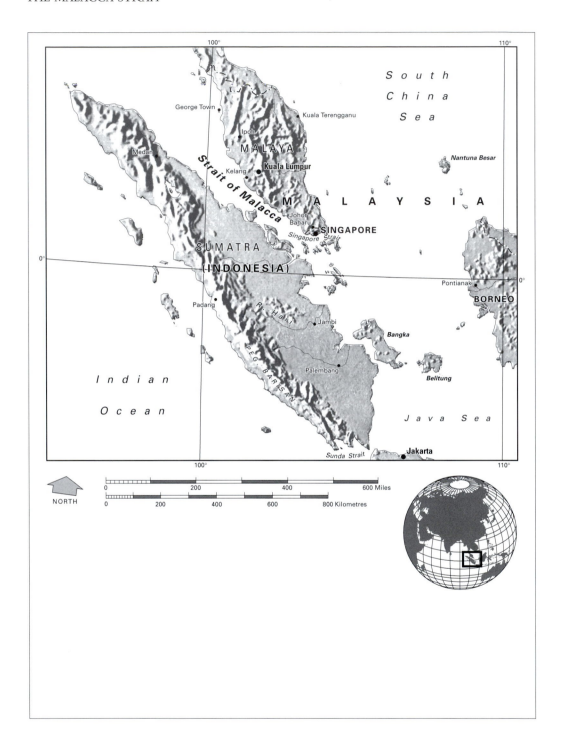

Given its location linking two major oceans, the Malacca Strait is both economically and strategically a key choke point. Use of any of the alternative straits – Sunda, Lombok and Ombia-Wetar – adds significantly to distance. In the case of the Yokohama–Persian/Arabian Gulf route, Sunda adds 9 per cent, Lombok 18 per cent and Ombia-Wetar 23 per cent. Very large cargo carriers (VLCCs) – those exceeding 200,000 dead-weight tonnage (dwt) – usually transit the deeper Lombok Strait on the outward journey, returning through Malacca. With the accelerating economic development of Singapore, following the incorporation of Hong Kong into China, and of ASEAN in general, the strait can only increase in economic importance. Indeed, Japan has established a Malacca Strait Council to monitor its long-term interests.

■ *Status*

Strategically, the Indian navy with its base in the Nicobar Islands, approximately 43 nml from the entrance to the strait, is well placed for surveillance. At the eastern end, the Chinese navy is expanding and increasing its interests throughout the South China Sea. In contrast, the Russian Pacific Fleet has left the Indian Ocean and the US Fleet has lost its main base in the Philippines. Thus, whether considered in economic terms or in the context of a potential naval vacuum, the Strait of Malacca must continue as a key potential flashpoint.

Alexander, L.M. (1988) Choke points of the world ocean: a geographic and military assessment, in E.M. Borgese, N. Ginsburg and J.R. Morgan (eds), *Ocean Yearbook 7*, Chicago, IL: University of Chicago Press, pp. 340–55

Cunha, D.D. (1991) Major Asian powers and the development of the Singaporean and Malaysian armed forces, *Contemporary S.E. Asia*, 13(1), pp. 55–71

Leng, L.Y. (1987) Access to S.E. Asian waters by naval powers, *Contemporary S.E. Asia*, 9(3), pp. 208–20

Naidu, G.V.C. (1991) The Indian navy and S.E. Asia, *Contemporary S.E. Asia*, 13(1), pp. 72–85

■ *Reading*

72

MALI

Situation ■ Mali is a 1.24 million km^2 landlocked state in West Africa with a relatively small population (10 million) and one of the lowest GDPs per capita in the world. The southern part of the country includes most of the headwaters of the Niger River, but the north is an arid desert and sand sea. The major long-term issue of drought is the same as that for other Sahelian states.

Issue ■ Formerly French Sudan, Mali is an Islamic state which obtained independence from France on 20 June 1960 as the Mali Federation. This was a two-country independence gained with Senegal, but the federation broke up within two months. One month later, the Union Soudanaise–Rassemblement Démocratique Africain (US–RDA) oriented the government towards socialism. At the same time, a pan-African policy with close ties to the Soviet Union, China and Cuba was launched.

Western hostility towards this approach compounded the many political, social and economic problems and, in February 1967, agreement was reached with France for re-entry into the French zone. However, following a coup on 19 November 1968, the new military regime under Moussa Traore opted for liberalisation and non-alignment. Military rule was legitimised in March 1979 with the creation of the Union Démocratique du Peuple Malien (UDPM). A further military coup followed on 26 March 1991 and Amadou Toure established a Conseil de Reconciliation Nationale (CNR). As a result, the entire political structure was redrawn and four parties contested the 1992 presidential election, which was won by the Alliance pour la Démocratie au Mali (ADEMA).

Meanwhile, the issue of the Tuaregs, a problem dating from the time of the French administration, was apparently settled between Algeria, Mali and Niger with the result that thousands of Tuareg refugees were repatriated. The Tuaregs, scattered between five states over an area of some 2.6 million km^2, number approximately 1 million, half of whom are in Niger, while the Tuareg population of Mali is put at between 300,000 and 400,000.

Status ■ Politically, and especially economically, Mali is still in crisis, but approaches other than outright repression – as practised by the military – are now being applied. Border demarcation disputes have been settled with Burkina Faso (1986) and Mauritania (1988). Accord on boundary security issues was reached with Algeria in February 1995. Thus, there appear to be the essentials of stability, but continuing internal issues and, more particularly, persistent droughts, pose massive problems.

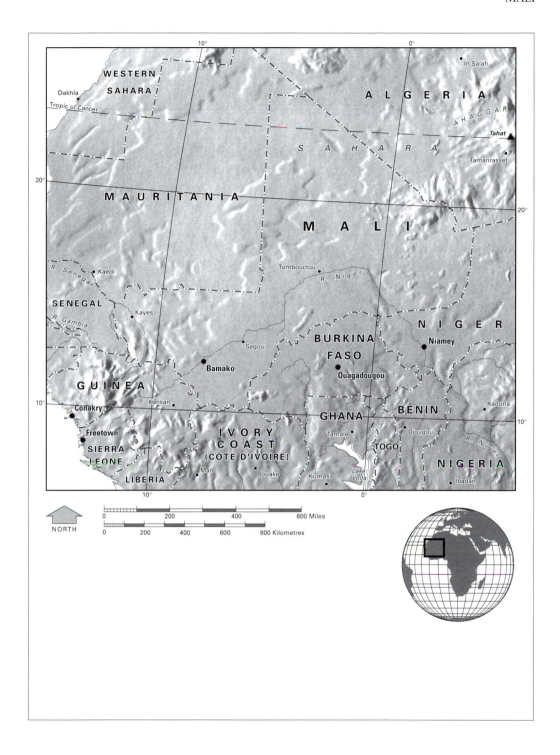

NORTH

| 0 | 200 | 400 | 600 Miles |
| 0 | 200 | 400 | 600 | 800 Kilometres |

MALI

Reading ■ Lode, K. (1997) *Civil Society Takes Responsibility: Popular Involvement in the Peace Process in Mali*, Oslo: International Peace Research Institute

Sandbrook, R. (1996) Transitions without consolidation, *Third World Quarterly*, 17(1), pp. 69–88

73

MAYOTTE ISLAND

Mayotte Island is part of the Comoros Group which lies astride the northern end of the Mozambique Channel. Geographically, the Comoros comprise four main islands – Njazidja, Nzwani, Mwali (Grande Comore, Anjouan, Moheli) and Mayotte (Mahore) – and many small islands. The group lies between 185 and 310 nml north-west of Madagascar. Politically, Mayotte is a territorial collective of France, while the remaining Comoros constitute an independent republic. The area of the Republic of Comoros is 2,235 km^2 and the population 653,000, of which 99.7 per cent are Muslim. Mayotte has an area of 372 km^2 and a population of just over 94,000, which is 99 per cent Muslim.

■ *Situation*

The Comoros were granted independence from France in 1975 but the population of Mayotte insisted on retaining French protection. In 1958, the Mouvement Populaire Mahorais (MPM) was founded to safeguard the interests of Mayotte. On 10 September 1972, in the Comoros Chamber of Deputies, the vote was taken to promote independence, in friendship and co-operation with France. This was opposed by the five MPM members.

■ *Issue*

On 15 June 1973, a Joint French–Comoros Declaration stated that independence would be attained within five years. On 22 December 1974, a referendum resulted in a 96 per cent vote in favour of independence, but in Mayotte there was a 63 per cent vote against. On 26 June 1975, the French Parliament passed the Comoros Islands Independence Bill, which required the establishment of a constitutional committee and island-by-island referendum. This was deemed unacceptable by the Comoros government and the Chamber of Deputies voted in favour of immediate independence on 6 July. The MPM delegates, who abstained from voting, telegraphed the French president, placing Mayotte 'under the Protection of the French Republic'. As a result, on 10 July, France stated that it would grant independence to the Comoros but not necessarily as one unitary state; later that month French troops left Grande Comore, but 200 Foreign Legionnaires remained on Mayotte.

On 10 December 1975, the French National Assembly passed a bill recognising the independence of the three Comoros Islands and providing for a referendum on Mayotte. On 8 February 1976, the first referendum produced a 99.4 per cent majority in favour of remaining with France and this stand was supported by France. However, on 21 October 1976, the UN General Assembly passed a motion by 102 votes to 1 calling on France to withdraw from Mayotte. This was followed on 6 December by a further resolution,

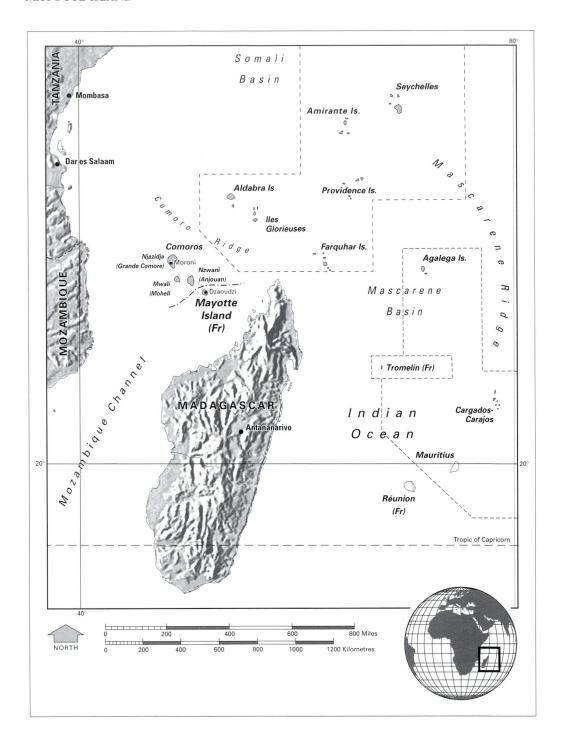

reaffirming Comoro sovereignty over Mayotte and calling for early negotiations. This was rejected by France as 'an impermissible interference in the internal affairs of France'.

Little further activity was reported until 1997 when riots on the island of Anjouan occurred in support of the demand by separatists for a return to French rule. OAU mediation proved unsuccessful and in February 1998 fighting between the secessionist factions on Anjouan broke out. The situation has placed a strain on the hitherto good relations between France and the Comoros.

Mayotte occupies a strategic position in the Mozambique Channel, and between it and Madagascar lie some of the best fishing grounds in the Indian Ocean. Politically, the case of Mayotte, and now possibly that of Anjouan, presents a classic example, like Gibraltar, of the last vestiges of empire. To the developing world, such territories represent a failure of decolonisation and even evidence for neo-imperialism. An alternative view is that they are simply examples of the right to self-determination.

Mayotte continues under its chosen system but problems with regard to maritime boundaries loom. The Comoros, Madagascar and the OAU are all strongly opposed to Mayotte's current status. However, Mayotte sends one deputy to the French National Assembly and, in the event of conflict, would expect the full support of the French military. The situation is complex and Mayotte is likely to remain a local flashpoint.

■ *Status*

The Economist (1989) *The Economist Atlas*, London: Economist Books/Hutchinson
Klen, M. (1998) Comores: l'archipel eclate, *Defense National*, decembre, pp. 109–19
Prescott, J.R.V. (1985) *The Maritime Political Boundaries of the World*, London: Methuen

■ *Reading*

74

MOLDOVA

Situation ■ Moldova is a small, landlocked state in the Black Sea Basin, denied access to the sea by a strip of Ukrainian territory some 40 km wide at its narrowest. It has a boundary to the north, east and south with Ukraine and to the west with Romania. On the west, the boundary is provided by the Prut River and on the east initially by the Dniester. However, the boundary extends for a narrow strip beyond the Dniester to take in an area known as Transdniester. This potential breakaway region is the major internal problem and is considered separately in this volume (see p. 45).

Moldova has an area of 33,700 km^2 and a population of 4.4 million, comprising 64 per cent Moldovans, 14 per cent Ukrainians, 13 per cent Russians and 4 per cent Gagauz. It has a relatively high population density for a country with a very low GDP per capita. Being agricultural, the country was one of the least developed of the Soviet republics.

Issue ■ Located on the major route from the Mediterranean and Southern Europe to Eurasia and Central Asia, historic Moldavia was subject to numerous invasions. The Moldavians are essentially Romanians, the ancestors of whom inhabited Bessarabia. This was conquered by the Russian Empire in 1812 but most of the territory reverted to Romania in 1918. It was later annexed by the Soviet Union in 1940. This history explains the strong Romanian connection and the efforts made first by the Soviet Union and then by Moldova to recognise a distinct identity. For example, the language issue arose strongly in the late 1980s and in 1989 the separate identities of Romanian and Moldavian were accepted.

Independence was declared on 27 August 1991 but, apart from massive economic problems, Moldova faced major difficulties over the issue of reunification with Romania and minority groups. Indeed, independence was preceded on 19 August 1990 by the declaration of the Republic of Gagauzia by the Turkic-speaking Gagauz minority in the south of the country. This was followed on 2 September 1990 by a proclamation from the Russian majority living to the east of the Dniester Valley of a Dniester Soviet Republic. On 7 January 1993 there was a call for a referendum on reunification with Romania which appeared to be supported by no more than 10 per cent of the population.

By 1 August 1995, the Gagauz conflict was over but the Transdniester issue remains. A joint statement with Russia and Ukraine asserted that the Transdniester region was part

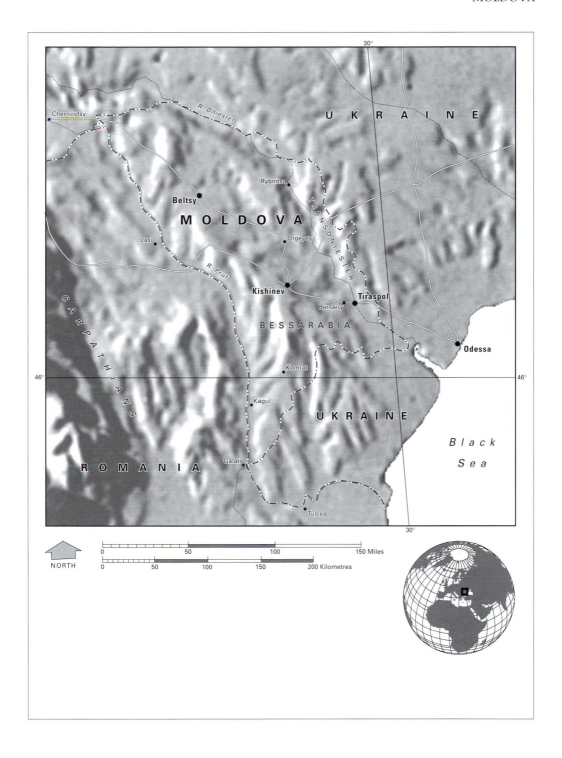

NORTH

of Moldova but should have special status. As a result, on 17 June 1996, an agreement was reached with Russia and Ukraine by which the region was described as 'a state-territorial formation in the form of a republic within Moldova's internationally recognised borders'.

While these major internal problems were being addressed, the GDP slumped by some 60 per cent between 1992 and 1994 and inflation reached 2,200 per cent at one point in 1992.

Status ■ While the economy still gives grave cause for concern, there have been major developments politically. Unification with Romania is no longer an issue and therefore Russian fears over its minority in Transdniester were allayed. Thus, Russian withdrawal of troops was planned for the end of 1997 but, after a slow start, the withdrawal is still not complete. On 16 March 1994, Moldova joined the PfP and, on 8 April, ratified membership of the CIS. While there remains a strong communist influence in government, Moldova has attained a degree of stability despite an imposing array of problems. However, the issue of the minorities has not been completely settled.

Reading ■ Waters, T. (1997) *On Crime and Corruption in the Republic of Moldova*, Camberley: Royal Military Academy Sandhurst (pamphlet)

Waters, T. (1997) *Moldova 1997*, Camberley: Royal Military Academy Sandhurst (pamphlet)

Waters, T. (1997) Problems, progress and prospects in a post-Soviet borderland: the Republic of Moldova, *Boundary and Security Bulletin*, 5(1), pp. 71–9

Waters, T. (1998*) Moldova: Armed Forces and Military Doctrine*, Camberley: Royal Military Academy Sandhurst (pamphlet)

75

MOROCCO

Morocco is located along the far north-western coast of Africa, the most westerly of the Arabic states. It has both Mediterranean and Atlantic coastlines and oversees the Strait of Gibraltar. Its area is 46,550 km^2, but to this is frequently added the 252,120 km^2 of Western Sahara. Two-thirds of Western Sahara were annexed in February 1976 and the remainder, upon the withdrawal of Mauritania, in August 1979 (see p. 364). Spanish enclaves still remain on the northern coast, the main two being Ceuta and Melilla (see p. 77). Morocco has largely unsettled boundaries with Algeria and Mauritania. The population is 21.7 million, very similar to that of its neighbour Algeria, which has an area more than five times that of Morocco. The country has important mineral deposits, most notably the world's largest reserves of phosphates.

(see p. 364)
(see p. 77)

■ *Situation*

Morocco, an ancient country long ruled by sultans, finally succumbed to European pressure in 1912 when France took over most of the territory and Spain established control of the northern coastal zone. This control resulted in the settlement on the best land of some half a million Europeans. A vast economic gulf developed between the Moroccans and the European settlers and an anti-colonial movement came into being in the 1940s. Independence was attained in 1956 but the sultan retained power as Muhammad V. He was succeeded by his son, Hassan II, who ruled from February 1961 until his death on 23 July 1999. During the major part of this period, the main opposition was provided by the Union Nationale des Forces Populaires (UNFP), the best-known leader of which was Ben Barka, who was kidnapped in Paris in 1965. Despite several coup and assassination attempts, the royal system has managed to combine repression with nominally democratic institutions. The image of the king gradually metamorphosed from that of a despot to that of a Middle Eastern peacemaker.

■ *Issue*

In 1975, the king himself led 350,000 Moroccans on the 'Green March' to claim Western Sahara, the phosphate-rich territory formerly held by Spain. Within the territory, a liberation movement, the Polisario Front, with aid from Algeria, maintained constant pressure on Morocco. Previously, the Polisario had announced the establishment of the Sahrawi Arab Democratic Republic (SADR). The king met with Polisario representatives early in 1989 and agreement has been reached on a referendum which it is hoped will take place in 2000.

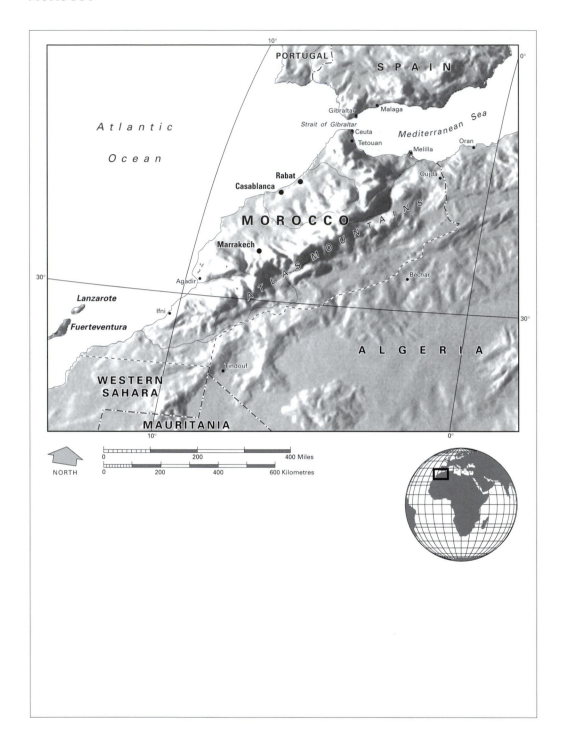

PORTUGAL

S P A I N

Atlantic

Ocean

Gibraltar • Malaga

Strait of Gibraltar • Ceuta

Mediterranean Sea

• Tetouan

• Melilla • Oran

Rabat

Casablanca • Oujda

M O R O C C O

Marrakech A T L A S M O U N T A I N S

• Béchar

Agadir

Lanzarote Ifni

Fuerteventura

A L G E R I A

• Tindouf

**WESTERN
SAHARA**

MAURITANIA

NORTH

0   200   400 Miles

0   200   400   600 Kilometres

Morocco occupies a strategic location at the entrance to the Mediterranean and is an important bridge between Europe and Africa. For more than 38 years, the king managed to maintain basic stability within the country but the key question must be asked about the political skill of his successor. As a direct descendant of The Prophet, the king will always have some legitimacy with the general population, but a subtle balancing act will be required if the problems of Western Sahara, Ceuta and Melilla are to be resolved, if religious fanaticism is to be kept at bay and if relations with Algeria are to be restored.

■ *Status*

Chopra, J. (1997) A chance for peace in Western Sahara, *Survival*, 39(3), pp. 51–65
Leveau, R. (1997) Morocco at the crossroads, *Mediterranean Politics*, 2(2), pp. 95–113

■ *Reading*

76

MURUROA ATOLL

Situation ■ Mururoa Atoll lies within the Tuamotu Islands, one of five island groups that comprise French Polynesia. French Polynesia is located approximately midway between South America and Australia and includes some 120 recognised islands, with a total area of some 4,000 km^2 and a population of 220,000. Mururoa Atoll has been used by France as its nuclear test site, the only one in the world operated by an extra-regional power.

Mururoa Atoll was originally selected for nuclear tests because of its isolation and the small, thinly dispersed population in the region. This made it suitable for atmospheric testing, while the structure of the island made it convenient for underground tests.

Issue ■ The post-war period in the South Pacific region has been dominated by the issue of French nuclear testing and moves between the islands for co-operation and independence. In 1947, the South Pacific Commission was founded by the relevant metropolitian countries: Australia, the UK, France, the Netherlands, New Zealand and the USA. Until 1974 it enjoyed only an advisory role, but from then on it became the governing body. In 1971, the South Pacific Forum was founded as a symbol and instrument of regional decision-making.

The first atmospheric tests took place on Mururoa in 1966 and these were followed by the first underground test in 1975. In 1985, the Treaty of Rarotonga established the South Pacific nuclear-free zone which was immediately recognised by the Soviet Union and China, but not by France, the UK or the USA. Global attention was further focused on French nuclear testing when in 1985 the *Rainbow Warrior*, a Greenpeace ship which had planned to impede explosions at Mururoa, was sunk in Auckland harbour by French secret agents.

Later that year, Australia approached the USA to put pressure on France, but to no avail; the USA re-confirmed its long-held view of the strategic primacy of the North Atlantic over the South Pacific and stated that the French decision was vital to the modernisation of its nuclear deterrent.

However, Australia continued to protest and stated that 'if France insisted on conducting these tests, it should do so on its home territory, especially if the tests were as harmless as France claimed'. France quoted a report produced by scientists from Australia, New Zealand and Papua New Guinea (1988), which asserted that the nuclear tests were completely harmless. Nevertheless, as Australia had pointed out, the report had not cleared the tests of long-term environmental consequences.

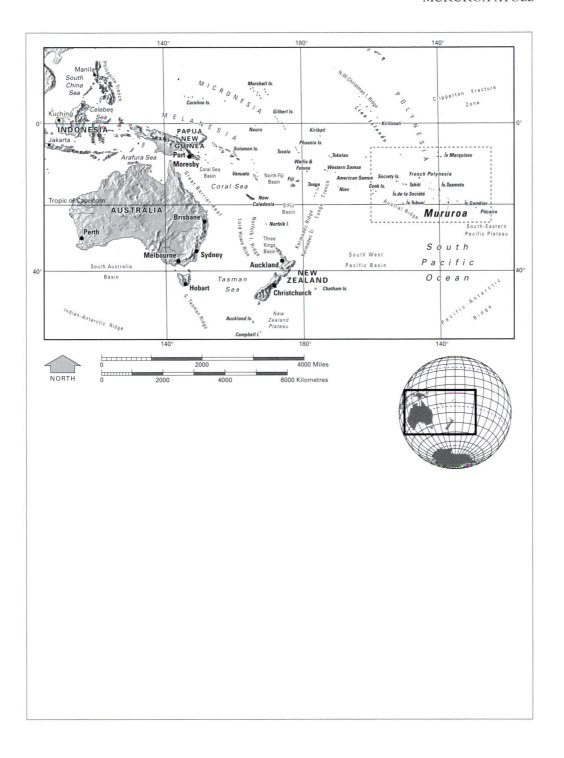

In June 1995 the decision by France to resume underground nuclear testing at Mururoa was widely opposed throughout the Pacific region and there were numerous protests. After the nuclear test of 5 September 1995, the worst violence in Tahiti's recent history erupted. In October there were two further tests and thousands of troops were deployed in Tahiti to try to prevent a recurrence of violence among the anti-nuclear and pro-independence groups. In November a fourth test was conducted and in December, despite international condemnation from Australia, New Zealand, Japan and the USA, there was a fifth test.

Status ■ French Polynesia is classified as an overseas territory and it sends two deputies to the French National Assembly. Within the islands there are numerous social and economic problems, many allied to the fear of rising sea levels. The majority of the population favours increased autonomy, while a growing minority supports independence. Given their strategic location and their importance for the global military reach of France, they are unlikely to be granted independence. With regard to nuclear testing, France considers that as the weapons and territory are French, the decision must be made by France. The regional position remains strongly opposed to testing. If the tests are harmful, they should be terminated; if they cause no harm, they should be conducted in metropolitan France. However, on conclusion of the test series, France intimated that no more tests were envisaged and signed the Comprehensive Test Ban Treaty (CTBT).

Reading ■ Dorrance, J.C. (1990) U.S. strategic and security interests and objectives in Australia, New Zealand and the Pacific Islands, in J.C. Dorrance *et al.*, *The South Pacific: Emerging Security Issues and U.S. Policy*, Cambridge, MA and Washington, DC: Institute for Foreign Policy Analysis, pp. 1–26

Thakur, R. (1990) Nuclear issues in the South Pacific, in J.C. Dorrance *et al.*, *The South Pacific: Emerging Security Issues and U.S. Policy*, Cambridge, MA and Washington, DC: Institute for Foreign Policy Analysis, pp. 27–51

77

MYANMAR (BURMA)

Myanmar is a medium-sized state located in a reasonably volatile part of the world between India, China and the former Indo-China. Like Thailand, it occupies a buffer position, but it has been less successful in avoiding colonialism. The area of Myanmar is 676,578 km^2 and the population 46.5 million, significantly less than that of Thailand. It is the largest country on the South-East Asian mainland and has boundaries with Bangladesh, India, China, Laos and Thailand. The population is 70 per cent Burman, but there are sizeable Karen and Shan minorities.

■ *Situation*

Myanmar (then known as Burma) gained full independence from the UK on 4 January 1948 and followed socialist ideology until the collapse of the Burma Socialist Program Party (BSPP) in 1988. On 18 September 1988, a military *junta*, the State Law and Order Restoration Council (SLORC) seized power and has remained in control of the country ever since. The SLORC has survived as a result of its large and well-trained army, its large-scale imprisonment of political opponents and the fact that it has maintained the most repressive regime in South-East Asia. Since its arrival in power, it has imposed martial law based upon the 1974 constitution. The civil service, police and judiciary are under martial law and all private organisations, including political parties and religious bodies, are tightly controlled.

■ *Issue*

In more than 50 years of civil war, government forces have fought armed factions of all the minority groups. A key to this constant turmoil is the profits of the opium trade – more than half the world's supply is grown in the 'Golden Triangle', which comprises adjacent sections of Burma, Laos and Thailand.

In 1991, the extremely repressive nature of the regime was highlighted when Aung San Suu Kyi, the long-term charismatic leader of the opposition who was being held under house arrest, was awarded the Nobel Peace Prize. Aung San was temporarily released from arrest in 1995 but the order was soon rescinded.

On 15 November 1997, the SLORC was dissolved and replaced by the State Peace and Development Council (SPDC), but it seems unlikely that the character of the regime will change. Conflict continues, together with ethnic cleansing and wholesale abuse of human rights. Myanmar is enmeshed in a catalogue of elements of the macropolitical agenda: narcotics, AIDS, refugees, conflict and environmental issues. Membership of ASEAN, announced on 23 July 1997, appears to have caused little amelioration.

■ *Status*

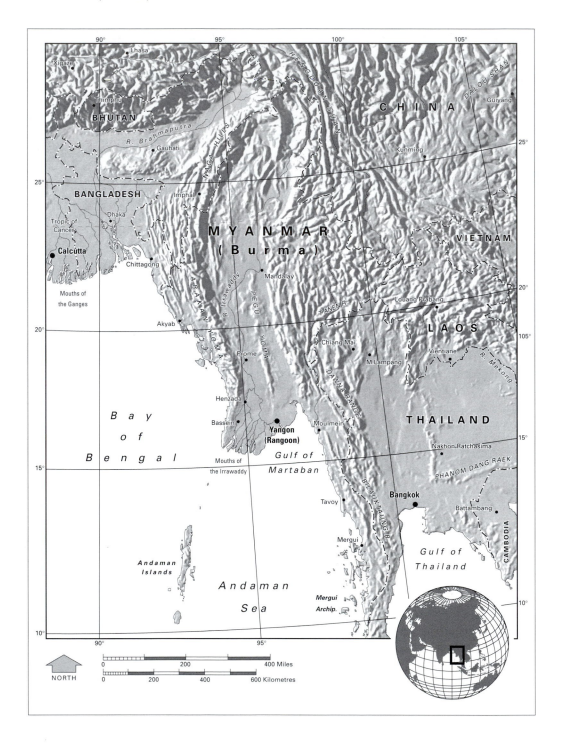

Although there are boundary problems, virtually all of the issues in Myanmar are internally generated. Therefore, it is unlikely to become anything other than a local flashpoint.

Conflict Studies (1997) From Burma to Myanmar: military rule and the struggle for democracy, London: Research Institute for Study of Conflict and Terrorism

Grundy-Warr, C. and Wong, E. (1997) Sanctuary under a plastic sheet – the unresolved problem of Rohingya refugees, *Boundary and Security Bulletin*, 5(3), pp, 79–92

IISS (1998) Myanmar's economic and political uncertainty: a silent coup in Yargon? *Strategic Comments*, 4(1)

Seekins, D. (1997) Burma–China relations: playing with fire, *Asian Survey*, 37(6), pp. 525–39

■ *Reading*

78

NAGORNO-KARABAKH

Situation ■ Nagorno-Karabakh is an autonomous enclave, populated by some 180,000 Christian Armenians but located in Muslim Azerbaijan. It is one of several enclaves in the Transcaucasus and, like the others, represents an attempt to rationalise a complex ethnic mosaic through political boundaries. As a result of its location, the conflict over Nagorno-Karabakh has particular geopolitical significance, with implications at the local, regional and global levels.

Issue ■ Ancestral hatred between the Armenians and the Azeris has existed for over a thousand years, but the most obvious causes of the conflict originated in the early 20th century. Within the light of the Armenian genocide, perpetrated by the Ottoman government during World War I, the close association between Azeris and Turkey was considered intolerable by the Armenian community. In 1918, the Armenians joined with the Russians to suppress a Muslim revolt, but later in the same year the Azeris, under Turkish protection, exacted revenge. The Treaty of Brest–Litovsk, in March 1918, placed Russian Armenia as an independent republic under German control. One month later Azerbaijan declared its independence. In 1919, following conflict over the enclave, the UK military administration awarded Nagorno-Karabakh to Azerbaijan. One year later, the Treaty of Sèvres established Greater Armenia as an independent state, but in the same year independence ended when Soviets and Turks together recaptured the Caucasus. Both Azerbaijan and Armenia were then proclaimed Soviet socialist republics and the communist leadership of Azerbaijan passed Nagorno-Karabakh to Armenia. However, this was reversed in 1923 when Stalin designated the enclave an autonomous region and awarded it back to Azerbaijan.

In 1924, Nakhichevan, populated by Azeris but separated from Azerbaijan by an area of Armenia, was established as an autonomous republic and attached to Azerbaijan. Thus, the picture became ever more complex.

Nevertheless, the incipient dispute remained dormant until the end of the Soviet era when more open political expression allowed renewed ethnic conflict. In 1985, Armenia demanded the incorporation of Nagorno-Karabakh into the Armenian Republic and serious clashes between the two communities over the issue had begun by 1988. By the end of 1988, there had been mass exchange of populations amounting to some 160,000 people moving in each direction. The deterioration in the enclave led the Soviet Union to impose direct rule over the region in January 1989, and in October 1989 the

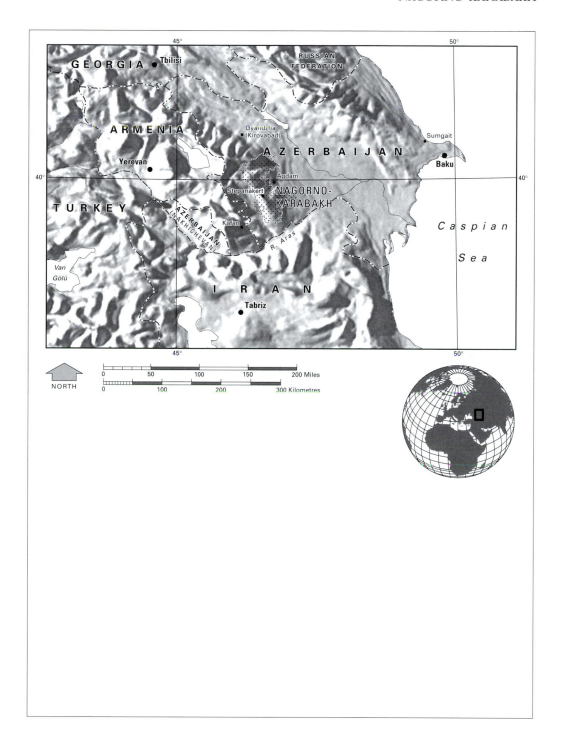

NORTH

| 0 | 50 | 100 | 150 | 200 Miles |

| 0 | 100 | 200 | 300 Kilometres |

Azerbaijani Popular Front and the Armenia Pan-national Movement were both legalised. Direct rule ended in November 1989 with jurisdiction over Nagorno-Karabakh handed back to Azerbaijan. On 1 December 1989, Armenia declared the enclave part of the Armenian Republic.

In January 1990, Nakhichevan declared its independence and the Baltic Council offered to mediate between representatives of the warring factions. By the middle of 1991, the Armenian and Azeri populations of Nagorno-Karabakh had completed their withdrawal into ethnically homogeneous zones. By June 1992, a corridor from Nagorno-Karabakh to Armenia had been cleared across the intervening territory of Azerbaijan, but later that year the military initiative returned to Azerbaijan. The continued fighting produced waves of refugees and the enclave was in receipt of international aid by mid-1993. Hostilities were largely ended with a Russian-brokered ceasefire on 16 May 1994. By that time, the forces of Nagorno-Karabakh had displaced approximately 600,000 Azeris and were in control not only of the enclave, but of certain surrounding districts.

Status ■ It is estimated that the war has cost at least 25,000 lives and up to 1.5 million refugees and internally displaced people. Approximately 20 per cent of the land area of Azerbaijan had been depopulated and all the settlements in Nagorno-Karabakh had suffered damage. The instability of the enclave has affected Georgia and, to an extent, the whole of the Transcaucasus region. It has also conflicted in various ways with both Russian and US interests in the area. Given the location of the enclave and the recent history of minorities in the Transcaucasus, it must be concluded that Nagorno-Karabakh is likely to remain a key geopolitical issue.

Reading ■ Glezer, O., Kolosov, V., Petrov, N., Streletsky, V. and Treyvish, A. (1991) A map of unrest in the Soviet Union, *Boundary Bulletin,* No. 2, pp. 16–20
Kaldor, M. (1997) *New Wars*, London: Pinter
Royal United Services Institute (1998) *The New International Security Review 1997*, London: Royal United Services Institute

79

NAVASSA ISLAND

The situation of Navassa Island is similar to that of several such islands which lie away from island groups in strategic waterways. They have potential military significance and, given the size of their potential EEZs, economic importance. Navassa Island is located in the Jamaica Channel, south of the Windward Passage choke point between Cuba and Haiti. The island lies approximately 30 nml west of Haiti and rather more than 90 nml east of Jamaica. It has an area of 5 km^2. There are no permanent inhabitants but tourists visit the island during the holiday season. There are regular 'flag-waving' landings by the US Coast Guard.

■ *Situation*

Under an Act of Congress of 1860, the USA claimed Navassa as a 'guano island' and, during World War II, a lighthouse was constructed there. Guano results from the concentration of seabird droppings and is a source of phosphate, a key agricultural fertiliser. Haiti also claims the island and during the 1950s built a church there for passing fishermen. The issue of Navassa Island rose to public prominence on 18 July 1981 when a group of six Haitians, having refused to seek landing permission from the USA, arrived by government helicopter and organised a symbolic occupation of the island. A crew from the Haitian national television service was in evidence and the Haitian Communications Authority allocated the island a Haitian radio-call prefix, to replace its American prefix. The occupiers were arrested by US marines and flown off the island.

■ *Issue*

The Windward Passage is an important choke point for the movement of strategic materials, particularly bauxite and alumina to the east coast of the USA from the Caribbean. Navassa Island is well located to provide surveillance over this traffic. Furthermore, ownership of Navassa would allow a claim of some 4,100 nml^2 of surrounding sea.

Cuba and Haiti have already agreed a maritime boundary which cuts into the Navassa equidistance area. Therefore there are already signs that the sea-bed claim resulting from ownership of the island will run into severe difficulties. Should significant sea-bed resources be discovered, US claims over Navassa would be questioned and the island could become a flashpoint.

■ *Status*

Day, A.J. (ed.) (1984) *Border and Territorial Disputes*, Harlow: Longman
Prescott, J.R.V. (1985) *The Maritime Political Boundaries of the World*, London: Methuen

■ *Reading*

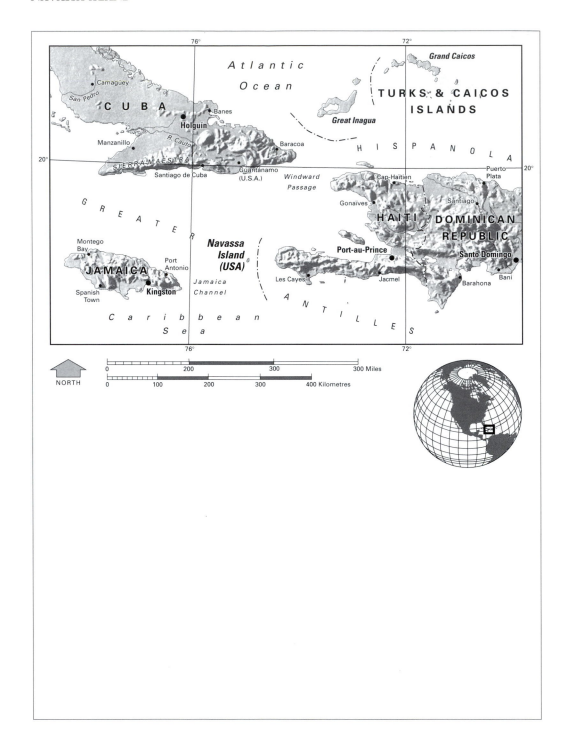

NORTH

0   200   300   300 Miles

0   100   200   300   400 Kilometres

80

NIGERIA

With a population of 111.7 million, Nigeria is easily Africa's most populous state. It has an area of 923,768 km^2 and is the largest West African state outside the Sahel. It is located at the head of the Gulf of Guinea and has boundaries with Benin, Niger, Chad and Cameroon. It extends from the tropical rainforest of the Niger delta to the savannah on the edge of the Sahel. Within the state there are numerous peoples, but the largest groups are the Hausa in the north, the Yoruba in the west and the Ibo in the east.

■ *Situation*

Nigeria gained independence from the UK on 1 October 1960. Since then, the country has had a troubled history with almost constant government instability. Military and civilian governments have proved equally incompetent and chauvinistic. Many of the problems can be traced to the colonial policy of 'divide and rule' to weaken and split nationalist movements. At independence, there were three political parties, each regional and based on one national group: the Northern People's Congress (NPC) based on the Hausa, the Action Group (AG) based on the Yoruba, and the National Council of Nigeria and the Cameroons (NCNC) based on the Ibo. Thus, the struggle for power was already developing along ethnic lines, to the detriment of political stability.

■ *Issue*

The First Republic was overthrown by a military coup in 1966 and subsequently there were four further military coups and the assassination of a military leader. In July 1967, the civil war between the federal government and Biafra (the new name given to the eastern region) erupted; this lasted until 13 January 1970.

Apart from the Arab states and Iran, Nigeria's oil reserves are among the largest in the world, but even improving economic standards did not bring political stability. Furthermore, corruption has been rife; for example, in 1995 Nigeria was a major importer of oil. There was also little respect for human rights, and when author Ken Saro-Wiwa and other members of the Movement for the Survival of the Ogoni People (MOSOP) were executed on 10 November 1995, Nigeria effectively became a pariah state and was suspended from the Commonwealth.

Despite the various upheavals, Nigeria has generally remained at peace with its neighbours and in 1975 helped establish ECOWAS. It also played a prominent role in 1963 in the formation of the OAU and, over the years, has given considerable financial support to liberation movements in Angola, Mozambique, Namibia, South Africa and Zimbabwe. Nonetheless, for a state with such vast natural resources, considerable human

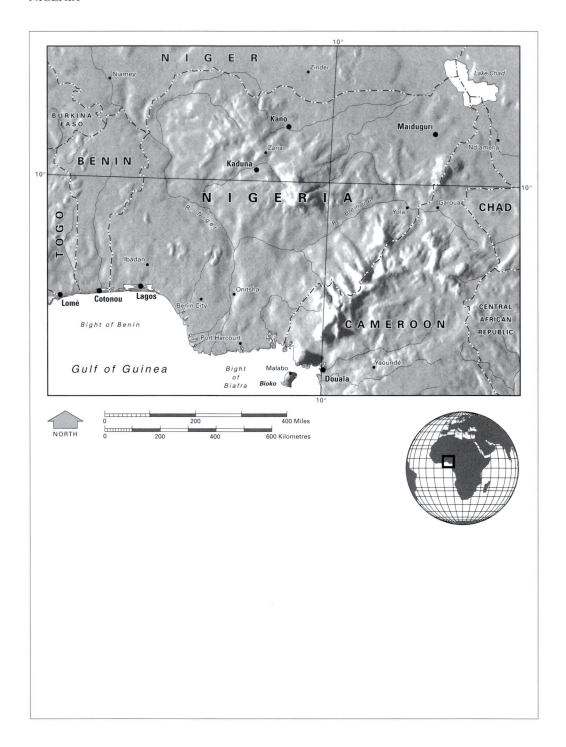

capital and a huge domestic market, Nigeria has been far from the leading state in Africa that its endowments might have indicated.

The new head of state, Abdulsalami Abubakar, who came to power in 1998, has an **■** *Status* opportunity to set Nigeria finally on the road to African leadership. Civilian rule was restored in February 1999 with the election victories of the People's Democratic Party. However, given the history of the country, there must be scepticism. Boundary problems with Benin and Cameroon remain, but there is clearly more stability than in the recent past. The key question must be whether co-operation can be developed between a civilian government and the military. If not, there must be a danger that the state itself may be Balkanised. Nigeria is potentially so powerful that any major political breakdown would have considerable regional impact.

Barling, K. (1998) The edge of the abyss, *The World Today*, 54(8–9), pp. 200–2 **■** *Reading*
IISS (1998) Divided Nigeria: a failing state? *Strategic Comments*, 4(6)
IISS (1998) Nigeria's transition to civilian rule: little prospect of real change, *Strategic Comments*, 4(2)

81

NORTHERN IRELAND

Situation ■ The territory of the British Isles is shared between two independent states: the United Kingdom and the Republic of Ireland. There are two main islands: Great Britain, which is divided between England, Scotland and Wales; and Ireland, which comprises Northern Ireland and the Republic of Ireland. The UK comprises England, Scotland, Wales and Northern Ireland, together with many of the smaller islands. Thus, Ireland is divided between two independent states and the boundary between them is international. Northern Ireland, the section of Ireland within the UK, comprises six counties: Derry, Antrim, Down, Armagh, Fermanagh and Tyrone. Its area is 14,120 km^2 and the population is approximately 1.6 million. Although it comprises only just 6 per cent of the territory and 3 per cent of the population of the UK, Northern Ireland has provided the focus for geopolitical attention for the past 30 years.

Issue ■ The society of Northern Ireland is riven by three fundamental cleavages. The most important is that between Roman Catholics, who comprise approximately 45 per cent of the population, and Protestants. A second division, which closely parallels the first, is between those who support the unification of Ireland and those who wish to remain within the UK. The former group includes the various shades of Republican opinion and the latter the Unionists and the Loyalists. The third cleavage is based on wealth. Between them, the three cleavages have resulted in two opposing camps, each labelled according to religion. Thus, broadly speaking, the Roman Catholics comprise the poorer elements of society and those who support Irish unification, whereas the Protestants include the wealthier people and, as a group, wish to retain ties with the UK. Since the Protestants are in the majority and the political parties, with one unfortunately ineffective exception, reflect the deep division of society, power-sharing has proved all but impossible.

The intractable nature of the Northern Ireland problem can be appreciated only in the context of the complex historical relationships between Great Britain and Ireland. In 1607 James I initiated the plantation of Ulster with English and Scottish Protestants. This laid the foundations for the divisions within Ulster and the cleavage between Ulster and the remainder of Ireland. The Catholics rebelled, but in 1649 they were crushed by Oliver Cromwell and Catholic landowners were dispossessed in favour of Protestants. The final disruption between the two religious groups occurred in 1690 when James II, supported by Catholic Irish, was defeated by William of Orange at the Battle of the Boyne. The Protestant victory is still celebrated annually in Northern Ireland and certain parts of Great Britain, such as Liverpool and Glasgow. Following the defeat, a new penal code was

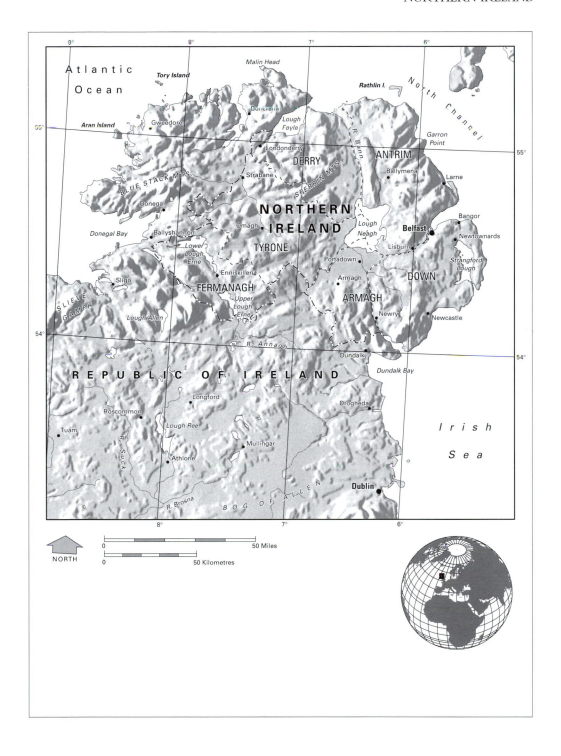

Atlantic
Ocean

Malin Head

Tory Island

Rathlin I.

North Channel

Aran Island

Gweedore

Dunerana

Lough
Foyla

Garron
Point

Londonderry

DERRY

R. Bann

ANTRIM

55°

BLUE STACK MTS.

Strabane

SPERRIN MTS.

Ballymena

Larne

Donegal

NORTHERN
IRELAND

Omagh

Bangor

Donegal Bay

Ballyshannon

Lower
Lough
Erne

TYRONE

Lough
Neagh

Belfast

Newtownards

Lisburn

Portadown

Strangford
Lough

Sligo

Enniskillen

FERMANAGH

Armagh

DOWN

SLIEVE
GAMPH

Upper
Lough
Erne

ARMAGH

Lough Allen

Newry

Newcastle

54°

R. Annagh

Dundalk

REPUBLIC   OF   IRELAND

Dundalk Bay

Longford

Drogheda

Roscommon

Irish

Tuam

Lough Ree

Sea

Mullingar

Athlone

R. Suck

R. Brosna

BOG OF ALLEN

Dublin

NORTH

0   50 Miles

0   50 Kilometres

245

introduced which denied Catholics any right to citizenship or ownership of property and the government of Ireland itself passed into the hands of a Protestant oligarchy.

In 1795 the Orange Order, a Protestant self-defence organisation, was established and the Act of Union (of Great Britian and Ireland) came into force in 1801. In 1846, as a result of the failure of the potato crop and constraints upon the entry of Irish wheat into world markets (due to US and British trading measures), there was a severe famine in which 1 million people died. A further 1,250,000 emigrated and thus the Irish population was reduced by almost 30 per cent. Unrest continued in Ireland and Irish Home Rule Bills were introduced to Parliament in 1886, 1893 and 1913, but they failed to survive. In 1898, the Ulster Unionist Party was established to provide a voice for Protestants and, in 1912, the Ulster Volunteer Force came into being as a Protestant defence militia. These developments were matched in the south by the formation of the Sinn Fein Party in 1905 and in 1913 by the establishment of a paramilitary National Volunteer Force.

In 1916, the Easter Rising in Dublin was put down and on 6 December 1921 the Anglo-Irish Treaty was signed. This established an Irish Free State, but Northern Ireland exercised its right to opt out and the Protestant Unionists retained control of six counties of Ulster within the UK. In 1925, the boundary between the Irish Free State and Northern Ireland was delimited and in December 1937 the independent state of Eire was proclaimed. The Republic of Ireland Act (1948) came into effect on Easter Sunday 1949, while at the same time the position of Northern Ireland as an integral part of the UK was guaranteed under the British government's Ireland Act (1949).

The Nationalist Volunteer Force, renamed in the early 1920s the Irish Republican Army (IRA), re-emerged in Northern Ireland in 1956 and continuing violence broke out in 1969. The UK took over responsibility for security and on 30 January 1972 direct rule was imposed. Violence continued and the one ray of hope was the Anglo-Irish Agreement signed in November 1985.

Status ■ The latest, and so far most successful attempt at ending the violence, came with the signing of the Northern Ireland Multi-party Peace Agreement in April 1998, the Good Friday Agreement. In May 1998, voters on both sides of the boundary gave their resounding support to the agreement and elections for the Northen Ireland Assembly took place in June 1998. Meanwhile, there was sporadic sectarian violence. The implementation of the agreement has yet to be completed. In particular, intransigence remains over the decommissioning of IRA weapons; members of the majority Unionist side demand that this must begin before the Assembly convenes. However, whether lasting agreement can be reached between the two sectors of society must be open to doubt and Northern Ireland is likely to remain the most entrenched boundary problem in Western Europe.

Hopkinson, W. (1998) Peace dividend? *The World Today*, 54(7), pp. 193–4

IISS (1998) A chance for peace in Northern Ireland, *Strategic Comments*, 4(4)

Lloyd, J. (1998) Ireland's uncertain peace, *Foreign Affairs*, 77(5), pp. 109–22

Schulze, K.E. (1998) Getting rid of guns, *The World Today*, 54(10), pp. 260–2

■ *Reading*

82

LAKE NYASA (MALAWI)

Situation ■ Lake Nyasa, a Rift Valley lake and the third largest lake in Africa, is situated at the southern end of the Great Rift Valley. It is 580 km long and varies in width from 24 to 80 km, giving it a surface area of 28,500 km^2. Its surface lies at an altitude of 437 m, although there are seasonal variations in lake level of up to 2 m, and it is almost 800 m deep.

Lake Nyasa illustrates the problem of boundary delimitation in lakes as opposed to seas. In any water body defined as a sea, which is normally taken to imply a natural connection with the world's oceans, UNCLOS agreements apply. In lakes, of which 52 occur on international boundaries, there are no such guidelines. A current example of a dispute over boundaries across lakes is that of the Caspian Sea, which could be defined as a lake or a sea (see p. 74).

The Malawi–Mozambique boundary was finalised by the Anglo-Portuguese Agreement of 18 November 1954, when the major part of the lake boundary was shifted from the eastern shore to the median line. As a result, of the 1,560 km-long boundary between the two countries, 328 km is lake boundary. The outcome was that Mozambique obtained some 8,472 km^2 of water surface. The Malawi–Tanzania boundary is approximately 472 km long, 320 km of which follow the eastern shore of Lake Nyasa to latitude 11° 34'S, south of which the Malawi–Mozambique boundary follows the median line. The point at issue is whether the Malawi–Tanzania lake boundary should also be a median line.

Issue ■ The original 19th-century boundary line was based on Anglo-German spheres of influence and an 1890 Anglo-German agreement described it as the eastern shore of Lake Nyasa. However, in practice German sovereignty extended to the median line until 1922 when Tanganyika (now Tanzania) came under British control. For the period 1916–34, official UK sources showed the boundary as a median line. From 1947 to 1961, British sources have generally abandoned the median line and depicted an eastern shore boundary in accordance with the 1890 agreement. When the Central African Federation of Rhodesia and Nyasaland was established in 1953, this position was reaffirmed.

However, on gaining its independence in 1961, Tanzania rejected the change on the grounds that it was both arbitrary and illegal, since Tanzania was at that time a UN trust territory. In January 1967, Tanzania raised the boundary issue again and restated its

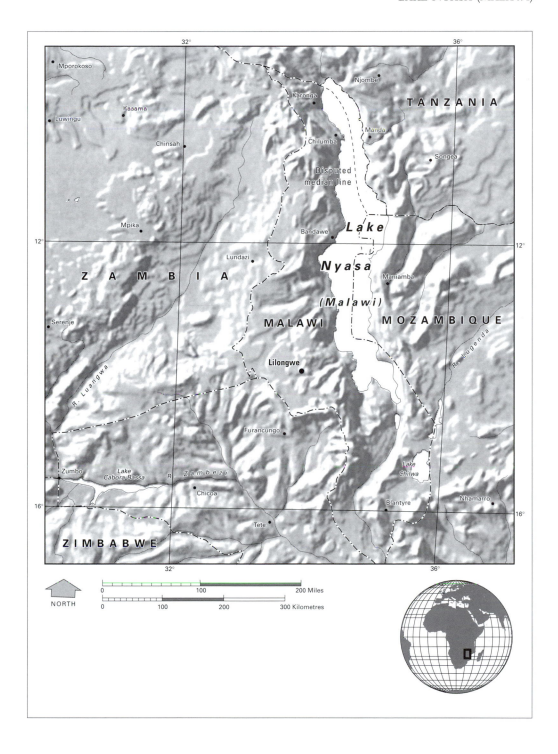

NORTH

0   100   200 Miles

0   100   200   300 Kilometres

claims. Malawi agreed to give the matter consideration. In September 1968, the president of Malawi put forward extravagant claims for the state's boundaries, based on Portuguese maps of the ancient empire of Maravi. These included the assertion that the boundary to the east was the Indian Ocean. On 27 September 1968, Zambia (an extensive part of which was also included in these claims) and Tanzania took a common stand, dismissing the claims of Malawi as having no substance. In 1977, the claims were dropped.

Status ■ There have been no further exchanges on the boundary issue since 1967 and the situation must be considered dormant. However, since it has not been officially settled, the boundary between Malawi and Tanzania must be deemed to be in dispute and the issue will be raised again. This could occur in the context of navigation, fishing or potential mineral rights.

Reading ■ Brownlie, I. (1979) *African Boundaries: A Legal and Diplomatic Encyclopaedia*, London: Royal Institute of International Affairs

Chambers World Gazetteer (1988) Cambridge: Cambridge University Press

US Department of State (1964) *Malawi–Tanganyika and Zanzibar Boundary,* International Boundary Study No. 37, October, Washington, DC: Office of the Geographer, Bureau of Intelligence and Research

US Department of State (1971) *Malawi–Mozambique Boundary*, International Boundary Study No. 112, August, Washington, DC: Office of the Geographer, Bureau of Intelligence and Research

83

THE OGADEN

The Ogaden is the semi-arid to arid area of grassland verging on desert between the core of Ethiopia and Somalia. It is inhabited by pastoral tribes who are ethnically Somali. The population, which varies over time as a result of environmental factors, is put at anything from 1 to 3 million. Somalia, itself an amalgamation of the former British Somaliland and Italian Somaliland, has an area of 637,657 km^2 and a population of 9.3 million. It is estimated that ethnic Somalis inhabit a further 328,000 km^2 beyond the borders of Somalia in Ethiopia, Djibouti and Kenya. This additional area is more than half the size of Somalia and indicates clearly the total lack of accord between political and ethnic boundaries. Indeed, the introduction of international boundaries by the colonial powers, using largely arbitrary lines, had little constraining effect upon the way of life of the nomadic peoples.

■ *Situation*

On achieving independence in 1960, Somalia immediately abrogated the boundary treaty agreed between Ethiopia and Britain in 1897. The aim appeared to be to awaken Somali irredentism and in 1963–4 there was a brief conflict between the troops of Somalia and Ethiopia over Somali support for guerrillas in the Ogaden. The OAU took immediate action to restore peace. Clashes between Kenya and Ethiopia ended with an agreement in 1968, but the continuing conflict between Somalia and Ethiopia led Somalia to sign a pact with the Soviet Union, permitting the establishment of Soviet bases.

■ *Issue*

With the overthrow of Haile Selassie and the arrival of the Marxist-based *Dergue* regime in 1974 (see p. 113), Somalia re-opened the boundary question. In 1977, the Somalis in Ogaden rebelled and received support from Somalian troops. There was a full-scale war which was won by Ethiopia as a result of support from the Soviet Union, which flew in 20,000 Cuban troops. From that time, the Soviet Union continued to support Ethiopian troops in Eritrea, Tigre and on the Somalia frontier. In consequence, Somalia became one of the few states that switched from Soviet to US protection during the Cold War. Somali forces were crushed by Ethiopia at Jijiga in March 1978 and the conflict subsided, although guerrilla forces remained active. The continuing guerrilla activity resulted in an estimated 1.5 million refugees by 1981.

Despite changes of regime in Ethiopia, fears of Ogaden independence remain. In August 1996, Ethiopian forces carried out military operations inside Somali territory, attacking the Islamic Union group, the aim of which is independence for Ogaden Province. In

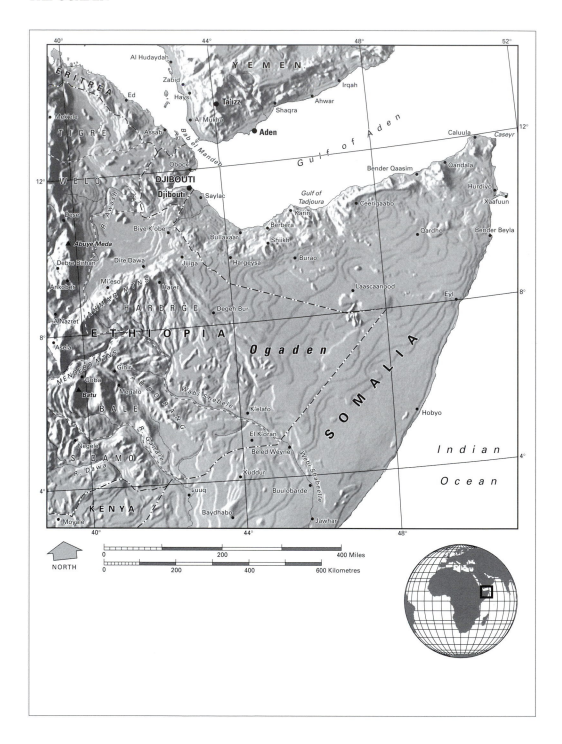

NORTH

0   200   400 Miles

0   200   400   600 Kilometres

January 1980, there were reports that the Ethiopian-Somali Democratic League and the Ogaden National Liberation Front had established a joint committee to facilitate plans to merge the two parties and establish a joint regional government. Later in the same year, Ethiopian troops provided support for the Somali National Front in its conflict with the Islamic Union.

The major problem of Somali irredentism remains unresolved and boundary clashes continue to be an ever-present possibility. The boundaries themselves are largely indefensible and have few control points, but the continuing conflict severely damages the regional economy in an area that is already frequently beset by natural hazards. Throughout most of 1999, the Ethiopian regime was engaged in a violent conflict with Eritrea and has been unable to use Eritrean Red Sea ports (see pp. 109 and 113). It has therefore developed closer ties with Djibouti and Somalia so that trade can be maintained. Meanwhile, Somalia presently lacks any overall government control (see p. 301). Thus, this whole region of the Horn of Africa is likely to remain a key flashpoint.

■ *Status*

■ *Reading*

Brownlie, I. (1979) *African Boundaries: A Legal and Diplomatic Encyclopaedia*, London: Royal Institute of International Affairs

Downing, D. (1980) *An Atlas of Territorial and Border Disputes*, London: New English Library

Griffiths, I.L.-L. (1985) *An Atlas of African Affairs*, London: Methuen

84

PAKISTAN

Situation ■ Located at the head of the Arabian Sea, Pakistan is part of the Indian subcontinent but has close links with the Middle East. It has an area of 796,095 km^2 and a population of 130 million, making it the most populous Muslim state in the world other than Indonesia. It has boundaries with Iran, Afghanistan, China and India. The Wakhan Panhandle of Afghanistan (see p. 360) separates it from Tajikistan and Central Asia. Geographically, it ranges from the deserts of Sind and Baluchistan to the mountains of the Karakoram, but the key element is the valley of the Indus.

Issue ■ Following the India Independence Act promulgated on 18 July 1947, the subcontinent of India was split according to religion and Pakistan was granted independence in the August. British India, Punjab and Bengal were all divided and Pakistan emerged as two territories, West and East Pakistan, separated by the breadth of India.

From the start, there were problems of attempting to reconcile an Islamic identity with the development of a modern state. Furthermore, there were great disparities between the different units with Punjabi predominance. The other major issue throughout the entire independence period has been the relationship between the military and civilian bureaucracy. The first military government took over in 1958 and for the next 30 years, with only a seven-year interlude, there has been military rule. Several different constitutional frameworks have been adopted, but the military remain closely involved.

Throughout the period, the major concern has been relations with India, with whom Pakistan has fought three wars. In 1971, India assisted East Pakistan, which broke away as the newly independent state of Bangladesh. The other two wars were fought over Kashmir, which remains a global flashpoint and is considered elsewhere in this volume (see p. 165).

Pakistan has been careful to retain close links with the USA and, as a member of the Central Treaty Organisation (CENTO) and the Baghdad Pact, received economic aid. However, with the Soviet invasion of Afghanistan in December 1979, Pakistan became a major recipient of US aid which it dispensed to selected Muslim rebel groups or *mujahidin*. However, relations with the USA have become strained as a result of Pakistan's nuclear programme.

A continuing issue is Pakistan's support for the *taliban*, the radical Sunni Islamic movement which runs most of Afghanistan (see p. 8). This has alienated Iran, and

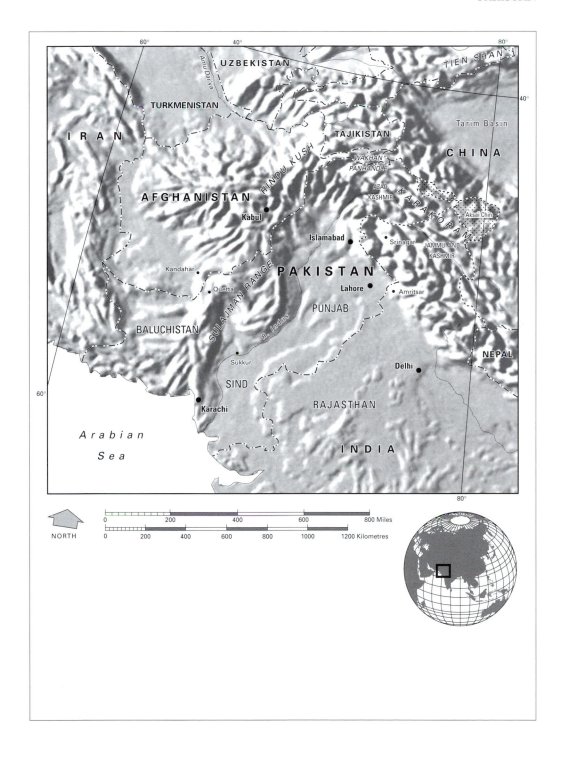

particularly the Shi'a minority which makes up some 18 per cent of its own population. Internal unrest has also been fostered by economic crisis, together with recurrent government scandals.

On 28 and 30 May 1998, Pakistan carried out a series of nuclear tests which have greatly heightened tension with India, currently ruled by the anti-Muslim Bharatiya Janata Party (BJP).

Status ■ With a burgeoning population, a lack of economic resources and a fragmented social and economic structure, Pakistan has major problems. Relations with the West have been damaged through support for the *taliban* and through nuclear testing. Throughout 1998 and 1999 there was ethnic violence, including bombings. Above all, the question of Kashmir remains and, during 1999, fighting on a small scale with India continued. Both internally and in its external relations, Pakistan is unstable and will remain a potential geopolitical flashpoint.

Reading ■ Ahmed, S. (1997) Pakistan at fifty: a tenuous democracy, *Current History*, 96(614), pp. 419–24

IISS (1998) Pakistan's growing crisis: in the shadow of Afghanistan, *Strategic Comments*, 4(8)

Rizui, H.A. (1998) Civil–military relations in contemporary Pakistan, *Survival*, 40(2), pp. 96–113

85

PALESTINE

The nascent state of Palestine comprises a number of autonomous areas, totalling 6,280 km^2. Of these, the Gaza Strip, excluding the Jewish settlements, with its area of 360 km^2 and the Jericho enclave with an area of 60 km^2 are fully autonomous. The remaining area, 5,860 km^2, is partially autonomous and is located in the West Bank. The population exceeds 1.6 million, with 660,000 in the Gaza Strip, 40,000 in Jericho and the remainder in the West Bank. The major geographical and political complication is that the Jewish settlements in the Gaza Strip and the West Bank remain under Israeli administration and jurisdiction (see p. 304). For most of the 20th century the region known as Palestine has been an area of conflict, not least because it contains holy sites of the three great monotheistic religions: Judaism, Christianity and Islam.

■ *Situation*

By 1914 Palestine, which was not then a separate political entity, had a population of approximately 650,000 Arabs, with a Jewish population of approximately 75,000. After World War I, Palestine became distinguished and was identified separately as a result of the division of the Middle East among the major European powers and the expressed wish of the Zionist movement for a national home for the Jews. Thus, it was clear from this time that the aims of Zionism and the aspirations of the Arab population of Palestine were incompatible.

■ *Issue*

Under the League of Nations mandate, Palestine was assigned to the UK which explicitly facilitated Jewish acquisition of land and immigration. As a consequence, the Jewish proportion of the population rose from 11 per cent in 1922 to 30 per cent in 1944. Conscious of the threat posed by Jewish immigration on such a scale, Arab nationalism developed and there was a full-scale uprising from 1936 to 1939.

The other factor that created moral support in the West for a Jewish homeland was the Holocaust, which united world Jewry behind Zionism. The 1947 UN plan for the partition of Palestine into separate Arab and Jewish states was rejected by the Palestinians and the Arab world in general and, with the declaration of independence by Israel, war ensued in 1948 and 1949. Israel defeated the Arab forces ranged against it, Palestine was obliterated as a potential state and the state of Israel occupied a large part of the territory, far more than originally planned by the UN. The remainders of Palestine not within the *de facto* boundaries of Israel were the West Bank, held by Jordan, and the Gaza Strip, held by Egypt. As a result of the war, some 700,000 Arabs left the area for the neighbouring Arab states. Few were ever allowed to return and a sizeable proportion have remained in refugee camps ever since.

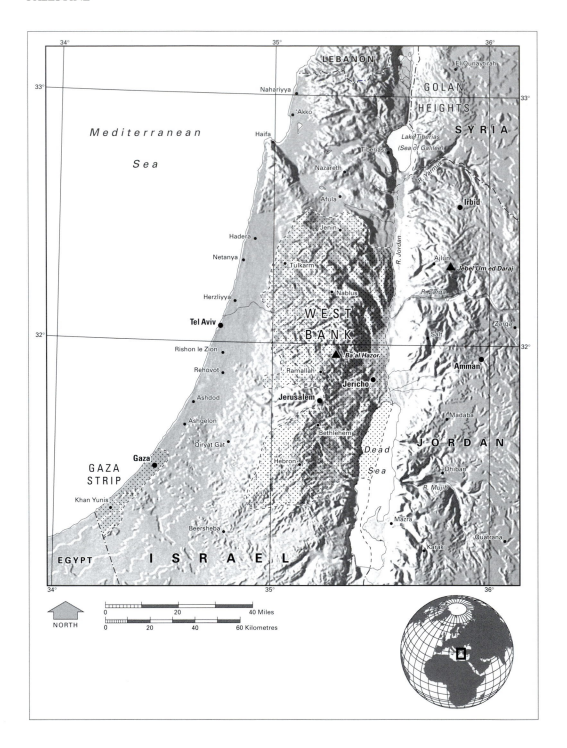

Mediterranean
Sea

LEBANON
GOLAN
HEIGHTS
SYRIA

El Qunaytirah
Nahariyya
'Akko
Haifa
Lake Tiberias
(Sea of Galilee)
Tiberias
Nazareth
Afula
Irbid
R. Yarmūk
Jenin
Ajlūn
Jebel Um ed Daraj
Hadera
Netanya
Tulkarm
Nablus
R. Zarqa
Herzliyya
WEST
BANK
R. Jordan
Tel Aviv
Zarqa
Salt
Rishon le Zion
Ba'al Hazor
Amman
Rehovot
Ramallah
Jericho
Ashdod
Jerusalem
Madaba
Ashqelon
Bethlehem
JORDAN
Qiryat Gat
Gaza
Dead
Sea
Dhiban
GAZA
STRIP
Hebron
R. Mujib
Khan Yunis
Mazra
Beersheba
Quatrana
Karak
EGYPT
ISRAEL

NORTH

0   20   40 Miles

0   20   40   60 Kilometres

The next conflict, the Six-Day War of 1967, resulted in Israeli occupation of Jerusalem, along with the West Bank, the Gaza Strip and the Golan Heights of Syria (see p. 126). Thus, Israel had taken over the whole of the former Palestine.

With the development of the Palestine Liberation Organisation (PLO) and the continuing marginalisation of Palestinians, the idea of a state of Palestine has been reinforced. In 1988, the PLO made a declaration for such a state, thereby explicitly offering recognition of Israel. The state would comprise the West Bank and Gaza Strip, with East Jerusalem as its capital, and to be viable and effective it would need some form of territorial contiguity under Palestinian Authority (PA) control. An initial step to demonstrate independence was the opening of Gaza International Airport on 25 November 1998.

After several unsuccessful attempts at negotiation, the Israeli–Palestinian Declaration of Principles, known as the Oslo Accords, was signed in September 1993. This followed the 1991 Madrid Peace Conference and was itself succeeded by the Wye River Memorandum signed on 23 October 1998. A comparison of these agreements shows that the land-for-peace formula which was originally espoused has been replaced by the concern for the security of Israel. Each percentage of the West Bank vacated by Israel now depends upon measures by the PA to safeguard what are described as Israel's 'vital security needs'. At the same time, Yasser Arafat, long-time leader of the PLO, has raised the PA's relations with the USA to the status of a security pact.

Apart from Fatah, every Palestinian faction has opposed the Wye Memorandum, which has also been denounced by several Arab states. Israel has a dilemma, in that it would like the PA to be strong enough to control militant groups such as Hamas, but not sufficiently strong that it could not be overcome by Israeli forces. The majority of Palestinians appear to remain sceptical about Israeli intentions and the US role in the peace process. The main explanation for this is that the Wye Memorandum did not directly address the key issues of Jerusalem or of the continuing establishment of Israeli settlements in the West Bank and Gaza.

Under Benjamin Netanyahu, Israel appeared to have no intention of stopping settlement activities or of accepting a Palestinian state within the 1967 boundaries. This increased pressure on the PA to declare statehood in May 1999.

The situation appears fraught, with Israel intransigent and the USA still offering it virtually uncritical support, despite the fact that Israel has occupied territory of other countries for 32 years. The issue of the Declaration of Statehood by Palestine is critical, but the situation may have been ameliorated with the election of a new Israeli Labour government under Ehud Barak in early 1999. However, the peace process must be seen

■ *Status*

in its regional context, characterised by the continuing issue of Iraq, the *rapprochement* between Iran and Saudi Arabia, and the various emerging Israeli relationships with Turkey, Azerbaijan and Afghanistan. Since the Middle East peace process began, there have been solutions to what appeared intractable disputes, most notably in South Africa, and these must give some cause for optimism. Despite foreboding in the region, it may be realised that the alternative to the implementation of the Oslo Agreements is too terrible to contemplate.

Reading ■ IISS (1998) The Palestinian Authority and the CIA: who will protect the guards?, *Strategic Comments*, 4(10)

Shikaki, M.K. (1998) Not yet dead but is it doomed? *The World Today*, 54(12), pp. 310–11

86

THE PANAMA CANAL

Strategically and economically, apart from Suez, Panama is the most important canal in the world. It allows transit between the Atlantic and the Pacific oceans across the centre of the American continent. It is the only inter-oceanic waterway between the North West Passage of northern Canada and the Magellan Strait in southern Chile. The canal cuts through Central America at its narrowest point, the Isthmus of Panama. ■ *Situation*

The Panama Canal is 80.5 km in length and transit takes from eight to ten hours. The maximum permissible draught is 11.4–12.2 m (depending on lake water levels), and special Panamax ships, with maximum dimensions of 274.3 by 32.3 m, have been designed to make optimum use of the canal. A boundary delimited on 8 km either side of the canal defines the 'Canal Area' (formerly known as the Canal Zone) and includes the cities of Cristobal and Balboa.

In 1880 – using a design by de Lesseps, the engineer of the Suez Canal – an attempt was made by France to breach the Isthmus of Panama. This was to be a sea-level waterway, but after a few years of effort it was abandoned as too expensive. In 1903, the USA put forward a different proposal for a canal. Colombia, the territory of which at that time included the Isthmus, was slow to respond and the USA organised the secession of Panama as an independent state, but under American tutelage. On 18 November 1903, the USA then concluded a treaty with the independent Republic of Panama which gave the USA unilateral control of canal operations, together with the civil and military administration of the newly delimited Canal Zone. ■ *Issue*

During the period 1904–14, a lock-based canal was constructed by the USA which officially opened on 15 August 1914. From 1975, a widening programme was started and in 1979 a new Panama Canal Treaty was negotiated. This took effect on 1 October 1979 when the Canal Zone (Canal Area) was formally transferred to Panamanian sovereignty, along with the cities of Cristobal and Balboa, the dry docks, the trans-isthmus railway and the naval base at Coco Solo. According to the treaty, by the year 2000 control of the canal was to pass to Panama and the USA was to have removed all its bases from the country.

In September 1995, discussions were initiated by Panama to extend the US military presence beyond the year 2000 to lessen the economic impact of withdrawal. By December 1997, a tentative agreement had been reached which involved, together with

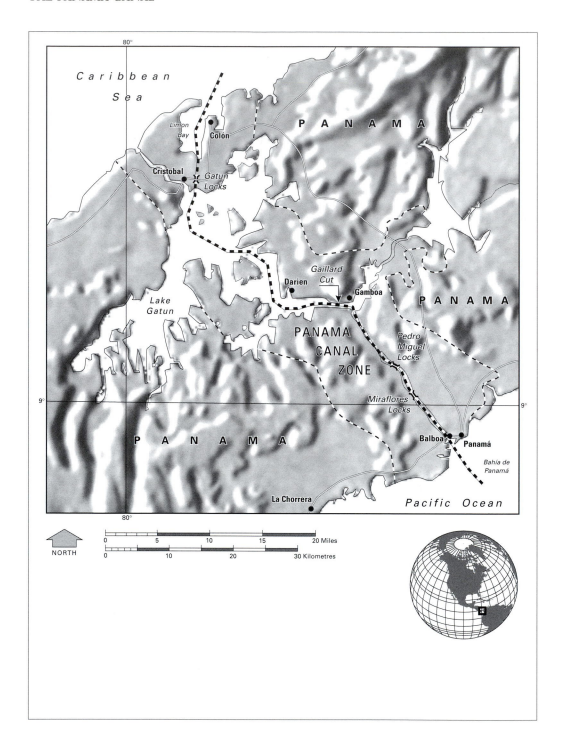

NORTH

0   5   10   15   20 Miles

0   10   20   30 Kilometres

Panamanian and other Latin American military and police forces, the establishment of a regional anti-drugs centre. By late 1998, agreement had still to be reached on the multilateral anti-drugs centre, but the transfer of the canal itself remained scheduled for 31 December 1999. Meanwhile, the USA has begun the search for new bases in Central and South America.

The Panama Canal is vital to US strategic interests, particularly for the redeployment of its navy between the Atlantic and the Pacific Oceans. 'Sea Lift', the replenishment of Europe from the USA in a time of emergency, is dependent upon the rapid transit of vessels between the two oceans. The canal is also vital to world shipping in general and to the US coastal shipping infrastructure.

Fears remain in Panama about the effects of US withdrawal and Panama's ability to operate the canal. However, it must be remembered that such fears were expressed about Egypt and the Suez Canal in 1956. The other major problem concerns congestion, as only one ship at a time can pass through the Gaillard Cut in the central highlands. Various proposals for improving the canal and for developing a more comprehensive integrated transport network alongside it have been put forward. The Panama Canal has never been a flashpoint but, in the light of its continuing strategic and economic importance, current problems may well result in increased tension.

■ *Status*

Drouhaud, P. (1997) Le Panama avant le retrocession du canal en 1999, *Defense Nationale*, Aout/Septembre, pp. 129–36

The Economist (1989) *The Economist Atlas,* London: Economist Books/Hutchinson

Times Books (1983) *Times Atlas of Oceans,* London: Times Books

■ *Reading*

87

THE PARACEL ISLANDS

Situation ■ The Paracel Islands form part of the complex maritime boundary dispute between China and Vietnam, which includes the Gulf of Tongking and the Spratly Islands, both of which are considered in this volume (see pp. 336 and 311).

The Paracels, known as the Xisha Qundao in Mandarin Chinese and the Quan Doa Hoang Sa in Vietnamese, lie approximately equidistant some 150–200 nml from Hainan Island and Vietnam. Two clusters are recognised, the Amphitrite and the Crescent groups. There are approximately 15 islets and a large number of reefs and shoals, scattered in a roughly oval shape, approximately 160 nml long in the Gulf of Tongking. Five islands are reported to be occupied by troops from China.

As a result of their location, both China and Vietnam have reasonable claims on the Paracel Islands. The Chinese base their case on the fact that the islands were discovered by Chinese navigators and used by Chinese fishermen for centuries, before being brought under Chinese administration from the 15th century. None of this was disputed until the 1930s. Vietnam, on the other hand, claims that the Paracels form part of the 19th-century empire of Annam, and that before then no country was in control of them.

Issue ■ The Paracels were annexed by France in 1932 and in 1939 they were occupied by Japan. Under the San Francisco Treaty of 1951, Japan renounced any claims but no statement was made as to the ownership of the islands. On 16 January 1974, in the 'One Hundred Minute War', the Chinese drove South Vietnamese forces out of the Paracels and established a garrison which has remained there ever since.

Discussions on the future of the islands, both separately and as part of the whole maritime boundary between China and Vietnam, continue to the present. In January 1995, in response to a Chinese claim to have discovered three uncharted islets in waters around the Paracel Islands, Vietnam restated its claim to the entire Paracel Island group. In 1996 and 1997, problems arose between the two disputants over exploration and exploitation rights. For example, in April 1997, China ceased petroleum drilling, following strong Vietnamese protests.

In April 1998, Vietnam issued a strong warning to China over reports that it planned to develop the Paracel Islands for tourism since this would constitute a violation of Vietnam's territorial integrity. In September 1998, in apparent retaliation for this event, the navy of Vietnam occupied two submerged reefs near the Spratly Islands. In October

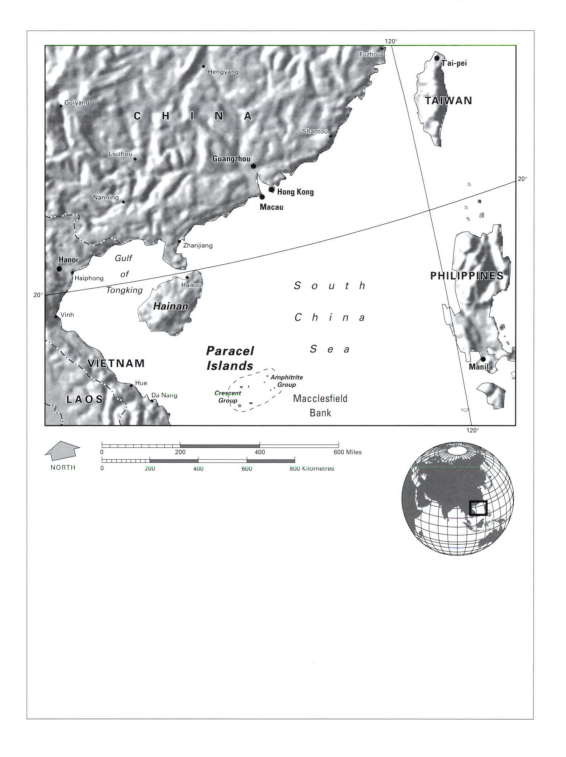

1998, relations were partly restored when the two countries agreed to accelerate negotiations to agree on both their land boundaries and the delimitation of the Gulf of Tongking by the year 2000.

Status ■ The islands remain strategically important with regard to shipping as the main sea-line between Singapore and Hong Kong passes between them and the Macclesfield Bank immediately to the east. More importantly, ownership would guarantee access to a large area of sea-bed with a potential for petroleum resources. The Paracels must also be seen in the context of China's overall claim to virtually the whole of the South China Sea, including the Spratly Islands. As the USA and Russia withdraw from the area and regional powers become established, the issue of the Paracel Islands could become a Pacific Rim flashpoint.

Reading ■ Bridge, J. (1994) South China Sea: the Spratly and Paracel Islands dispute, *The World Today*, 50(6), pp. 109–12

Dzurek, D.J. (1985) Boundary and resource disputes in the South China Sea, in E.M. Borgese and N. Ginsburg (eds), *Ocean Yearbook 5*, Chicago, IL: University of Chicago Press, pp. 254–84

Park, C. (1980) Offshore oil development in the China Seas: some legal and territorial issues, in E.M. Borgese and N. Ginsburg (eds), *Ocean Yearbook 2*, Chicago, IL: University of Chicago Press, pp. 302–16

Weatherbee, D.E. (1987) The South China Sea: from zone of conflict to zone of peace?, in L.E. Grinter and Y.W. Kihl (eds), *East Asian Conflict Zones*, Basingstoke: Macmillan, pp. 123–48

88

PERU

Peru, a large country at 1,285,216 km^2, is located on the western side of South America and has a long Pacific littoral. As with other Andean states, there is a major geographical difference between the highlands of the Andes and the lowlands of the interior. Its population of 23.5 million is larger than that of all the other South American states except Colombia, Argentina and Brazil. Peru has boundaries with Ecuador, Colombia, Brazil, Bolivia and Chile.

■ *Situation*

As with several other Latin American states, events in the 19th century exercised a significant influence on those in the 20th century. Following independence in the 1820s, Peru had a succession of military rulers and, as a result of its defeat by Chile in the War of the Pacific (1979–83), faced dire economic problems.

■ *Issue*

For some 30 years, from the 1930s onwards, the major conflict was internal: between the new political party, the Alianza Popular Revolucionaria Americana (APRA), and the army. As elsewhere in the continent, the army stood for the interests of the elites while the politicians represented the middle classes. A major political change occurred with the coup of 1968, led by Juan Alvarado, which resulted in notable reforms, including the legitimisation of the Marxist union confederation.

In 1979 a new constitution was produced and the following year Peru returned to civilian rule, which lasted until 5 April 1992 when Alberto Fujimori suspended the constitution, Congress and judiciary. He justified this on the grounds that the economy was virtually bankrupt. Unemployment and underemployment had reached 70 per cent, inflation had run at more than 7,000 per cent during 1990 and for most of the previous 15 years net economic growth had been negative. Bankruptcy had been avoided only by the informal sector, perhaps as high as 40 per cent of the economy, and the illegal sector, based on cocaine.

Apart from the economy, the other major problem from the 1960s had been the radical guerrilla movement Shining Path or Sendero Luminoso (SL). The movement thrives particularly on the major cleavage between core and periphery, typical of many Latin American states. SL launched a new wave of guerrilla attacks in April 1991, but on 12 September 1992 its leader was captured. The other similar movement is the Tupac Amaru Revolutionary Movement (MRTA), which achieved worldwide publicity when it stormed a reception at the Japanese embassy in Lima on 17 December 1996. The resulting seige lasted for 126 days, the longest in Latin American history.

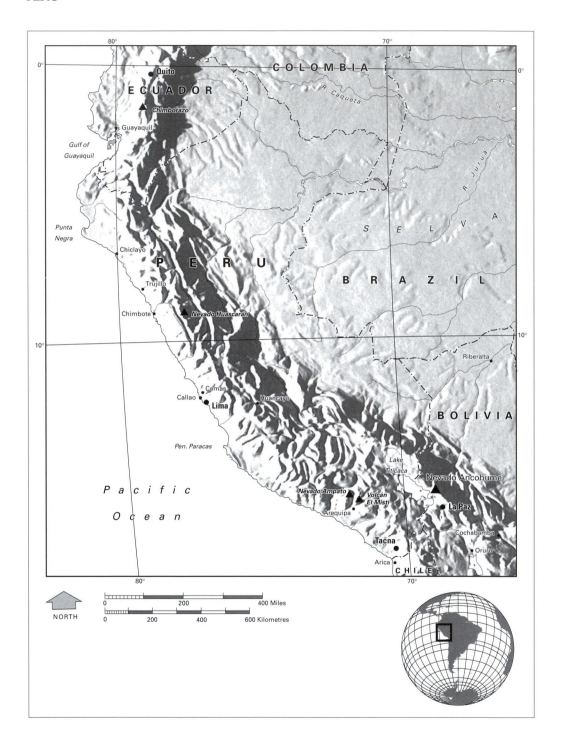

NORTH

0   200   400 Miles

0   200   400   600 Kilometres

Foreign policy has been dominated by the traditional suspicion of Chile, but more importantly by the boundary dispute with Ecuador (see p. 103). In 1995, this latter dispute appeared to be giving rise to a mini arms race.

Despite the dire internal problems, particularly of the economy, Peru does appear to have a measure of stability under the present government. Following negotiations throughout 1998, an agreement was signed with Ecuador in October which formally ended the territorial dispute. It has been agreed that the issue will be decided by four guarantor countries and a demilitarised zone has been established. In November 1998, the government announced the capture of the MRTA leader. It is almost impossible to believe that there will not be further internal upheavals in Peru, but relations with its neighbours seem settled and it cannot be characterised as a potential geopolitical flashpoint.

■ *Status*

Foron, J. (1997) The future of revolutions at the fin-de-siècle, *Third World Quarterly*, 18(5), pp. 791–820

Robinson, L. (1997) A Shogun in Peru, *World Policy Journal*, Winter, pp. 55–61

■ *Reading*

89

THE RANN OF KUTCH

Situation ■ The Rann of Kutch is a desolate area of salt marshes, brackish lakes and isolated rocky elevations located between Sind (Pakistan) and Gujarat (India). For part of the year it is inaccessible; between June and November, with the onset of the south-west monsoon, it is largely inundated, forming a large body of shallow water with a maximum depth of 1–2 m. As the monsoon ends, the water level drops and the area becomes basically salt flats. The Rann is approximately 20,500 km^2 in extent and it is important because its northern edge provides a 403 km-long stretch of the India–Pakistan boundary. The award was made by the Indo–Pakistan Western Boundary Case Tribunal in 1968.

Issue ■ Prior to independence, the British Indian Province of Sind and the British suzerainties of Kutch, Santalpur, Tharad, Suigam, Wav and Jodhpur abutted on to the Rann of Kutch. Following a dispute over the southern limits of Sind in 1913, a partial demarcation of the boundary was achieved in 1923–4. With the India Independence Act of 18 July 1947, Sind was allotted to Pakistan, while on the expiry of the suzerainties, the remainder acceded to union with India. Following its independence, in July 1948 Pakistan raised the question of the Sind–Kutch frontier boundary delimitation east of this demarcated section. However, although the issue arose periodically, it remained low key until 1965, when there were frontier clashes. Hostilities terminated when the UK persuaded the combatants to submit the dispute to the Indo–Pakistan Western Boundary Case Tribunal. In February 1968, the tribunal presented its award, determining the boundary. The award referred to approximately 9,000 km^2 of uninhabited territory.

As in many such instances, the case rested primarily on the geographical definition of the Rann of Kutch. Pakistan submitted evidence to prove that Sind extended south of the Rann before and after the period of British administration. Furthermore, it considered the Rann to be a maritime feature and therefore, as in the case of a bay, that equitable distribution should be achieved by a median line. The equidistant line claimed by Pakistan roughly accorded with latitude 24°N. In contrast, India contended that the boundary ran along the northern edge of the Rann and cited the 1923–4 demarcation line in support of its case. The tribunal decided on a compromise position close to the northern edge of the Rann.

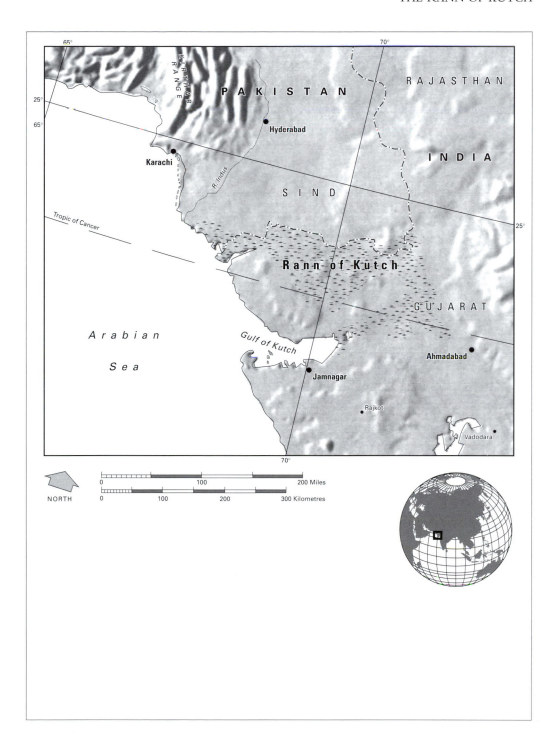

Status ■ Despite the settlement, there remains a possibility of instability in the region, given the deteriorating relations between India and Pakistan. More likely, is dispute over oil since the area has petroleum potential. At present, the Rann of Kutch must be considered a dormant flashpoint.

Reading ■ Boyd, A. (1991) *An Atlas of World Affairs*, London: Routledge

US Department of State (1968) *India–Pakistan (Rann of Kutch),* International Boundary Study No. 86, February, Washington, DC: Office of the Geographer, Bureau of Intelligence and Research

90

ROCKALL AND ST KILDA

Located on the Rockall Bank at 57° 36′N, 13° 41′W, the islet of Rockall is 225 nml west of the Hebrides and is in an extremely isolated location. It consists of a very small rock platform which is uninhabitable, but has been formally annexed by the UK. Apart from the UK, claimants to Rockall have been Ireland and, from 1985, Iceland and Denmark.

The dispute between the UK and Ireland hinged, as with many maritime disputes, upon differing legal principles. According to Britain, there should be a strict median line, using all offshore islands as base points. In contrast, the Irish approach has been for an 'equitable' equidistance line based on a variety of factors such as habitability and population. The claims of Iceland and Denmark (through the Faeroes) are based on the argument that the Rockall–Faeroes plateau is a natural prolongation of their land mass, rather than that of Great Britain or Ireland. The Rockall Trough in fact separates the continental shelf off the British Isles from a series of banks which link Rockall with both the Faeroes and Iceland.

During the 1960s and 1970s there were unsuccessful negotiations between the UK and Ireland. Both claimed large areas of sea in a series of rounds of designation. However, following Irish proposals in 1976 and early 1977, on 21 February 1977 the UK agreed to arbitration. In 1980, Ireland agreed to a five-man tribunal, but progress was minimal as both sides awaited results from several other ICJ cases. In 1985, the emergence of claims by both Iceland and Denmark spurred the UK and Ireland to move away from arbitration to a negotiated practical settlement. It was rightly considered that an arbitration court would need to take the new Scandinavian claims into account and this would greatly complicate the issue.

On 8 November 1988, agreement on the delimitation of the continental shelf was reached and the result was unique in such settlements in that it comprised a stepped line. Such a line might be useful in the delimitation of oil exploration concessions, but it poses obvious problems for ships trying to locate their position. In the agreement, no mention was made of Rockall.

Despite this settlement, there remain the claims of Denmark and Iceland, while Ireland still considers the status of Rockall itself to be a live issue. The underlying fear has been not only that as an island Rockall might generate a vast Atlantic continental shelf for the UK – as much as 120,000 nml^2 or approximately one-quarter as much again as the size

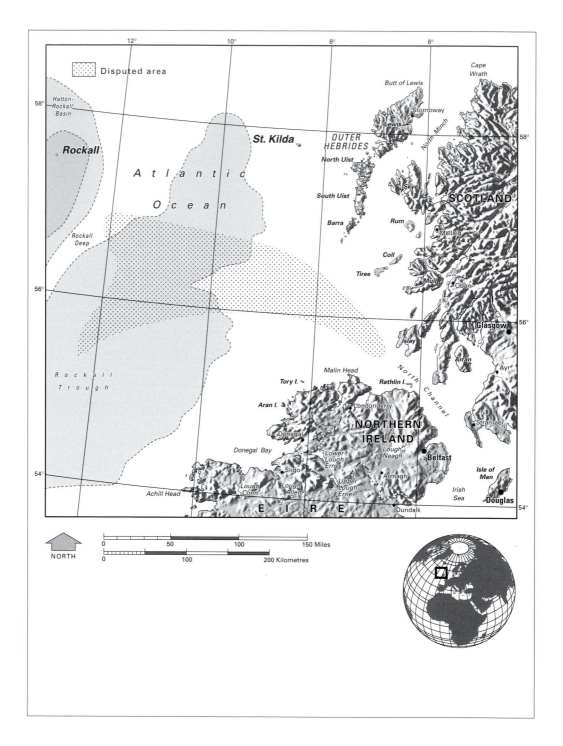

Disputed area

12°   10°   8°   6°

Hatton-
Rockall
Basin

Cape
Wrath

Butt of Lewis

Stornoway

Rockall

58°

St. Kilda

Lewis

OUTER
HEBRIDES

North Minch

58°

A t l a n t i c

North Uist

Skye

SCOTLAND

O c e a n

South Uist

Rum

Mallaig

Rockall
Deep

Barra

Coll

Tiree

Mull

Oban

56°

R o c k a l l
T r o u g h

Islay

Glasgow

56°

Arran

Ayr

Malin Head

North Channel

Tory I.

Rathlin I.

Stranraer

Aran I.

Londonderry

NORTHERN
IRELAND

Donegal

Lough
Neagh

Belfast

Isle of
Man

Donegal Bay

Lower
Lough
Erne

Sligo

Armagh

Irish
Sea

Douglas

54°

Lough
Conn

Lough
Allen

Upper
Lough
Erne

54°

Achill Head

E I R E

Dundalk

NORTH

0   50   100   150 Miles

0   100   200 Kilometres

of the UK – but that it might be used as a base point in any further continental shelf delimitation. All of this is highly relevant in an area not only important for fishing but with great potential for petroleum discovery.

In 1997, the new UK government decided to accede to the UN Law of the Sea Convention (UNCLOS) and accept that the UK fishery limits could not be defined by Rockall as it is not a valid base point under Article 121(3) of the Convention. The new limits are based on St Kilda, with a loss of some 60,000 nml^2. However, this new delimitation still overlaps with the claims of Denmark and Iceland and the question of the 12 nml limit around the rock remains in dispute with Ireland. While Rockall is no longer a flashpoint, it is possible that similar disputes could erupt over St Kilda. Iceland has contended that it is uninhabited and should not be used as a base point. The dispute might now develop into one between the UK and Ireland on the one hand and Iceland and Denmark on the other. Thus the issue of maritime delimitation in the region remains contentious.

■ *Status*

Lysaght, C. (1990) The Agreement on the Delimitation of the Continental Shelf between Ireland and the United Kingdom, *Irish Studies in International Affairs*, 3(2), pp. 83–109

Symmons, C.R. (1989) The UK/Ireland Continental Shelf Agreement 1998: a model for compromise in maritime delimitation, in *International Boundaries and Boundary Conflict Resolution*, Conference Proceedings, Durham: IBRU, University of Durham, pp. 387–412

Symmons, C. (1998) Ireland and the Rockall dispute: an analysis of recent developments, *Boundary and Security Bulletin*, 6(1), pp. 78–93

■ *Reading*

91

RUSSIA

Situation ■ Despite the dismemberment of the Soviet Union, Russia – with an area of 17,075,400 km ^{2} – remains easily the largest state in the world, almost twice the size of the USA and, from Moscow to the Bering Strait, it spans ten time zones. The main statistical effect of the independence of the republics was the reduction in population to just under 148 million, a reduction of around 100 million and down from a position of approximate parity with the USA. As a result of its economic problems, Russia has one of the world's highest external debts.

Issue ■ In December 1991, the Soviet Union was dissolved and the Russian Federation (Russia) claimed the status of legal successor. Thus, for the first time since 1922, there was an independent Russian state. This extraordinary change had been precipitated over the previous few years by the last president of the Soviet Union, Mikhail Gorbachev. Through *glasnost* and *perestroika* he advocated for government openness and restructuring respectively. The result was the attempted coup of August 1991 and the final collapse of the Soviet Union. Instability ensued with, at one time, more than 150 conflicts extant. Russia must be regarded as a complex of flashpoints.

Attempts to move the state towards democracy and a market economy from the rigid command structure that had been in place for more than 70 years proved, not unexpectedly, extremely difficult. Until his resignation on the eve of the millennium, the political system was dominated by the president, Boris Yeltsin, who was in extremely poor health. There is a plethora of weak political parties and the general level of public support in the populace for parties is low.

The economy is in a state of collapse and is causing alarm throughout the free states of the FSU. Since 1991, policies have been aimed at rapid marketisation and privatisation, but the freeing of prices in January 1992 led to vast increases, corruption and burgeoning crime. Indeed, it is considered by some financial experts that complete collapse is required before a viable structure can be built.

Apart from these visceral issues, there is the question of the territorial integrity of the republic. More than 80 per cent of the population is Russian but there are 36 minorities with populations in excess of 100,000. The largest of these comprises 5.5 million Tatars, who in March 1992 voted for a sovereign state. Chechnya declared its independence in autumn 1991 and this is considered in the next section. In March 1992, all the main

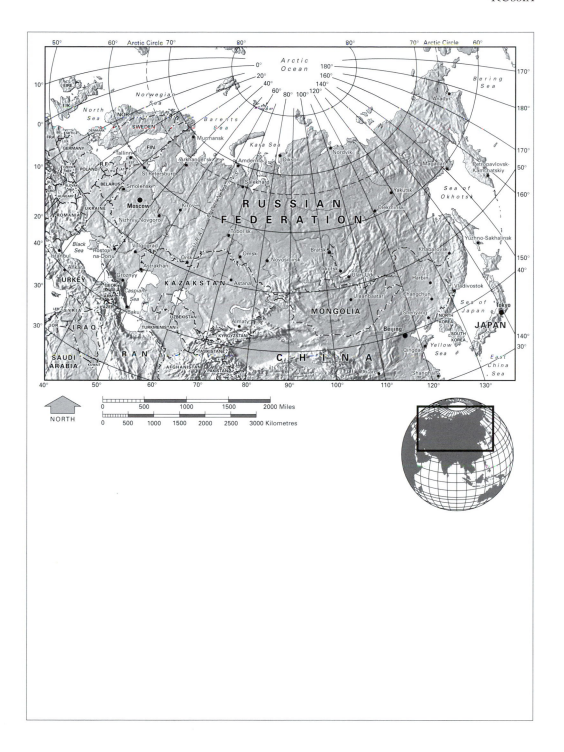

NORTH

0	500	1000	1500	2000 Miles	

| 0 | 500 | 1000 | 1500 | 2000 | 2500 | 3000 Kilometres |

minority republics other than Tatarstan and Chechnya signed a federal treaty with Russia. A further concern is the 26 million Russians living beyond Russia's current boundaries in the 'near abroad'. This problem is closely related to that of international boundaries, a major concern for the FSU. The plight of the military is also a key issue; on 10 September 1998, Yeltsin was advised that the armed forces could not be relied upon to defend the regime in the face of mass protest.

The political problems can be classified as internal, within the FSU or international. Internally, Chechnya has dominated events but there were other problems in the North Caucasus, notably Dagestan (see p. 283). The North Caucasus has become a major arsenal of weaponry and ammunition and it is not surprising that, apart from these two, there have also been serious tensions in Ingushetia and North Ossetia. The North Caucasus is also a major routeway and is deeply involved in the development of petroleum in the Caspian Sea Basin. Therefore it is also not surprising that, internally, the North Caucasus has been the most important Russian flashpoint.

In the FSU, various agreements, culminating in that of May 1997, have resulted in accord with Ukraine over the future of the Black Sea Fleet and its bases. The significant point has been Russian recognition of the Crimea and Sevastopol as Ukrainian territory. In Moldova (see p. 224), Russia has made great efforts to achieve a settlement of the Transdniester problem and relations appear to have been normalised between the two entities after an agreement signed on 8 May 1997. Relations with Belarus have remained close (see p. 39), but the question of re-integration is dogged by the extremely authoritarian approach of the president of Belarus which was still evident in 1999.

A major focus is, however, on the Southern Caucasus which presents an extremely volatile geopolitical landscape since it now appears to be considered an area of vital interest by the USA. Competition between the two military superpowers over rival spheres of influence has, particularly given the resource issue, become focused on this region. The minority problems in Georgia, Azerbaijan and Armenia have all occupied Russia, which is clearly not happy with an incipient Azerbaijan–Georgia–Ukraine link.

In Central Asia, Russia has supplied guards for most of the external boundaries of the FSU. The main concern seems to be the prevention of destabilisation within the area, particularly as a result of the civil war in Tajikistan (see p. 330), and the maintenance of a key role. Abroad, relations with Japan have been improved considerably. As a result, there was Japanese support for Russia to become a full member of the G7 (Group of Seven) nations. An agreement was also reached on the settlement of the Kurile Islands dispute (see p. 188) by the year 2000. In January 1992, Russia and Finland signed a Mutual Co-operation Agreement and it seems unlikely that the question of Karelia (see p. 162) will become a serious issue. However, the major concern has obviously been the eastward expansion of NATO against the wishes of Russia. In early 1999, Poland, the Czech Republic and Hungary acceded. So far, none of the FSU states have joined NATO but there are strong pressures from the Baltic states. On 27 May 1997, Russia signed an agreement with NATO known as the Founding Act, which gives Russia a voice, but not a veto, in NATO decision-making. While remaining opposed to any further NATO expansion, Russia has shown – through its relative inactivity over Kosovo – its need to remain in good standing with the USA in order to obtain further International Monetary Fund (IMF) loans.

The economic and social conditions of Russia remain dire, but it did achieve continuity of government in the person of Yeltsin. However, there remains the feeling that the federation is neither a nation nor a state but a territory within which a high proportion of the Russian peoples live. Just as the territorial integrity of the state has, in a sense, been breached, so have most of the norms of ordinary life. To be plunged from superpower status to penury in perhaps two years is a transformation that few could contemplate with equanimity. There has been an exponential rise in the rate of crime and the Russian mafia has already established key global links. Coupled with the vast haemorrhaging of resources abroad, the state has proved unable to collect taxes. For some analysts, the situation appears terminal. If recovery does not prove possible, then the most likely outcomes are either a military takeover or fragmentation into a plethora of small states. If the first were to occur, this would in all probability pressage a return to Cold War relations, while the second is not likely to result in anything other than long-term chaos.

■ *Status*

If progress is maintained towards a democracy and market economy, the close relationships being developed with China, Japan and India could result in a total reorientation of global geopolitics.

Blandy, C. (1998) *Prigorodnyy Rayon: The Continuing Dispute*, Camberley: Royal Military Academy Sandhurst (pamphlet)
Herd, G. (1998) Regional meltdown? *The World Today*, 54(10), pp. 251–2
IISS (1998) Russia's desperate military, *Strategic Comments*, 4(9)

■ *Reading*

92

RUSSIA: CHECHNYA

Situation ■ Chechnya has an area of 10,680 km^2 and a population of about 1.1 million. It is located in the Northern Caucasus and borders on Georgia, North Ossetia, Dagestan and the Russian Federation (Stavropol *Kray*). The Chechens are Sufi Muslims and have inhabited the area from the earliest times.

Issue ■ In December 1922, the Chechen were granted an autonomous *oblast* (administrative region) which in December 1934 was merged with that of the Ingush to form the Chechen–Ingush *oblast*. This unit was then raised to the state of autonomous republic in December 1936.

The key event in its subsequent history was the mass deportations from the republic ordered by Josef Stalin in 1944. Almost half a million people were removed to Kazakstan and Uzbekistan. From the 1950s onwards, repatriation gradually occurred, although the lands relinquished in 1944 had since been settled by Russians. Feelings rose during the 1980s and, with the demise of the Soviet Union in 1991, independence was demanded. However, the Ingush population expressed a wish to remain within the Russian Federation. Although not recognised by Russia, Dzhokhar Dudayev was sworn in as president of Chechnya in November 1991 and independence was declared. Tension between Chechnya and what had then become the Russian Federation increased and a financial and economic blockade was imposed. In retaliation, in March 1992, Chechnya cut the oil pipelines from the Grozny fields to Russia.

As the economic situation in Chechnya worsened, Dudayev adopted repressive measures and three of the 18 *rayons* (sub-republic political units) declared their intention to break away both politically and economically from Chechnya. On 11 December 1994, the Russian military intervened until the Khasavyurt Accords of late August 1996 brought a cessation of hostilities and the removal of Russian troops. However, the question of the status of Chechnya was postponed until 31 December 2001. The inability to subdue a small state illustrated clearly the current weakness of at least part of the Russian army. The war with Russia resulted in the destruction of much of the Chechnya infrastructure and indirectly in the growth of the illegal economy.

Status ■ Chechnya remains blockaded and the long drawn-out invasion by Russian troops has continued into 2000. However, Russia still appears to have no policy for the North Caucasus. The fact that on 6 November 1997 an announcement was made that

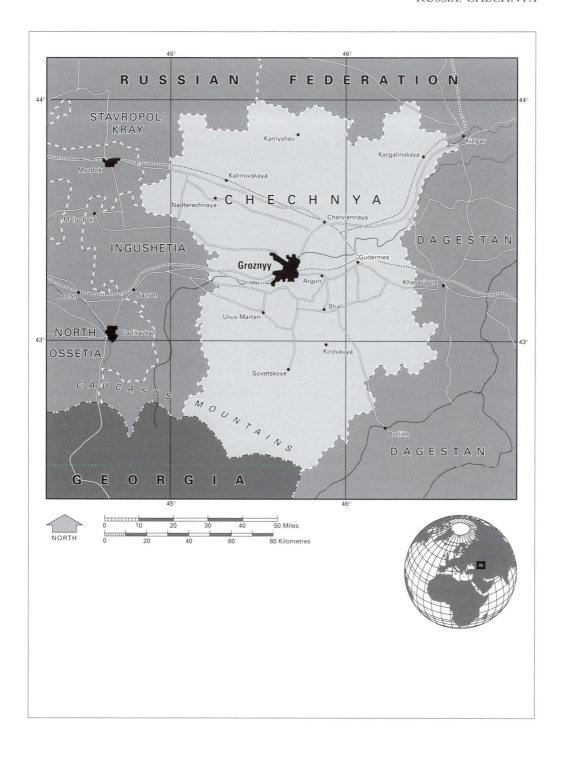

NORTH

0 10 20 30 40 50 Miles
0 20 40 60 80 Kilometres

281

Chechnya would henceforth be known as the Islamic Republic of Chechnya did little to improve the situation. It is the sixth state in the world to use the word 'Islamic' in its official title and the first such entity in the Russian Federation. However, Western support for independence – or even to halt the invasion – is unlikely to be forthcoming in view of the effect this would have upon relations with Russia.

Reading ■ Blandy, C. (1998) *Chechnya: A Beleaguered President*, Camberley: Royal Military Academy Sandhurst (pamphlet)

Blandy, C. (1998) *Chechen Status – Wide Differences Remain*, Camberley: Royal Military Academy Sandhurst (pamphlet)

93

RUSSIA: DAGESTAN

Dagestan has an area of 50,300 km^2 and a population of approximately 1.8 million. It is located on the Caspian Sea in the Northern Caucasus and borders on Azerbaijan, Georgia, Chechnya and the Russian Federation (the *Krays* of Stavropol and Kalmyukia). It therefore occupies an even more strategic position than Chechnya. It lies on the main Russian transport link to the Transcaucasus and the only route through which petroleum from Azerbaijan can be transported to the West. The loss of Dagestan would therefore ensure that the main oil route would have to be constructed through Georgia to Ceyhan in Turkey. Additionally, with Chechnya's initial secession, the loss of Dagestan could result in major turmoil in the North Caucasus.

■ *Situation*

Dagestan was established as a Soviet republic on 20 January 1921 and declared its sovereignty in May 1991. It is distinctive in that the name relates to territory rather than to an ethnic group and there are in fact 32 ethnic groups within its borders. It is one of the most ethnically complex republics of Russia. It is strongly Islamic in character and is situated in a volatile region.

■ *Issue*

Throughout the period of sovereignty there has been rising ethnic tension, with open clashes occurring in 1993. Should one group in this ethnic mosaic gain ascendency, there could be a disastrous domino effect. There is evidence that the problem is being exacerbated by new criminally based networks. There are also potential problems with radical Muslim groups, which receive strong support from Chechnya. Indeed, there is a fear among the leadership that Chechnya is pursuing an alliance with Dagestan which would result in the Northern Caucasus being removed from Russian rule altogether. Thus, as opposed to the sudden events in Chechnya, in Dagestan there is a slow waning of Russian control.

With Russia's declining power in the region and ambiguity over the status of the Caspian Sea, there is a clear danger that Dagestan may become more of a flashpoint than Chechnya. Furthermore, as a result of petroleum, there are strong Western interests in the region and Russian relations with the Islamic world may be at stake.

■ *Status*

Blandy, C. (1998) *Dagestan: the Gathering Storm*, Camberley: Royal Military Academy
  Sandhurst (pamphlet)
IISS (1998) Moscow's rule crumbles in Dagestan, *Strategic Comments*, 4(7)

■ *Reading*

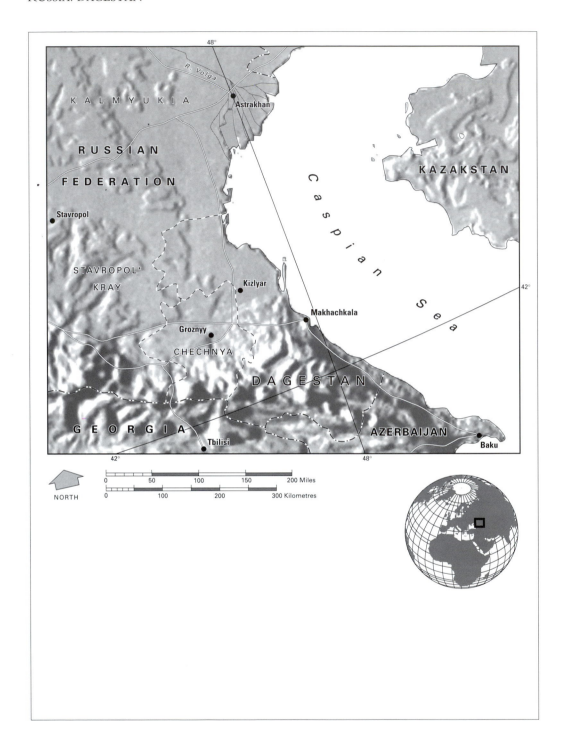

NORTH

0   50   100   150   200 Miles

0   100   200   300 Kilometres

94

RWANDA

Rwanda is a small landlocked state in the Great Lakes region of Africa, immediately to the north of Burundi. With an area of 26,338 km^2, it is very similar in size to Burundi, but its population of just under 8 million is somewhat larger. The distribution of ethnic groups, with 85 per cent Hutu, 14 per cent Tutsi and 1 per cent Twa, is within 1 per cent to that in Burundi. The histories and development of the two countries have remained closely intertwined (see also p. 60). Rwanda has boundaries with Uganda, Tanzania, Burundi and the Democratic Republic of the Congo. After World War I, the country came under Belgium as a League of Nations mandate and a UN trust territory. As in Burundi, Belgian policies expanded the power of chiefs, which favoured the Tutsi. However, inequalities fuelled protests and there was a revolution from 1959 to 1961, as a result of which Belgium moved its support to the Hutu. In 1961, the monarchy was abolished and on 1 July 1962 Belgium ceded power to a republic which was Hutu-dominated.

■ *Situation*

Affected in part by the massacre of Hutus in Burundi, there was violence in 1972 and 1973 which ended in a coup by the military under Juvenal Habyarimana. He continued with single-party rule until 1992, by which time his Mouvement National Rwandais pour le Developpement (MNRD) was in a weakened state.

■ *Issue*

Political reform had been delayed from 1990 by an invasion in that year of the Tutsi-dominated Rwandan Patriotic Front (FPR). The advance was repelled by French, Belgian and Zairean troops and a ceasefire was agreed. Amid tension, talks to broaden the government continued and, on 4 October 1993, the UN established a UN Assistance Mission for Rwanda (UNAMIR).

The death of Habyarimana – who died along with the president of Burundi in an aircraft on 6 April 1994 – sparked an orgy of violence greater than anything previously seen. This reached a crescendo following the reduction of UNAMIR and in the absence of Western troops. The death toll reached a total between 200,000 and 800,000 and was described by the UN as 'genocidal'. By early May 1994, some 1.5 million refugees had crossed into neighbouring countries and the conflict was seen as a major international disaster. On 19 July 1994, the FPR installed a new transitional government.

The Office of the UN High Commissioner for Refugees (UNHCR) encouraged refugees to return home from Zaire (now the Democratic Republic of the Congo), but

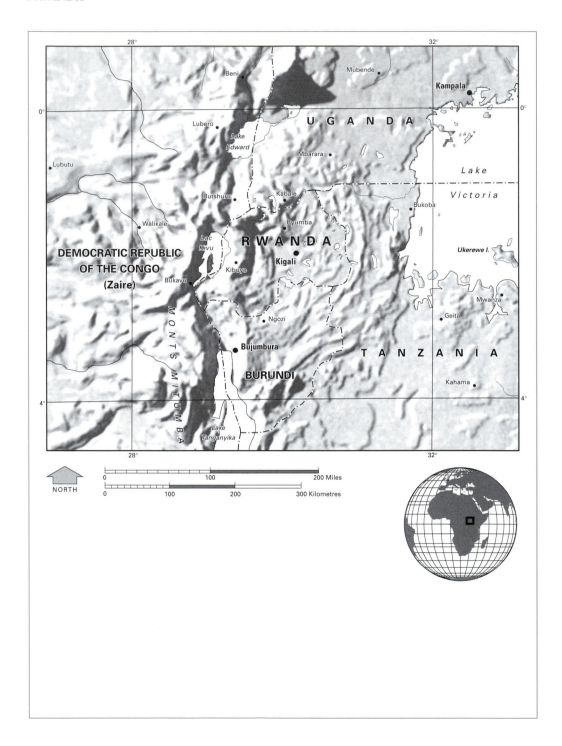

in September 1994 this policy was suspended. On 8 November, the UN Security Council established an International Criminal Tribunal (ICT) for Rwanda, but the first trial did not take place until 3 January 1997.

Meanwhile, there had been clashes with Zaire over the repatriation of refugees, amid claims that Rwanda was preparing to attack the camps. In 1997, Rwanda, with five other African nations, supported Laurent Kabila in his campaign in Zaire (see p. 86).

Violence continued throughout 1998 and 1999 and so far the FPR has failed in its attempts at national reconciliation. Guerrilla attacks continue and it appears that their only objective, in which they are largely successful, is to make Rwanda ungovernable. Rwanda will remain a local flashpoint, but such events, if they happen in Central Africa, will continue to be viewed differently by the international community from similar events in Europe.

■ *Status*

Dowden, R. (1996) The state has melted, the killing continues, *The World Today*, 52(12), pp. 304–6

Plant, M. (1994) Rwanda: looking beyond the slaughter, *The World Today*, 50(8–9), pp. 149–53

Prunier, G. (1999) *Rwanda in Zaire: From Genocide to Continental War*, London: C. Hurst

■ *Reading*

95

THE SENKAKU AND RYUKYU ISLANDS

Situation ■ The Senkaku Islands, known to the Chinese as the Tiaoyu or Tiao Yu Tai Islands, are situated some 200 nml west of Okinawa and about 100 nml north-east of Taiwan. They comprise a small, uninhabited group of five coral islands and scattered islets, the largest of which is only 4 km long and 1.5 km wide. Although physically distinct, the Senkaku Islands are frequently considered in association with the Ryukyu Islands.

The Ryukyu Islands form a chain 650 nml long, dividing the East China Sea from the Pacific. They stretch in a virtually straight line, south-south-west from Kyushu (Japan) and have a total area of 2,246 km^2 and a population of over 1 million. The principal island is Okinawa, which is 1,176 km^2 in area and lies 285 nml from Kyushu. Given their location, both groups of islands have, in their different ways, economic and strategic significance.

Issue ■ In 1874, China relinquished its claims to the Ryukyu Islands and they became part of the Japanese Empire. In 1895, Japan occupied the Senkaku Islands. At the end of World War II, both islands were placed under US military control and in 1951 the San Francisco Peace Treaty included the Senkaku Islands with the Ryukyu group. On 14 May 1972, according to the treaty between Japan and the USA, both island groups reverted to Japan. The major point of stress between Japan and the USA has been Okinawa, on which the USA retained rights to a base.

Previously, on 11 June 1971, Taiwan had claimed the Senkaku Islands, and on 30 December 1971 China also claimed them, as part of its greater claim on Taiwan. In February 1972, the government of Taiwan announced the incorporation of the Senkakus into Taiwan. On 17 February 1972, Japan protested and later issued a document stating that under the Treaty of Shimanoseki (1895) the islands had been incorporated into Japanese territory, along with Taiwan itself and the Pascadores Islands.

On 12 August 1978, Japan and China signed a Treaty of Peace and Friendship, but later that year Chinese fishing boats began operating in the territorial waters of the Senkakus. However, following the treaty it was assumed that China had, for all practical purposes, recognised Japanese control of the Senkaku group. On 21 October 1990, Japanese coastguard patrol boats turned back two Taiwanese vessels, which had been seeking to assert Taiwan's authority over the Senkakus.

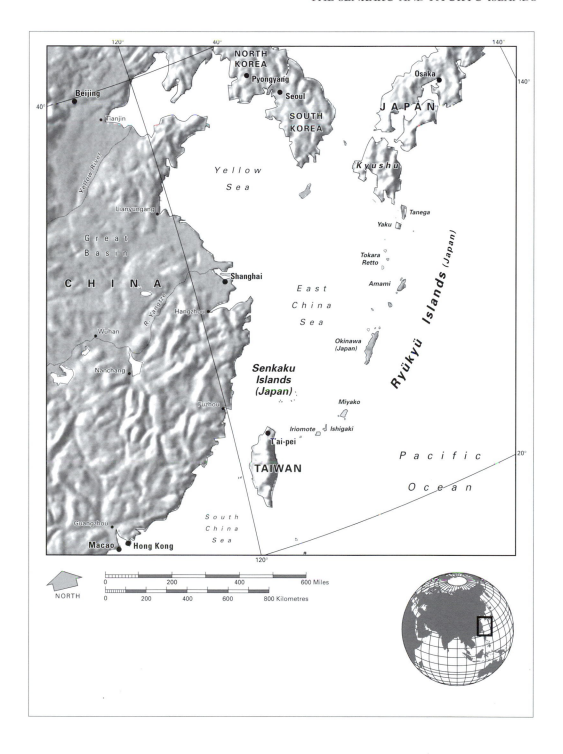

NORTH
KOREA
Pyongyang
Seoul

Beijing

Tianjin

SOUTH
KOREA

Osaka

J A P A N

K y u s h u

Yellow
Sea

Tanega

Yaku

Lianyungang

G r e a t
B a s i n

C H I N A

Shanghai

E a s t
C h i n a
S e a

Tokara
Retto

Amami

Ryūkyū Islands (Japan)

Hangzhou

Wuhan

Okinawa
(Japan)

Nanchang

Senkaku
Islands
(Japan)

Miyako

Fuzhou

Iriomote
Ishigaki

T'ai-pei

TAIWAN

P a c i f i c

O c e a n

Guangzhou

Macao Hong Kong

S o u t h
C h i n a
S e a

NORTH

| 0 | | 200 | | 400 | | 600 Miles |
| 0 | 200 | 400 | 600 | 800 Kilometres |

During 1996, tension again increased. In August, China reiterated that the Senkaku Islands were an inseparable part of Chinese territory. This followed Japanese landings on the islands, which also resulted in protests, not only in China but also in Taiwan and Hong Kong which were worried by what was perceived as a revival of Japanese militarism. Following further stand-offs, in October 1996 a flotilla of 41 vessels from Taiwan, Hong Kong and Macao converged on the Senkaku Islands and were intercepted by 50 Japanese patrol boats. Talks followed, but no progress was made, although no more landings occurred. In May 1997, the Senkaku dispute resurfaced with another Japanese landing on an island. By the end of the year, a new fisheries agreement had been signed between China and Japan, but the issue of the Senkaku Islands remains.

Status ■ The Senkaku Islands are strategically located at the southern end of the East China Sea but, more importantly, their value relates to fishing rights and potential petroleum exploitation. The Ryukyus and Okinawa also guard the approaches to and exits from both the East China Sea and the Sea of Japan. The Senkaku Islands continue to be an issue in the relationship between China and Japan that could well be significant in any period of tension between China and Taiwan. Given the obvious feelings that their occupation arouses, the Senkaku Islands must be considered an important potential flashpoint.

Reading ■ *Chambers World Gazetteer* (1988) Cambridge: Cambridge University Press
Day, A.J. (ed.) (1984) *Border and Territorial Disputes*, Harlow: Longman
Downing, D. (1980) *An Atlas of Territorial and Border Disputes*, London: New English Library

96

THE SHATT AL ARAB

The Shatt al Arab is the river that results from the confluence of the Tigris and the Euphrates at Qurna. Its flow is enhanced by a major tributary, the Karun, the drainage basin of which is entirely in Iran. The Shatt al Arab is 209 km long and has an average width of 400 m, reaching 1 km at the estuary. The average depth along the main shipping reach from Faw to Basrah is 7 m and the navigable channel has been extended by dredging. Throughout much of its course the waterway flows through low, marshy ground into which it loses a major part of its discharge. Since the implementation of Iraq's marsh draining policy, it can only be assumed that these losses have been enhanced.

■ *Situation*

The importance of the Shatt al Arab is that it marks not only the boundary of Iraq and Iran, but also that between the Arab and Persian worlds. At the same time, it provides access to the major Iraqi ports of Faw and Basrah and the key Iranian oil ports of Abadan and Khorramshahr.

The boundary along the Shatt al Arab originates, in the first instance, from the Treaty of Erzurum (1847). The delimitation placed the boundary on the left (east or Persian) bank of the Shatt al Arab, leaving the waterway under Turkish sovereignty but allowing freedom of navigation. This alignment was confirmed by the Constantinople Protocol of 4 November 1913, which delimited the entire boundary in detail and stated specifically that the Shatt al Arab, except for certain islands, was under Turkish sovereignty. Meanwhile, demarcation was complete by October 1914 and the boundary followed the low-water mark on the Persian side of the Shatt, with the exception of the area around Khorramshahr, where it followed the *thalweg* (line of deepest water). In 1934, Iran challenged both the treaty and the protocol and there followed on 4 July 1937 a Frontier Treaty between Iran and Iraq which reaffirmed it with the exception of the Abadan area where, as in the Khorramshahr area, the boundary was moved from the low-water mark to the thalweg. Thus, Iraq controlled the waterway except for the two main Iranian port areas.

■ *Issue*

However, there were still Iranian fears over freedom of navigation and on 6 March 1975, in a joint communiqué between the two countries, Iraq conceded a *thalweg* boundary throughout the length of the Shatt. In return, Iran ceased providing aid for Kurds in northern Iraq.

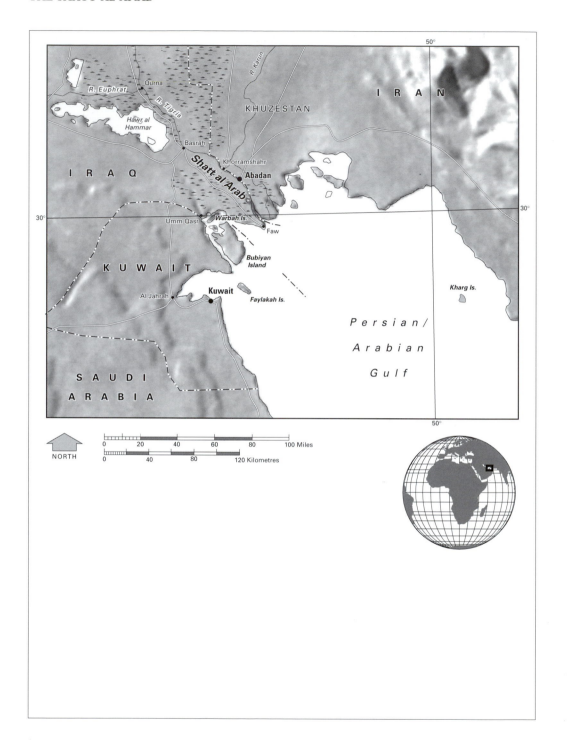

NORTH

0 20 40 60 80 100 Miles

0 40 80 120 Kilometres

In 1980, Iraq abrogated the Joint (Algiers) Communiqué as the two countries moved into their long, drawn-out conflict (see p. 150). In 1990, following the Iraqi invasion of Kuwait and the resultant UN sanctions, Iraq looked to Iran for support. In return, Iraq agreed to return to the *thalweg* boundary. Since the end of the Gulf War in 1991, and following Iraqi military attacks upon the Marsh Arabs, the southern area of Iraq, including the Shatt al Arab, has been protected as a NATO-protected no-fly zone.

The overwhelming significance of the Shatt al Arab is as an outlet to the sea for Basrah and for Abadan and Khorramshahr, Iran's most important ports. For Iraq, with less than 50 km of coastline on the Persian/Arabian Gulf, the Shatt al Arab is critical. Its only other possible outlet is from Umm Qasr, which involves transiting a narrow waterway that is partly under Kuwaiti control. As relations between Iraq and its neighbours have swung violently back and forth, the regime has focused its attention on either Umm Qasr and Khorzubair or on Basrah and the Shatt al Arab. It is inconceivable that the Shatt al Arab and its immediate environs will not remain a key geopolitical flashpoint.

■ *Status*

Amin, S.H. (1984) *Political and Strategic Issues in the Gulf*, Glasgow: Royston

Anderson, E.W. and Rashidian, K. (1991) *Iraq: the Continuing Middle East Crisis*, London: Pinter

Blake, G.H., Dewdney, J. and Mitchell, J. (1987) *The Cambridge Atlas of the Middle East and North Africa*, Cambridge: Cambridge University Press

■ *Reading*

97

SIERRA LEONE

Situation ■ Sierra Leone is a small West African state with an area of 71,740 km² and a population of 4.5 million. It developed as a haven from slavery and conflicts, but conflict now seems endemic. Indeed, Sierra Leone is commonly cited as a state that best illustrates the trend of global anarchy. Its early development trend was very different, dependent upon agriculture and mining, particularly diamonds, which allowed the development of an outstanding educational system.

Issue ■ After the All People's Congress (APC) beat the Sierra Leone People's Party (SLPP) in the elections of 1967, the state was re-built in a highly centralised form by Siaka Stevens who led the government, with one brief military interregnum, from 1967 until 1985. In 1978, the APC became the only legal party. It brought internal stability but at the cost of a growth in inequality, and violence was not far beneath the surface. The successor to Stevens continued in the one-party mode until the coup of 1992 when Valentine Strasser became chairman of the National Provisional Ruling Council (NPRC). As the economy has declined, so ethnic tensions between north and south have increased. In 1994, government troops were reported to have been involved in banditry and proved unable to halt the activities of the Revolutionary United Front (RUF), an offshoot of Taylor's National Patriotic Front of Liberia (NPFL).

By 1994, most of the country was effectively lawless and on 18 May 1995 ECOWAS was called in to negotiate with the rebels. On 16 January 1996, Strasser was overthrown in a coup and a new government promised free and fair elections. These took place during 1996 and the SLPP, together with its candidate for presidency, Ahmed Kabbah, were successful. However, there was sporadic fighting throughout 1996 and 1997 and the government was overthrown. The *junta* abolished the constitution and banned political parties which resulted in further extreme violence and human rights abuses. When fighting took place between the forces of the *junta* and ECOWAS troops, 300,000 people fled the country. On 13 February 1998, ECOWAS forces captured Freetown and on 10 March Kabbah was reinstated.

Status ■ At the present time, it is doubtful whether Sierra Leone qualifies for classification as a sovereign state. ECOMOG troops control, on behalf of the current leadership, some 90 per cent of Sierra Leone, but there seems little chance of any stability after their departure. The government faces the devastating problems of resurrecting an economy that is virtually prostrate, re-integrating thousands of internal and external refugees and

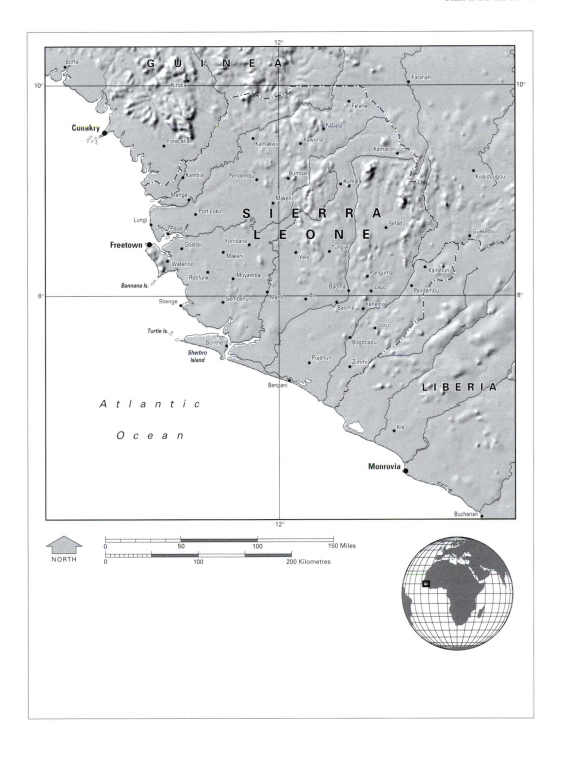

bringing the remainder of the country, together with the RUF, back into society. As with several other small countries in Africa, Sierra Leone will remain a geopolitical flashpoint, but one of only local interest.

Reading ■   Olonisakin, F. (1998) Mercenaries fill the vacuum, *The World Today*, 54(6), pp. 146–8

Riley, S. (1996) *Liberia and Sierra Leone: Anarchy and Peace in W. Africa?* Conflict Studies 287, London: Research Institute for Study of Conflict and Terrorism

Shearer, D. (1997) Dial an army, *The World Today*, 53(8–9), pp. 203–5

Shearer, D. (1998) Private Armies and Military Intervention, *Adelphi Paper* 316, Oxford: Oxford University Press

98

THE SINO-RUSSIAN/SOVIET UNION BOUNDARY

Stretching from the Pamir plateau of Central Asia to the Pacific Ocean, the 6,640 km boundary between China and Russia is divided into two sections by Mongolia. The eastern sector, separating Manchuria from Siberia, runs for 3,700 km, primarily along the courses of the rivers Argun, Amur and Ussuri. The western sector between Sinkiang and the FSU states of Kazakstan, Kyrgyzstan and Tajikistan is 3,000 km in length and crosses some of the highest mountains in the world.

■ *Situation*

In the eastern sector, control of certain areas was established by both the Chinese and the Russian empires in the 17th century and there was sporadic fighting between them. The Treaty of Nerchinsk in 1689 fixed the boundary between the two empires north of the Amur River, along the line of the Stanovoi mountains. As China weakened and Russian strength grew, the balance changed and the Treaty of Aigun (1858) gave Russia sovereignty over some 480,000 km^2 north of the Amur River, while a further 330,000 km^2 east of the Ussuri River were placed under joint Sino-Russian sovereignty. Later in 1858, these changes were confirmed at the Treaty of Tientsin (Tiajin), and at the subsequent Treaty of Peking in 1860 Russia gained the area east of the Ussuri and defined the Central Asian boundary. However, Chinese control in Sinkiang (Xinjiang) was tenuous and at the Treaty of Chuguchak (1864) the Russian claim for 900,000 km^2 territory that had been under China's control was accepted.

■ *Issue*

By 1871, Russia had occupied the Ili and Tekkes valleys up to Kulja and by 1877, with Russian aid, Xinjiang was finally subdued by China. At the Treaty of St Petersburg (1881), Russia agreed to evacuate half the territory it had occupied in return for retention of the other half and territorial concessions further north, to the east of Lake Zaysan. Thus, by the end of the 19th century, with Russian expansion into the Pamir Knot, the delimitation of the Sino-Russian border was complete.

There then followed the overthrow of the Chinese Empire in 1911 and the Bolshevik revolution in 1917. The new regime in China demanded the abrogation of all the 'unequal treaties' while, with the Karakhan Declaration of 25 July 1919, the Soviet Union stated that past treaties were null and void and it renounced seizures of territory. Significantly, the treaties of Aigun, Peking and Chuguchak were not mentioned in the declaration. On 31 May 1924, there was a Sino–Soviet agreement to annul the treaties

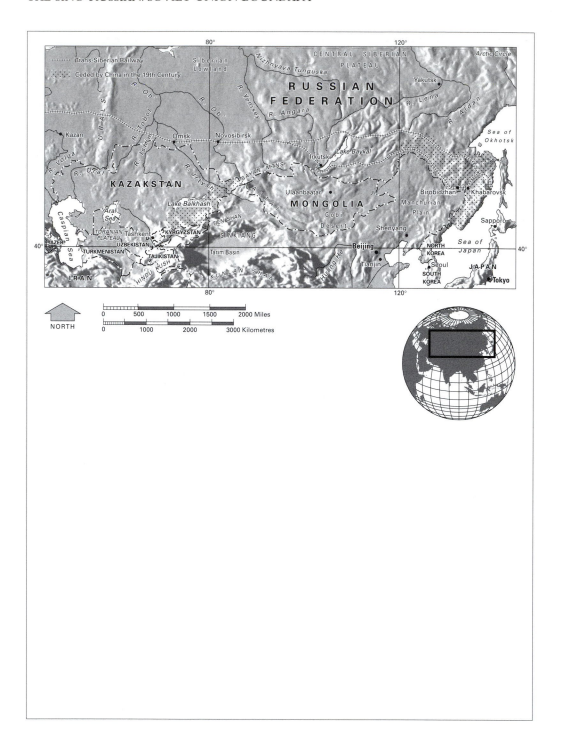

and demarcate the boundaries again, but pending the completion of this, the current boundaries were to be maintained. Following the communist victory in China in 1949, a 30-year Treaty of Friendship, Alliance and Mutual Assistance was signed with the Soviet Union in 1950.

From the 1960s until recently, relations between China and the Soviet Union/Russia deteriorated; there were numerous boundary clashes and the maps produced by each side were disputed. A particularly violent confrontation took place along the eastern sector in 1969, and China also identified 20 areas in Xinjiang that were in dispute. In total, some 1.5 million km^2 were at issue, including the Russian outlet to the Pacific and part of the trans-Siberian railway.

With *glasnost* and the collapse of the Soviet Union, relations with China have improved greatly. A new boundary agreement was reached on 16 May 1991, one element of which included the return to China of a section of territory in the far east of Siberia. In October 1995, a border agreement was signed settling the disputes over the western sector, but at the time it was stated that the eastern sector was already the subject of agreement. In April 1997, Russia and China discussed boundary issues with Kazakstan, Kyrgyzstan and Tajikistan. By November 1997, it was announced that, with the exception of two islands in the Amur River, all issues connected with demarcating the eastern side of the boundary had been settled and both sides stated their willingness to start demarcation of the western sector.

While the boundary issue itself is largely settled, Russian fears have grown in the light of Chinese predominance in the Far East. The Russian Far East increasingly depends economically upon north-east China and there is concern over the future territorial integrity of the area. However, at the local level military forces in the boundary region have been reduced by both sides, and at the international level there have been strong Russian initiatives to develop a triangular partnership with China and India. In the western sector, Russian anxiety continues over cross-border conflicts in Afghanistan and Tajikistan, while Chinese concerns about possible separatist movements in Xinjiang Province continue. Therefore, although the boundary issues appear to be finally settled, the border region, both in the east and the west, is likely to remain a key geopolitical flashpoint.

■ *Status*

Garnett, S. (1998) *Limited Partnership: Russia–China Relations in a Changing Asia*, Washington, DC: Carnegie Endowment for International Peace

Karan, P.P. (1964) The Sino-Soviet border dispute, *Journal of Geography*, LXIII(5), pp. 216–22

■ *Reading*

Kim, W. (1994) Sino-Russian relations and Chinese workers in the Russian Far East: a porous border, *Asian Survey*, 34(12), pp. 1064–76

US Department of State (1974) *China–U.S.S.R. Boundary*, International Boundary Study No. 64 (revised), January, Washington, DC: Office of the Geographer, Bureau of Intelligence and Research

99

SOMALIA

Located along the coast of the Horn of Africa, Somalia today is an amalgam of former colonial territories. It is a large country with an area of 637,657 km^2, but with a population of only around 9.3 million. This can be compared with the populations of its neighbours: Ethiopia has more than 56 million and Kenya has in excess of 30 million. Besides Kenya and Ethiopia, Somalia also has a boundary with Djibouti, the former French Somaliland. It is strategically located near the entrance to the Red Sea but has been severely weakened by constant conflict.

■ *Situation*

The Somalis, a homogeneous group of pastoralists, had long roamed the whole Horn of Africa when European colonialism intervened in the latter part of the 19th century. The UK established the Somaliland Protectorate in northern Somalia in 1886, France established French Somaliland in 1888 and in 1905, Italy took over southern Somalia. During the same period, the Ogaden was ceded to Ethiopia and the Northern Frontier District became part of Kenya. These were particularly traumatic events for a people of one language, one religion and one ethnicity. In the event, the spark for resistance was generated by Islam.

■ *Issue*

After World War II, the spirit of nationalism grew and independence was obtained for British Somaliland on 26 June 1960. Five days later, it joined with southern Somalia to become the new nation, the Somali Republic. However, the new multi-party state was soon beset with tensions between north and south, as well as economic problems and a war over the boundary with Ethiopia. On 21 October 1969, the military government – the Supreme Revolutionary Council (SRC) – took over, led by Mohammed Siad Barre. The country became socialist and was renamed the Somali Democratic Republic.

The Siad Barre regime lasted until January 1991, but never overcame the problems resulting from the harsh environment of the country and the difficulties of attempting to produce a stable state from an essentially tribal pastoral economy. Furthermore, there has been constant hostility with Ethiopia and a full-scale war which cost thousands of lives in 1997–8. Additionally, internal unrest had increased with the rise of the Somali National Movement (SNM).

Subsequent to the regime of Siad Barre, there has been no stable government. Numerous factions have competed for power under a variety of warlords, the best known of whom was Farah Aidid. Eventually, in August 1992, with reports of mass starvation, the UN

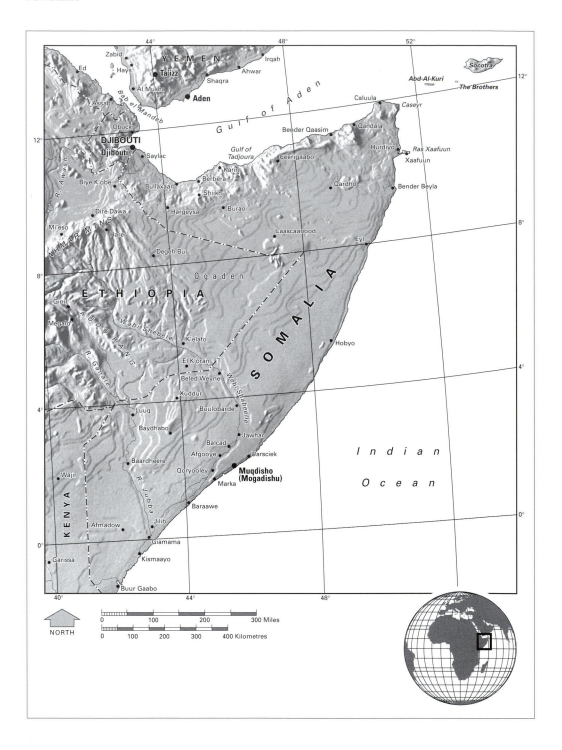

44°   48°   52°

Zabid   YEMEN   Irqah   Socotra   12°
Ed   Hays   Ta'izz   Shaqra   Ahwar   Abd-Al-Kuri   The Brothers
Al Mukha   Aden   Caluula
Assab   Gulf of Aden   Qandala   Caseyr
Obock   Bender Qaasim   Qandala
DJIBOUTI   Hurdiyo   Ras Xaafuun
Djibouti   Saylac   Gulf of   Xaafuun
Biye K'obe   Tadjoura   Ceerigaabo
Bullaxaar   Karin   Qardho   Bender Beyla
Dire Dawa   Berbera   Shiikh   Burao
Mi'eso   Hargeysa   Laascaanood   Eyl   8°
Harer   AHMAR MTNS   Degeh Bur
Ogaden   SOMALIA
ETHIOPIA
Ginir   Wabi Shebele   K'elafo   Hobyo
Megalo   AUDO RANG   El K'oran
R. Ganale   Beled Weyne   4°
Luuq   Xuddur   Wabi Shabeelle
Baydhabo   Buulobarde
Balcad   Jawhar   Indian
Baardheere   Afgooye   Uarsciek   Ocean
Wajir   Qoryooley   Muqdisho
KENYA   Marka   (Mogadishu)
R. Jubba   Baraawe   0°
Afmadow   Jilib
Garissa   Giamama
Kismaayo
Buur Gaabo

40°   44°   48°

NORTH

0   100   200   300 Miles
0   100   200   300   400 Kilometres

dispatched a peacekeeping force to guard relief supplies. In December 1992, the USA sent forces to Somalia as part of a multinational United Task Force (UNITAF) which comprised some 35,000 men. After some reverses, the US forces withdrew and peacekeeping operations were handed over to a new UN Operation in Somalia (UNOSOM II). However, intense fighting continued and, being unable to reconcile the many rival Somali factions, the UN withdrew UNOSOM II in late March 1995.

Aidid continued his offensive, but died on 1 August 1996. Nevertheless, hopes for any improvement were dashed when the Somali National Alliance (SNA) elected Aidid's son as the interim president of Somalia. Finally, in mid-November 1996, 26 groups, including all the major factions except that of Aidid, agreed at a meeting sponsored by the OAU to the creation of a National Salvation Council (NSC).

In December 1997, most of the factions signed a new peace accord. This provided for an ■ *Status* end to conflict, a three-year interim government shared by the various factions and the elimination of the Green Line sectoral demarcation in the capital Mogadishu. The Green Line had delineated the different zones of the warlords. Somalia is at present essentially stateless, but it is not anarchic. What has happened is that the main zones of the country have developed their own political structures. There is still conflict in the south and tensions remain with Ethiopia, but there is more stability. It was the strategic location of Somalia in the first place that attracted huge levels of foreign aid and military assistance, while the colonial period had produced artificial divisions. Somalia will remain important because of its location, but there must be some hope that it can now, without the interference of West or East, develop a new, more suitable, Somali structure.

Menkhaus, K. (1998) Somalia: political order in a stateless society, *Current History*,   ■ *Reading*
    97(619), pp. 220–4
Peterson, D. (1998) Finding African solutions to African problems, *Washington Quarterly*,
    21(3), pp. 149–58
Prunier, G. (1998) Somaliland goes it alone, *Current History*, 97(619), pp. 225–8

100

SOUTH LEBANON

Situation ■ Located centrally in the Levant at the eastern end of the Mediterranean, Lebanon is at the historical crossroads of the world and has been the scene of virtually continuous conflict since shortly after its independence in 1943. It has an area of 10,400 km^2 and a population of just over 3 million. Despite its small size, Lebanon is characterised by great variations in relief, including mountains which provide it with far more rainfall than any of its neighbours. More significantly, Lebanon has an extremely complex social mosaic, well illustrated by the religious differences. The population is just under 60 per cent Muslim and just over 40 per cent Christian, but the Muslims are divided into Shi'a, Sunni and Druse in the approximate ratio of 6:4:1 respectively, and the Christians comprise (as percentage of the total population) Maronites (25 per cent), Greek Orthodox (7 per cent), Armenian Orthodox (5 per cent) and Greek Catholic (4.5 per cent).

In 1943, France, which held the League of Nations mandate for the region, developed the 'National Pact' as a basis for power-sharing between Christians and Muslims in Lebanon. The pact was based on a census conducted in 1932, which showed Christians and Muslims to be in the ratio 6:5, and it was agreed that the offices of state would be awarded according to religion. Thus, the structure was rigid and based upon an earlier census, the validity of which can only be conjectured. Furthermore, since 1943 the population has undergone constant change which has produced an ever-increasing number of Muslims.

Tensions in Lebanon have arisen from internal conflicts, the Arab–Israeli confrontation and incursions from both Syria and Israel. The current key issue is the future of South Lebanon and the security zone established there.

Issue ■ After the Arab–Israeli wars of 1948–9 and 1967 (see p. 257), large numbers of Palestinian refugees settled in Lebanon, altering the delicate population balance. Then, following its expulsion from Jordan in 1970, the headquarters of the Palestine Liberation Organisation (PLO) was established in Lebanon. The history of South Lebanon as a distinctive entity and battleground dates effectively from about 1970. Between 1970 and the major Israeli invasion of 1982, the area endured almost continuous turmoil as a result of the Arab–Israeli conflict. By 1975, there were some 400,000 Palestinian refugees, mostly in camps in South Lebanon. The plight of the refugees attracted some support from fellow Arabs, but hostility from the Maronites, and Palestinian cross-border raids brought Israeli reprisals. In 1973, the Maronite militia first came into conflict with the Palestinian

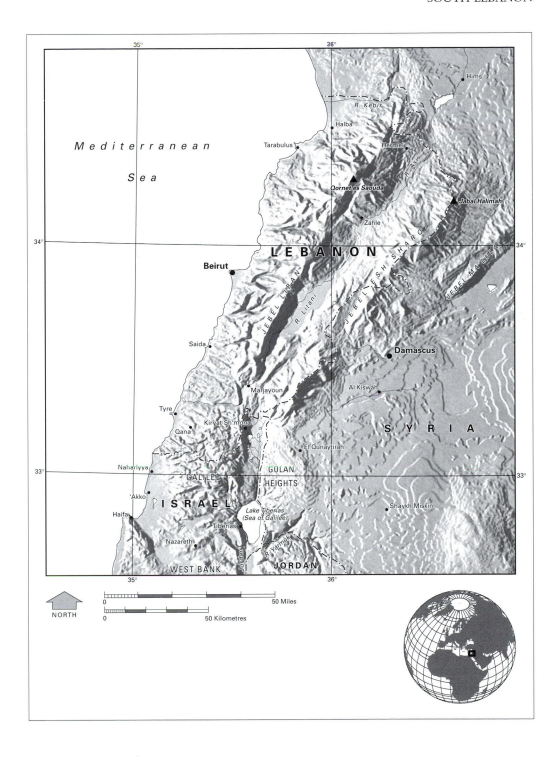

guerrillas and in the following few years a number of more extreme organisations emerged. In 1974, the Shi'a Muslims began to organise Amal groups (freedom fighters) and by mid–1975, there was full-scale civil war. However, Syria imposed a provisional settlement, although in the south fighting resumed between Palestinians and Christians. In response to this and PLO attacks across the boundary, Israeli forces invaded as far north as the Litani River. The result was that at the ceasefire of July 1978, the key military positions were handed over to the Lebanese Christian militia and a semi-independent state of Free Lebanon was established. In promoting the disintegration of Lebanon, Israel was providing itself with a buffer zone to ensure the security of northern Galilee.

Israeli attacks on Palestinian positions continued in the early 1980s and then on 6 June 1982, in 'Operation Peaceful Galilee', the Israeli military advanced as far as west Beirut. The aim was the removal of the PLO and this was achieved, following an agreement of 19 August 1982. However, the invasion, together with two massacres in Palestinian refugee camps (Chattila and Sabra), brought international condemnation. Given a guaranteed demilitarised zone adjacent to its northern border, Israel offered to withdraw and an agreement was reached on 17 May 1983. The security zone, extending some 10 km from the boundary and patrolled by the Israeli-backed South Lebanon Army (SLA), was set up and Israel retained a right of re-entry into the zone. The security zone of South Lebanon constitutes the one almost continuously active front between Israel and the Arabs.

Status ■ South Lebanon is the one area in which Israel continues to suffer regular military losses. In April 1996, Hezbollah (an Islamic guerrilla group) had shelled the Israeli settlement of Kiryat Sh'mona and Israel in response initiated 'Operation Grapes of Wrath' which led to a massacre at Qana in which 110 civilians were killed. The name of Qana remains symbolic throughout the Arab world. The new Israeli government of 1999 has declared that it will leave South Lebanon, but in doing so, it would lose a significant bargaining tool. Peace in the region depends upon Israel's relationship with Syria and this must at some stage include the evacuation of the whole or part of the Golan Heights (see p. 126). At present, Israel and Syria can exert pressure on each other through South Lebanon, but it appears that there is strong popular pressure in Israel for a withdrawal which would bring an end to the Israeli military death toll. Furthermore, Hezbollah may now be not only militarily stronger but also more effective than the Israeli army and the SLA in South Lebanon. South Lebanon is one of the most critical global geopolitical flashpoints.

Reading ■ Garfinkle, A. (1997) Israel's abiding troubles in Lebanon, *Orbis*, 41(4), pp. 603–12
Gordon, S. (1998) *The Vulture and the Snake. Counter Guerrilla Air Warfare: The War in Southern Lebanon*, Jaffa: Israel Centre for Strategic Studies

Hinnebusch, R. (1998) Pax-Syriana? *Mediterranean Politics*, 3(1), pp. 137–60
Rapoport, D.C. (ed.) (1988) *Inside Terrorist Organizations*, London: Frank Cass

101

SPITZBERGEN (SVALBARD)

Situation ■ Spitzbergen, an archipelago comprising several large and many small islands, lies some 400 nml north of the Norwegian mainland. On 9 February 1920, Norway gained undisputed sovereignty of the archipelago by means of a treaty signed by 13 countries and, later, acceded to by 36 states, including the Soviet Union. The treaty conferred upon Norway full sovereignty over all islands within an area bounded by latitudes 74° and 81°N and longitudes 10° and 35°E. However, all parties to the treaty enjoyed equal fishing and hunting rights on the islands and in the territorial waters and had equality in all maritime, industrial, mining and commercial activities. These activities were limited to peaceful uses and, as a result, in the late 1940s Norway was able to resist Soviet pressure to station a military garrison in Spitzbergen.

The population of the islands comprises approximately 2,000 Russians, based at Barentsberg and Pyramiden, and 1,000 Norwegians, centred at Longyerbyen, both communities being concerned with coal mining.

Issue ■ The 1920 treaty made no provision relating to the continental shelf beyond territorial waters; the area, including Spitzbergen itself, covers almost 400,000 nml^2. Problems arose in 1970 when Norway asserted jurisdiction over the shelf surrounding Spitzbergen, claiming it as a natural prolongation of Norway's mainland continental shelf. In contrast, the Soviet Union maintained that Spitzbergen had its own continental shelf and it was only to that that the treaty should apply.

In 1970, Norway introduced a fisheries protection zone as part of a Norwegian EEZ. The effect of this 200 nml EEZ extension was that all sea-lines to the northern ports of the Soviet Union passed through waters under Norway's jurisdiction. Given the vital importance of the Kola Peninsula bases to the Soviet Union (see p. 174), attempts were made to persuade Norway to accept joint administration. Fearing that this would in effect give the Soviet Union control, Norway refused. As Soviet military activity in the region increased during the 1970s, there were numerous violations of the 1920 treaty.

Status ■ The maritime boundary issues remain unresolved, but the end of the Cold War has resulted in a major decrease in tension. Future developments depend upon political and economic changes in Russia in general and, specifically, upon future military requirements for the Kola Peninsula. Geopolitically, the issue of Spitzbergen must be considered dormant.

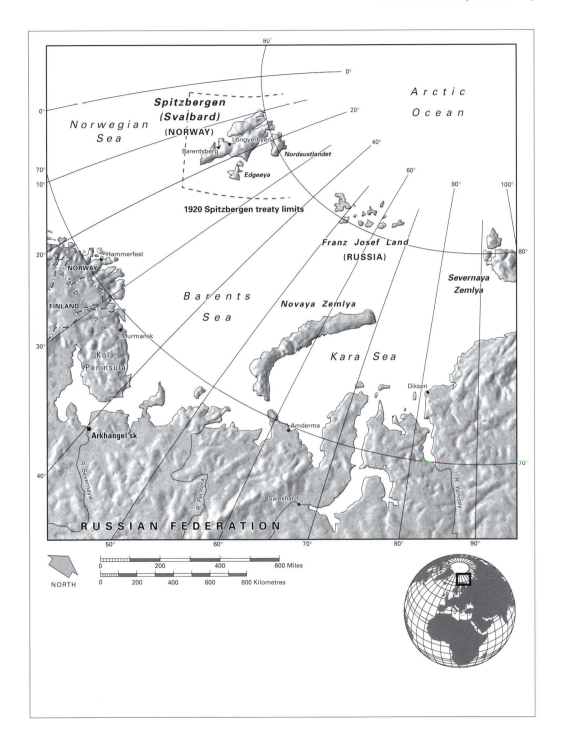

Spitzbergen
(Svalbard)
(NORWAY)

Longyerbyen

Barentsberg

Nordaustlandet

Edgeøya

1920 Spitzbergen treaty limits

Norwegian
Sea

Arctic

Ocean

Franz Josef Land
(RUSSIA)

Severnaya
Zemlya

Hammerfest

NORWAY

FINLAND

Barents
Sea

Novaya Zemlya

Murmansk

Kola
Peninsula

Kara Sea

Dikson

Amderma

Arkhangel'sk

R. Severnaya

R. Pechora

Salekhard

R. Yenisey

RUSSIAN FEDERATION

NORTH

0   200   400   600 Miles

0   200   400   600   800 Kilometres

SPITZBERGEN (SVALBARD)

Reading ■ Armstrong, T., Rogers, G. and Rowley, G. (1978) *The Circumpolar North*, London:
Methuen
Leighton, M.K. (1979) *The Soviet Threat to NATO's Northern Flank*, Agenda Paper No.
10, New York: National Strategy Information Center
Luton, G. (1986) Strategic issues in the Arctic region, in E.M Borgese and N. Ginsburg
(eds), *Ocean Yearbook 6*, Chicago, IL: University of Chicago Press, pp. 399–416

102

THE SPRATLY ISLANDS

On British Admiralty charts the vast expanse of reefs, shoals and islands in the South China Sea is referred to predominantly as 'Dangerous Ground' and the 'Reed Bank', but there is a small group labelled 'Spratly Islands'. It is now common parlance to refer to the entire area, with all its different kinds of eminence, as the 'Spratly Islands'. The islands are located approximately 300 nml west of the Philippine island of Palawan, 300 nml east of Vietnam and 650 nml south of Hainan (China). The Four Claim Area covers approximately 70,000 nml^2 and ranges from 7–12°N and 11–118°E. The islands are very small; the largest, Itu Aba, is only 960 by 400 m (36 ha) and rises just over 2 m above the water.

All five claimants to the Spratly Islands cite geography, particularly proximity, as the factor in their favour. The claims of China, Taiwan and Vietnam are based entirely on distance. This is only possible in the case of China through a different view of geopolitics. The claim of the Philippines follows its 1956 Proclamation, in which an attempt was made to establish the independent state of Kalayaan (Freedom Land) in the Spratlys. This claim was presented on 7 June 1978. The claim of Malaysia is based on geology, in that the islands stand on the Malaysian continental shelf. There are, as a result, overlapping claims, with each of the islands claimed by at least two states. No island is claimed by more than four states. Of the other regional states, the claims of Brunei do not overlap with those of other disputants and Indonesia claims only the Natuna gas field at the southern end of the area.

As part of its larger claim to Indonesia, France annexed the Spratly Islands in 1933. China and Japan protested, the latter claiming continuous commercial occupation since 1917. In 1939, Japan annexed the islands, but in 1946 a Chinese (Kuomintang) naval expedition took possession and garrisoned Itu Aba. At the Treaty of San Francisco in 1951, Japan renounced its claim, but in 1954, after the division of Vietnam, South Vietnam lodged a claim. From that time until the present, there have been claims and counter-claims, with sporadic conflict. In May 1956, the first claim by the Philippines was made and in August 1956 a South Vietnamese garrison was established in the islands. By September 1973, several islands were occupied and South Vietnam promulgated a decree incorporating the Spratlys into its adjacent province. However, on 11 January 1974, China made a general protest and expelled the South Vietnamese from the Paracel Islands (see p. 264). In May 1976, the Philippines announced that a consortium would

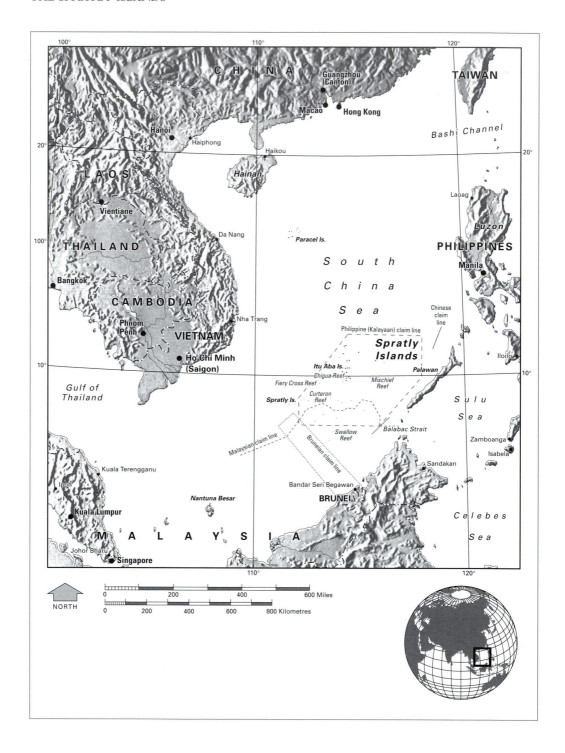

start exploration for petroleum in the area and the Provisional Revolutionary Government (South Vietnam), China and Taiwan protested. With the reunification of Vietnam in July 1976, there was further confrontation with China over the islands. By March 1978, the Philippines had set up garrisons on seven islands.

In 1978, agreements and counter-claims proliferated, and on 14 September 1979 the Philippines stated that its claim was only to the seven islands occupied. This brought forth an immediate protest from Vietnam. Nevertheless, in 1988 these claims and counter-claims were partly resolved by action, when forces from China landed on Fiery Cross and Curteron Reefs. An island-hopping race with Vietnam began. On 14 March, the Chinese and Vietnamese forces clashed near Chigua Reef and three Vietnamese ships were damaged and two sunk. China was accused of obstructing rescue attempts and the Vietnamese were alleged to be 'continuing to seize Chinese islands on the pretext of carrying out rescue operations'. By April, China had control of 6 islands and reefs, and Vietnam had an extra 15, making a total of 21. A Vietnamese call for negotiations was rebuffed but on 13 April 1990, China made a proposal for the joint development of the Spratly Islands. In May 1991, the position became even more complex when Malaysia announced the development of Terumba Layang-Layang Atoll (Swallow Reef) as a tourist resort. This brought forth storms of protest and, as a result, Vietnam reaffirmed its sovereignty in April and in May, while China increased its military activity. In February 1995, Chinese forces occupied Mischief, a territory claimed by the Philippines. This was the first time China had seized territory from any country other than Vietnam, and the Philippines protested strongly.

Tensions between the two states finally eased in November 1998 with an agreement on the joint use of resources on and around Mischief Reef. Meanwhile, in September 1998, Vietnam had occupied two submerged reefs. By the end of November 1998, tension between China and the Philippines had risen again with the arrest of Chinese fishermen and the seizure of six boats, which were claimed to have been fishing near a Philippine island in the Spratlys. On 18 January 1999, the Philippines reported that China had deployed two missile-carrying frigates near Mischief Reef.

■ *Status*

The Spratly Islands, virtually unnoticed until the 1930s, now furnish what many consider to be the key potential flashpoint in South-East Asia and possibly the entire Pacific region. The islands have a certain strategic importance in that major shipping lanes pass around them and their ownership would allow claims of the order of 150,000 nml^2 of sea and sea-bed. All five states maintain their claims and all five occupy some territory in the group. Given the problems of maritime delimitation in the area, the Spratly Islands must remain a key flashpoint.

Reading ■   Bristow, D. (1998) The future of territorial disputes within SE Asia, *The International Security Review*, pp. 317–23

Dzurek, D. (1997) *The Spratly Islands Dispute: Who's on First?* Maritime Briefing, 12(1), Durham: IBRU, University of Durham

Leng, L.Y. (1989) The Malaysian–Philippine maritime dispute, *Contemporary Southeast Asia*, 11(1), pp. 61–74

Townsend–Gault, I. (1998) Preventative diplomacy and pro-activity in the South China Sea, *Contemporary Southeast Asia*, 20(2), pp. 171–90

103

SUDAN

With an area of 2,505,813 km^2, Sudan is the largest state in Africa. Its population of 28 million is Muslim in the north and non-Muslim in the south, thereby making it an effective bridge between Africa and the Middle East. However, it is this division that has been perpetuated in recurrent crises and conflicts since 1930.

■ *Situation*

Sudan has boundaries with Egypt, Libya, Chad, Central African Republic, Democratic Republic of the Congo, Uganda, Kenya, Ethiopia and Eritrea. It has also established a shared resources zone across the Red Sea with Saudi Arabia.

Independence was achieved on 1 January 1956, when the Nationalist United Party (NUP) rejected union with Egypt. Before independence, the country had been designated the Anglo-Egyptian Sudan. However, immediate political rivalry resulted in the first military coup on 17 November 1958. A state of emergency was declared and a full range of repressive measures was imposed. As the conflict in the south deepened, there were several unsuccessful coup attempts and eventually civil war resulted in the October revolution of 1964. Following this, Sudan began a cycle of ineffective civilian and military regimes and a succession of unstable coalitions.

■ *Issue*

With the military coup of Ja'afar Nimeiri on 25 May 1969, there was at least continuity in that his regime remained in power until April 1985. Initially, he aligned himself with the communists, but tensions arose between them and his Revolutionary Command Council (RCC). The regime was further transformed in September 1983 when Shari'a (Islamic) law was decreed. The result was a wave of uprisings in the south, led by John Garang and the Sudan People's Liberation Army (SPLA). The civil war then entered the international arena in that Garang received support from Ethiopia, Libya, Cuba and even Israel, while Nimeiri became the major beneficiary in Africa (after Egypt) of US economic and military aid.

After Nimeiri's downfall in 1985, the cycle of regimes was resumed. Continuity of government followed the military coup of 30 June 1989, which initiated the regime of Omer Hassan el-Bashir. However, despite various peace initiatives, the war in the south continued and there seems little prospect of its termination. Apart from the civil war and the chronic economic instability, Sudan also had problems involving boundary delimitation, conflict overspill and refugees with its neighbours, in particular, Ethiopia, Eritrea, Uganda and Egypt.

315

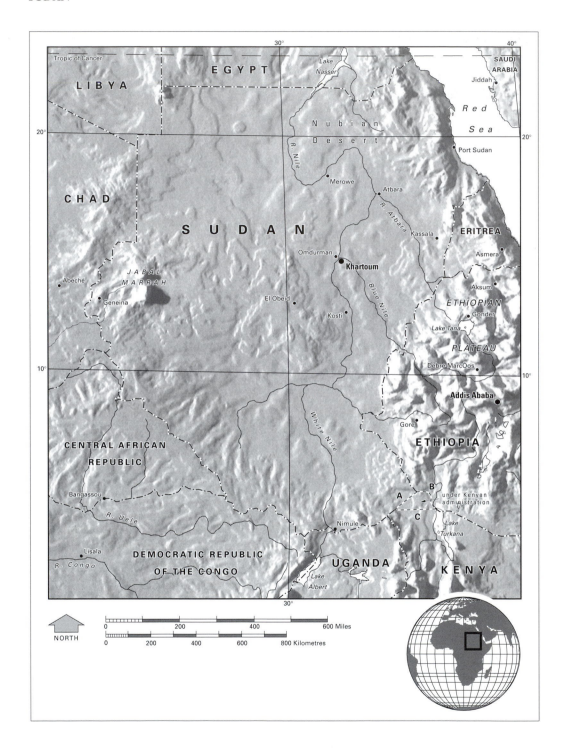

NORTH

| 0 | 200 | 400 | 600 Miles |
| 0 | 200 | 400 | 600 | 800 Kilometres |

While liberalisation has occurred in many parts of Africa, Sudan has constantly been accused of human rights violations against its non-Muslim ethnic groups. The long-running war has now become internationalised and has lost Sudan the support of Western nations. The fact that the war is being fought across a major religious and ethnic fault line has undoubtedly led to its longevity. Sudan is being torn apart by the very factors that make a microcosm of Africa and a bridge with the Middle East. With so many boundaries and boundary issues, it seems certain that Sudan will remain, for the foreseeable future, a major African flashpoint.

■ *Status*

Ahmed, A. (1998) World without honour? *The World Today*, 54(10), pp. 246–8

Deng, F. (1998) Africa's dilemmas in the Sudan, *The World Today*, 54(3), pp. 72–4

Stern, J. (1998) Apocalypse never, but the threat is real, *Survival*, 40(4), pp. 176–9

■ *Reading*

104

THE SUEZ CANAL

Situation ■ Suez is the most important canal in the world, providing the only waterway through the World Island (the main global landmasses of Asia, Europe and Africa). The only other alternatives are the Cape of Good Hope route to the south and, to the north, the North East Passage which, as a result of severe ice conditions, has never been developed. The Suez Canal links the Mediterranean to the Red Sea by way of Suez and, unlike the Panama Canal, it is at sea level. In 1869, the 165.8 km-long Suez Canal, designed by Ferdinand de Lesseps, was opened.

Originally 21.9 m wide and 7 m deep, by 1956 the maximum permissible draft had risen to 10.7 m and this was increased in 1961 to 11.3 m, in October 1980 to 16.1 m and then to the present maximum of 19.5 m. From October 1980, the width was increased to 270 m, with the result that the canal could then take tankers up to 150,000 tonnes, fully laden. Phase two, postponed as a result of the world shipping recession and the decline in oil consumption, would have produced an increase in width to 315 m and in depth to 23.5 m, thereby allowing the passage of ships of 250,000 tonnes. The average transit time is 24 hours and approximately 80 ships per day use the canal.

Issue ■ In 1875, Britain acquired a half share of the Suez Canal Company and in 1882, largely to guarantee its control of the canal, occupied Egypt. The position of Britain was recognised internationally by the Constantinople Convention of 1888. A series of strategic locations which linked Britain with India – Gibraltar, Malta, Suez and Aden – became known as the 'imperial lifeline' and the canal's protection became a major British occupation.

When Egypt nationalised the Canal Company in 1956, the UK and France, in collusion with Israel, declared war on Egypt in order to protect their interests, but the hostilities were opposed by both superpowers and the conflict ended quickly. However, the canal itself was blocked by wrecked ships and was closed from October 1956 until April 1957. It was again closed in June 1967 as a result of the Six-Day War and, owing to political problems, not re-opened until June 1975. Due to the lengthy closure, the infrastructure of world shipping reorganised itself with the construction of the SUMED pipeline – which provided an alternative to the Suez Canal – and the development of the Cape route. The other major factor was the emergence of supertankers which were designed to combat the extra costs of the Cape route but were too large to transit Suez.

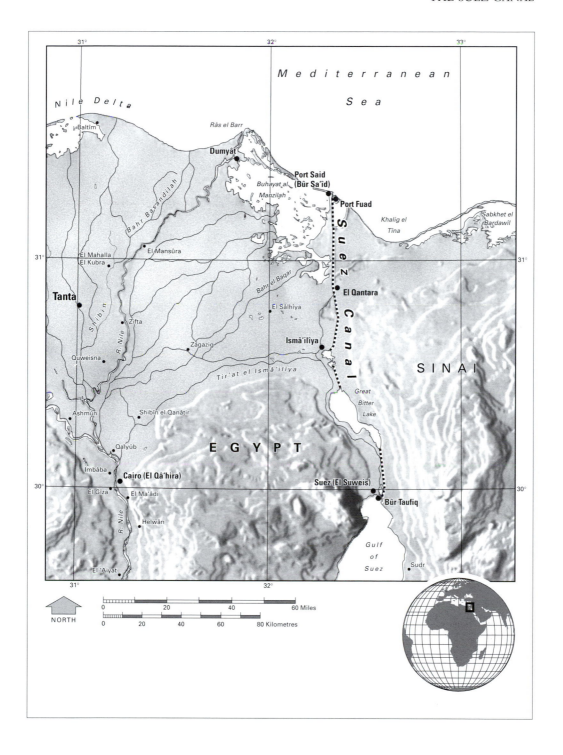

Mediterranean
Sea

Nile Delta

Baltìm

Râs el Barr

Dumyât

Port Said
(Bûr Sa'îd)

Buhayat al
Manzilah

Port Fuad

Khalig el
Tîna

Sabkhet el
Bardawîl

Bahr Basândilah

El Mahalla
El Kubra

El Mansûra

Suez Canal

Tanta

Bahr el Baqar

El Qantara

El Sâlhîya

Shibîn R. Nile

Zifta

Zâgazig

Ismâ'ilîya

SINAI

Quweisna

Tir'at el Ismâ'ilîya

Ashmûn

Shibîn el Qanâtir

Great
Bitter
Lake

E G Y P T

Qalyûb

Imbâba

Cairo (El Qâ'hira)

El Gîza

El Ma'âdi

Suez (El Suweis)

Bûr Taufiq

Helwân

R. Nile

Gulf
of
Suez

Sudr

El 'Aiyât

NORTH

0   20   40   60 Miles

0   20   40   60   80 Kilometres

319

As a result of these changes, the Suez Canal may never regain its former pre-eminence. Furthermore, the opening of SUMED, a 336 km-long double pipeline in 1975, further reduced trade. Indeed, SUMED is now the main oil routeway from the Red Sea to the Mediterranean.

Status ■ As Western Europe and the USA come to rely increasingly upon oil from the Persian/Arabian Gulf region, so the importance of the Suez Canal should at least be maintained, if not increased. The volume of oil transiting via the Suez will depend largely upon any further pipeline construction. However, the development of the Caspian Basin oilfields will produce significant west-to-east oil movements through the canal and its geopolitical importance is therefore likely to be enhanced. Since it can be so easily blocked, the Suez Canal as a key transport mode must always be a potential flashpoint.

Reading ■ Blake, G.H., Dewdney, J. and Mitchell, J. (1987) *The Cambridge Atlas of the Middle East and North Africa*, Cambridge: Cambridge University Press

Gerges, F. (1994) *The Superpowers and the Middle East*, New York: Westview

Lapidoth, R. (1975) *Freedom of Navigation with Special Reference to International Waterways in the Middle East*, Jerusalem: The Hebrew University

Pickering, J. (1998) *Britain's Withdrawal from East of Suez: the Politics of Retrenchment*, Basingstoke: Macmillan

105

SURINAME

Suriname, the former Dutch Guiana, closely resembles its neighbour, Guyana. The country is, for the most part, densely forested and the majority of the population live on a narrow coastal strip where the chief hazards are potential sea-level rise and saline incursions. The area of Suriname is 163,265 km^2 and the population is 423,000. There is a complex mosaic of ethnic variation and religious adherence. Furthermore, Suriname is virtually a one-product economy, completely dominated by the bauxite industry. This accounts for about 80 per cent of export earnings and it also ensures US interest in the country. Bauxite, an ore of aluminium, is relatively strategic in that there are a limited number of producers, many of which are politically volatile. Suriname is a major supplier to the USA. Politically, the military are dominant and Dutch aid was frozen after a military coup in 1990. Suriname has boundary disputes in both the west and the east. That in the west with Guyana has already been considered in this volume (see p. 132); that in the east – with French Guiana – concerns an area between the Litani and Marouini rivers, both of which are tributaries of the Marowijne River (known as the Maroni in French Guiana, and in both countries as the Lawa). The area at issue is some 5,000 km^2 of thickly forested, mountainous terrain which rises to form the Tumac-Humac (Tumucumaque) range, the common border with Brazil.

In 1680, the French and Dutch agreed on the Maroni River as the boundary between their territorial claims. Although this was only navigable for some 40 km inland, beyond that neither country was interested. However, in the early 19th century differences arose as to whether the boundary followed the Tapanahoni River or the Awa River.

The Portuguese–French Treaty of 1815 and Convention of 28 August 1817 stated that the western boundary of French Guiana was the Tapanahoni River, but the Netherlands protested. In 1861, a French–Dutch commission was unable to decide which river constituted the Upper Maroni and discussions lapsed until 1876. On 29 November 1888, it was agreed to submit the case to arbitration, the selected arbitrator being Alexander III, Tsar of Russia. The arbitration body decided, on 25 May 1891, in favour of the Dutch, as the Awa was defined as the upper course of the Maroni.

The development in the south of the country resulted in further disputes over the tributaries and a conference in early 1905 recommended that the boundary should be the thalweg (line of deepest water) from the Maroni estuary and along the Maroni, Awa and Itany (Litani) rivers. On 30 September 1915, this was modified by agreement when a

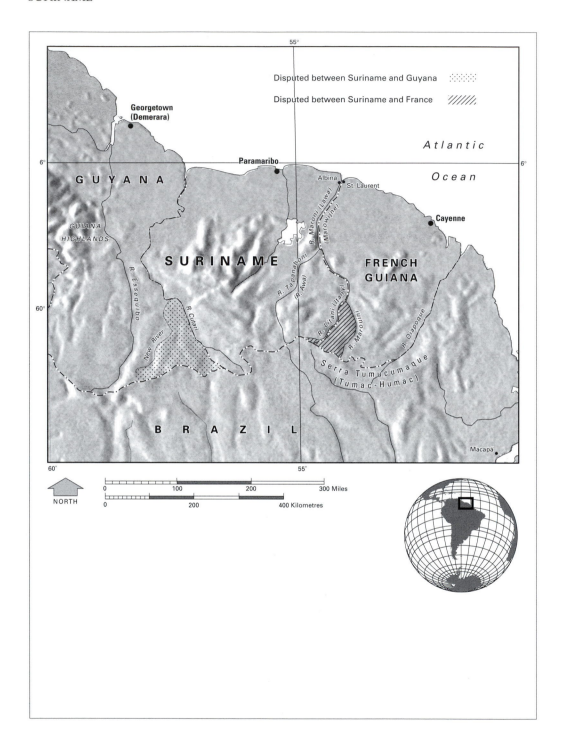

Disputed between Suriname and Guyana

Disputed between Suriname and France

Atlantic

Georgetown
(Demerara)

6°

Paramaribo

Albina

St. Laurent

Ocean

6°

GUYANA

Cayenne

GUIANA
HIGHLANDS

S U R I N A M E

FRENCH
GUIANA

R. Essequibo

R. Tapanahoni

R. Maroni (Lawa)
(Marowijne)

R. Awa)

R. Litani (Itany)

R. Marou

R. Maron

R. Oiapoque

60°

New River

R. Cutari

Serra Tumucumaque
(Tumac-Humac)

B R A Z I L

Macapá

60°

55°

NORTH

0   100   200   300 Miles

0   200   400 Kilometres

median line was substituted for the *thalweg* in the estuary. However, despite the recommendation, the area between the Litani and the Maroni was still claimed by the Netherlands and, since its independence in 1975, by Suriname.

Negotiations in November 1975 and February 1977 formulated a treaty whereby Suriname would recognise French sovereignty over most of the area in return for 500 million francs' development aid for joint development of the mineral wealth of the region. This treaty was initialled on 15 August 1977 but no real progress was made.

Suriname remains a poor country with a legacy of incompetent military rule, but it is a key supplier to the West, particularly the USA, of bauxite. Its boundary dispute with French Guiana remains dormant. The dominant problem is internal conflict over dissatisfaction with the distribution of national wealth. Five armed groups (the Jungle Commando, Tukuyana Amazones, the Mondela, the Angulla and the Koffie Make) have all been effectively disarmed, but the growth of such movements has been unusual in that they have had an economic rather than a political objective. Thus, Suriname is very likely to remain a local flashpoint.

■ *Status*

Brana-Shute, G. (1993) An inside-out insurgency, *Journal of Commonwealth and Comparative Politics*, 31(2), pp. 54–69

Brana-Shute, G. (1995) Suriname: the nation against the state, *Current History*, 94(580)

Child, J. (1985) *Geopolitics and Conflict in South America*, Stanford, CA: Praeger/Hoover Institution Press

The Economist (1989) *The Economist Atlas,* London: Economist Books/Hutchinson

■ *Reading*

106

TACNA

Situation ■ Tacna, a coastal region and town in the far south of Peru, is the focus of the Bolivia–Chile–Peru territorial dispute involving, in particular, Bolivia's loss of access to the sea. It is an arid region at the northern end of the Atacama Desert and is significant mainly for the extraction of nitrates and phosphates.

Issue ■ In 1866 an agreement was reached between Chile and Bolivia for a boundary along latitude 22°S and for profits from the nitrate and guano (phosphate) industries located between latitudes 23° and 25°S to be shared. Eighty-five per cent of the population of Antofagasta Province, the central province covered by the agreement, was Chilean, and this so alarmed Bolivia that it made a secret Treaty of Alliance with Peru in February 1873. Following the seizure of Chilean nitrate companies by Peru in 1875 and Bolivia in 1878, Chile declared war on its two neighbours in 1879. The 'War of the Pacific' ended in defeat for the Peru–Bolivia army in November 1883. With the subsequent Treaty of Ancon on 20 October 1883, Peru ceded to Chile unconditionally and in perpetuity the province of Tarapaca and agreed that the provinces of Tacna and Arica should remain under Chilean administration for 10 years before a plebiscite was taken. A year later, a truce was achieved between Chile and Bolivia as a result of which Bolivia lost its nitrate industry and, far more importantly, access to the Pacific Ocean. This was converted into the Peace Treaty of October 1904 when the absolute and perpetual dominion by Chile over the former Bolivian territory was confirmed and the boundary was demarcated using 96 boundary points. In addition, the Arica–La Paz railway was to be built at Chilean expense, and Bolivia's right to full and free transit through Chilean territory to the Pacific was recognised in perpetuity.

In 1913 the railway was completed, but in 1918 Bolivia demanded an outlet via a sea port in either Tacna or Arica province. Since Chile had failed to provide for the plebiscite, there was US intervention and on 3 June 1929 the Washington Protocol to the Treaty of Ancon awarded Arica to Chile and Tacna to Peru, while Bolivia gained nothing. Furthermore, a provision in the protocol stated that no territory originally belonging to Peru could be ceded to a third party (that is, Bolivia) without Chilean approval. This vastly complicated Bolivia's quest for access to the Pacific. One result was an attempt to gain access to the Atlantic in the Chaco War with Paraguay. A minor compensation was that Bolivia gained right of access to the Atlantic via Paraguay and the Parana River, with the use of Puerto Casado (Paraguay) as a free port.

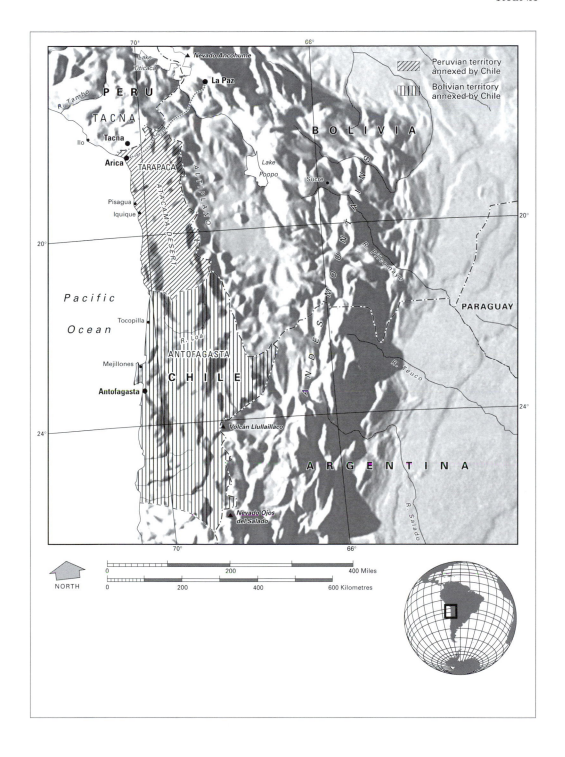

Peruvian territory annexed by Chile

Bolivian territory annexed by Chile

PERU

Lake Titicaca

Nevado Ancohume

La Paz

TACNA

Ilo

Tacna

Arica

TARAPACA

Pisagua

Iquique

ATACAMA DESERT

ALTIPLANO

BOLIVIA

Lake Poopo

Sucre

R. Tambo

Pacific

Ocean

Tocopilla

R. Loa

ANTOFAGASTA

CHILE

Mejillones

Antofagasta

Volcán Llullaillaco

ANDES MOUNTAINS

R. Pilcomayo

PARAGUAY

R. Teuco

ARGENTINA

Nevado Ojos del Salado

R. Salado

NORTH

0   200   400 Miles

0   200   400   600 Kilometres

325

TACNA

In the early 1970s, the threat of a second War of the Pacific loomed and in December 1975, in attempting to solve the Pacific access issue, Chile proposed that Bolivia should:

a) cede an equal amount of territory in return for a corridor;
b) purchase the Chilean section of the Arica–La Paz railway;
c) allow Chile full use of the waters of the Lauca River;
d) demilitarise the corridor; and
e) pay compensation for use of port facilities.

In November 1976, Chile refused to consider a new set of Peruvian proposals whereby Bolivia would receive a 13.5 km-wide corridor along the Chile–Peru frontier, just over 3 km north of the Arica–La Paz railway. An International Zone would be set up, there would be joint control of the Arica port and Bolivia would be allowed to establish a port under its sole sovereignty in a buffer zone which could claim territorial waters.

The latest move occurred on 19 January 1992, when Peru made a concrete proposal for Bolivian access to the Pacific via the Peruvian port of Ilo. It was further agreed that Ilo should be a duty-free port.

Status ■ With the offer by Peru, it appears that the Tacna issue has been settled. However, the long and painful history of disagreement over territory between the three states must mean that, as a flashpoint, Tacna can only be classified as dormant.

Reading ■ Child, J. (1985) *Geopolitics and Conflict in South America*, Stanford, CA: Praeger/Hoover Institution Press

Gamba-Stonehouse, V. (1989) *Strategy in the Southern Oceans*, London: Pinter

Glassner, M.I. (1970) *Access to the Sea for Developing Land-Locked States*, The Hague: Martinus Nijhoff

Glassner, M.I. (1983) The transit problems of landlocked states: the cases of Bolivia and Paraguay, in E.M. Borgese and N. Ginsburg (eds), *Ocean Yearbook 4*, Chicago, IL: University of Chicago Press, pp. 366-89

107

TAIWAN

Taiwan is one major and several smaller islands with a total area of 35,742 km^2, separated from the Chinese mainland by the 160 km-wide Taiwan Strait. It has a population of 21.5 million. Taiwan is held by both the communist Chinese government in Beijing and the nationalist Chinese government in Taipei to be a province of China rather than an independent country. Nevertheless, its continuing status poses major geopolitical problems for the future.

After losing the Sino–Japanese War in 1895, China ceded Taiwan to Japan. After World War II, it was again ceded, but this time to the Republic of China (ROC) – at that time run by the Nationalist Government – and the Kuomintang (KMT) under Chiang Kai-shek. Having been driven from mainland China by the communists in 1949, the KMT moved to Taiwan. The corruption and repression of the government was such that an uprising occurred in 1947 which resulted in a deep division between the 1.5–2 million Chinese new settlers and the Taiwanese.

With the outbreak of the Korean War in 1950, the USA revived support for the KMT and, therefore, Taiwan. With government planning and assistance, multinationals were attracted and the economy of Taiwan grew extraordinarily rapidly. Foreign investment and science were employed to develop a range of industries and services which completely transformed Taiwan society.

However, political development did not keep pace and the People's Republic of China (PRC) was awarded the Chinese seat at the UN on 25 October 1971. As a result, the ROC is recognised by none of the major powers, despite the fact that it has extensive trade relations with them. The visit of President Nixon to the PRC in February 1972 confirmed the US position that Taiwan was part of China.

With the death of Chiang Kai-shek in 1975, the regime became less authoritarian and the opposition was able to establish a party, the Democratic Progressive Party (DPP) in 1986. Meanwhile, the estrangement from the USA continued and on 1 January 1979 it was announced that diplomatic relations, together with the Mutual Defence Treaty, would be terminated. This was a selective policy in that trade continued and, in 1992, US fighter aircraft were sold to Taiwan to balance the purchase of similar aircraft by the PRC from Russia.

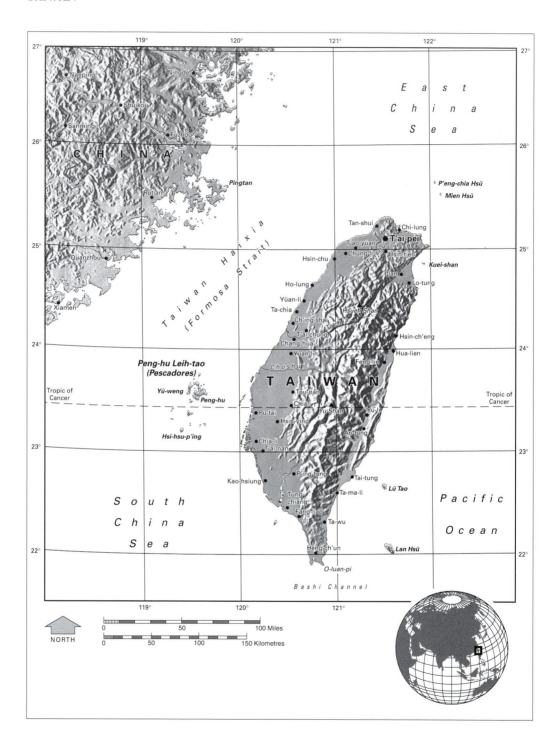

Following the planned return of Hong Kong to China in 1997, and the return of Macao ■ *Status*
on 20 December 1999, the remaining territory to be reunified will be Taiwan. The date
for this has been put tentatively at 2010, but China may not wish to wait that long.
Taiwan remains a non-state entity, but is an Asian tiger economy, alongside South Korea.
With the decline of the KMT, the major opposition party, the DPP, which advocates
independence may achieve ascendency. However, there have been improved contacts
and the first-ever Taiwan–China project – oil exploration in the Taiwan Strait – was
agreed in June 1998. Nonetheless, during the 1996 elections in Taiwan, the PRC
exerted intimidatory military pressure. Given its commitment to the defence of Taiwan
under the 1979 Taiwan Relations Act, the USA responded by sending a powerful task
force. This event must raise the question as to whether the USA would be prepared to
indulge in what would be a highly destructive war in the defence of Taiwan. This
potential confrontation represents a major geopolitical flashpoint of the future.

Bridges, B. (1998) Keeping a cool distance, *The World Today*, 54(6), pp. 162–3   ■ *Reading*
Lijun, S. (1998) *The Evolution of China's Perception of Taiwan*, Canberra: Strategic and
    Defence Studies Centre
Tucker, N. (1998) China–Taiwan: US debates and policy choices, *Survival*, 40(4),
    pp. 150–67
Yang, A. (1997) *Crisis, What Crisis?* Taipei: Policy Studies

108

TAJIKISTAN

Situation ■ With an area of 143,100 km^2, Tajikistan is the smallest of the five Central Asian FSU states, but its population of more than 5.8 million is greater than those of either Kyrgyzstan or Turkmenistan. Unlike the other languages of the Central Asian states, which are within the Turkic group, Tajik is related to Farsi and this has resulted in ties with Iran rather than with Turkey. The state has boundaries with Uzbekistan, Kyrgyzstan, China and Afghanistan. The boundaries with the two Central Asian states are particularly contorted in the area of the Fergana Valley, a high-profile global flashpoint (see p. 191). Relations with Uzbekistan are complicated by the fact that almost 25 per cent of the population of Tajiskistan is Uzbek.

Issue ■ The state was conquered by the Red Army and became a Russian republic and, eventually, a separate union republic in 1929. It continued as an intergral part of the Soviet Union until, following rioting in early 1990, sovereignty was declared on 25 August 1990, with the conservative Communist Party structure in control. Independence was declared in August 1991 under the Tajik Socialist Party (TSP), in fact, the renamed Communist Party of Tajiskistan (CPT). The presidential elections later that year saw the TSP candidate elected and also the formation of an alliance between the Tajik Democratic Party (TDP) and the Islamic Renaissance Party (IRP).

The power struggle between those who wished to preserve the old system with a neo-Soviet government and those who looked to something new in the post-Soviet period, erupted in civil war in mid-1992. The situation was exacerbated by other ethnic and regional concerns and despite a variety of peacekeeping moves, conflict continues. In April 1993, the Russian Supreme Soviet voted to send a peacekeeping force to join CIS contingents from Kazakstan, Kyrgyzstan and Uzbekistan. The UN-sponsored talks produced a ceasefire accord on 18 September 1993, but this did not reduce hostilities. By mid-1995, the CIS peacekeeping force numbered some 25,000, the majority of whom were Russian. During 1996 the fighting intensified, but the fall of Kabul to *taliban* forces (see p. 8) provided a spur to peace efforts. A further peace accord was signed between the government and the IRP in Moscow on 23 November 1996. This held for a while and allowed the establishment of a transitional National Reconciliation Commission (NRC). However, in January 1998, the United Tajik Opposition (UTO) suspended its participation in the NRC and a further spate of killings and hostage-taking ensued. Fighting between the government and UTO forces continued until the end of 1998.

NORTH

0   100   200 Miles

0   100   200 Kilometres

Status ■ There has been civil war in Tajikistan almost continuously since its independence. Although resulting largely from internal factors, the situation has undoubtedly been exacerbated by the fear of religious extremism in the neighbouring countries. The success of the *taliban* in Afghanistan and the continuing civil war in that country have cast a shadow over Central Asian development, but nowhere more obviously than in Tajikistan. Apart from the continuing conflict, the governments have also been handicapped by an extremely weak economy; at independence, the weakest among the Central Asian states. The issue of conflict overspill is considered a key problem in the neighbouring states and Tajikistan appears set to remain, for the foreseeable future, the main flashpoint among the FSU states of Central Asia.

Reading ■ Atkin, M. (1997) Tajikistan's civil war, *Current History*, 96(612), pp. 336–40
Brenninkmeijer, O. (1996) Tajikistan's elusive peace, *The World Today*, 52(2), pp. 42–5
Open Society Institute (1998) *Tajikistan: Refugee Reintegration and Conflict Prevention*,
    New York: Open Society Institute

109

THE STRAIT OF TIRAN

The Strait of Tiran links the Red Sea with the Gulf of Aqaba and is therefore vital as the choke point controlling maritime access from Eilat (Israel) and Aqaba (Jordan). It is 7 nml long and 4 nml wide, varying in depth between 73 and 83 m. Tiran and Sanafir Islands are located in the strait and vessels need to transit through two narrow channels, Enterprise Passage and Grafton Passage. The strait is within the territorial waters of two riparian states: Egypt and Saudi Arabia. Saudi Arabia extended its territorial waters from 3 to 6 nml in 1949, and Egypt followed suit in 1951. Later, in 1958, both extended to 12 nml. However, even before the earlier increase, the territorial waters of both riparians included the strait in general and the navigable channels in particular. In the past, the ownership of Sanafir Island has been questioned, but it is now agreed that it belongs to Saudi Arabia, which exercises control over Egyptian development.

■ *Situation*

In 1948, with the hostilities between Israel and the Arab states, the Strait of Tiran was closed to Israeli vessels and in 1950 Egypt took possession of the islands of Tiran and Sanafir. In 1957, after the Suez campaign, transit was granted to vessels of all nations and UN Emergency Force (UNEF) troops were stationed on the western shore at Sharm el Sheikh and Ras Nasrani to guarantee freedom of passage.

■ *Issue*

In May 1967, Egypt requested the withdrawal of UNEF and again closed the strait to ships bound for Eilat. In June, following the Six-Day War, Israeli troops occupied the western side of the strait and the islands upon which the strait was re-opened to all flags and the right of innocent passage was guaranteed. In 1979, as part of the implementation of the Camp David Accords, Israel returned the islands to Egypt. They formed part of Zone C which was to be supervised by Egyptian police and UN forces. Since then, agreement on Sanafir Island has been reached with Saudi Arabia.

The periodic closure of the Tiran Strait to Israeli shipping has been justified on a number of counts. It has been argued that the Gulf of Aqaba is an internal sea of the Arabs and Israel is not considered a legitimate riparian. However, following the 1986 arbitration which ended in Egypt's favour over Taba (a boundary marker disputed between Egypt and Israel), the boundary south of Eilat clearly has international recognition. Egypt argues that since Egypt, Jordan and Saudi Arabia are separate states, there is not a single riparian and the Gulf of Aqaba must be multinational; therefore the idea of an internal sea does not apply. The second argument involves the concept of an historic bay, but it would be very difficult to apply such a concept in a multinational situation. The third main point

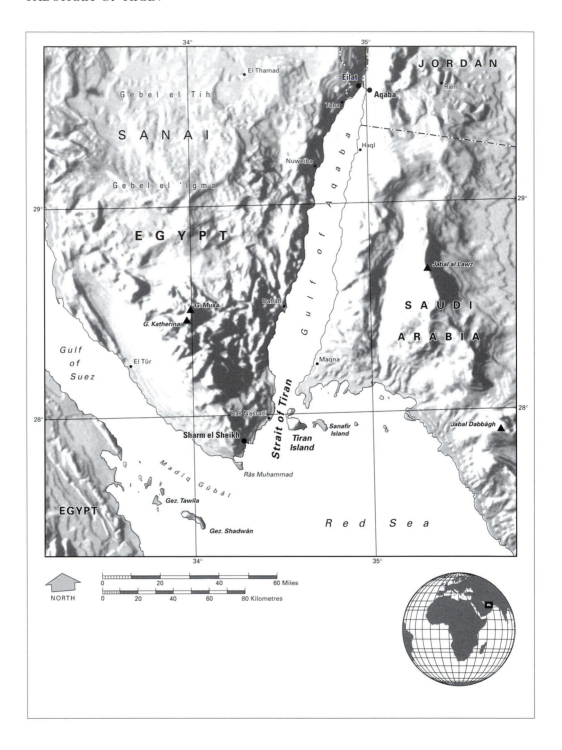

raised is that when a state of belligerency occurs, there is a right to mount a blockade. Clearly this can be supported, but is not tenable after the end of active hostilities.

By normal definitions, the Strait of Tiran appears as an international strait: it is a natural maritime passage which uses the territorial waters of more than one state; it is used for international navigation; it links two parts of the high seas and it links the high seas to the territorial seas of foreign states. Furthermore, it allows passage from the high seas to the territorial seas of states which are not themselves riparians.

The Strait of Tiran is vital as a maritime outlet for Jordan. This was shown both during the Iran–Iraq War and the Gulf War, when Iraq was largely sustained by Jordan through the port of Aqaba. It also provides Israel with the only alternative to its Mediterranean coast ports. Thus, given the continuing volatility in the region, the Strait of Tiran must be considered a flashpoint.

■ *Status*

Lapidoth, R. (1975) *Freedom of Navigation with Special Reference to International Waterways in the Middle East*, Jerusalem: The Hebrew University

Prescott, J.R.V. (1985) *The Maritime Political Boundaries of the World*, London: Methuen

Times Books (1983) *Times Atlas of the Oceans* London: Times Books

■ *Reading*

110

THE GULF OF TONGKING

Situation ■ Together with the Paracel Islands and the Spratly Islands (see pp. 264 and 311), the Gulf of Tongking is the third clear flashpoint involving the maritime boundary dispute between China and Vietnam. The gulf is bounded by Vietnam to the west, the mainland of China to the north and Hainan Island (China) to the east. It has an area of 24,000 nml^2 and a maximum depth of about 80 m. The gulf is 170 nml wide at its widest and has two outlets: the Hainan Strait between Hainan Island and the Liuchow Peninsula, approximately 19 nml in width; and the major passage to the south, 125 nml wide at its narrowest point. In their repeated claims about the violation of territorial rights, some level of conflict between China and Vietnam appears, if not inevitable, at least likely. The area is of particular significance because of its potential for petroleum resources.

Issue ■ On 26 June 1887, the maritime boundary between China and Indo-China (now Vietnam), was apparently consigned at the Sino-French Convention. However, the outcome of this convention remains central to the current dispute. In April 1973, North Vietnam was reported to have signed an agreement with Ente Nationale Idrocarburi (ENI) for oil prospecting in the gulf. The outer edge of the ENI-proposed Exploration Zone coincided roughly with the median-line boundary between North Vietnam and China.

Maritime boundary negotiations proposed by North Vietnam were accepted by China on 18 January 1974 provided that prospecting should not take place in the area bounded by latitudes 18° and 20°N and longitudes 107° and 108°E, and also that no third country should be involved. No agreement was reached and, on 12 May 1977, Vietnam issued a declaration on its territorial sea, EEZ and continental shelf. As a result, on 7 October negotiations on both the land and the maritime boundaries began. Nevertheless, China refused to discuss its land boundary unless Vietnam gave up its claim that the maritime boundary already existed as a result of the 1887 convention. Stalemate continued until 13 December 1979, when Vietnam protested about alleged contracts signed by China for petroleum exploration in the gulf. The outer edge of the proposed Chinese zone approximated to the median line in the gulf and Vietnam feared that any exploration agreements might eventually result in a *de facto* recognition of Chinese claims. On 12 November 1982, Vietnam implemented its 1977 declaration on baselines, which were promptly declared 'null and void' by China.

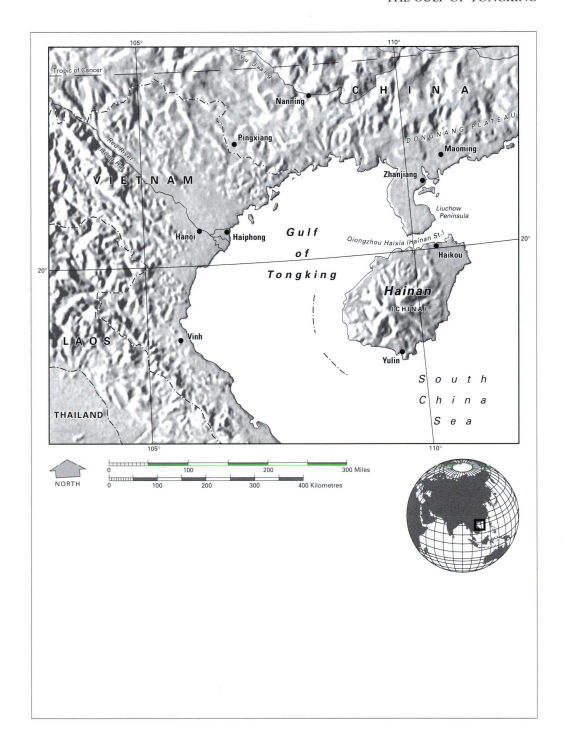

NORTH

0   100   200   300 Miles

0   100   200   300   400 Kilometres

The key remains the Sino-French Convention of 1887 in which the relevant section reads: 'The islands which are east of the Paris meridian of 105° 43′E (108° 3′E of Greenwich), that is to say that the north–south line, passing through the eastern part of Taha's Kau or Quan Chou (Tra Co), which forms the boundary, are also allocated to China.' China contends that such treaties between Imperial China and the West were 'unequal'. Moreover, if the line described were extended to include the whole of the gulf, it would be more than 130 nml from the coast of Vietnam and only about 30 nml from Hainan, giving approximately two-thirds of the area of the gulf to Vietnam. The key limitation of the Vietnamese claim is that no end points are proposed for the meridians indicated. Furthermore, since the concept of maritime sovereignty is comparatively recent, it seems very unlikely that the line proposed by the convention was intended as a maritime boundary. It may well have been used merely to separate island groups.

Status ■ The three focuses of maritime boundary disputes between Vietnam and China all include strategic and economic elements, together with aspects of national honour. Given the statements made by both sides and the protracted nature of the abortive negotiations, the Gulf of Tongking must remain a potential flashpoint.

Reading ■ Amer, R. (1997) The territorial disputes between China and Vietnam and regional security, *Contemporary Southeast Asia*, 19(1), pp. 86–113

Gerhard, W. (1998) *China and Vietnam: Chances and Limitations of Bilateral Cooperation*, Köln: Bundesinstitut für östwissenschaftliche und internationale Studein

Grinter, L. and Kihl, Y.W. (1987) *East Asian Conflict Zones*, Basingstoke: Macmillan

Pao-Min, C. (1997) Vietnam and China: new opportunities and new challenges, *Contemporary Southeast Asia*, 19(2), pp. 136–51

111

TRANSYLVANIA

Transylvania is a triangular plateau of approximately 62,000 km^2. It has comparatively easy access to Hungary in the north but only two main passes to the south, through the Transylvanian Alps. The population is approximately 8 million and includes a high proportion of the Hungarians living in Romania. The Hungarian population is put at something between 1.7 and 2 million, depending on the source of the statistics. After the geopolitical changes of 1989, nationalism emerged as perhaps the most powerful political force in East Central Europe. Part of this process involved the revival of the Transylvanian issue, a Hungarian–Romanian dispute with a long history, representing a potentially explosive ethnic conflict.

■ *Situation*

In 1003, Transylvania was conquered by King Stephen of Hungary and during the following two centuries, there was a substantial influx of Germans. The so-called 'Three Nations' (Romanians, Magyars and Germans) enjoyed self-government under the Hungarians and, after 1526, under Ottoman suzerainty. In the 17th century, Transylvania came under the domination of the Austro-Hungarian Empire but became the scene of violent conflict in 1848–9 as the Hungarians attempted to remove Austrian domination. Transylvania was eventually incorporated into the Hungarian part of the Austro-Hungarian Empire in 1867.

■ *Issue*

With the aim of obtaining Transylvania, Romania entered World War I in 1916 on the side of the Allies and duly gained the territory. It remained Romanian until the 'Vienna Award' of 1940, when the northern half was returned to Hungary. At the same time, Romania lost Bessarabia and Northern Bukovina to the Soviet Union and Southern Dobruja to Bulgaria. As a result of the Paris peace treaties between the Allies, Hungary and Romania in 1947, Hungary was forced to return northern Transylvania to Romania.

During the 1960s, Romania placed various restrictions upon the minorities in Transylvania, but on 24 February 1972, the 1948 Treaty of Friendship Co-operation and Assistance between Hungary and Romania was nevertheless renewed for a further 20 years.

Throughout the early 1990s, a constant theme of the external relations of Romania was discord with Hungary over the status of the ethnic minority population in Transylvania. In 1994, the Romanian Parliament passed legislation curbing Hungarian-language education and making the display of the flag or singing of the anthem of another state a

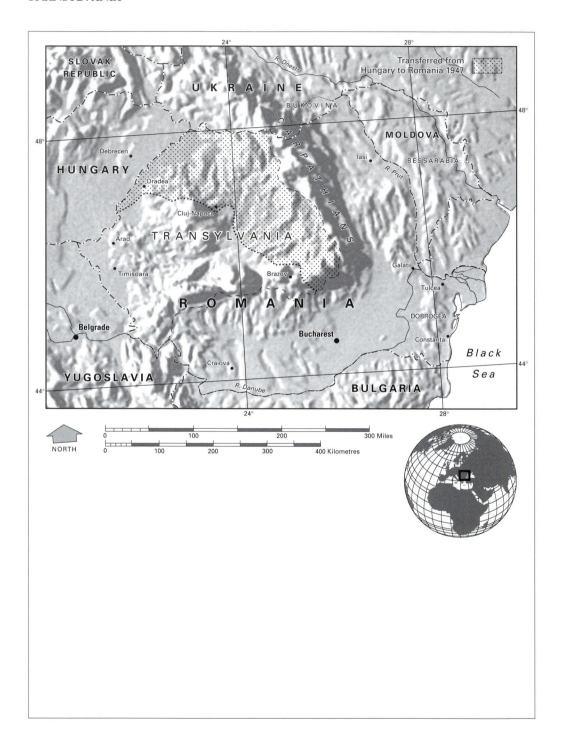

Transferred from
Hungary to Romania 1947

SLOVAK
REPUBLIC

UKRAINE

BUKOVINA

CARPATHIANS

HUNGARY

Debrecen

Oradea

Cluj-Napoca

TRANSYLVANIA

Arad

Timisoara

Brazov

ROMANIA

MOLDOVA

Iasi

R. Prut

BESSARABIA

Galati

Tulcea

DOBROGEA

Belgrade

Bucharest

Constanta

Craiova

Black
Sea

YUGOSLAVIA

R. Danube

BULGARIA

R. Dnestr

NORTH

0   100   200   300 Miles

0   100   200   300   400 Kilometres

criminal offence. Conditions greatly improved following the signing of a new Romanian–Hungarian Friendship and Co-operation Treaty on 16 September 1996. As a result, Hungary renounced any claim to Romanian territory populated by ethnic Hungarians if Romania guaranteed ethnic minority rights. In February 1997, the two countries agreed to the formation of a joint peacekeeping force and, in June 1997, the two nations signed a Friendship Treaty confirming existing borders.

Possible conflict in Transylvania seems to have been defused further with an agreement by Romania in October 1998 to the establishment of the Hungarian- and German-language Petofi-Schiller University. However, although relations seem to be settled between the two countries at governmental level, the issue of ethnic Hungarians remains a problem. The Hungarian minority, which has been represented in the national government since November 1996, is unwilling to co-operate in building Romanian national institutions and appears determined to remain a separate national entity. There is a continuing strong belief that Transylvania includes part of the natural cultural core of Hungary. Given Romania's other boundary problems to the east with Moldova (see p. 224), further dispute over Transylvania cannot be discounted.

■ *Status*

Beleanu, V. (1995) *Political Nationalism in Transylvania*, Camberley: Royal Military Academy Sandhurst (pamphlet)

Beleanu, V. (1998) *Romania at a Historic Crossroads*, Camberley: Royal Military Academy Sandhurst (pamphlet)

Downing, D. (1980) *An Atlas of Territorial and Border Disputes*, London: New English Library

■ *Reading*

112

TROMELIN ISLAND

Situation ■ Tromelin is a tiny isolated island, approximately 1 km^2 in area, located at 15° 52′S, 54° 25′E, 280 nml east of Madagascar and approximately 340 nml north of Mauritius and Réunion. It is the summit of a volcano which rises some 4,000 m from the ocean floor and is topped by a coral plateau. Apart from maritime claims, it has no obvious economic importance and access from the sea is difficult. There is no water and no agriculture, but a landing strip has been built for light aircraft.

Issue ■ The island was discovered in 1722 by French sailors and there is no record of any dispute over it until the 20th century. The only effective occupation remains a permanent French meteorological station which was established on 7 May 1954. However, it was at a World Meteorological Organisation (WMO) Congress in 1959 that Mauritius stated that it considered Tromelin to be part of its own territory. This suggestion was immediately refuted by France.

In 1960, when Madagascar (from which Tromelin had been administered) became independent, it also laid claim to the island. Nevertheless, this claim was waived in favour of Mauritius in 1976 when, on 2 April, Mauritius officially claimed Tromelin. The case of Mauritius is based on an interpretation of the wording of the Treaty of Paris (30 May 1814) under which Britain restored certain Indian Ocean islands taken from France in 1810: 'except the Isle of France (Mauritius) and its dependencies, especially Rodrigues and the Seychelles'. The key word is 'especially', which was defined by Mauritius in its claim as 'in particular, among others or notably'. The interpretation is that, in addition to Rodrigues and the Seychelles, there were other minor dependencies (including Tromelin) which remained British, and therefore came under Mauritius following independence on 12 March 1968.

On 17 December 1976, France officially rejected the claim of Mauritius. France interpreted 'especially' in the text of the treaty to be equivalent to 'namely' and that therefore Tromelin was French from 1814. In the French text, the term used was '*nommement*', and since French was held to be the language of diplomacy at that time, that text was said to be superior. Indeed, on 2 April 1973, Britain stated that there never had been nor was there any Franco-British dispute over Tromelin. However, on 20 June 1980, Mauritius announced that its constitution had been amended to add Tromelin to a list of dependencies; the island was included in its sea–bed claim.

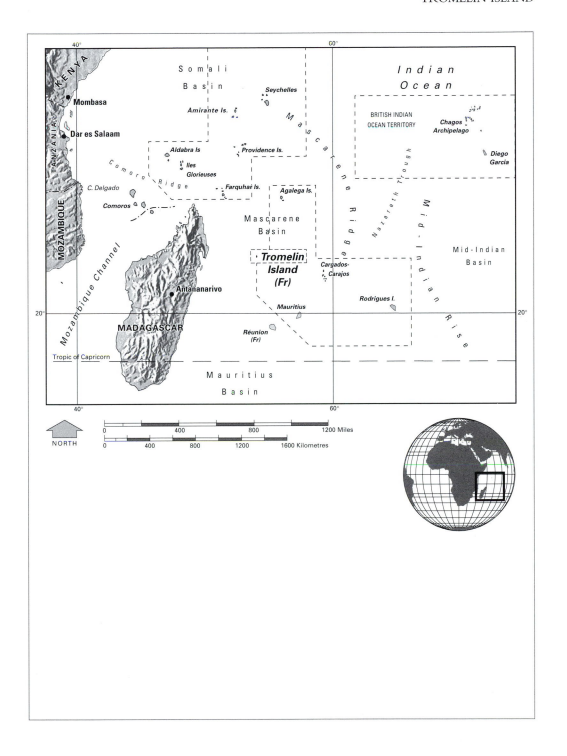

NORTH

| 0 | 400 | 800 | 1200 Miles |
| 0 | 400 | 800 | 1200 | 1600 Kilometres |

Status ■ In 1990, during the president's tour of the Indian Ocean region, France agreed to Franco–Mauritian discussions on the future of Tromelin. However, the island is still occupied by France and its status appears to remain unchanged. The only potential issue of importance is the possibility of sea and seabed claims if resources are found in the area. Tromelin is unlikely to be the subject of any major dispute.

Reading ■ Cottrell, A.J. and Hahn, W.F. (1978) *Naval Race or Arms Control in the Indian Ocean,* Agenda Paper No. 8, New York, National Strategy Information Center
Day, A.J. (ed.) (1984) *Border and Territorial Disputes*, Harlow: Longman
Prescott, J.R.V. (1985) *The Maritime Political Boundaries of the World*, London: Methuen

113

TURKEY

Turkey has a population of 61.6 million and an area of 774,815 km^2, making it second only in terms of population to Iran in the Middle East. Its location between Europe, the Middle East and Asia is one of the most strategic in the world. Control of the Turkish Straits was vital during the Cold War and remains crucial in the context of the economic development of the Black Sea region and the Caspian Sea Basin. With a position that is partly in Europe and partly in Asia, Turkey has boundaries with Bulgaria, Greece, Georgia, Armenia, Iran, Iraq and Syria, together with a very short length shared with the Azerbaijan autonomous region of Nakhichevan. Only the Russian Federation has more boundaries, spread between two continents.

■ *Situation*

Following the demise of the Ottoman Empire and World War I, Turkey, as a new state, was created as a result of a nationalist struggle from 1919 to 1922. The conflict was external against the army of Greece, supported by the West, and internal against the forces of the sultan. The victory was confirmed by the Treaty of Lausanne in July 1923. In the final internal struggle, the radicals of Kemal Ataturk were successful and a republic was established on 29 October 1923. The ruling party of Ataturk was the Republican People's Party (RPP) and in 1924 the caliphate was abolished and Turkey became a secular state, the first Muslim country to disestablish Islam. Ataturk wished to found a modern Western-style state, but found it necessary to impose a high degree of state intervention.

■ *Issue*

After World War II, the one-party system was opposed and the Democrat Party which was formed ruled from 1950 until 1960. During that period, the country benefited from the US-funded Marshall Plan for rebuilding post-war Europe, but impatience with the pace of economic development resulted in a takeover by the military on 27 January 1960. Turkey returned to a two-party system through the Justice Party which won the elections of 1965 and 1967 and great efforts were then made to integrate the armed forces into the political system. However, political instability eventually ensued and a further military takeover occurred on 12 March 1971, after which the country lived under martial law until the elections of October 1973. In 1973, the RPP re-emerged, but in coalition with the Islamist National Salvation Party (NSP). In July 1974 came the military intervention in Cyprus, which is discussed elsewhere in this volume (see p. 97).

Political and economic instability towards the end of the 1970s resulted in the third military takeover on 12 September 1980. The army tried to depoliticise the system, but

TURKEY

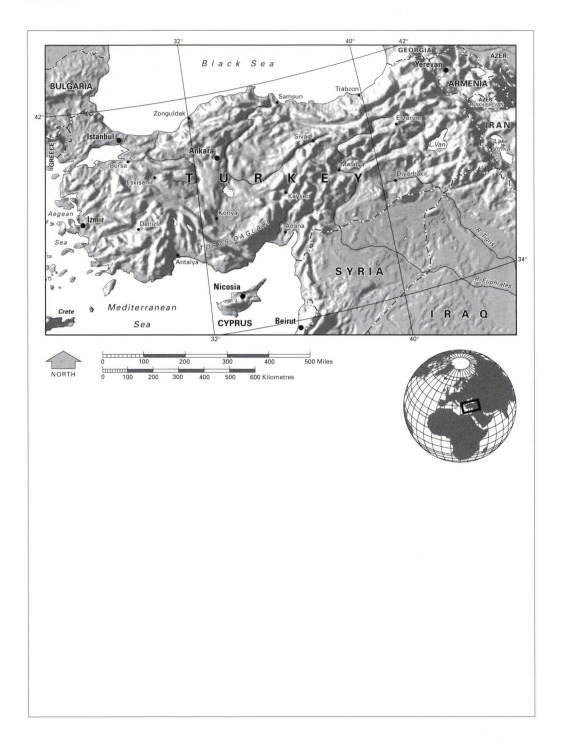

NORTH

0	100	200	300	400	500 Miles

0	100	200	300	400	500	600 Kilometres

in 1983 the Motherland Party of Turgut Ozal came to power and eased the transition back to democracy. The election of October 1991 produced a victory for the True Path Party of Sulaiman Demirel in coalition with the Social Democratic Populist Party (SHP), formerly the RPP. However, Ozal had become president and, before he died in 1993, his influence was strongly felt internationally in the development of a twin-track policy towards both Europe and the Middle East and in the initiating of the South-East Anatolian Project (GAP), the world's largest irrigation and water control scheme under construction. After Ozal, there followed an array of short-lived governments, including that of Necmettin Erbakan, the first Islamist to hold such an office. An important fact has been that there has been no return to military rule.

Throughout, Turkey has maintained close relations with the West, being admitted to NATO in 1952 and the Baghdad Pact, later the Central Treaty Organisation (CENTO), in 1955. Problems occurred in the 1960s over Cyprus and in 1967 the country almost went to war with Greece. Apart from the issue of Cyprus, there is also the problem of the maritime delimitation of the Aegean, and relations with Greece were further strained in 1996 over the ownership of a small islet known as Imia to the Greeks and Kardak to the Turks (see p. 5).

In its long-running battle with the Kurdish Workers' Party (PKK), Turkey had reached agreement on 'hot pursuit' with Iraq, but in 1990 the country sided with the Alliance after the Iraqi invasion of Kuwait. A key factor in the imposition of sanctions following the Gulf War has been the closure by Turkey of the Iraqi pipeline to Dortyol on the Turkish Mediterranean coast. Furthermore, the 'no-fly' zones in Iraq have been maintained only through the use of air bases in Turkey. In 1992, Turkey faced a particular dilemma with the conflict in Bosnia (see p. 54) when Muslims appealed for support.

Status

Regarded as a model for the way a Muslim country might operate a democratic political system, Turkey has, since 1980, avoided military intervention, although it has not been politically stable. By early 1999, the fourth coalition government in three years had collapsed. Meanwhile, relations with Europe cooled when Turkey was omitted from the list of countries for EU enlargement which was published in December 1997. Particularly galling was the fact that the long-term loyal NATO ally, Cyprus, was on the list. Problems with the PKK continue and the high-profile trial of its leader, Abdullah Ocalan, will clearly affect Turkey's international standing, especially in the wake of events in Kosovo (see p. 180). There is also a continuing underlying problem of religion in that there is a very strong desire, particularly among the military, to maintain a secular state and to avoid any taint of Islamic fundamentalism but, at the same time, the government has developed strong links with Israel. Meanwhile, confrontation with Greece, a fellow NATO member, continues on a number of fronts.

Therefore, Turkey is currently riven by a number of contradictory forces. Nonetheless, it remains vital not only for the security of the Eastern Mediterranean but also for the economic development of the whole Black Sea region and the export of petroleum from the Caspian Sea Basin. Whatever happens in either area, transport by pipeline across Turkey and through the Turkish Straits will remain a necessity. Thus, while Turkey itself is unlikely to be a flashpoint, it is almost certain that one of the issues in which it is involved will become a major geopolitical focus.

Reading ■   El-Shazly, N. (1999) Arab anger at new axis, *The World Today*, 55(1), pp. 25–7
Hale, W. (1999) In deep trouble, *The World Today*, 55(1), pp. 22–5
IISS (1998) Tougher Turkey: growing cooperation with Israel, *Strategic Comments*, 4(9)
Waxman, D. (1998) *Turkey's Identity Crisis: Domestic Discord and Foreign Policy*, London: Research Institute for Study of Conflict

114

TURKMENISTAN

Turkmenistan is a large FSU Central Asian state, with an area of 488,100 km^2, virtually the same size as the neighbouring Uzbekistan. However, with a population of only 4 million, as compared with Uzbekistan's 22.8 million, the country is very thinly peopled. The population is comparable with those of Kyrgyzstan and Tajikistan, but Turkmenistan is between two and three times larger than both of those states. Geographically, Turkmenistan extends from the foothills of the surrounding mountains to the Amudarya River and the Caspian Sea but the interior consists of the Karakum Desert, and so the population is distributed mainly in the foothills, along the river and along the coast.

■ *Situation*

In 1924, the territory of the former emirates of Bukhara and Khiva was divided between the union republics of Turkmenia and Uzbekistan. Of all the Central Asian republics, Turkmenistan remained the most tightly under communist control until the break-up of the Soviet Union. The elections of 1990 promoted Communist Party leader Saparmurad Niyazov to the presidency, which he has retained. Independence was declared in October 1991 and in December the Turkmen Communist Party (TCP) became the Democratic Party of Turkmenistan (DPT). By this means, the state officially dispensed with the doctrine of communism while retaining its procedures.

■ *Issue*

In early 1992, Turkmenistan was admitted to the Organisation for Security and Co-operation in Europe (OSCE) and, later in the same year, it also joined the UN, the IMF and the International Bank for Reconstruction and Development (IBRD). It also became a member of the Organisation of the Islamic Conference (OIC).

In sharp contrast to Tajikistan, there has been no internal conflict and relations with its neighbours have remained generally stable. In May 1992, it was announced that a gas pipeline from Turkmenistan to Europe would be constructed through Iran and Turkey. There are nascent boundary problems, but the only crucial issues concern the delimitation of the Caspian Sea (see p. 74) and the ownership of the Kyapaz–Serdan Caspian oilfield, disputed with Azerbaijan. While there has been no problem of conflict overspill from Afghanistan, agreement was reached for the deployment of Russian troops along the southern frontier.

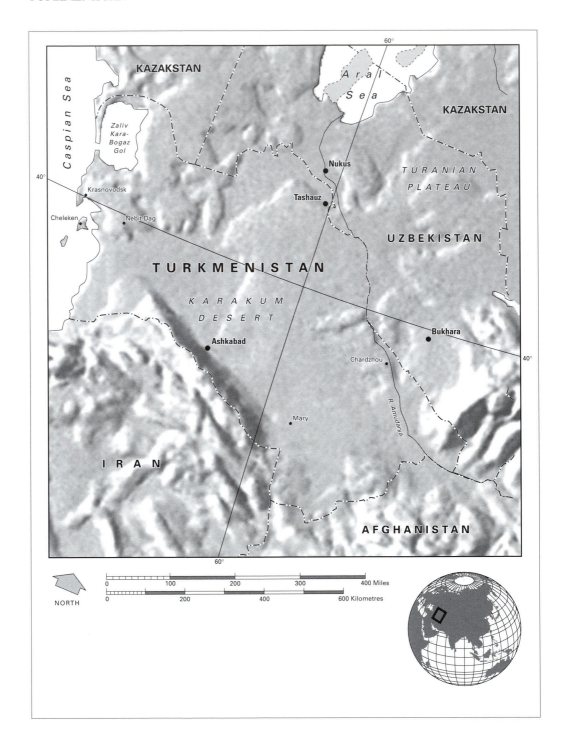

KAZAKSTAN

Caspian Sea

Zaliv
Kara-
Bogaz
Gol

Aral
Sea

KAZAKSTAN

40°

Nukus

TURANIAN
PLATEAU

Krasnovodsk

Tashauz

Cheleken

Nebit Dag

UZBEKISTAN

TURKMENISTAN

KARAKUM
DESERT

Ashkabad

Bukhara

40°

Chardzhou

R.Amudarya

Mary

IRAN

60°

AFGHANISTAN

60°

NORTH

0	100	200	300	400 Miles
0	200	400	600 Kilometres

Although opposition activity has been muted, there are signs of disquiet with the economy and the personality cult of the president. However, political expression is effectively illegal and, given the small and widely dispersed nature of the population, it seems unlikely that firm control will not continue. Good relations have been developed with both Turkey and Iran and, in May 1996, a link was established with the railway system of Iran. Turkmenistan takes a relatively conciliatory line towards the *taliban* in Afghanistan, although this may be connected with the desire to construct oil and gas pipelines through Afghanistan to Pakistan. Lacking a strong military, Turkmenistan has adopted a neutral posture and has been the only Central Asian state absent at recent NATO conferences. With regard to the Caspian Sea, Turkmenistan made it clear in February 1998 that it agrees with Iran that all five littoral states should be jointly involved. Due to its petroleum reserves, Turkmenistan is potentially a wealthy country. It is politically stable and has far fewer environmental problems than its neighbours. Of all the FSU Central Asian states, Turkmenistan is the least likely to become a flashpoint.

■ *Status*

Curtis, G. (1997) *Kazakstan, Kyrgyzstan, Turkmenistan and Uzbekistan*, Country Studies, Washington, DC: US Library of Congress

■ *Reading*

115

UKRAINE

Situation ■ Ukraine is the third largest and second most populous of the states of the FSU, with an area of 603,700 km^2 and a population of 51.6 million. Located between the newly independent states of Central Europe and the Russian Federation, Ukraine has a unique role to play in future European stability. It has boundaries with Moldova, Romania, Slovakia, Poland, Belarus and the Russian Federation. Other than Turkey, it has the longest Black Sea coastline of any state.

Issue ■ Although it has a long history, the Ukraine was divided at the time of the Russian Empire and it was only in 1940 that the western area was incorporated from Poland and Ukrainians were once again within a single political entity. During the Soviet period, great privation was suffered as a result of collectivisation and subsequent famine and the territory was subject to Russification policies. In July 1990, sovereignty was announced and then, in late 1991, independence. However, within Ukraine there are sharp cleavages along religious, ethnic, regional and class fault lines. Western Ukraine is the centre of nationalism and of support for the Ukrainian popular front, Rukh. Russians comprise 22 per cent of the population and they are concentrated in the south and east. They constitute a majority in the Crimea, which was ceded to Ukraine in 1954.

Ukraine has a wide variety of natural resources, including oil, gas and minerals, but is best known as one of the most productive farming areas in the world. However, mismanagement and corruption have resulted in unemployment and high inflation, and in 1997 the economy was ranked 23rd out of the 25 former Soviet bloc nations monitored by the European Bank for Reconstruction and Development (EBRD). After initial government changes, the present leader, Leonid Kuchma, came into office in 1994.

Apart from the west–east split between Ukrainians and Russians, and between the Uniate Church and the Orthodox Church, the other major internal conflict has been over the Ukrainian autonomous republic of Crimea. On 31 January 1994, the leader of the Republican Movement of Crimea (RDK), a secessionist body, was elected president of the republic. This issue has in turn complicated relations with Russia. After years of dispute, which included discussions on the future of the Black Sea Fleet, it was only in May 1997 that Russia finally recognised the Crimea and the city of Sevastopol as Ukrainian. There have also been boundary problems with Romania and Moldova, but these appear to have been settled.

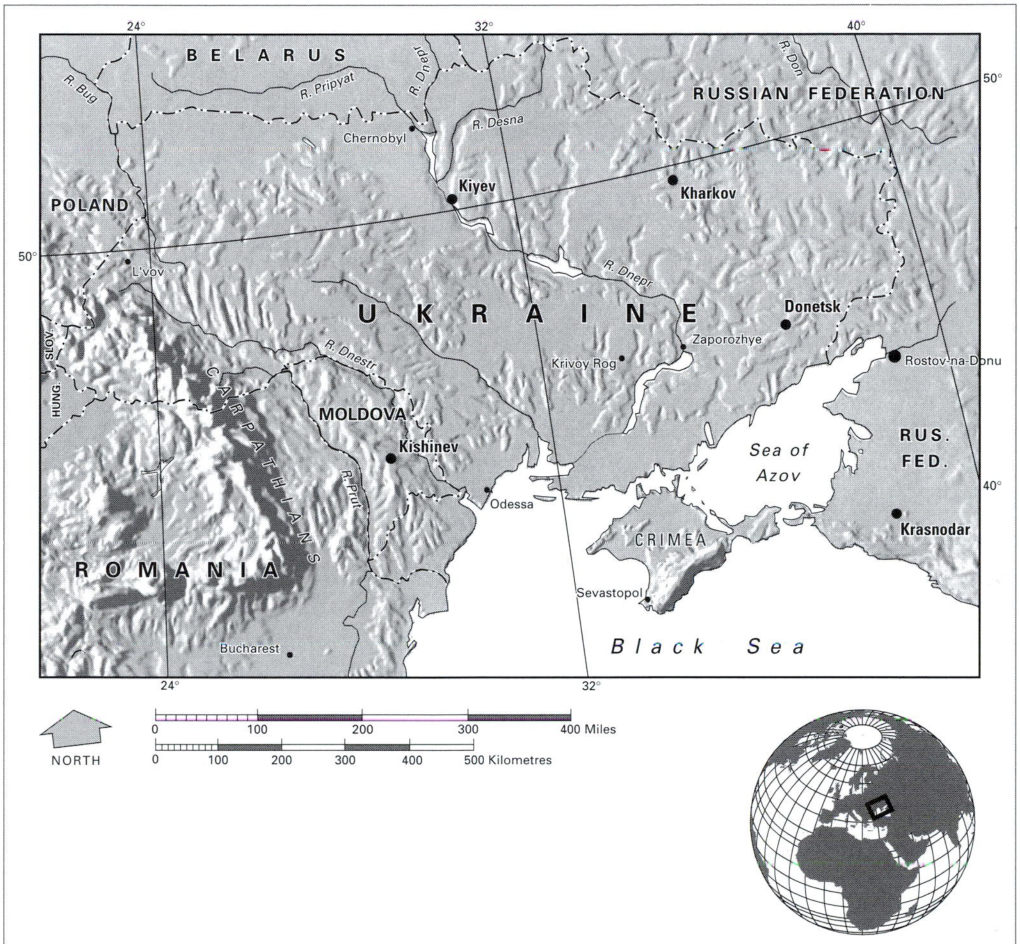
BELARUS
RUSSIAN FEDERATION
POLAND
UKRAINE
MOLDOVA
ROMANIA
RUS. FED.
HUNG.
SLOV.
CARPATHIANS
CRIMEA
Sea of Azov
Black Sea
R. Bug
R. Pripyat
R. Dnepr
R. Desna
R. Don
R. Dnestr
R. Prut
Chernobyl
Kiyev
Kharkov
L'vov
Donetsk
Zaporozhye
Krivoy Rog
Rostov-na-Donu
Kishinev
Odessa
Krasnodar
Sevastopol
Bucharest
24°
32°
40°
50°
NORTH
0 100 200 300 400 Miles
0 100 200 300 400 500 Kilometres

Despite not being an independent state, Ukraine was a founding member of the UN in 1945 and was admitted to the IMF and the World Bank in September 1992, having earlier joined the OSCE and the CIS. There was some delay before START I and the Non-Proliferation Treaty were endorsed on 1 June 1996, when Ukraine had completed the programme of nuclear disarmament by transferring its warheads to Russia.

The other major nuclear issue, and that for which Ukraine is most widely known, was Chernobyl – the site of the world's worst civilian nuclear disaster in 1986. In April 1997, agreement was reached on Western support and on closing the plant by 2005. However, Ukraine claims to spend 12 per cent of its budget on the plant and it is known that the sarcophagus is in an increasingly unstable state.

Status ■ Despite government patronage and corruption, and a sharp rise in crime, Ukraine has survived with more internal stability than several of the other newly independent states. However, there remain fears of its possible future dismemberment by Russia. In July 1998, Ukraine signed a co-operation charter with NATO with the establishment of a NATO–Ukraine Commission which gives Ukraine direct access to NATO in the event of any external threat. The state has yet to decide upon the issue of NATO membership, but it did accede to the PfP. Ukraine therefore attempts to maintain a delicate balancing act between West and East. At the same time, it has developed Black Sea initiatives, in particular, a good relationship with Turkey. Ukraine is not a flashpoint, but its future development will provide a clear indication of the likely long-term relationship between Russia and the West.

Reading ■ Arel, D. (1998) Ukraine: the muddle way, *Current History*, 97(621), pp. 342–6
IISS (1998) Kleptocracy in Ukraine: putting the country at risk, *Strategic Comments*, 4(4)
Sherr, J. (1998) *Ukraine's New Time of Troubles*, Camberley: Royal Military Academy
    Sandhurst (pamphlet)

116

UZBEKISTAN

Located on one of the world's historic routeways, Uzbekistan has long been a major centre for trade between Europe and China. It has an area of 447,400 km^2 and, at 22.8 million, the largest population among the Central Asian FSU states. It has boundaries with Turkmenistan, Kazakstan, Kyrgyzstan, Tajikistan and Afghanistan; it is the only state to have boundaries with all four Central Asian states. Compared with those with Turkmenistan and Tajikistan, the length of boundary shared with Afghanistan is short, being rather less than 150 km. Uzbekistan is therefore landlocked and has no access to the Caspian Sea, although it does share the Aral Sea with Kazakstan.

■ *Situation*

The state appeared in 1924 when the Soviet Union divided Turkestan between the republics of Turkmenia (later Turkmenistan) and Uzbekistan. Independence was declared in September 1991, after which the Uzbek Communist Party (UCP) became the People's Democratic Party (HDP) of Uzbekistan.

■ *Issue*

The state has a range of resources, including oil and natural gas, but is chiefly known for its irrigated agriculture and the virtual monoculture of cotton. The effect on the Amudarya River and, in similar circumstances, the Syrdarya in the north in Kazakstan, was catastrophic and the result is seen in the increasing desiccation of the Aral Sea.

Like its neighbour Turkmenistan, Uzbekistan has retained tight communist-style control of the political system and is effectively a one-party state, the nationalist Unity Party (Birlik) having been prevented from registration. Elected originally as president on 24 March 1990, Islam Karimov retains power. In 1992, Uzbekistan joined the UN, the IMF, the World Bank and the OSCE. In July 1994, it became a member of the PfP.

Relations with its neighbours have been fairly stable and in January 1994 Uzbekistan joined Kazakstan and Kyrgyzstan to form the Central Asian Economic Union (CAEU). Whether this will eventually lead to a united states of Central Asia is debatable, given the present position in Tajikistan (see p. 330) and the degree of Turkmenistan's self-imposed isolation. The main threat is seen as spillover from the civil war in Tajikistan and this has prompted the development of closer relations with Russia. Uzbekistan is reported to be providing assistance to Abdul Rashid Dostam in the war in Afghanistan.

As in Turkmenistan and Kazakstan, the presidential term has been extended, without the need for re-election. This shows clearly the emphasis placed on stability, and doubts about the benefits of multi-party democracy. In September 1997, Uzbek troops

■ *Status*

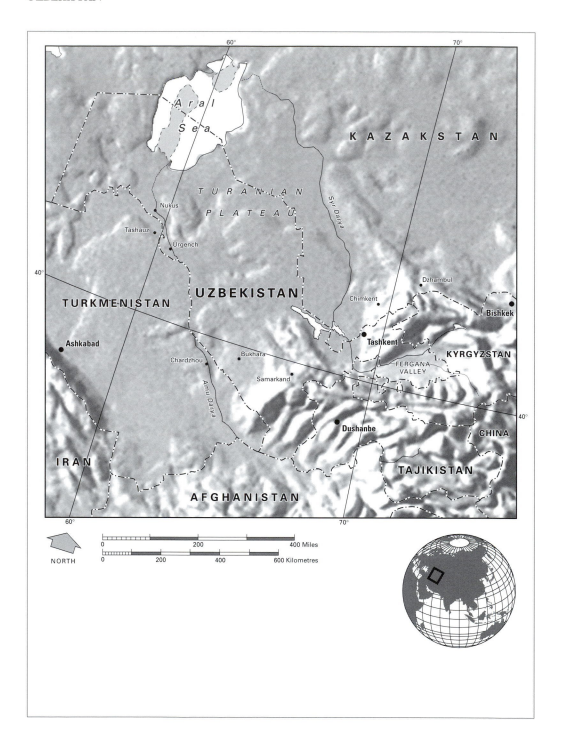

participated with the USA, Kazakstan and Kyrgyzstan in PfP exercises, thereby indicating the country's concern to retain some balance between West and East. However, massive economic problems remain, particularly in the context of agriculture and water supply. There has been tension between Uzbeks and Muslim groups and the government has taken a hard line to discourage religious extremism. Uzbekistan undoubtedly has the potential to become the leading market economy in the region but environmental and transnational issues, particularly in the Fergana Valley, loom large. The Fergana Valley is already recognised as a geopolitical flashpoint (see p. 191).

Curtis, G. (1997) *Kazakstan, Kyrgyzstan, Tajikistan, Turkmenistan and Uzbekistan,*
    Country Studies, Washington, DC: US Library of Congress

Weisbrode, K. (1997) Uzbekistan: in the shadow of Tamerlane, *World Policy Journal,*
    Spring, pp. 53–60

■ *Reading*

117

THE WAKHAN PANHANDLE

Situation ■ The Wakhan Panhandle extends 350 km from Eshkasham at its western end to beyond the Vakjir Pass at its eastern extremity. At its widest, where it includes the Nicholas Range, the Panhandle is 65 km wide and at its narrowest, at its western entrance, is only 18 km wide. The Wakhan Panhandle lies along the greatest watershed in the world, the mountain range of the Hindu Kush, with peaks between 5,000 and 6,500 m. The people, who are ethnically Tajiks, are herders, scattered among a number of isolated villages. The main regional settlement is Fayzabad to the north-west of the Panhandle, which has a population of 65,000 and is the route focus of the region. The nearest road crosses the Pamir Mountains from Tajikistan, 85 m north of the Wakhan boundary. Travel within the Panhandle is along trails and tracks and movement by wheeled vehicles is virtually impossible. Throughout the winter, the region is snow bound and between May and July travel is seriously hampered by flooding. There are some 20 passes through the Panhandle.

Issue ■ The Wakhan Panhandle is a creation of 'The Great Game' of the 19th century. As the British and Russian empires struggled for hegemony in south Central Asia, the British created what is effectively a buffer strip. To maintain a unified buffer area between north-western India and the expanding Russian Empire, the British distended the boundary of Afghanistan. The western two-thirds of the region were delimited by the Russo-British Agreement of 31 January 1873, and the demarcation was confirmed by Afghanistan and the Soviet Union between 1947 and 1948. This part of the boundary was also covered by the Treaty Concerning the Regime of the Soviet–Afghanistan State Frontier (18 January 1958).

The eastern third, from Sari Qul, was delimited by a Russo-British Exchange of Notes, dated 11 March 1895, and confirmed by the Afghanistan–Soviet Union Treaty on Border Demarcation of 16 July 1981. This last treaty was, of course, signed during the Soviet occupation of Afghanistan, including the Panhandle. Indeed, the Panhandle was considered of such strategic importance, particularly as a conduit for the movement of arms to the *mujahidin* (freedom fighters), that it was controlled directly by the Soviet Military Southern Headquarters at Tashkent, in what is now Uzbekistan.

The 1981 treaty was greeted by a storm of protest from China. On 22 July 1981, China declared the treaty to be illegal and invalid as the Soviet Union had no right to conclude a boundary treaty involving a line with a third country. This referred to some 20,000 km^2

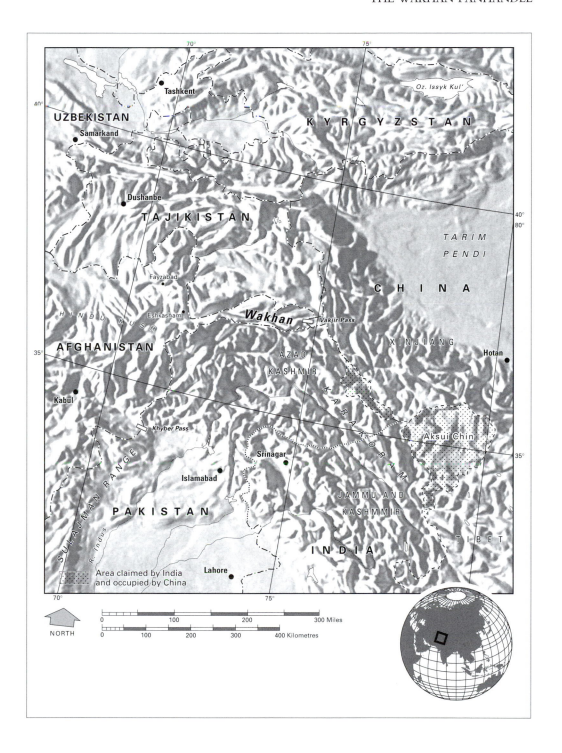

Area claimed by India
and occupied by China

NORTH

| 0 | 100 | 200 | 300 Miles |

| 0 | 100 | 200 | 300 | 400 Kilometres |

of territory to the north, which had been in dispute between China and the Soviet Union (Russia) for approximately 90 years. However, China stressed it had no outstanding territorial disputes with Afghanistan and supported the Agreement of November 1963 which regulated the 70 km China–Afghanistan border at the eastern end of the Panhandle.

Status ■ The Wakhan Panhandle remains of strategic and geopolitical significance. It separates the Central Asian states of the FSU from the Indian subcontinent and, with the continuing problems of Kashmir (see p. 165) and instability to the north, it can still be a key buffer. Indeed, Russian anxiety has focused upon cross-border conflict in Afghanistan and Tajikistan, while Chinese concern continues over possible separatism in Xinjiang Province. Therefore, despite its inaccessible terrain, Wakhan is at the focus of a major potential flashpoint. During the 1980s and the civil war in Afghanistan, and again in 1990 when support was provided for the Islamic uprising in Xinjiang, the Wakhan Panhandle was an important route for arms smuggling.

Reading ■ Anderson, E.W. and Dupree, N.H. (eds) (1990) *The Cultural Basis of Afghan Nationalism*, London: Pinter

US Department of State (1974) *China–USSR Boundary*, International Boundary Study No. 64 (revised January 1974), Washington, DC: Office of the Geographer, Bureau of Intelligence and Research

US Department of State (1983) *Afghanistan–USSR Boundary*, International Boundary Study No. 26 (revised September 1983), Washington, DC: Office of the Geographer, Bureau of Intelligence and Research

118

WARBAH AND BUBIYAN ISLANDS

Warbah and Bubiyan are two strategically located, low-lying uninhabited islands at the head of the Persian/Arabian Gulf. They lie between Kuwait and Iraq, but are the territory of Kuwait. Warbah is 11 km long and 3 km wide and Bubiyan measures 41 by 21 km. Bubiyan lies within 1 nml of the Kuwaiti mainland and within 5 nml of Iraq, while the nearest part of Warbah is 2 nml from Kuwait and less than 1 nml from Iraq. ■ *Situation*

Kuwait came under British protection in 1899 and in the Anglo-Turkish Agreement of 1913 Kuwaiti ownership of Warbah and Bubiyan islands was recognised. However, owing to the start of World War II, the agreement was never ratified. Iraq became independent in 1932 and Kuwait in 1961 and both are, of course, major oil-producing states. ■ *Issue*

The revolution in Iraq in 1958 ended British influence and the protectorate officially terminated in 1961 when Iraq immediately claimed the whole of Kuwait. The claim was based on the fact that Kuwait was part of the former Ottoman province of Basra and it was later reinforced by the construction of a commercial port and naval base at Umm Qasr on the Khor Zubair. The UK had previously constructed a port at Umm Qasr during World War II but this was later dismantled. Kuwait requested British support and troops were deployed along the Kuwait–Iraq boundary, to be replaced later by a joint Arab Force. Two years later, Iraq dropped its claim to the whole of Kuwait but persisted in pressing for ownership or a long-term lease on Warbah and Bubiyan. Clearly, Warbah Island influences the security of the approach to Umm Qasr, a port that is vital to Iraq, particularly when there have been disputes with Iran along the Shatt al Arab (see p. 291). This point was illustrated in 1969 when there was a border violation near Umm Qasr. This was justified by Iraq, then in dispute with Iran, as necessary port protection. Further violations occurred in 1972 and 1973.

Following the Iran–Iraq agreement over the Shatt in 1975, Kuwait put pressure on Iraq to remove its forces from the Umm Qasr area. Iraq agreed, but requested that Warbah and Bubiyan should be the subject of a long-term lease agreement. Kuwait rejected this idea and, to assert its sovereignty and reinforce control, a 4 km-long bridge was built from the mainland to Bubiyan Island.

In 1981, Iraqi claims to the island were revived, and in 1990 the Gulf War was triggered when the whole of Kuwait was occupied and designated the '19th province' of Iraq. In

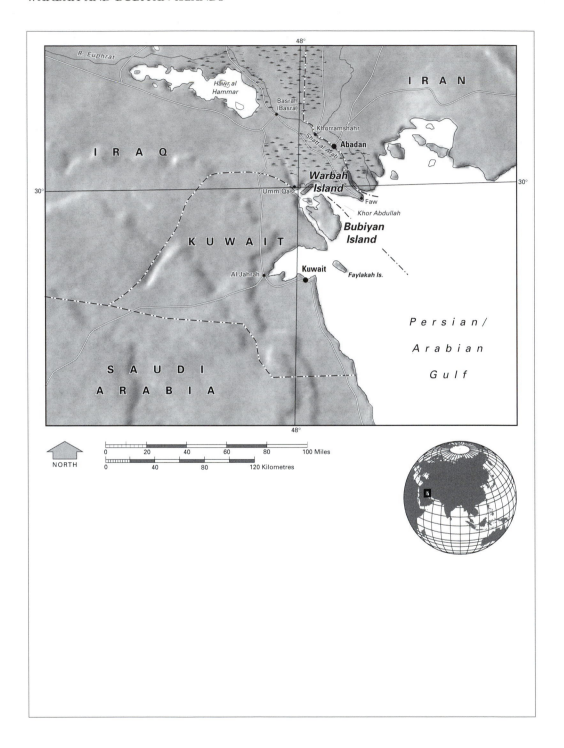

early 1991, as a result of Operation Desert Storm, Iraq was ejected from Kuwait. A protection zone was established along the whole of the boundary between Kuwait and Iraq and, under UN sponsorship, the land and maritime boundary was re-demarcated. Demarcation and delimitation ended in March 1992 with the Khor Abdullah between Iraq and Warbah Island being defined by a median line.

Intrinsically, the two islands are of no value. However, ownership of them would safeguard the entry to Umm Qasr and allow Iraq to claim a far greater proportion of the resources of the Persian/Arabian Gulf. Problems over the Shatt al Arab and the islands can both be related originally to the fact that Iraq has only 30–40 km of coastline on the Gulf.

Iraq's restricted access to the Gulf remains an unresolved factor and a highly sensitive issue. While Warbah and Bubiyan islands remain part of Kuwait, the question of some accommodation with Iraq must be a possibility. Meanwhile, the islands and the approach to Umm Qasr remain a key potential flashpoint.

■ *Status*

■ *Reading*

Anderson, E.W. and Rashidian, K. (1991) *Iraq and the Continuing Middle East Crisis*, London: Pinter

Peterson, J.E. (1985) The islands of Arabia: their recent history and strategic importance, *Arabian Studies*, VII, pp. 23–5

Schofield, R. (1994) *The Kuwaiti Islands of Warbah and Bubiyan and Iraqi Access to the Gulf*, London: UCL Press

Swearingen, W.D. (1981) Sources of conflict over oil in the Persian/Arabian Gulf, *The Middle East Journal*, 33(5), pp. 314–30

119

WESTERN SAHARA

Situation ■ A desert country on the seaboard of north-west Africa, Western Sahara has an area of 270,000 km^2 and a population of approximately 182,000. To the north is Morocco and there is a short length of boundary with Algeria, but otherwise the country is surrounded to the east and south by Mauritania. Relative to Western Sahara, all three of the surrounding countries are considerably more developed and militarily far stronger. The one major resource of the country is phosphate. The native peoples are nomadic Sahrawis who were absorbed by the Arabs in the 13th century.

Issue ■ Following its 1860 defeat of Morocco in 1884–6, Spain established a protectorate over the southern part of Western Sahara known as Rio de Oro. Morocco itself was then divided into Spanish and French protectorates and the northern part of Western Sahara, Saguia el-Hamra, came under Spanish jurisdiction in 1904.

Morocco became independent from France in 1956 and had established sovereignty over most of Spanish Morocco by 1958. However, Spain retained the whole of Western Sahara. At that time, Moroccan aspirations extended not only to Western Sahara but also the whole of Mauritania and the Tindouf region of Algeria.

In 1967, Spain granted home rule for the Sahrawi people but Morocco, Algeria and Mauritania had in the meantime decided to co-operate to end colonial rule. By the mid–1970s, anti-Spanish forces were joined by the Polisario Front (Popular Front for the Liberation of Saguia el-Hamra and Rio de Oro), a guerrilla movement backed initially by Algeria. However, at the same time, the original threefold alignment collapsed, with Morocco and Mauritania both lodging claims for Western Sahara while Algeria supported independence.

On 14 December 1972, a UN resolution called for the independence of Spanish Sahara and Spain announced that there would be a referendum in 1975. Then, on 13 December 1974, the UN approved a further resolution, sponsored by Morocco and Mauritania, urging that advice should be obtained from the ICJ on the status of Spanish Sahara. The ICJ opinion, given on 16 October 1975 – which is now regularly cited as one of the defining cases of national self-determination – stated that although there were 'certain ties of allegiance' between Western (Spanish) Sahara and both Morocco and Mauritania at the time of colonisation by Spain in 1884, these did not support a claim of territorial sovereignty.

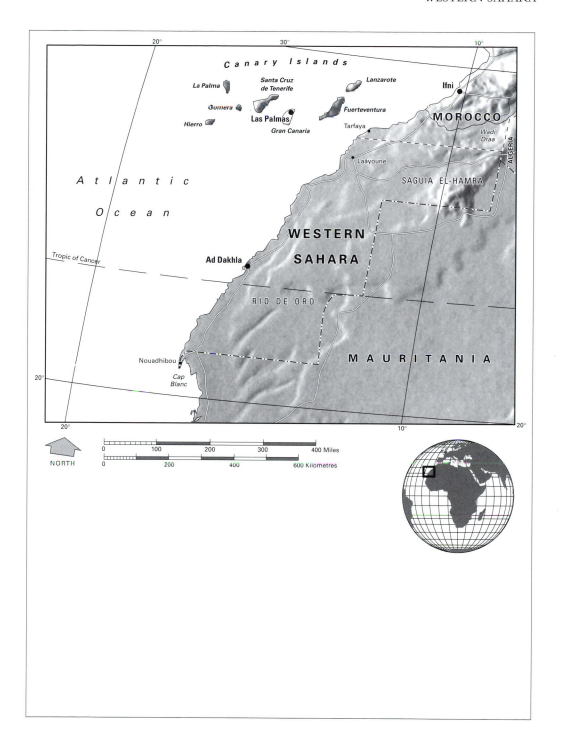

NORTH

| 0 | 100 | 200 | 300 | 400 Miles |
| 0 | 200 | 400 | 600 Kilometres |

365

However, on 14 November 1975 the Madrid Agreement was concluded under which Spain agreed to withdraw from Spanish Sahara and, despite the ICJ advisory opinion, to hand the territory over to Morocco and Mauritania. Accordingly, Morocco and Mauritania partitioned Western Sahara, using the ancient division between Saguia el-Hamra in the north and Rio de Oro in the south. The Polisario Front, backed by Algeria, strongly opposed this act of neo-colonialism, declaring an independent Sahrawi Arab Democratic Republic (SADR) and forming a government in exile.

Following Polisario successes and a military coup, Mauritanian troops were withdrawn from Western Sahara by August 1979. Morocco seized the opportunity to take over the southern part of Western Sahara, which it renamed Oued Addahab. To support its position, in 1980 Morocco commenced the building of a defensive wall to seal off Western Sahara from Mauritania. This structure, stretching from Wadi Draa in southern Morocco to immediately north of Nouadhibou at Western Sahara's southern boundary, was completed in 1987. In August 1988, Morocco and the Polisario Front accepted a UN-sponsored ceasefire formula under which a referendum would determine the wishes of the people of Western Sahara. However, six years after it began, the UN Mission for the Referendum in Western Sahara (MINURSO) had failed to accomplish its goal. In March 1997, a former US secretary of state was appointed as the UN secretary general's special envoy for the Mission.

Status ■ Preparations continue for the referendum, but the enforcement of the result could well produce hostilities. Moroccan feelings about Western Sahara remain strong, but there is likely to be overwhelming support for the decolonisation of Africa's last remaining colony. Therefore, Western Sahara will remain a flashpoint but, like so many areas of geopolitical concern in Africa, one that is likely to excite little more than local interest.

Reading ■ Boyd, A. (1991) *An Atlas of World Affairs*, 9th edn, London: Routledge
Chopra, J. (1997) A chance of peace in Western Sahara, *Survival*, 39(3), pp. 51–65
Munroe, D. and Day, A.J. (1990) *A World Record of Major Conflict Areas*, London: Arnold
Zunes, S. (1996) Western Sahara: peace derailed, *Current History*, 95(601), pp. 228–33

120

YEMEN

Yemen has an area of 527,968 km^2 and a population of 14.5 million, rather less than that reported for Saudi Arabia. The state occupies a strategic location on the south-west corner of the Arabian Peninsula, overlooking Bab el Mandeb and the entrance to the Red Sea. Having high mountains and more rainfall than the remainder of the peninsula, it was known from ancient times as Arabia Felix, which had been settled for thousands of years. Yemen has boundaries with Oman and Saudi Arabia, together with a maritime boundary in the throes of delimitation with Eritrea. The modern state results from the union of two separate Yemeni states in May 1990.

■ *Situation*

The highland area of Arabia Felix became an independent state, North Yemen, with the demise of the Ottoman Empire in 1919. Society was divided between the north, which was loyal to the Zeidi branch of Shi'a Islam, and the centre and south which comprised the Shafei population, loyal to the Sunni branch of Islam. Initially, power was in the hands of the Zeidis, led by Imams, but in 1962 the Imamate was replaced in a nationalist coup by the Yemen Arab Republic (YAR). There followed a civil war, with Saudi Arabia and the UK on the side of the tribes and Egypt on the side of the republic. In 1970, peace was agreed and in 1978 Ali Abdallah Salih assumed power which, through all the vicissitudes, he has held ever since. The economy relied heavily on remittances from expatriate workers throughout the oil-rich Arab states, and in 1984 oil was discovered in the YAR itself.

■ *Issue*

The state of South Yemen resulted from British occupation of Aden as a coaling and strategic location in 1839. To ensure the security of Aden, the neighbouring sheikhdoms were cultivated and the Federation of South Arabia was achieved in 1962. In November 1967, the UK withdrew and power was taken by the National Liberation Front (NLF) in the form of a radical one-party state. As a Soviet-supported Marxist state, the country was renamed the People's Democratic Republic of Yemen (PDRY), but there were few resources other than the port of Aden, which declined rapidly. Thus, the state was largely reliant upon aid from the Soviet Union.

Despite wars between them in 1972 and 1979, the two Yemens achieved full union as the Republic of Yemen in May 1990. Although there was now the promise of greater oil resources in the south than in the north, the distribution of power within the new state was weighted heavily towards the north. Tensions rose and fighting broke out in 1994. The south seceded on 21 May but, by 7 July, the civil war had ended along with the

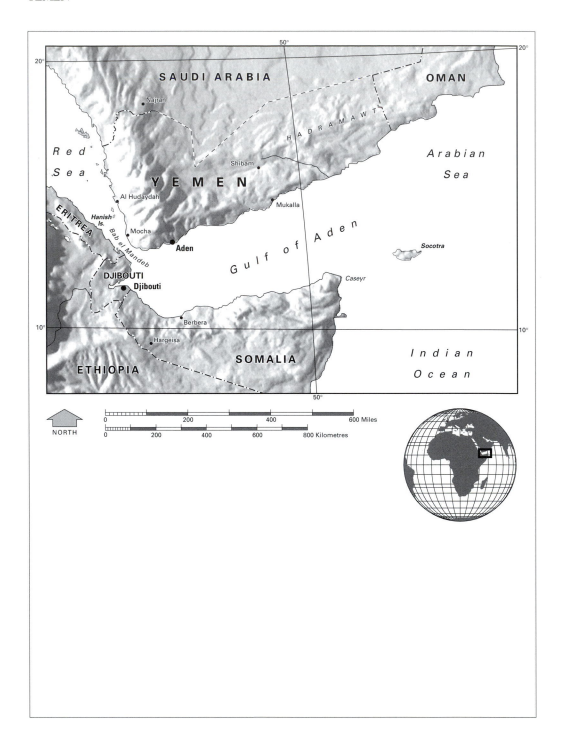

NORTH

0   200   400   600 Miles

0   200   400   600   800 Kilometres

short-lived secession. The election of 1997 was won by the General People's Congress (GPC) of Salih – the Yemeni Socialist Party (YSP), supported predominantly in the south, boycotted the elections.

The major foreign policy issue since unification resulted from Iraq's attack on Kuwait in 1990 (see p. 153). Yemen abstained in both the UN Security Council and the Arab League votes against Iraq and, as a result, Saudi Arabia withdrew the privileges granted to Yemeni citizens. It is claimed that this led to the repatriation of approximately 1 million Yemeni nationals. Friction over the border conflict with Saudi Arabia also peaked in 1992. By 1995, following clashes in the boundary zone, a Memorandum of Understanding was drawn up between the two countries to demarcate the boundary. In fact, the section from the Red Sea coast to Najran had been demarcated under the 1934 Treaty of Taif. However, from approximately Najran eastwards to the boundary with Oman, the border still needs to be allocated. The maritime boundary has also not been delimited and, following a minor skirmish of Duwaimah Island in June and July 1998, the question has some urgency; the maritime boundary between Yemen and Eritrea was delimited in December 1999. Following the dispute over the Hanish Islands, an arbitration awarded in favour of Yemen (see p. 24).

The economy of Yemen remains in a poor state, in large part at least as a result of its relations with Saudi Arabia. In May 1998, Saudi Arabia resumed the issue of visas to Yemeni nationals, but recovery will take a long time. Meanwhile, the key factor from Yemen's viewpoint is the delimitation of the boundaries that would allow the exploitation of petroleum resources to accelerate. Given its heavy dependence upon Saudi Arabia, Yemen has looked elsewhere for support, but has been refused membership of both the Commonwealth and the Gulf Co-operation Council (GCC). However, the USA is currently carrying out feasibility studies of Aden and Mocha as future naval bases. Having been considered something of a 'pariah' state following the Gulf War, Yemen now has generally good relations with all its neighbours, including Oman, with whom its boundary was demarcated in 1992.

■ *Status*

Halliday, F. (1997) Yemen's uneasy elections, *The World Today*, 53(3), pp. 73–6
IISS (1995) *Conflict in Yemen*, Oxford: Oxford University Press
Pelletiere, S. (1996) *Yemen and Stability in the Persian Gulf*, Carlisle, PA: US Army War College

■ *Reading*

121

YUGOSLAVIA

Situation ■ Until its demise in 1992, the Federal People's Republic of Yugoslavia (FPRY) comprised six constituent republics: Bosnia-Herzegovina, Croatia, Macedonia, Montenegro, Serbia and Slovenia. It covered 255,800 km^2 and had a population of almost 24 million. The successor state, the Federal Republic of Yugoslavia, has an area of 102,173 km^2 and a population of just over 10.5 million. The successor state therefore retains 40 per cent of the area and 44 per cent of the population of the FPRY. Yugoslavia now comprises Serbia and Montenegro, together with two regions that have been considered semi-autonomous, Kosovo and Vojvodina, both in Serbia. Kosovo, which is considered elsewhere in this volume (see p. 180), has a population that is 90 per cent ethnic Albanian, while Vojvodina has a significant Hungarian minority.

Issue ■ On 3 October 1929, the kingdom of the Croats, Serbs and Slovenes was formally named Yugoslavia and was a tightly controlled state, dominated by Serbia. The Croats became disaffected and their antagonism continued through World War II, when resistance to the Axis powers was led by two groups, the Chetniks and the Partisans. At the end of the war, the Partisans assumed power under Tito, himself a Croat. On 29 November 1945, the monarchy was abolished and the FPRY was proclaimed.

Although orthodox communists, Yugoslavia did not follow Soviet directives and was expelled from the communist bloc in 1948. With Western help, it then developed its own form of democratic socialism. On 4 May 1980, Tito died and the leadership was rotated on an annual basis. This resulted in political and economic problems and, like the Soviet Union, Yugoslavia began to witness its own disintegration. In 1990, Slovenia, Macedonia and Croatia declared their full sovereignty, while Serbia stripped Kosovo and Vojvodina of autonomy status. The further breakdown which followed is discussed in the relevant sections in this volume (see pp. 54, 89, 180 and 206). By the end of 1991, the original state of Yugoslavia had ceased to exist. On 15 January 1992, the independence of Croatia and Slovenia was recognised and, on 12 February, Serbia and Montenegro agreed to remain a state that would constitute the continuation of Yugoslavia. Bosnia-Herzegovina became independent on 1 March and, by the end of the month, Macedonia had followed. The president, Slobodan Milosevic, though a proponent of 'greater Serbia', was forced to accept the plan for the cantonisation of Bosnia-Herzegovina in May 1993. Milosevic was bitterly blamed for this, particularly when, in April 1995, Croatia recovered what had been announced as the Republic of Serbian Krajina.

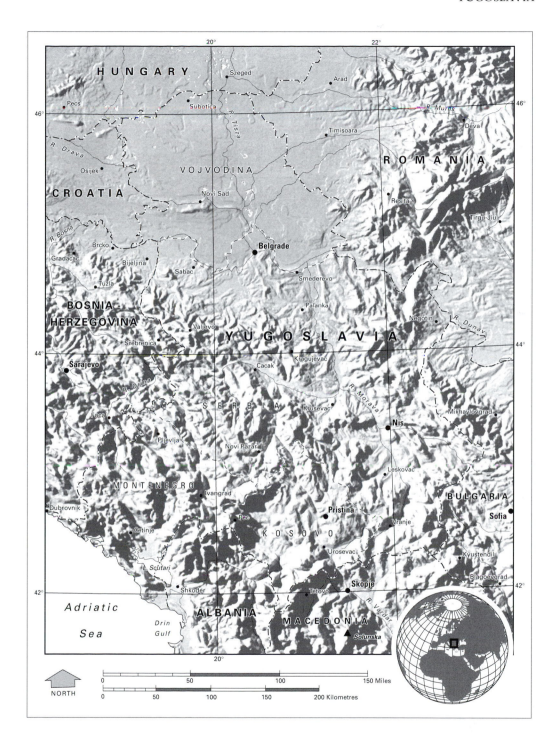

NORTH

0   50   100   150 Miles

0   50   100   150   200 Kilometres

Meanwhile, relations with Kosovo remained in crisis and the conflict between the Albanians in Kosovo and Serbia intensified throughout 1997. The Kosovo Liberation Army (KLA) began a guerrilla war and, early in 1998, the Serbian police responded violently. As the crisis deepened, so it became a matter for global concern and in 1999, with the failure to reach agreement, NATO attacked Serbian forces in Kosovo.

Status ■ The post-mortem of the Kosovo conflict has yet to take place. It is certain that Kosovo itself has been severely damaged and many cities in Serbia have been greatly reduced, while traffic on the Danube has been halted and, for a variety of reasons, pollution has become a major problem. This was brought about in no small measure by NATO's use of depleted uranium weapons. The only uncontested facts seem to be that NATO attacked without sanction from the UN and therefore, technically, its action was illegal. With the NATO bombardment, ethnic cleansing by Serbia, which had been proceeding on a relatively small scale, increased exponentially so that a high proportion of the Albanian population of Kosovo was moved. There are now severe refugee problems, not least in Macedonia which has tried to maintain a delicate balance between its ethnic groups and now finds itself with a greatly enlarged Albanian population. Serbian actions in Kosovo certainly constitute war crimes, but it appears unlikely that anyone will be brought to trial in the immediate future. Given the hatred between Serbs and Albanians, in and immediately outside Kosovo, it is likely that some form of UN presence will be required for a very long time to come if any form of stability is to be maintained. Meanwhile, Kosovo remains technically part of Yugoslavia, as does Montenegro which made no attempt to help the Serbian troops and may, in the future, seek independence. The entire region, and Serbia in particular, will remain a flashpoint for the foreseeable future.

Reading ■ IISS (1998) Montenegro and Yugoslavia: moving towards secession? *Strategic Comments*, 4(6)

Poulton, H. (1993) *Balkans: Minorities and States in Conflict*, London: Minority Rights Publications

Rand Corporation (1997) *Anticipating Ethnic Conflict*, San Francisco, CA: The Rand Corporation

Schierup, C. (1999) *Scramble for the Balkans*, Basingstoke: Macmillan

122

ZAMBIA

Zambia has an area of 752,618 km^2 and a population of 9.4 million. It is therefore almost ■ *Situation* twice the size of its neighbour, Zimbabwe, but has a smaller population. It is located centrally in southern Africa and has boundaries with eight countries: Tanzania, Democratic Republic of the Congo, Angola, Namibia, Botswana, Zimbabwe, Mozambique and Malawi. The boundary with Botswana is only at a tripoint and that with Namibia is through the Caprivi Strip (see p. 71). If the number of contiguous states can be related to the likelihood of conflict, Zambia, like the Democratic Republic of the Congo and Sudan (see pp. 86 and 315), is likely to be prone to boundary instability. However, unlike the other two states, Zambia has remained relatively stable, but it is nevertheless in a pivotal geopolitical position.

The country was annexed by the British South Africa Company as Northern Rhodesia in ■ *Issue* 1898, and became one of the world's leading copper producers. Initially, it was administered jointly with Southern Rhodesia (Zimbabwe), but was a separate protectorate from 1924. Zambia was joined with Southern Rhodesia and Nyasaland (Malawi) from 1953 until 1963 in the Federation of Rhodesia and Nyasaland.

By the 1950s, nationalism was growing and both Northern Rhodesia and Nyasaland were unwilling to continue under the dominance of white-ruled Southern Rhodesia. On 24 October 1964, Northern Rhodesia became an independent republic within the Commonwealth, taking the name of Zambia, after the Zambezi River. The state was ruled by Kenneth Kaunda and his party, the United National Independence Party (UNIP). Kaunda remained in charge of the country until 1991, but there were several political crises during that period, in part connected to white rule to the south and economic problems aligned with declining commodity prices. Economic ties had been with the south and Kaunda cut these to help end white rule in southern Africa. When copper prices slumped there were major problems, and in 1972 Kaunda set up a one-party state.

Increasing disillusion resulted in the formation of the Movement for Multiparty Democracy (MMD) and pressure for elections, which were eventually held in October 1991. Frederick Chiluba and the MMD were installed and still lead the country. However, economic mismanagement has continued, together with examples of corruption, and the country was placed in a state of emergency in 1993, a condition which was only lifted in March 1998.

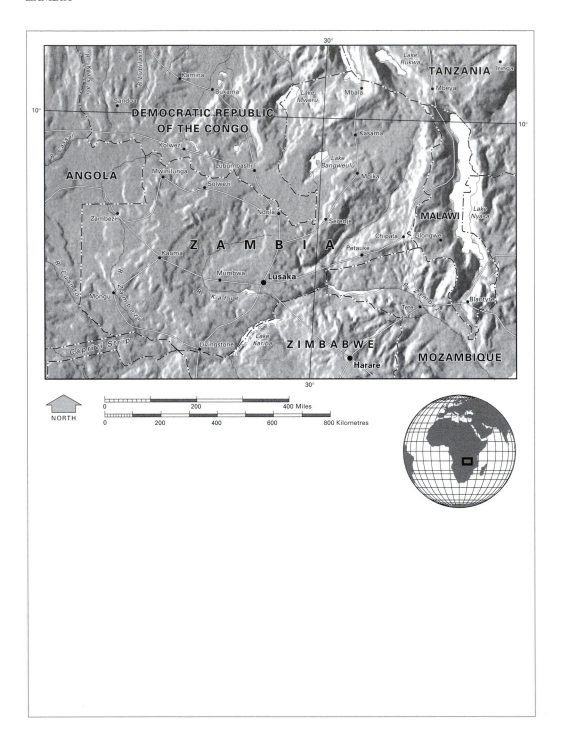

NORTH

0   200   400 Miles

0   200   400   600   800 Kilometres

Throughout the 1980s, foreign relations were dominated by the question of racial discrimination in southern Africa. Zambia became the sanctuary for numerous exiled groups and Lusaka became the headquarters of the African National Congress (ANC). In efforts to lessen reliance on South African trade routes, Zambia was prominent in attempting the resurrection of the Benguela Railway through Angola and the Tanzam Railway to Dar es Salaam (see p. 42). During this period there were also border problems with Malawi, Zaire and Mozambique.

Given its location and the many problems besetting Zambia, a reasonable level of stability has been maintained. Zambia must also take a great deal of the credit, since it paid the price, for the eventual advent of majority rule in both Zimbabwe and the Republic of South Africa. For much of his period in office, Kaunda was one of the voices of reason in Africa when there was apparent chaos elsewhere. The only current potential flashpoint is in the copper belt, which is contiguous with the potentially volatile Shaba Province of the Democratic Republic of the Congo. Apart from copper, both produce cobalt, one of the most strategic minerals. ■ *Status*

Bull, T. (1996) Zambia: boom, doom or merely gloom? *The World Today*, 52(10), pp. 258–60 ■ *Reading*

Simutanyi, N. (1996) The politics of structural adjustment in Zambia, *Third World Quarterly*, 17(4), pp. 825–39

123

ZIMBABWE

Situation ■ Zimbabwe is located in Central Africa, immediately south-east of Zambia, and is bounded by the Zambezi and the Limpopo rivers. It has an area of 390,757 km^2 and a population of 11.5 million. It has boundaries with Mozambique, Zambia, Namibia, Botswana and the Republic of South Africa. The boundary with Namibia is through the tripoint at the terminus of the Caprivi Strip (see p. 71). It has a more diversified economy than Zambia, having agricultural products and a number of key minerals, most notably chromium. Like Zambia, it is landlocked and relies upon South Africa and Mozambique for trade routes.

Issue ■ The country was colonised by the British South Africa Company in the 1890s and was administered jointly with Northern Rhodesia until 1924. From 1953 until 1963, it was part of the Federation of Rhodesia and Nyasaland and then, when that federation broke up upon the independence of the other two states, the white minority of Rhodesia made a Unilateral Declaration of Independence (UDI).

The white minority government followed the policies of South Africa and maintained racial discrimination in all sectors of life. In response, liberation movements developed and resorted to guerrilla tactics. Eventually, after various initiatives by the UK, two nationalist groups – the Zimbabwe African National Union (ZANU) and the Zimbabwe African People's Union (ZAPU) – forced a negotiated settlement in 1979. On 18 April 1980, Zimbabwe became independent and elections produced a clear victory for ZANU. As a condition of independence, protection had been built in for the white minority and the new government, while including a majority from ZANU, also had membership from ZAPU and the white-settler Rhodesian Front (RF). Robert Mugabe and ZANU have remained in charge of the country. Initially, there were problems between ZANU and ZAPU, but the Unity Accord, signed in March 1986, signalled the merger of the two parties and the achievement of a one-party state.

Opposition has been generated by the fact that the government has been unable to provide the expected changes, but there has been progress, including land redistribution and the resettlement of refugees. However, the economy has been largely dominated by dependence upon South Africa which maintained a policy of destabilisation. In 1980, the Southern African Development Co-ordination Council (SADCC) was established, which helped lessen dependence upon South Africa. Throughout, Zimbabwe has remained an outspoken critic of South African human rights policy and must take some credit for the changes that have occurred there.

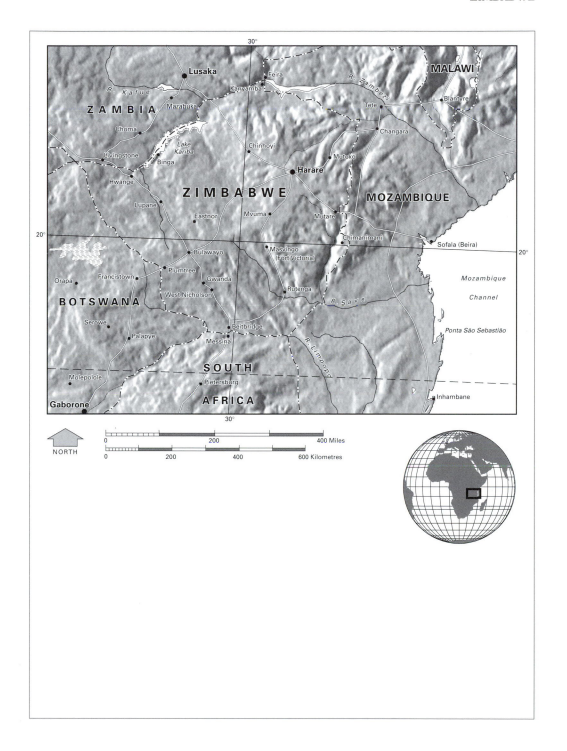

NORTH

0   200   400 Miles

0   200   400   600 Kilometres

Boundary problems have arisen with Mozambique, Zimbabwe and Malawi and efforts have been made to co-ordinate border security. In February 1997, a defence agreement was signed with South Africa which, in its rejuvenated form, still dominates the international relations of Zimbabwe.

Status ■ Given its 'frontline' position with regard to South Africa, Zimbabwe has made commendable progress in many spheres. However, the economy is flagging badly and there is growing public concern over corruption. Mugabe has responded by taking increasingly repressive measures and, in particular, promising to repossess 5 million ha of primarily white-owned commercial farmland. This resulted in a 40 per cent depreciation of the Zimbabwe dollar in December 1997. Mugabe is therefore in a parlous position. If he abandons the policy, he loses rural support, but if he expropriates the land, the effect on the economy could be disastrous. Throughout 1998, there were clashes ranging from riots in Harare over food price increases to a nationwide strike against tax increases and battles with students. It was announced in March 1998 that the land seizure programme had been altered to include compensation awards. Although Zimbabwe is beset with problems, it retains a key role in the development of southern Africa.

Reading ■ Abiodun, A. (1994) *Brothers at War*, London: British Academic Press
IISS (1998) Pressure for political change in Zimbabwe, *Strategic Comments*, 4(3)

INDEX

Note: This index allows readers to locate references to many locations and geographical features that do not merit an entry of their own in the main alphabetical sequence of the text. It is also designed to supplement the cross-references already supplied in the text by showing additional links between many of the flashpoints discussed. Index entries are also included for significant individuals, political parties, issues that may give rise to conflict, and for some types of conflict. Bold type is used to highlight the pages on which the main discussion of any particular topic is to be found. Alphabetical arrangement is word-by-word, ignoring prepositions, conjunctions, definite and indefinite articles, etc. in the arrangement of subheadings.

Index compiled by Ann Kingdom